eCulture

Cultural Content in the Digital Age

Alfredo M. Ronchi

eCulture

Cultural Content in the Digital Age

Alfredo M. Ronchi
Politecnico di Milano
HyperMediaGroup
Piazza Leonardo da Vinci 32
20133 Milano
Italy
alfredo.ronchi@polimi.it

ISBN 978-3-540-75273-8   e-ISBN 978-3-540-75276-9
DOI 10.1007/978-3-540-75276-9
Springer Dordrecht Heidelberg London New York

Library of Congress Control Number: 2008936491
ACM Computing Classification (1998): H.4, H.5, J.5, K.4

© 2009 Springer-Verlag Berlin Heidelberg
This work is subject to copyright. All rights are reserved, whether the whole or part of the material is concerned, specifically the rights of translation, reprinting, reuse of illustrations, recitation, broadcasting, reproduction on microfilm or in any other way, and storage in data banks. Duplication of this publication or parts thereof is permitted only under the provisions of the German Copyright Law of September 9, 1965, in it current version, and permission for use must always be obtained from Springer. Violations are liable to prosecution under the German Copyright Law.

The use of general descriptive names, registered names, trademarks, etc. in this publication does not imply, even in the absence of a specific statement, that such names are exempt from the relevant protective laws and regulations and therefore free for general use.

Cover design: KünkelLopka, Heidelberg
Typesetting and Production: le-tex publishing services oHG, Leipzig, Germany

Printed on acid-free paper

9 8 7 6 5 4 3 2 1

Springer is part of Springer Science+Business Media (www.springer.com)

Introduction

Creativity is one of the highest forms of human energy. It is a defining human trait that enables us to design and to use tools, and it gives us the ability to solve problems. In the modern world, creativity and its outcome—innovation— are credited as the greatest predictors for economic advancement, equal to or surpassing investments. Creativity can be a vehicle for empowerment and fulfilment or, if denied or abused, it can lead to frustration, apathy, alienation, and even violence.

The role of creativity has been magnified by the explosive developments in Information and Communication Technologies.

ICTs are the most powerful means to produce, preserve and communicate the fruits of human creativity, including information, know-how, knowledge, and works of art.[1]

---

[1] Passage from the "Vienna Conclusions" of the conference ICT and Creativity: Towards a Global Cooperation for Quality Content in the Information Society, held in Vienna, Austria, 23 June 2005, http://www.wsa-conference.org/data/viennaconclusions_051104.pdf

Acknowledgements

This book aims to synthesise some of the experiences that I have accumulated after working in the field of eCulture for two decades. It has been a great pleasure to be able to merge two of my main interests, technology and culture.

Computer graphics provided one of the first opportunities to merge these different interests, using drafting and solid modelling applications, in the 1980s. This application of computer graphics was propaedeutic to my first attempts to make use of virtual reality technology in the field of culture, and (at almost the same time) it also proved instructive when the potential advantages of applying the Internet in a cultural context were first considered, starting with "networks of virtual museums" early in the 1990s.

I should like to begin here by thanking Prof. Giovanni degli Antoni for his suggestions and encouragement, as well as all of the students and the researchers that actively cooperated with me in developing concepts, ideas and projects. There are a number of colleagues that I would like to thank for their valuable contributions: Francesco Antinucci, who introduced me to the "human side of ICT" and shared his deep knowledge of human perception; Fabrizio Funtò, Marcello Pappagallo and Antonella Guidazzoli, all of whom were perfect partners in many projects; Michele Gianni and Umberto Parrini, who provided close links to the humanistic side of my work; and Sergio Conti, one of the main supporters of the European Commision's MOSAIC project. Significant contributions were also provided by Derrick de Kerckhove and his vision of eSociety as well as by Ranjit Makkuni, multifaceted artist and scientist who introduced me to the possible relation between cutting edge technologies and craftmanship.

Special thanks are due to Kim H. Veltman, my partner in a number of projects and initiatives; Mario Verdese, my partner in the establishment of the EC MEDICI Framework of Cooperation as it was conceived in 1995; Sylviane Toporkoff, for promoting my studies in the Global Forum community; Senator Pierre Laffitte who introduced me to the experimental laboratory for the future of Sophia Antipolis; Eleanor Fink, Kimmo Aulake, Lynn Thiesmeyer, Michio Umegaki, my main contributors and partners in *On Culture in a World-Wide Information Society*; Elisa Liberatori Prati for her continuous and kind cooperation; Terje Nyphan for his studies of monument conservation and economics; Georges Mihaies and Shinji Matsumoto and their constant participation in MEDICI initiatives; Frederic Andres and ACM initiatives; Alvise de Michelis and his vision of the "reuse" of digital images and a number of other cultural initiatives; Judith Gradwhol, for introducing relevant innovative concepts in virtual collections management; Joachim Sauter, for introducing the art and magic of ART+COM, Garegin Chookaszyan, for offering me a close look at Armenian culture and traditions; Gerfried Stocker "Master" in creativity and "Ars Electronica"; Wolfgang Kippes, an active partner in MEDICI initiatives and a true example of a "cultural enterprises" manager; as well as Giovanni Alliata di Montereale. Piero Fantastichini and Paolo Micciché "creators" of impressive digital artefacts.

I would like to thank all of the experts that actively cooperated with the MEDICI Framework. Finally, a special thank you to Larissa Zoni and Ileana Baronio for her long-term close cooperation.

Foreword

The aim of the present book is to provide a comprehensive vision of a very relevant sector of the *digital landscape*: electronic content, or more precisely, cultural content. The relevance of *content and services* is now evident due to the contribution provided by the two phases of the World Summit on the Information Society, held in Geneva (2003) and Tunis (2005).

The creation and provision of high-quality content and services are key actions to bridging the digital divide. A special initiative that addresses these goals, the so-called *World Summit Award*, was started during the Summit.

Scope

This work is subdivided into three main parts: the first is devoted to the main issues and general guidelines; the second to technological fundamentals and the main solutions; and the third to applications and services.

Starting from the basics, the reader will be introduced to issues and achievements associated with virtual museums, cataloguing, digitising, publishing, the sustainable exploitation of cultural content, and a relevant case study. Drawing upon the many years of experience and achievements *in digital cultural content* of the author, this last part aims to provide a comprehensive overview of the issues and achievements associated with digital collections and cultural content.

Target Audience

Cultural content managers, publishers, memory institutions, digital collections developers.

Background Knowledge

A basic knowledge of information and communications technologies.

Background

The present section outlines basic issues and achievements in the field of the application of ICT and advanced technologies to cultural heritage, where *heritage* is considered to be the "path toward today's society and culture".

The extension of the concept of a *cultural heritage* to new classes of "objects", both tangible and intangible, and the relationship between conserving them and experiencing them provide new challenges, such as the combined utilisation of various online databases, and the creation of supranational and multilingual thesauri.

The rapid obsolescence of technologies focuses our attention on data storage and access from a long-term (i.e. after ten, twenty or more years) perspective. However, the aspects that attract the online user the most are both the interface and the provision of easy access to different subjects and contents.

We conclude by considering how to shape eSociety while also bridging the increasing gap between those who are online and those who are offline.

A significant number of charters, principles, and guidelines, including the *Nara Document on Authenticity* (1994), the *Burra Charter* (1999), the *International Charter on Cultural Tourism* (1999), and the *Principles for the Conservation of Heritage Sites in China* (2002) have emphasised the fundamental role of sensitive and effective interpretation in heritage conservation.

The general theme of *Universal Access to Information*, launched on the occasion of the *32nd UNESCO General Conference*, the *World Summit on the Information Society*, and the implementation of the documents adopted by the *Summit* lead us to consider (amongst others) the technological and cultural aspects of this.

Universal Access to Information, by UNESCO

Let us "historically" frame this subject with an overview of the main events that have characterised the evolution of the applications of information and communications technology (ICT) that are dedicated to cultural and social issues.

Going back over a decade, to the early 1990s, we may refer to both the US project entitled *Super Information Highways*[1] and to the *Bangemann Report*[2] that, in partial antithesis, presented the "European path" towards the Information Society.

Super information highways and the Bangemann Report

---

[1] The term "information superhighway" was popularised by Al Gore (then the US Vice President) in 1994.

[2] See: http://www.medicif.org/Dig_library/ECdocs/reports/Bangemann.html or http://ec.europa.eu/archives/ISPO/infosoc/backg/bangeman.html.

In February 1995, the European Commission organised the first meeting on the Information Society, in Brussels[3]. During the meeting, a list of eleven pilot projects was approved:

The eleven pilot projects

- Global Inventory (of projects)
- Global Interoperability
- Cross-Cultural Education and Training
- Bibliotheca Universalis
- Multimedia Access to World Cultural Heritage
- Environment
- Global Emergency
- Government Online
- Global Healthcare
- Global Marketplace for SMEs
- Maritime Information Systems.

The aim of these projects was to trace the guidelines of the Information Society.

G7 Summit in Halifax and ISAD Conference

In June 1995, a worldwide *G7*[4] *Summit* was held in Halifax, Canada. The *G7 Group* approved and adopted the abovementioned list of projects. As a consequence, practical demonstrations followed during the ISAD Conference (Information Society and Developing Countries) held in Midrand, South Africa in May 1996. During this conference, four demo projects were selected[5], representing the four principal sections identified by the project *Multimedia Access to World Cultural Heritage*.

Multimedia Access to World Cultural Heritage

Focusing on European initiatives, the combined initiatives led to the birth of a new framework of understanding. The reference document was largely a *Declaration of Intent* that was initially signed by 240 museums and institutions. In this context, there was the development of a likely organic approach to the use of multimedia and more generally of ICT in the field of cultural heritage. The *Memorandum of Understanding for Multimedia Access to Europe's Cultural Heritage*, or more simply the *MoU*, is usually considered to bè the Act of Incorporation for the "Information Company on European Cultural Heritage".

Memorandum of Understanding for Multimedia Access to Europe's Cultural Heritage—MoU

The MoU lasted, as stated in the document itself, for two years, and then the European Commission issued a "call for tender"—it asked for follow-up

---

3   The European vision moves the focus away from mere technology toward both cultural and social dimensions.

4   The G7 comprise Canada, England, France, Germany, Italy, Japan and the USA.

5   The four sections principally referred to the specific contents of museums and art galleries: 3D Acquisition (originally called Laser Camera), a laser camera presented by the National Research Council, Ottawa; Filing, of the Museo di Storia della Scienza in Florence; Visualisation of the Nefertari Tomb, developed by Infobyte, Rome; "SUMS" Navigation, developed by SUMS Corporation, Toronto.

Background

projects. MoU was mainly a declaration of intent; the follow-up had to be much more pragmatic.

In 1997, a new "agency" called the *MEDICI Framework* was launched. A partnership has since been developed between the MEDICI initiative and the Council of Europe in the application of new information technologies to the field of culture.

MEDICI Framework of Cooperation

The goal of MEDICI is to promote the use of advanced technologies to access, understand, preserve and to promote the economics of cultural heritage. The aim of this is to create conditions that permit the development of new economic activities that promote cultural heritage, mainly through the use of new media, and to create new employment opportunities in related sectors.

The official MoU progress report dated April 1996 reported that a third area that can be defined as application and testing "will be made up of projects that are market-oriented and based on the enjoyment of cultural heritage. This area will include projects aiming at producing advanced cultural applications by using the present technological resources in key sectors (education, entertainment, cultural tourism, disadvantaged users etc.)."

In this area, an assessment of museum initiatives highlights that the World Wide Web has assumed a leading position within the *Multimedia Access to World Cultural Heritage project*.

Following this trend, the MEDICI Framework, who had been involved in web technology from the very beginning[6], began to cooperate closely with the *World Wide Web Conference* initiative. Following interesting discussions at WWW7, held in Brisbane (April 1998)[7], a set of sessions called the *Culture Track* devoted to outlining a comprehensive scenario on emerging technologies and trends in "networked arts" was created, care of MEDICI, for WWW9, held in Amsterdam (May 2000)[8].

The World Wide Web Conference and the Culture Track

Specifically referencing virtual museums, this Culture Track[9] explored how multimedia technology could be employed to improve the way that visitors presently perceive a visit to a museum or art gallery.

In order to explore the whole scenario, additional topics included benefits associated with ICT applications, real issues related to museums and archives, e-society, e-commerce and e-services. In terms of e-commerce, one of the main ideas at that time was to apply a market model based on image copyright to

---

6   Active contribution to WWW 3 and the development of online Ricci Oddi Modern Art Gallery (1994) and the De Architectura online portal (1993–94)

7   The 7th World Wide Web Conference, held in Brisbane, April 1998
    see: http://www7.scu.edu.au.

8   The 9th World Wide Web Conference, held in Amsterdam May 2000,
    see: http://www.www9.org.

9   Culture Track of the 9th World Wide Web Conference, held in Amsterdam,
    see: http://www.medicif.org. (see references to Chap. 5, Ronchi 2004)

online exhibits. An additional discussion topic was the "increasing digital gap" or the "digital divide".

Culture Counts

From October 4th to 7th 1999, a relevant event took place in Florence: *Culture Counts—Financing, Resources and the Economics of Culture in Sustainable Development (World Bank 1999).* As expressed in the title, the main focus of the conference was economics, but related concepts such as sustainability, access and the digital divide were also considered and discussed in depth too.

The important role of culture in sustainable development was examined, as was the need for new partnerships among multilateral development agencies, the private sector, foundations, nongovernmental organisations and academia to support this work. In addition, the importance of reducing cultural poverty in sustainable development programs was considered.

The event, which gathered key contributions from around the world, was organised and supported by the Government of Italy, the World Bank, and the United Nations Educational, Scientific and Cultural Organization. As stated in the official programme, "the premise of the conference was that culture is crucial to advancing sustainable development."

The objectives of the conference were to:
- Promote the expansion of the economic analysis of, and the resources available to, culture in sustainable development programs
- Expand the range of institutions and actors involved in culture from a developmental perspective
- Increase the number of instruments that can be used in these programs.

Culture Counts provided an important forum for experts and key decision-makers to discuss the full range of economic and financial issues associated with the cultural dimensions of poverty alleviation in developing countries.

Specific emphasis was placed on archives, because both current records and historical archives document the actions of individuals and states:

The role of records and archives

"On the one hand, records provide the evidence governments need to function and be accountable, to develop and implement policy, and to protect citizens' rights. On the other hand, being archives, they constitute a vital element of cultural heritage by preserving the collective memory of a nation and forming an essential link in the chain of human history. Records and archives management have key implications for development, often overlooked[10]."

The documentary evidence conserved in the archives of a particular country helps to ensure accountability, and thus good governance, in both the public and the private sectors of the economy. Therefore, the digitisation of existing archives and the preservation of *digital duplicates* are key issues (World Bank 1999), as is the broadening of digital access in order to establish a true Information Society.

---

10 *In Archives and Sustainable Development* (organised by the World Bank in Latin America).

XIV **Background**

Amongst other activities and official presentations, a set of workshops were held, which included: *Cathedrals for Environment: Financing Culture and Nature for Generation to Come* (organised by the IUCN and the Mountain Institute); *Cultural Economics, Identity and Poverty Reduction* (organised by the World Bank); the *Culture and National Millennium Commissions* (organised by The White House in the USA); *Cultural Conservation in East Asia* (organised by The World Bank in Asia); *Sharing the Wealth: Improved Sustainability Through Integrated Conservation Planning* (organised by the World Monuments Fund); *Valuing Heritage—Beyond Economics* (organised by ICCROM); *Museums: Conservation and Management of Cultural Heritage* (organised by CIVITA); *Cultural Policy and Sustainable Development, a New Partnership* (organised by the Council of Europe); *Culture and Private Sector Support* (organised by Arts and Business); *Sustainable Development in Communication and Education: Pilot Projects and Case Studies* (organised by Scuola Normale Superiore di Pisa, Soprintendenza Archeologica di Pompei, MEDICI Framework, European Commission, Istituto Centrale per il Restauro); *Financing Cultural Site Management* (organised by The World Bank); *Growth and Culture in Urban and Regional Proximity* (organised by INTERARTS Observatory and UNESCO); *Strategies and Guidelines for Architectural Heritage: Technical and Financial Aspects* (organised by ICOMOS, UNESCO, Council of Europe); *Supporting Cultural Enterprises for Local Development* (organised by Ford Foundation); *Cultural Tourism and Development* (organised by the Touring Club of Italy).

Culture Counts: workshops

On the occasion of the Special European Council held in Lisbon on March 23rd and 24th 2000, delegates launched a guideline document entitled e-Europe[11]. This document provides some guidelines for developing e-society, starting with ensuring cheaper Internet access, accelerating e-commerce, providing fast Internet connections for researchers and students, smart cards to secure electronic access, and risk capital for high-tech SMEs, enabling e-participation for the disabled and online health care, intelligent transport, and for allowing access to government services online.

Special European Council—Lisbon: eEurope

As expressed within the document:

e-Europe is a political initiative to ensure the European Union fully benefits for generations to come from changes the Information Society is bringing. Those changes, the most significant since the Industrial Revolution, are far-reaching and global. They are not just about technology. They will affect everyone, everywhere. Bringing communities, both rural and urban, closer together, creating wealth, sharing knowledge, they have huge potential to enrich everyone's lives.

Managing this transformation represents the central economic and social challenge for the Union. It will impact profoundly on European employment,

---

11   See: http://ec.europa.eu/information_society/eeurope/2005/index_en.htm.

Background   XV

growth and productivity for the next five years (2000–2005) and for decades afterwards.

e-Europe is intended to accelerate positive change in the Union. It aims at ensuring this change towards the Information Society is cohesive, not divisive. Integrating, not fragmenting. Information Society is an opportunity not a threat. In essence, e-Europe aims at bringing the benefits of the Information Society to the reach of all Europeans.

An opportunity not a threat

The key objectives of e-Europe are:

The key objectives of e-Europe

- To bring every citizen (even at home or at school) and every business and administration into the digital age, and enabling them to get online;
- To create a digitally literate Europe supported by an entrepreneurial culture that is ready to finance and develop new ideas;
- To ensure that the whole process is socially inclusive, building consumer trust and strengthening social cohesion.

More recently, a number of different global initiatives aimed at predicting and possibly solving different problems related to the provision of universal access to information have been activated. These include, in relation to cultural preservation, UNESCO's Intangible Heritage Task Force (2002) and South Eastern Pacific Archives (supported by Keio University); in relation to the digital divide, the G8's Digital Opportunities Task Force (2000)[12], UNESCO OCCAM's Infopoverty Programme (2001), the two phases of the World Summit on the Information Society (WSIS), the first of which was held in Geneva in December 2003 and the second held in Tunis in November 2005 (organised by UNO and ITU), and the creation of the Global Alliance for ICT and Development (GAID, in 2006).

Intangible Heritage Task Force

WSIS: World Summit on the Information Society

On the occasion of the G8 Summit in Kyushu-Okinawa (2000), the *Charter on Global Information Society* was adopted.

In the Okinawa Charter, the G8 leaders agreed to establish a Digital Opportunity Task Force (DOT Force) aimed at integrating efforts to bridge the digital divide into a broader international approach.

Digital Opportunity Task Force (DOT force)

The Charter noted in paragraph 18 that the DOT Force, in close consultation with other partners and in a manner responsive to the needs of developing countries, would:

- Actively facilitate discussions with developing countries, international organizations and other stake holders to promote international co-operation with a view to fostering policy, regulatory and network readiness; improving connectivity, increasing access and lowering cost; building human capacity and encouraging participation in global e-commerce ;
- Encourage the G8's own efforts to cooperate on IT-related pilot programmes and projects;
- Promote closer policy dialogue among partners and work to raise global public awareness of the challenges and opportunities;

---

12 Subsequently evolved into GAID (Global Alliance for ICT and Development).

- Examine inputs from the private sector and other interested groups such as the Global Digital Divide Initiative's contributions;
- Report its findings and activities to G8 personal representatives before our next meeting in Genoa 2001.

The DOT Force was formed in the fourth quarter of 2000. Forty-three members participated in its work.

Following the G8 summit in Genoa (July 2001), the Global Forum 2001: Expanding the Global e-Society was held in Newcastle (UK) in October 2001, during which the WWW10 panel presented its report, *On Culture in a World Wide Web Information Society*. Other contributions to this Forum, such as *Time Rich Time Poor* (Lindskog 2001), also addressed cultural aspects.

Global Forum 2001: Expanding the Global e-Society

In November 2001, a joint event managed by the Council of Europe (see *New Information Technologies and the Young*; Council of Europe 2000) and UNESCO, Cultural Industries and New Technologies, was held in Strasbourg (France).

UNESCO: Cultural Industries and New Technologies

Fig. 0.1 Global Development Gateway portal (Development Gateway Foundation, Inc.)

A publication entitled *Vital Links for a Knowledge Culture* (Jeffrey 2001) was issued during this event. Vital Links deals with the complex relationships between NICTs (new information and communication technologies) and culture across Europe (Council of Europe 1999).

Vital Links

The publication is structured as follows:
- The context: vital links for a knowledge culture and the deep structure of knowledge societies;

Background   XVII

- Dealing with public access to new information and communication technologies in Europe through statistics and indices;
- Some focused contributions on the many dimensions of access in Europe;
- Discussions of policy frameworks, including *Cultural Policy in the Knowledge Society, Towards a Strategic Evolutionary Cultural Policy*, and *A Policy Networks Model*.

Around this time, the World Bank created the Development Gateway, a global support portal for developing countries.

The World Summit on the Information Society

In order to fight the digital divide and promote the positive use of ICT, a two-phase process was launched, the *World Summit on the Information Society* (WSIS). It represented one of the first occasions on which different representatives from governments, institutions, and civil society met in order to try to shape the future of society.

Both phases were structured in a set of Preparatory Committees (PrepCom) held at both national/continental level and global level. The final event of the first phase was the summit held in Geneva, on December 2003, involving thousands of people from around the world. Three main *layers* were tackled in Geneva: political, NGO and civil society issues.

Two years later, as foreseen by the original project, a second set of Preparatory Committees led to the final summit held in Tunis on November 2005.

In the general framework of the WSIS, a relevant initiative promoting quality digital content creation and the potential reduction of the digital divide was created: the *World Summit Award* (WSA).

World Summit Award (WSA)
The WSA is a global initiative to select and promote the world's best e-content in eBusiness, eCulture, eEntertainment, eGovernment, eHealth, eInclusion, eLearning, and eScience.

Potential platforms and channels covered by the award are: broadband/online; mobile content; crossmedia; offline/DVD; CD-ROM or video materials; games platforms; interactive TV; interactive computer graphics; content tools; interface design.

The project was launched in cooperation with the WSIS 2003–2005, and it received support from numerous national and international nonprofit organisations, as well as substantial contributions from the private industry sector.

In 2003, 136 countries participated in the WSA and 40 finalists were selected out of 803 submissions by a worldwide expert network.

In 2005, 168 countries applied, and over 320 international expert representatives from Africa, Asia, Arab nations and the Middle East, South and Latin America, North America, Australia, New Zealand and Europe teamed up to ensure the independence, diversity and inclusiveness of the WSA global contest. More than 30 countries launched a national preselection process.

The same happened for the 2007 contest. In this case, evaluations were held in Brijuni (Croatia), while the awards ceremony was held on November in Venice (Italy).

Fig. 0.2 The World Summit on Information Society (WSIS) Logo

Global Alliance for ICT and Development

In 2006, the *Global Alliance for ICT and Development*, a new initiative from the UNO, was launched. The *Millennium Declaration* of 2000 and the outcome of the 2003–05 World Summit established a clear set of internationally agreed development goals. The WSIS forged a global consensus on the importance of information and communication technologies (ICT) as tools for achieving these development goals.

As a follow-up to the DOT Force and to actively support the main role of ICT, on 28 March 2006 the United Nations Secretary-General approved the establishment of the Global Alliance for ICT and Development (GAID). The decision was based on the internationally recognized need for an open, multi-stakeholder forum that brings together governments, international organisations, civil society, the private sector, media and other stakeholder constituencies in order to enhance the utilisation of ICT—including community media and other traditional mass broadcast media such as radio and television, as well as communications media such as fixed and mobile phones—in order to encourage its development. The alliance is an embodiment of the *Millennium Development Goals* (MDG): to develop a global partnership for development and, "in cooperation with the private sector, make available the benefits of new technologies, especially information and communication technologies". In accordance with the *Outcome Document*[13] of the UN World Summit held in 2005, the Global Alliance will also "enhance the contributions of NGOs, civil society, the private sector and other stakeholders in national development efforts, as well as the promotion of the global partnership for development".

The mission of the Global Alliance for ICT and Development is to aid the transformation of the spirit and vision of the WSIS into action and to promote the application of ICT in order to achieve of internationally agreed development goals, including the Millennium Development Goals. It will do so by providing

Global Alliance for ICT and Development

---

13 A/RES/60/1 (http://www.un.org/summit2005/documents.html).

an inclusive multi-stakeholder global forum and platform for cross-sectoral policy dialogue and advocacy, and by catalysing multi-stakeholder action-oriented partnerships that are encouraged under the GAID umbrella. GAID itself will not have any operational or implementational role. The Alliance will provide multi-stakeholder input to intergovernmental bodies, including the Economic and Social Council and the Commission for Science and Technology for Development.

The long-term objectives of the Alliance were outlined during the open global consultation in 2005. This event, which paved the way to the launch of the Global Alliance, identified six broad objectives that the Alliance will pursue over its lifetime:

- Mainstream the global ICT agenda into the broader United Nations development agenda;
- Bring together key organisations and other stakeholders involved in ICT for development in order to enhance collaboration and their effectiveness in achieving the internationally agreed development goals;
- Raise the awareness of policymakers on ICTD policy issues;
- Facilitate the identification of technological solutions for specific development needs and goals, and launch pertinent partnerships;
- Promote the creation of an enabling environment and innovative business models for pro-poor investment, innovation, entrepreneurship and growth, and for empowering people living in poverty and other marginalized communities;
- Provide the Secretary-General with advice on ICTD-related issues.

Within the framework of these objectives, specific attention will be given to mainstreaming ICTD into the United Nations development agenda, raising the awareness of policy-makers, and providing advice to the Secretary-General on ICTD policy issues.

References

7th WWW Conf. (Brisbane, Australia, May 1997): http://www7.scu.edu.au

9th WWW Conf. (Amsterdam, The Netherlands, May 2000): http://www.www9.org

M. Bangemann et al. (2003) Europe and the global information society ("Bangemann Report"; Recommendations to the European Council): http://ec.europa.eu/archives/ISPO/infosoc/backg/bangeman.html and http://www.medicif.org/Dig_library/ECdocs/reports/Bangemann.htm

P.A. Bruck et al. (2005) Vienna Conclusions. In: Proc. Conf. "ICT and Creativity: Towards a Global Cooperation for Quality Content in the Information Society", Vienna, Austria, 2–3 June 2005 (see http://www.acten.net/cgi-bin/WebGUI/www/index.pl/newsletter27 and http://www.acten.net/cgi-bin/WebGUI/www/index.pl/newsletter27?wid=934&func=viewSubmission&sid=1466 or, for the full discussion version, http://buziaulane.blogspot.com/2005_06_06_buziaulane_archive.html)

Central Institute for Cataloguing and Documentation (the body within the Ministry for Cultural Heritage and Activities (MiBAC) that defines the standards and tools for the cataloguing and documentation of national archaeological, architectural, art history and ethno-anthropological heritage in agreement with the regions. It also manages the General Information System for cataloguing and carries out high-level training and research in the cataloguing sector. The Institute conserves and evaluates collections of photography and aerial photography held in their own archives, which are open for public consultation): http://www.iccd.beniculturali.it

CIVITA group: http://www.civita.it/

Community Research & Development Information Service (CORDIS): http://cordis.europa.eu/en/home.html

Constitution of the United Nations Educational, Scientific, and Cultural Organization: http://www.icomos.org/unesco/unesco_constitution.html

Council of Europe (1999) Digital culture in Europe: A selective inventory of centres of innovation in the arts and new technologies. Council of Europe Publishing, Paris

Council of Europe (2001) New information technologies and the young. Council of Europe Publishing, Paris

Council of Europe: http://www.coe.int

Development Gateway Foundation: http://www.developmentgateway.org/index.do

EC (1995) G7 members and the European Commission decide to identify a number of selected Pilot Projects. At: Information Society Meeting, Brussels, Belgium, 25–26 Feb. 1995: http://admi.net/archive/www.telecom.gouv.fr/english/activ/techno/g7piproa.htm

EC (1996a) G8 Global Information Society Pilot Projects Matrix – Pilot project number 5: Electronic Museums and Galleries – http://ec.europa.eu/archives/ISPO/intcoop/g8/i_g8pp_matrix.html

EC (1996b) Memorandum of understanding for multimedia access to Europe's cultural heritage: http://ec.europa.eu/archives/ISPO/docs/topics/docs/mou_cultural_all.zip

EC (1999) eEurope—an Information Society for all: http://portal.etsi.org/eEurope/

EC (2000) Presidency conclusions. At: Lisbon European Council, 23–24 March 2000: http://www.europarl.europa.eu/summits/lis1_en.htm

EC (2005) e-Europe and i2010—a European Information Society for growth and employment: http://ec.europa.eu/information_society/eeurope/2005/index_en.htm

European Commission: http://ec.europa.eu/index_en.htm

European Commission Framework Programme 7: http://cordis.europa.eu/fp7/home_en.html

European Commission MEDICI Framework: http://www.medicif.org

European Parliament: http://www.europarl.europa.eu

European Union: http://europa.eu

G7 Summit (Halifax, Nova Scotia, Canada, 15–17 June 1995) information: http://www.chebucto.ns.ca/Current/HalifaxSummitG7/index.html

G8 Digital Opportunities Task Force (DOT Force): http://www.mofa.go.jp/policy/economy/summit/2000/genoa.html#1

Getty Information Institute (1998) Demonstrable projects: methodologies, tools, and guidelines: http://www.ninch.org/PROJECTS/Future/Getty.html

Global Alliance for ICT and Development (GAID): http://www.un-gaid.org

IFLA (1999) G7 Information Society Conference Brussels 1995, Information Policy: G-7 Information Society Resources: http://www.ifla.org.sg/II/g7.htm

Infopoverty Programme: http://www.infopoverty.org

Information Society: http://ec.europa.eu/archives/ISPO

International Centre for the Preservation and Restoration of the Cultural Property (ICCROM): http://www.iccrom.org

International Computing Centre (ICC), Geneva, Switzerland: http://www.unicc.org

International Council of Museums (ICOM): http://icom.museum/ or www.icom.org

International Council on Monuments and Sites (ICOMOS): http://www.icomos.org

International Telecommunications Union (ITU): http://www.itu.org

ISAD (Information Society and Development) (1996a) Chairperson's view concerning ideas emerging from the fora discussions on global information society and development. In: ISAD Conf., Midrand, South Africa, 13–15 May 1996

ISAD (Information Society and Development) (1996b) Chair's conclusions. In: ISAD Conf., Midrand, South Africa, 13–15 May 1996: http://ec.europa.eu/archives/ISPO/docs/promotion/past_events/isad_conclusioin.doc

Istituto Centrale per il Restauro (ICR; founded in 1939 when it was felt that there was a need to plan restoration on a scientific basis and so unify intervention methodologies for works of art and archaeological findings in Italy): http://www.icr.beniculturali.it

Istituto per le Tecnologie Applicate ai Beni Culturali of the National Research Council (CNR): http://www.itabc.cnr.it

L. Jeffrey (2001) Vital links for a knowledge culture. Council of Europe Publishing, Paris

Keio University Shonan Fujisawa Campus (SFC) South Eastern Pacific Archives: http://www.sfc.keio.ac.jp/index.html.en

Key Action 3, "Multimedia content & tools" (within the IST programme): http://ec.europa.eu/archives/ISPO/topics/i_MM.html

XXII **Background**

Lerici Foundation (Politecnico di Milano, Italy; the first institution in Italy to introduce non-invasive methods for the location and identification of buried archaeological structures): http://www.lerici.polimi.it/english/index.htm

H. Lindskog (2001) Time rich time poor. Proc. Global Forum 2001 (see http://www.items.fr)

B. Mannoni (1996) Bringing museums online: http://membres.lycos.fr/mannoni/cacm.htm

Observatory for Cultural and Audiovisual Communication (OCCAM): http://www.occam.org

Opificio delle Pietre Dure (OPD; an autonomous Institute of the Ministry for Cultural Heritage, whose operational, research and training activities find expression in the field of conservation of works of art): http://www.opificiodellepietredure.it/

Organisation for Economic Cooperation and Development (OECD): http://www.oecd.org/home/0,2987,en_2649_201185_1_1_1_1_1,00.html

Politecnico di Milano: http://www.polimi.it

M. Prensky (2001) Digital natives, digital immigrants. On the Horizon 9:5 (see http://www.marcprensky.com/writing/Prensky%20-%20Digital%20Natives,%20Digital%20Immigrants%20-%20Part1.pdf)

Scuola Normale Superiore di Pisa: http://www.sns.it

Scuola Normale Superiore Sant'Anna: http://www.sssup.it

The Interdisciplinary Centre for Research, Planning and Management of Cultural Heritage at Scuola Normale Superiore di Pisa: http://www.sns.it/en/laboratori/laboratorilettere/gestpatr/

The Lund Principles (on 4 April 2001, under the Swedish EU Presidency, the European Commission organised an expert meeting with representatives from all Member States in Lund. The conclusions and recommendations derived from this meeting are known as the Lund Principles and were further developed in the Lund Action Plan, which establishes an agenda for actions to be carried out by Member States and the Commission): http://cordis.europa.eu/ist/digicult/lund-principles.htm

Touring Club of Italy (TCI; founded in 1894 with the aim of spreading and developing the social and cultural values of tourism, promoting the defence, conservation and proper enjoyment of the country's national heritage, landscape and environment, and producing publications on travel and for travellers): http://www.touringclub.it/english/index.asp

UN (2003) Universal access to information. Launched at: 32nd UNESCO Gen. Conf., Paris, France, 29 Sept.–17 Oct. 2003 (see http://portal.unesco.org/en/ev.php-URL_ID=16639&URL_DO=DO_TOPIC&URL_SECTION=201.html)

UN (2005) World Summit on Information Society 2005 Outcome Document: http://www.un.org/summit2005/documents.html

UNESCO Intangible Heritage: http://portal.unesco.org/culture/en/ev.php-URL_ID=34325&URL_DO=DO_TOPIC&URL_SECTION=201.html

United Nations (UN): http://www.un.org

United Nations Development Programme (UNDP), New York: http://www.undp.org

United Nations Economic and Social Council: http://www.un.org/ecosoc

United Nations Educational, Scientific and Cultural Organization (UNESCO) Paris, France: http://www.unesco.org

United Nations Industrial Development Organization (UNIDO), Vienna, Austria: http://www.unido.org

World Bank (1999) Proc. "Culture Counts: Financing, Resources, and the Economics of Culture in Sustainable Development", Florence, Italy, 4–7 October 1999 (see http://wbln0018.worldbank.org/Institutional/SPRConferences.nsf/conferences/Culture+Counts?OpenDocument)

World Bank: http://www.worldbank.org

World Intellectual Property Organization (WIPO), Geneva, Switzerland: http://www.wipo.int/portal/index.html.en

World Monuments Fund (safeguards the world's irreplaceable heritage): http://www.wmf.org

World Summit Award (a contribution that aims to help bridge the digital divide): http://www.wsis-award.org

World Summit on the Information Society (two phases, 2003–2005): http://www.wsis.org

Contents

Part I
Cultural Content and the Information Society

1   Digital Content   **3**

2   e-Society and the Social Divide   **5**

3   Quality Content   **9**

4   Digital Content and Creativity   **13**

5   Cultural Content   **15**

    5.1   Tangible and Intangible Digital Heritage   **19**

    5.2   UNESCO's "Intangible Heritage"   **19**

6   Digital Communication: the Role of Context   **21**

7   Cultural Diversity and Cultural Models   **23**

    7.1   On Culture in a Worldwide Information Society   **26**

8   Content, Communication and Tools   **33**

    8.1   Why is Digital Communication Revolutionary?   **33**

    8.2   Memetics and the Internet   **36**

    8.3   The Evolution of the Digital Species   **39**

    8.4   Historical Background   **42**

    8.5   Nonlinear Versus Linear, and Many Media Versus Just One Medium   **49**

    8.6   Technology: From the Stylus to the Computer   **51**

    8.7   From Standalone Computers to the Internet and Wireless Communication   **57**

    8.8   Digital Convergence and the History of Movies   **64**

    8.9   Information Transmission   **66**

    8.10   Some Concluding Remarks   **68**

    References   **71**

Part II
The General Technological Framework

9 Native Digital Content **81**
  9.1 Data Creation **81**
  9.2 Native "Nondigital" Content **82**
  9.3 Data Acquisition and Digitisation **83**

10 Datasets and Formats **101**
  10.1 Data Types **101**
  10.2 Image Compression **108**
  10.3 Archiving Tools and Standards **109**
  10.4 Colours and Palettes **109**
  10.5 The Most Popular Graphics File Formats **110**

11 Data Visualisation and Display Technologies **113**
  11.1 From Two-Dimensional to Three (and Higher)-Dimensional Views **114**
  11.2 Computer Graphics and Virtual Reality **118**
  11.3 Evolution of Virtual Reality **119**
  11.4 Enhanced Reality **131**
  11.5 Telepresence and Robots **133**

12 Interaction Design **139**
  12.1 Interaction Design and Affective Aspects **142**
  12.2 Tyrannical or User-Friendly Technology? **142**
  12.3 Expected Product Life and Life Cycles **144**
  12.4 Sustainable Development of Menus and Options **147**
  12.5 Accessibility **149**
  12.6 Usability **153**

13 Computer Games, Edutainment and Theme Parks **155**
  13.1 Information Technology and the Young **155**
  13.2 Computer Games and Digital Cultures **156**
  13.3 Games **158**
  13.4 Interactivity and Immersivity **160**
  13.5 Abstract Games **160**
  13.6 Simulations **161**
  13.7 Simulators, Dark Rides and Other Nonlinear Formats **163**
  13.8 A Brief History of Computer Games **169**

13.9 The History of Computer Games Viewed From an Application Perspective 173

13.10 Other Kinds of Entertainment 176

13.11 Creative Activities 177

13.12 Smart Phones 178

13.13 Theme Parks and High-Tech Shows 179

14 Customer Relationship Management 181

15 Smart Labels, Smart Tags and RFID 183

16 Standards and Protocols for Interoperability 185

16.1 More on Interoperability 186

17 Data Tags and the Semantic Web 187

17.1 Markup Languages and Data Tagging 187

17.2 Content, Structure, Format and Reference 189

17.3 Data and Metadata 190

17.4 Semantic Web 191

17.5 Advanced Online Services 193

17.6 Advanced W3C Design and Evaluation 199

18 Ambient Intelligence 201

19 Long-Term Preservation of Digital Archives 203

19.1 Graffiti From the Digital Era 203

19.2 Already Lost... and To Be Lost 205

19.3 Historical Background of Initiatives 207

19.4 Digital Fragility: Problems and Issues 208

19.5 The Rationale Behind Preservation 210

19.6 Economy and Infrastructure 213

19.7 Some Closing Remarks 214

20 The Future: the Weave of the Digital Fabric 219

20.1 Predicting the Future 219

20.2 Institutes for the Future 220

References 223

Part III
Exploitation, Applications and Services

21 Content, Communication and Tools 237

21.1 Culture, ICT and Emerging Technologies 238

21.2 Which Role? 238

Contents • *XXVII*

21.3 Cultural Content **238**

21.4 Standards and Good Practices **239**

21.5 Sustainability and Economic Models **239**

21.6 Data Acquisition and Digital Preservation **240**

21.7 Comparing Classification Schemes **240**

21.8 Data Structure and Interoperability **240**

21.9 Maintenance of Large Databanks **240**

21.10 Navigation Tools, Interfaces and Metaphors **241**

21.11 Experiencing Cultural Heritage **241**

21.12 Information Policies: Frameworks and Intellectual Property Rights **242**

21.13 Monument Conservation **243**

21.14 Education and Training **243**

22 Exploitation, Applications and Services **245**

22.1 Accessing European Cultural Heritage **247**

23 Prioritisation in Digitalisation **249**

24 Cataloguing Standards and Archiving Tools **251**

24.1 Historical Background of Cataloguing **252**

24.2 Data Standards **255**

24.4 Some Basic Problems That Must be Solved When Cataloguing Historical Items **266**

24.5 Catalogues and Database Management Systems **267**

25 Virtual Museum Networks **269**

25.1 MCN and the CIMI Initiative **271**

25.2 Recent Applications **272**

26 Unique Object ID **277**

26.1 One of the Proposed Solutions **279**

27 Different Channels and Platforms **283**

28 Intellectual Property Rights **287**

28.1 Introduction **287**

28.2 Copyleft **287**

28.3 Free Access **289**

28.4 Freeware **289**

28.5 Copyright **290**

28.6 Digital Uncertainties **294**

28.7 Image Scanning and Image Security **294**

28.8 The Malaysian Experiment **296**

28.9 Creative Commons **300**

28.10 The Products **304**

28.11 Creativity, Production and Market **305**

28.12 Final Considerations **305**

28.13 Digital Rights Management and Clearance **306**

28.14 Protecting Rights **307**

28.15 Digital Object Identifiers **310**

29 Technology and Privacy **313**

29.1 Privacy and Personal Data Management **314**

30 Usability, Accessibility and Platforms **317**

31 Content Repackaging **321**

31.1 The Evolution of Hypertext Markup **324**

32 Experiencing Cultural Content **325**

32.1 Impact of the Interface on the Enjoyment of Cultural Content **332**

32.2 A Quick Overview **334**

32.3 Advanced Interaction Models for Cultural Content **341**

33 Cultural Tourism **359**

33.1 Application Trends **363**

34 Games and Edutainment Applications **375**

35 Hands-On and Interactive Museums **379**

35.1 Science and Technology Museums **380**

35.2 Theme Parks **383**

35.3 From Conventional to Hi-Tech Exhibits **393**

36 Educational Market **395**

36.1 The Role of Memory Institutions **398**

37 Culture Counts: the Economic Dimension **401**

37.1 Some of the Basic Conditions Required to Develop the Cultural Heritage Market **404**

37.2 Cultural Heritage as Value Generator in a Post-Industrial Economy **405**

37.3 Economic Promotion of Cultural Heritage: Problems and Issues **411**

37.4 Cultural Services and Markets **412**

37.5 Emerging Professional Profiles **413**

37.6 Cultural Services and Markets: the Challenge **415**

37.7 The European ICT Market **418**

Contents **XXIX**

37.8 A European Knowledge Society **420**

37.9 The Challenge: Fostering Creativity **421**

37.10 The Art Market and Digital Media **423**

38 Quality **427**

38.1 Affective Quality **430**

39 Conclusions and Future Trends **435**

References **437**

Subject Index **453**

Part I   Cultural Content and the Information Society

1 Digital Content

Content and services (subsequently termed simply "content") represent the added value provided by ICT through "super information highways". We tend to call them eContent ("e" for "electronic"), although some elements of some services do not even have a "digital" structure (e.g. RFID).

Over the centuries, mankind has produced an ever-increasing amount of *content* in different formats, using different techniques and technologies. It is intended that some of this *content* will survive become our legacy to future generations, while most of the *content* is initially maintained but eventually becomes obsolescent and disappears.

Formats, techniques and technologies differ very much both from culture to culture and from era to era. *Oral traditions* live on as a major tool for preserving and communicating *content* in several different areas of the world. *Performing arts and rituals* form the backbones of many different cultures, while most of the world uses *signs*, *symbols*, *ideograms* and *alphabets* as tools for writing and printing.

Oral traditions and performing arts

The printing press was one of the last true revolutions in *content management*; a true milestone that enables the unlimited reproduction of texts at limited cost.

Bill Gates said: *The Internet is something fundamentally different. It will change our world the same way like the invention of the printing press and the coming of the industrial age. The internet is something fundamentally different. Technology is growing so rapidly, and we are only at the very beginning of a new society.*

Fig. 1.1 Metropolitan graffiti (photo by the author)

The Digital Age	Today we are facing a potential new revolution thanks to the *Digital Age*. Digital communication is the newest link in a long chain, which started with nonverbal communication and gestures, evolved to languages, signs and writing, which led to the development of printing, broadcasting and other media and formats. As an extension of this, interactive virtual reality provides a powerful tool for knowledge and complex structured information transfer.

Furthermore, the electronic industry is now moving from the Internet era, where connectivity and intelligence was built into certain products, to the *ubiquitous network society*, where everyday objects possess such capabilities.

After the "I" and "e" eras, we are now entering the "u" (for "ubiquitous") era. This next phase in technological evolution has been given different names: *ubiquitous computing* in Japan, *pervasive computing* in the US, and *ambient intelligence* in Europe. There are, as usual, slight differences between the approaches taken in these different regions: universal access and computational power or "transparent" computer support and cooperative behaviour from the digital environment.

2 e-Society and the Social Divide

What is the role and what are the effects of the *digital revolution*? Which opportunities and threats are associated with digital information?

Digital revolution

In the present context, the term *digital information* is better than *electronic information* because it more accurately captures the essential aspects of the topic. From an ontological point of view, we are dealing with a new class of objects. Digital information and its related technologies have the potential to make a huge impact on culture and society.

In the general framework of the innovations and transformations associated with *e-society,* let us now focus our attention on developing countries.

As already outlined by the author on the occasion of the *Smart Communities Symposium* held in Rome in 1997[1], the advent of *e-society* will, in the current scenario, dramatically increase the gap between the industrialised countries and the developing ones, and even the gaps between the industrialised countries themselves. At that time I called this issue *the increasing gap*; now we use the term *the digital divide*. On the one hand, this is a big problem, but on the other, it presents an incredible opportunity. Thinking *positive*, let us consider it to provide *digital opportunities*. This is the basic idea behind the WSA initiative.

The increasing gap

It used to be said that *there are more phones in Manhattan than in some developing countries;* now, however, there is a shift of paradigm, and access to *the network* provides the discriminatory factor. This means that both a lack of physical access to the network and an inability to handle digital technologies can cause a loss of competitiveness.

The network discriminates

As outlined in the last reports on the diffusion of the Internet, there are large areas of the globe that are almost inaccessible for technological, political, social, economic and/or religious reasons. In some regions, while it is possible to connect to the network, in reality it is too expensive to do so. Digital networks have vastly increased the speed at which it is possible to communicate, providing real and tangible benefits to *power users*. Communications, information and assets exchanges, commerce and many other activities have increased their own potentials using such networks.

---

1   Smart Communities Forum: *Economic Development in a Global Information Society*, September 1997, Sophia-Antipolis, Nice, France and Rome, Italy.

eEconomy

The rise of the Internet has triggered the development of new skills, as well as new job opportunities, new services and new enterprises—all pillars of the so-called *e-economy*, an economy based largely on intangible goods (something immaterial which sometimes even disappear completely, as in the case of investors that have lost their capital).

The starting point of this development can be traced back to 1994, and right now its growth is more than doubling every year. This progression will create an enormous gap between *wired* and *unwired* people/countries in just a few years time. The growth of the Internet is important, and users are developing new market models every day.

Even if this seems to be mainly an infrastructural issue, there are many possible solutions that can be used to *bridge the gap*. Wireless networks on the Earth or those based on satellites represent one possible solution.

The gap as an opportunity

In such a situation the *gap* might provide an *opportunity* to skip some "technological *generations*. The major benefits of doing this are that it negates the need for *noninterchangeable infrastructure* and *backward compatibility*.

A few years ago, as a result of the second *Infopoverty* conference, a kit that provided a *satellite uplink* powered by solar energy was assembled, based on the experiences of a *Solar Village* in Honduras.

Solar Village

The results from the Solar Village indicated that, even in isolated villages, access to digital technology creates new job opportunities. More recently, a more extensive study was carried out in Tunisia and the results were showcased during the *World Summit on Information Society in Tunis* (November 2005).

Industrialised countries

In industrialised countries, the *digital era* can be considered to be an incredible opportunity to stimulate new initiatives, create new working and business models, provide jobs for young, old and even retired people, and to bridge gaps in education and training by transferring knowledge in a more efficient way thanks to technology.

We need to adequately consider these problems as we launch and develop the *e-society*. In addition, a number of new and emerging *professional profiles* have arisen or will arise due to the arrival of *e-society*. Some of these were or will be created from scratch, while others have evolved or will evolve from traditional skills.

Access to resources

However, network-based services may not be of any use to emerging countries if end-users are unable to access the information. Access to archives, cultural services, educational and training services need to be provided in *e-format* because of the added value but we must also ensure that this added value can be exploited by end-users.

When dealing with cultural issues, we often face problems such as the preservation of *cultural identity* or *cultural diversity* in some technologically remote areas of the world. How do we safely store and offer oral traditions or storytelling for local public enjoyment, for instance? Steaming audio and video across the Internet requires some bandwidth in addition to the basic technology and web access, so that sometimes the only way to ensure that end-users are able to experience them is to use VHS cassettes, an "easy access" technology which is widely available, cheap and the de facto standard.

Reciprocity and biopiracy

This aspect is very relevant, because if it is important to preserve cultural assets—to keep records of rites, oral traditions, and performances—as a legacy to humanity, then we must also provide the content holders/owners with a copy of the final, released version of the *contents* in an enjoyable format, as well as a percentage of any revenue obtained from it, as compensation[2]. It is therefore important to consider how IPR should be managed. Communities that involve themselves in technological evolution must share information within a tailored legal framework.

Emerging technologies such as *PDAs*, *smart phones* and *enhanced portable communication systems* may represent a solution on the *client (application) side*. The presence of a client side does not necessary imply the corresponding presence of a *server side*; *peer-to-peer* connections offer an attractive alternative approach that enables new interpersonal services (e.g. communities, social services, etc.).

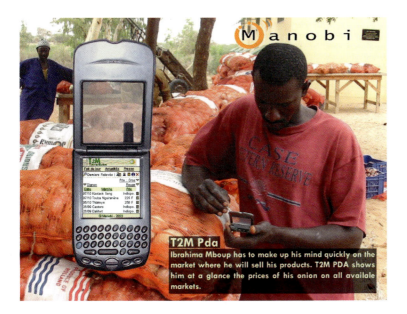

Fig. 2.1 Time to Market (produced by MANOBI, Senegal): WSA 2003 eInclusion winner

---

2   If there is not a "return on investment" for the owners, it is known as "biopiracy".

3 Quality Content

Quality content is essential in order to foster the development of the *Information or Knowledge Society*[3]. Early examples of *digital content* sometimes provoked a negative reaction due to the poor quality of both the content and the format. Some of the early products look more like a bare porting of paper-based books without the physical look and feel of a real book and its typical "easy to use" approach. Perhaps you remember some "digital cookbooks" that required that a PC with a keyboard and mouse was installed in your kitchen?!

A basic taxonomy

Quality content leads to the creation of *added value services*. Some of the *key sectors* that take advantage of digital content are[4]:

Key eContent sectors

- **e-Business**: Involves the support and optimisation of business processes; the creation of new business models in e-commerce and m-commerce, business-to-business, business-to-consumers, internet security and other areas; the support of SMEs in the marketplace.
- **e-Culture**: Involves preserving and presenting cultural heritage in line with the challenges of the future; exhibiting valuable cultural assets clearly and informatively using state-of-the-art technology.
- **e-Entertainment**: Involves supplying digitised entertainment products and services; entertaining the user in a variety of languages and in line with diverse cultures; supporting data transfer (one-way or two-way; single or multiple players), interactive entertainment and the synergy between analogue and digital platforms.
- **e-Government**: Involves empowering citizens and serving public services clients; fostering the quality and efficiency of information exchange and communication services in governmental and public administrative processes; strengthening participation of citizens in Information Society decision-making.
- **e-Health**: Involves developing the consumer-centred model of health care, where stakeholders collaborate, utilizing ICT, and internet technologies are used to manage health issues as well as the health care system.

---

3 Following an idea promoted by the European Commission: first step: Information Society; second step: Knowledge Society.

4 We refer to content categories used for the World Summit Award.

3 Quality Content   9

- **e-Inclusion**: Encompasses all measures that support the integration of less developed countries into the Information Society; reducing the "digital divide" and "content gap" between technology-empowered and technology-excluded communities and groups, such as those in rural areas and women; binding society together through multimedia.
- **e-Learning**: Involves enabling learners to acquire knowledge and skills for a complex and globalising world; transforming schools, universities and other educational institutions through interactive, personalised and distributed learning resources; creating active e-learning communities and target models and solutions for corporate training; supporting first steps in multimedia creation.
- **e-Science**: Involves fostering global collaboration in key areas of science, and the next-generation infrastructure that will enable it; providing measures to promote and demonstrate scientific processes and make them accessible to citizens; the realisation of scientific projects via new media.

It is easy to pick out some subcategories of these sectors, such as museum portals, virtual museums, electronic art artefacts and cultural services and applications under the eCulture umbrella. Note that other sectors are also now appearing on the scene, including: eDemocracy, eParticipation, eWork, eArt, eSecurity, eEnvironment...

eSecurity, eEnviroment

Platforms and channels

On the technological and infrastructural side, some of the more commonly used platforms and channels are:
- *Broadband/Online/Web*: All web and internet content and applications, especially those showing the potential of broadband experiences involving high interactivity, global connections, real-time and streaming media, and up-to-date communication.
- *Content tools and interface design*: Powerful content tools, content management systems and technological innovations concerning new approaches to interface design.
- *Cross and mixed media*: Projects based on the use of many different media to obtain flexibility, media adequacy and high usability.
- *Game platforms*: Pulsating contents with high-speed interactions that are highly involving and provide a rush to users.
- *Interactive computer graphics*[5]: Visually explosive content that transforms reality and seduces users into virtual worlds with cyberworld narratives.
- *Interactive TV and video*[6]: Fully digitised broadcast content that involves the user.

---

5   This platform was widely used in the field of cultural heritage.
6   Including, of course, digital terrestrial and satellite television.

I Cultural Content and the Information Society

- *Mobile content*[7]: Innovative content and applications that make use of the potential of compact, mobile and communication-intensive platforms, and focus on new multimedia solutions.
- *Offline/DVD, CD-ROM*: Classical and future multimedia projects with a strong emphasis on telling a story in an emotional, expressive and media-rich way.

An additional category might be *position-related content and services*, resulting from the combined use of a basic platform plus a GPS-based service. A number of emerging cultural services are based on navigators or pocket PCs and smart phones equipped with GPS units.

Fig. 3.1
Palmtop Navigator (photo by Francesca Ronchi)

---

7   This is an emerging channel due to the development of triple and quadruple players.

4 Digital Content and Creativity

The idea of the Knowledge Society is to add value to ideas, creativity and interactions. In the new scenario of an enlarged Europe there is a need to catalyse a common understanding that encourages the richness resulting from cultural diversity but also censures the unwanted effects that can sometimes arise from such diversity (e.g. clashes between cultures), thus leading to a common vision of the European Society. Young people and their special creativity could play an important role in such a scenario, particularly if supported by digital technologies. One of our aims is to promote creativity by maximising the cultural and educational potential of new technologies. Digital technology affects our lives in so many areas, including health, security, safety, work and similar fields, and particularly in the fields of cultural interests, creativity, entertainment, communication and relationships.

Creativity and interaction

Digital media have dramatically increased the possibilities available to the artist, by creating new forms of expression and by lowering the costs of producing certain artforms to such a degree that they become within the reach of individuals. As well as specifically digital media, music, still images and video are three significant areas where the costs of producing a finished work have dropped so dramatically that it has encouraged the emergence of new young talents.

Digital media and artists

Digital technology, and in particular the Internet, has completely overturned traditional ideas about distribution. *Any work that can take a digital form can be infinitely reproduced at minimal cost.* Young people in particular will be encouraged if they feel that others will see their efforts.

The instant global network provided by the Internet has made the building of special-interest groups unprecedentedly easy. These spaces are where artists talk, and they are excellent places to gauge the state of a scene.

Peer-to-peer technology enables on-the-fly exchange of content, and thus provides unlimited opportunities to share personal content and to activate added-value chains of cooperation.

Peer-to-peer

Creativity must be encouraged, and new interactive cultural expressions must be stimulated. Knowledge is not about the circulation of information. It is about adding value to ideas. A Knowledge Society must provide people with opportunities to think in new ways.

Up to now, ICT has often led to the creation of *libraries without books* and *highways without cars*—the technological infrastructure is in place but we can't do anything useful with it—while ICT companies are still looking for

Libraries without books

killer applications. However, there are some applications and technologies that are still at the development stage but should provide users with useful services.

Software availability is very patchy. The least widely available software includes video/audio authorware, and software for composing music and computer graphics as well as 3-D modelling.

Digital literacy

There is a need to channel the creative energies of young people by promoting *digital literacy* in the field of new ICT-enabled or empowered creativity and expression. There is also a need to create a proactive environment that enhances the overall quality of eContent products. Digital and social divides must be bridged in order to provide access and added value to citizens. Digital technologies and ICT tools provide an incredible opportunity to encourage growth and prosperity. Digital content and services empowered by broadband communications, both wired and wireless, could have a significant impact on society. One of the first steps in this direction is to promote *human networking* and the exchange of experiences and skills amongst different groups and communities.

Fig. 4.1 "Cyber" sheep at the TLC Museum in Frankfurt (photo by the author)

5 Cultural Content

"Culture is not one of life's luxuries, it is life itself. Culture is the soil that provides society's nourishment and the basis on which it defines its value system, traditions, and behaviour. It contains morals and ethics of the community, governs society's conception of its own future and selects the means of getting there."

From The Power of Culture (Royal Danish Ministry of Foreign Affairs 2000)

"Information and communication technology (ICT) is an engine of growth and change for the world economy. If this technology is to be harnessed to enhance democratic principles, it must contribute to the creation and enrichment of an educated, informed citizenry; it must incorporate the accumulated knowledge and creativity of the past; and it must anticipate and enhance creativity for the future.

In this context, it is essential that ICT embrace a cultural agenda. Development effectiveness depends to a great extent on "solutions" that resonate with a community's sense of identity and culture creates that sense of identity. Culture encompasses human knowledge, values, beliefs, behaviour, customs, language, ideas, codes, institutions, heritage, rituals, and creative expression all of which constitute essential signposts for understanding who we are and what we do. If advances in health, commerce, education, and economic growth are to be implemented and sustained, understanding culture is critical.[8]"

A cultural agenda

---

[8] From the report *On Culture in a Worldwide Information Society (see* http://www.medicif.org/Activities/Culture/future%20online%20culture%20G-8%20report%20final%204.htm*)*. People who helped shape this report: Eleanor Fink, The World Bank Report author; Co-chair, "The Future of Online Culture" Alfredo Ronchi, Politecnico di Milano, Co-chair of the session on "The Future of Online Culture" at WWW10; Andrew Cameron, Maplehurst Consultants, Canadian Heritage Information Network; Mercedes Giovinazzo, Council of Europe; David Green, Founding Director, National Initiative for a Networked Cultural Heritage; Kim Machan, Director, Multimedia Art Asia Pacific; Ranjit Makkuni, Xerox, Palo Alto Research Center; Liddy Nevile, Senior Research Fellow, University of Melbourne and WWW10 Culture Track Chair; Bernard Smith, Head of Unit, Cultural Patrimony Applications, European Commission; Lynn Thiesmeyer, Director, Southeast Asia Online Archive, Keio University; Friso Visser, Expert for Cultural Patrimony Applications, the European Commission; and Shelley Sperry, report editor.

Fig. 5.1 Ara Pacis (virtual reconstruction by Infobyte S.p.A., Italy)

The *G8's DOT Force* was launched to help bridge the digital divide and create a *global Information Society*. However, it is unclear whether the G8 understand the information requirements that must be addressed in order to promote online culture.

Cultural heritage

Before looking in depth at the relationship between cultural heritage and technology, we will try to define which class of objects we associate with the words *cultural heritage*. Our "heritage" can be considered to be the long path that ends with our present environment and way of life.

The term *cultural heritage* often brings to mind works of art, such as *paintings*, *frescoes*, *sculptures* and sometimes *monuments*. However, in doing so we actually overlook most cultural heritage[9].

From a purely legal point of view, we can consider anything realised by *human beings* more than fifty years ago to be potentially protected. Therefore, many objects can be enlisted for protection, such as the first *Bakelite radio set* issued, *post-war period cars,* and the *first electronic equipment*[10]. Generalising this approach, the *heritage* that should be looked after ranges from archaeological excavations to blue jeans to frescoes and industrial design products.

---

9   Most cultural heritage consists of "minor" cultural and artistic objects, such as medals, coins, plasters, silver, furniture, musical instruments, knick-knacks, ethnographic collections, etc.

10 These considerations are particularly applicable to the activation phase of a true communications market involving the enjoyment of cultural heritage, a market which up to now has been widely based on the simple assignment of image copyright. Consequently the Japanese are deeply interested in protecting this new class of objects, due to their prominent role in the development of communications technology.

Fig. 5.2 Old television set (photo by the author)

Furthermore, if we consider ethnographic collections, , then pictures (which have already been protected for almost fifty years), movies and TV recordings constitute an irreplaceable fountain of information to protect and hand down to posterity. In addition to *tangible heritage,* we must also preserve *intangible heritage.*

Let us prepare ourselves to face new types of collections, and consequently let us consider, in addition to the traditional ones, new types of maintenance and presentation[11]. Once we have defined the new types of cultural heritage to be protected, we will move the *focus* back to objects that are traditionally held in museums and collections.

How should we "structure" our heritage? A first attempt at classification should consider:

Natural, cultural and mixed heritage

- Natural heritage
- Cultural heritage
- Mixed heritage

---

11 During the preparation of the *Memorandum of Understanding*, the European Commission identified seven different types of museum, based on content: fine arts; natural history; archaeology; modern art; sciences; maritime; and ethnographic.

5 *Cultural Content*   17

Tangible and intangible cultural heritage

Cultural heritage can be subdivided into:
- Tangible cultural heritage
- Intangible cultural heritage

Immovable and movable heritage

Tangible heritage is usually then subdivided into:
- Immovable
- Movable

where immovable heritage is typically represented by built heritage, monuments and archaeological sites, and movable heritage, including paintings, sculptures, furniture, coins, and even frescos[12].

World Heritage Sites

Following this classification, UNESCO decided to define a selection of natural, cultural and mixed heritage sites as World Heritage Sites[13]; the main guidelines that are used to define such sites are included in the Convention Concerning the Protection of the World Cultural and Natural Heritage (1972)[14]. An updated list of the monuments and sites that form part of the cultural and natural heritage that the World Heritage Committee considers to have outstanding universal value is available online[15]. In July 2007, this list included over eight hundred sites. In addition, UNESCO defined *masterpieces* in a list[16] of relevant intangible heritage *objects*. New masterpieces are added to the list after a selection process and a proclamation.

Masterpieces

By 2007, 90 objects had been proclaimed as being masterpieces by Director-General Koïchiro Matsuura:
- In May 2001, 19 masterpieces were chosen from 32 proposals
- In November 2003, 28 were chosen from 56 proposals
- In November 2005, 43 were chosen from 64 proposals.

The 90 proclaimed cultural expressions and spaces are located in 70 countries from all regions of the world: 14 masterpieces are located in Africa, 8 in the Arab states, 30 in the Asia–Pacific region, 21 in Europe, and 17 in Latin America and the Caribbean.

---

12 They are termed "movable" because they can be (and often are) detached from the wall.

13 Heritage is our legacy from the past, what we live with today, and what we pass on to future generations. Our cultural and natural heritage are both irreplaceable sources of life and inspiration. Places as unique and diverse as the wilds of East Africa's Serengeti, the Pyramids of Egypt, the Great Barrier Reef in Australia and the Baroque cathedrals of Latin America make up our world's heritage. (Passage from UNESCO's *World Heritage* website; see http://whc.unesco.org/en/about).

14 Available at http://whc.unesco.org/?cid=175.

15 Available at http://whc.unesco.org/en/list.

16 Available at http://www.unesco.org/culture/ich/index.php?pg=00107.

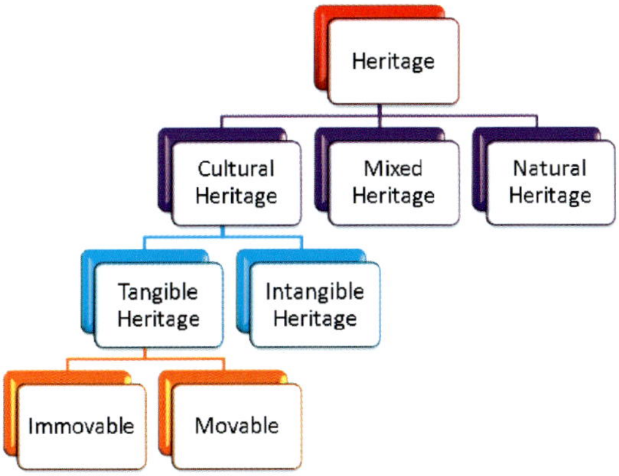

Fig. 5.3 Schema of Heritage taxonomy

5.1 Tangible and Intangible Digital Heritage

Cultural heritage should be considered to be the sum of the experiences that shaped the society in question, and so it should include art, history, and even food.

If we focus solely on the arts as a form of world cultural heritage, Western art tends to be visual art, Eastern art is largely associated with the performing arts, and Southern art is mainly based on oral traditions. UNESCO termed the last two kinds of content *intangible heritage,* and launched a task force to draw up guidelines aimed at preserving intangible heritage all over the world.

5.2 UNESCO's "Intangible Heritage"

The term "intangible cultural heritage" refers to the practices, representations, expressions, knowledge, and skills—as well as the instruments, objects, artefacts and cultural spaces associated with them—that communities, groups and, in some cases, individuals recognise as being part of their cultural heritage.

Representations, expressions, knowledge, skills...

This *intangible cultural heritage*, which is transmitted from generation to generation, is constantly recreated by communities and groups in response to their environment, their interactions with nature, and their history, and provides them with a sense of identity and continuity, thus promoting respect for cultural diversity and human creativity.

For the purposes of the convention defined in 5.2.1, only the intangible cultural heritage that is compatible with current international human rights, as well as with the requirements of mutual respect among communities, groups and individuals, and of sustainable development, is considered.

5 Cultural Content

5.2.1 The Convention

Convention for the Safeguarding of the Intangible Cultural Heritage

The *Convention for the Safeguarding of the Intangible Cultural Heritage*[17] defines intangible cultural heritage (as mentioned earlier) as the practices, representations, expressions, as well as the knowledge and skills, that communities, groups and, in some cases, individuals recognise as being part of their cultural heritage. This is sometimes known as *living cultural heritage*, and it is manifested, inter alia, in the following domains:
- Oral traditions and expressions, including language as a vehicle of intangible cultural heritage;
- Performing arts;
- Social practices, rituals and festive events;
- Knowledge and practices concerning nature and the universe;
- Traditional craftsmanship.

The term safeguarding refers to measures aimed at ensuring the viability of intangible cultural heritage, including the identification, documentation, research, preservation, protection, promotion, enhancement, transmission, particularly through formal and informal education, as well as the revitalisation of the various aspects of this heritage.

Fig. 5.4 Live Heritage (Living Heritage/2020 Communications Trust, New Zealand)

---

17 See http://www.unesco.org/culture/ich/index.php?lg=EN&pg=home.

6 Digital Communication: the Role of Context

Early in the 1990s, as a follow-up to a set of concrete experiences, I wrote some papers and articles entitled *Real Virtuality...,* to emphasise some concrete results and a case study that could aid the generation of new ideas regarding— and potential future applications of—virtual reality in the field of culture.

Real Virtuality...

Today, more than fifteen years after interactive virtual reality was first exploited, and more than ten years after the "explosion" of the Internet, a wide range of technologies are on the shelf, a number of applications and services are available, so what is missing? What are the opportunities and the threats?

Opportunities and threats

Many relevant players in both the museum and ICT communities invested time and resources into creating pilot projects and applications ranging from 3-D reconstructions, image-based rendering, to *virtual museums*. We are now in a position to consider whether such investments are effectively useful and really do increase and promote knowledge of the arts, sciences and history, and whether they satisfy users' requirements. Do virtual museums really provide added value to end-users? Are museums, content providers and users ready and willing to apply new technologies to cultural heritage? In the twenty-first century, the Information Society era, does the nineteenth century's encyclopaedic approach to museums still survive? Do ICT tools really help content holders and/or end-users?

Do virtual museums really provide added value to end-users?

As we have already stated, digital communication is the most recent link in a long chain, which started with nonverbal communication and gestures, evolved into languages, signs and writing, and then developed into printing, broadcasting and other media and formats. Do we use digital communication in the best way? Just how much are we really exploiting the potential offered by digital media? Is multimedia simply the sum of different media, or is it more than this? Does virtual reality merely refer to navigation through digital replicas of the *real* world?

One idea, following the approach suggested by Renée Descartes, is to start from *tabula rasa* (from scratch), and to look at the past in order to pick out some signs and clues that will allow us to choose the best format for the new digital media.

Tabula rasa

New technologies that enable new media and formats, such as interactive virtual reality or online multimedia, provide a good opportunity to (re)discover new ways of communicating and, in particular, of bringing some "lost" formats back to life.

"Lost" formats

Some technologies are (re-)enabling (new) communication formats. Today, people have the opportunity to create digital objects—a new *class* of objects from an ontological point of view—and they can use multimedia technologies and the Internet, which are both powerful communication tools, but still immature technologies that have yet to fulfil their full potential.

Virtual and enhanced reality also represent powerful tools for the transfer of information and knowledge, because they move away from transferring information in the usual *symbolic* way (i.e. by reading) and make use of a more perceptive-motory approach, where (even abstract) items can be explored and *touched*.

By making use of these tools, we will shift our current emphasis on the symbolic transfer of information and knowledge to an emphasis on an *experimental*, hands-on mechanism of information transfer. Last but not least, digital communication provides the opportunity to offer both the *object* and an *enriched context*, making it possible to preserve spatial and geometrical contextualisation. This means that we will be able to enjoy contextualised cultural information and visual 3-D or 4-D[18] reconstructions of objects that have their original shapes and spatial organisation.

---

18 In other words, including the dimension of time. Such reconstructions offer the opportunity to navigate in space and time in a virtual universe. Some early examples of such reconstructions are that of St. Peter's Cathedral by Infobyte S.p.A., and that of Bologna's historical city center by Cineca.

7 Cultural Diversity and Cultural Models

Globalisation is one of the key terms used to describe future trends, but there are many aspects of this concept that should be carefully considered, such as our *cultural identity*.

Cultural diversity is an asset that needs to be preserved, and to do so cultural models must be considered. *Cultural diversity* is the engine of cultural and economic growth; it provides incredible richness as well as traditions.

Even if we consider the "old Europe", with just fifteen countries, we must still face the issue of cultural diversity; since it encompasses 350 million people, 12 languages and at least three different cultural models (Mediterranean, German and Nordic).

Since May 1st 2004, the *cultural diversity* of Europe has increased significantly due to the inclusion of new countries and their cultural assets. Some languages still provide barriers (to science, tourism, etc.), as do some cultural and semantic aspects.

When we consider the application of ICT to culture, semantic aspects are not solely tied to the implementation of the *Semantic Web*, a web of machine-readable data that allows software agents to carry out rather complex tasks for humans automatically. At a lower level, semantic aspects are the basis for the interoperability of cultural content.

Such problems must be faced and possibly solved whilst developing transnational cultural applications.

The idea of creating a working group that deals with cultural issues in the Information Society era was launched by MEDICI[19] in the year 2000 in cooperation with a number of institutions. A panel was held on the occasion of the

On Culture in a Worldwide Information Society

---

19 The MEDICI Framework (Multimedia for EDucation and employment through Integrated Cultural Initiatives) is a framework of co-operation that was established and supervised by the European Commission. A partnership aimed at the application of new information technologies to the field of culture is being developed between the MEDICI initiative and the Council of Europe. MEDICI operates not just in Europe but across the world. The goal of MEDICI is to promote the use of advanced technologies to access, understand, preserve and promote the economics of Europe's cultural heritage.

10th WWW[20]; as a follow-up, an official final report was submitted to the G8 during the *G8 Summit* held in Genoa in June 2001.

The report and recommendations highlight:

- The value of the cultural agenda in development
- The potential of information and communications technologies to implement the cultural agenda by transforming information from a scarce, unequally distributed and fragmented commodity into a true public commodity
- The importance of integrating the cultural agenda and ICT into the G8 program for advancing a worldwide Information Society.

A number of suggestions and remarks were gathered, such as those regarding the Western-style top-down scrolling behaviour of web browsers and the limited number of character sets displayable on a single page (Asian servers need to be able to handle Thai, Chinese, Korean and Vietnamese).

Following the summit held in October 2001 in Genoa, the *Global Forum 2001: Expanding the Global e-Society* held in Newcastle (UK) saw the presentation of the report from the WWW10 Panel as well as other contributions that addressed cultural aspects, such as the paper *Time Rich Time Poor*[21].

Cultural industries and new technologies

As already mentioned, a joint event managed by the Council of Europe and UNESCO, *Cultural Industries and New Technologies*, was held in November 2001 in Strasbourg (France). A publication entitled *Vital Links for a Knowledge Culture was issued during this event. Vital Links* deals with the complex relations between NICTs[22] and culture across Europe. It starts with a discussion of the general context (culture, ICT, new technologies) and the deep structures of the Knowledge Society. It then describes public access to new information and communication technologies in Europe through statistics and indices, and provides contributions devoted to various aspects of access in Europe. The last part of the publication is devoted to policy frameworks, and contains chapters entitled *Cultural Policy in the Knowledge Society, Towards a Strategic Evolutionary Cultural Policy, and A Policy Network Model.*

XI World Wide Web Conference and Indigenous Space and Cyberspace

During WWW2002[23], a panel on culture was held (as usual), and the two distinguished panellists made some relevant remarks. The first contribution,

---

20 Held in Hong Kong in May 2001.

21 Helena Lindskog elaborated on another aspect of the digital divide, namely the divide between the time-rich and the time-poor, and the impact of this divide on the e-society. If the e-society wishes to provide services that are accessible at any time, anywhere, and in any way, it must satisfy the needs of both the time-rich and the time-poor, and address both time and financial issues alike. Market segmentation is currently based on time, and this may have to change in the future.

22 NICT means "new information and communication technologies".

23 Held in Honolulu on 7–11 May 2002.

from Lynn Thiesmeyer[24], was dedicated to *Indigenous Space and Cyberspace: Online Culture and Development in Southeast Asia*.

The contribution outlines the chances of preserving cultural representations that are not simply object- or text-based thanks to the WWW technology. Examples of such cultural representations in mainland Southeast Asia include *life practices*, such as the use of space and time, which are closely associated with different agricultural models.

These practices include female-based culture and economic activities, indigenous medicine, the creation and use of hand tools, cultural adaptation to diverse geographies and climates, and indigenous knowledge. All of these rely not just on static objects or spaces, but also on movements through household, communal, agricultural, and forest spaces for a variety of interlinked purposes. Conventional databases, as well as conventional data-gathering techniques, have so far failed to adequately capture the intangibles of space, movement and indigenous knowledge.

This is the challenge and the ultimate goal of the Multimedia Online Project for Southeast Asia: to create a practical multimedia archive with the capacity to handle several new forms of information, and to maintain a direct real-time visual link to onsite sources in rural Asia. In addition, the multimedia archive must comply with the *reciprocity* principle, thus providing added value to the *owners* of cultural content.

Reciprocity

Kimmo Aulake[25] introduced the second topic, *cultural policies*, starting with the *Intergovernmental Context for Culture in the Information Society*, which included a list of key organisations such as UNESCO, the European Union, the Council of Europe, WTO, OECD, and the G8.

Cultural policies are legitimised by national constitutions, national laws, and international instruments and commitments. There are two main principles to consider in a discussion of cultural policies: *public access and cultural diversity*.

Public access to information is a prerequisite for the development of a democratic Information Society. Recalling *Vital Links*, meaningful public access must be *affordable, available and usable*: "Access is a cultural phenomenon and meaningful access is composed of a literate user having access to meaningful content and services."

Public access

Affordable, available and usable

The second principle, *cultural diversity,* is one of the main assets of the human race. *Cultural diversity* and its preservation are crucial to discussions of globalisation.

Cultural diversity

---

24 Dr. Lynn Thiesmeyer, Coordinator, Mekhong Region Development Net / Women and Development Online, Faculty of Environmental Information Keio University, Shonan–Fujisawa Campus Endo 5322, Fujisawa, Japan 252-8520. See: http://www.sfc.keio.ac.jp/~thiesmey/widmain.html.

25 Kimmo Aulake, Ministry of Education and Culture, Finland.

Unfortunately, there are some issues associated with *cultural diversity,* such as the proliferation of different policies with an increasing level of interaction but unfortunately often with poor coordination. This is particularly true in relation to the rapid expansion of the scope and coverage of multilateral trade policy (GATS and TRIPS).

"La culture, ce n'est pas une marchandise comme les autres"

The main difference between *cultural and trade policies* is the modus operandi applied; uniformity or diversity, liberalisation or (de)regulation, blindness or sensitivity, not forgetting that *la culture, ce n'est pas une marchandise comme les autres* (i.e. culture is different—it is not merchandise).

All of this implies that the following actions are key to the proper inclusion of culture in a worldwide Information Society:
- Clarifying the cultural objectives
- Understanding the implications of increased interaction between policies
- Developing the international aspects of cultural policies and cultural cooperation
- Guaranteeing cross-sector cooperation
- Engaging the affected sectors.

There are *no contradictions* between the objectives of cultural policy and other policies. Cultural policy serves essential societal values and objectives. Culture, cultural diversity and access to information are at the very core of the development of an Information Society.

7.1   On Culture in a Worldwide Information Society

This section summarises a report[26] that describes the achievements of panels and contributions on this topic. The report distils over three years of activity in this area, will enable us to outline some of the *critical issues* and *policy needs* that must be addressed and to make recommendations about pilot projects that should be launched to fully demonstrate the role of culture in development and poverty reduction.

The report outlines how the members of the G8 can include a cultural agenda in their efforts to promote global participation and empowerment in order to advance the development goals of poverty reduction, economic growth, education, health, sanitation, and global e-commerce.

---

26 This section is an excerpt from a report entitled *On Culture in a Worldwide Information Society,* based on the activity of the panel *The Future of Online Culture* (co-chairs: E. Fink and A.M. Ronchi) at the 10th International World Wide Web Conference (see http://www.medicif.org/Activities/Culture/future%20online%20 culture%20G-8%20report%20final%204.htm and http://www.medicif.org/events/ MEDICI_events/Www10/Fink_Ronchi.htm, respectively).

The *Okinawa Charter on Global Information Society*, created at the July 2000 G8[27] meeting in Okinawa, Japan, affirmed the importance of using ICT in for developmental purposes:

Okinawa Charter

Information and Communications Technology (ICT) is one of the most potent forces in shaping the twenty-first century. Its revolutionary impact affects the way people live, learn and work, and the way government interacts with civil society. It is fast becoming a vital engine of growth for the world economy.
The essence of the IT-driven economic and social transformation is its power to help individuals and societies to use knowledge and ideas. Our vision of an Information Society is one that better enables people to fulfil their potential and realize their aspirations[28].

The recommendations of the report are structured into four main sections:
- Cultural content
- Standards and good practices
- Access and information policies
- Frameworks and intellectual property rights.

We will now consider each of these topics in turn.

7.1.1   Cultural Content

The first section discusses *how developing cultural content* still represents a formidable challenge:

Develop a critical mass of cultural content. We are currently in a digital dark age with respect to lack of content. Without a critical mass of information, technological capacity is a hollow structure, like a highway without cars.

It is even difficult to make high-quality content available through digital *channels*, due to the lack of an appropriate *format.*[29]

During the evolution of communication from oral traditions to manuscripts to printed books, and later on to movies and radio and television broadcasting, a specific format was adopted or readopted at each evolutionary phase. How-

---

27 The "G8" group of nations includes Canada, France, Germany, Italy, Japan, Russia, the United Kingdom and the United States. The G8 are the world's largest industrial economies, representing a combined $30 trillion of the global gross domestic product (GDP), or about two-thirds of the world's economic output.

28 Available at http://www.g8.fr/evian/english/navigation/g8_documents/archives_ from_previous_summits/okinawa_summit_-_2000/okinawa_charter_on_global_ information_society.html.

29 Alfredo M. Ronchi, The bias of printing, proceedings "Cultural Heritage, Networks, Hypermedia".

ever, even though we have now entered the multimedia era, we are yet to find a proper format for multiple media channels; we are still *porting* books online.

Creativity must be encouraged, and new interactive cultural expressions must be stimulated. As stated earlier, "Knowledge is not about circulation of information. It is about adding value to ideas. A Knowledge Society must provide people with opportunities to think in new ways"[30].

The creation of a fully interactive online culture would transform links between computers into connections between people that can stimulate ideas and new skills. We must create mechanisms that encourage the participation and empowerment of all people in developing and developed countries and allow them autonomy and control.

7.1.2   Standards and Good Practices

The second section of the report, entitled *Standards and Good Practices*, develops standards for creating and managing digital collections and *guides to good practices* for creating cultural content:

"Developing standards to formulate and manage data and to migrate data to new platforms is essential and will require significant investments, which in turn demand standards and terminology to ensure long-term viability of electronic information and the ability to search across databases. Good practices are needed in order to help smaller institutions and developing nations avoid reinventing the wheel" (see NINCH 2001 for a good example).

The adoption of de facto standards and the use of Internet technologies guarantees interoperability and reuse of investments.

The report, in addition, suggests the construction of a portal containing international data standards, good practices, and policy frameworks in order to promote and encourage the harmonisation of cultural content. This portal should be a basic mechanism that allows information about international standards and policies to be disseminated as quickly as possible.

In terms of enabling technologies, during the same event (WWW10), *Extensible Mark-up Language (XML)*—which was first introduced during WWW7 in Brisbane in 1998—was endorsed as a standard by the World Wide Web Consortium (W3C).

---

30   Suggested by Dr. Shalini Venturelli (Associate Professor of International Communication Policy, American University), in a lecture on *Knowledge, Civil Society & Culture in the Information Society: Toward a New Model of IT Policy for Developing Countries*, World Bank, Washington, DC, July 2001.

Many major organisations[31], including *memory institutions* (libraries, museums, archives) and galleries, have also adopted the *Dublin Core (DC)*[32] metadata standard and the *Resource Description Framework (RDF)*[33], which were developed to aid the discovery of objects and content harmonization.

Technological aspects are not enough, however; the *economic sustainability* of cultural services must be ensured, meaning that institutional awareness of *new economic models* must be promoted. Some surveys have indicated that cultural institutions can earn revenue from ICT when they market their cultural resources[34] to media companies (in a business-to-business—B2B—fashion) or produce their own value added products and services (in a business-to-customers—B2C—model)[35].

New economic models: B2B and B2C

If the cultural institutions are to extend their range of operations to include online services and content provision, the creation of a web of links with related organisations implies the hiring and training of qualified staff. Institutions must develop *training programs* for technicians and managers of online resources. The development of *training programs* at various levels (local, regional, national, international, and also institutional) is essential[36].

Training programs

---

31 The United Nations Economic, Scientific, and Cultural Organization (UNESCO), the International Council of Museums (ICOM), and the Council of Europe have published policy frameworks and conventions that advocate the use of standards. A good example of key policy frameworks that advocate standards is the UNESCO convention concerning the Protection of the World Cultural and Natural Heritage, which includes a provision that a World Heritage Committee be established and that each party submit an inventory of its national heritage to this committee. The UNESCO convention on the Means of Prohibiting the Illicit Import, Export and Transfer of Ownership of Cultural Property advocates the use of the Object ID metadata standard as a means of protecting cultural property and reporting property that has been stolen. The Council of Europe has published useful guidelines on this topic, including their *Declaration on a European Policy for New Information Technologies* (Council of Europe 1999), which includes recommendations for public access to and freedom of expression in networked information. The Declaration can be found online at https://wcd.coe.int/ViewDoc.jsp?BackColorInternet=9999CC&BackColorIntranet=FFBB55&BackColorLogged=FFAC75&id=849061.

32 The Dublin Core (see http://dublincore.org/) was developed by PURL (see http://www.purl.org) and OCLC.

33 An online RDF primer is available at http://www.w3.org/TR/rdf-primer/.

34 Cultural content should include restoration processes, investigations, "the making of" digital reconstructions, etc.

35 For more information on these issues, see the proceedings of MEDICI panels held during CeBIT, available online at http://www.medicif.org.

36 Information and analysis contributed by Friso Visser, expert for Cultural Patrimony Applications, European Commission.

Collaboration and cooperation with the private technology sector must be promoted in order to encourage and establish standards that will ensure the sustainability of digital technology.

Conserving for long periods of time

Rapid changes in technology make the preservation of digital content a challenge. Taking into account the huge amount of data to be filed, the amount of time needed to accomplish this task, and the length of time that we need to store such information, we must objectively consider a problem that has been largely underestimated so far: how to approach the long-term *conservation of digital information*.

Detailed consideration of this subject leads us to explore two aspects: technological obsolescence and the *temporary nature* of so-called *permanent supports*. The typical timescale of technological turnover for ICT (quarters) is much shorter than the timescales usually associated with cultural heritage (centuries).

Digital formats suddenly become obsolete and disappear. Even an unusually long-lived solution, such as PC/DOS, which was popular for over twenty years, is only a short-lived phenomenon compared to the lengths of time that many documents have spent in state owned archives.

The magnetic diskette is an example of a storage medium that gradually degrades; it has an operational lifespan of thousands of hours, this is not long enough to be considered a *permanent* storage solution for cultural information.

What are the long-term implications if we rely on current digital technology to preserve our cultural memory?[37]

7.1.3 Access

The third section of the report, *Access*, deals with some well-known topics, such as radio and satellite access, even those powered by solar energy or "Western" interfaces and video audio content.

An interesting suggestion for merging traditions and technology states: *It might be useful to provide opportunities for re-using the hand skills and expertise of craftsmen in designing delivery devices*[38].

One subsection states the need to *Encourage development of multilingual capabilities, and create new modes of mapping and indexing information and new conceptual search capabilities beyond the Semantic Web*. This subsection contains an interesting reference to new conceptual models for interfaces aimed at easing information retrieval and knowledge representation. Experiences such

---

[37] For more information on these issues, see MacLean and Davis (1999).

[38] Suggestions provided by Ranjit Makkuni, Xerox PARC, with reference to the Crossings Project. Information about the Crossings Project is available at http://www.sacredworld.com/crossing.htm.

as *Smithsonian Without Walls: Revealing Things* [39], *American Bytes/History Wired* [40] and other mapping systems are directly referenced as fields of further investigation.

7.1.4 Information Policies: Frameworks and Intellectual Property Rights

This section of the report promotes the adoption *of clear, publicly available national and international information policy frameworks*, with specific reference to developing countries that should be assisted by industrialized countries in establishing common policy frameworks.

Lastly, the section also promotes proactive *intellectual property rights* that emphasise the public good. The lack of a comprehensive policy framework for handling *intellectual property rights* is currently one of the major barriers to global information access. Content integrity and source certification must be included within the policy framework.

---

39 Judith Gradwhol for the Smithsonian Institution in 1998: *Revealing Things*; see: http://www.si.edu.

40 *Treemap* and *Treemaps For Space-Constrained Visualization of Hierarchies* by Ben Shneiderman: see: http://www.cs.umd.edu/hcil/.

7 *Cultural Diversity and Cultural Models*

8 Content, Communication and Tools

Having considered the general framework and related problems and issues, the present chapter is devoted to *communication processes* and potential benefits and problems associated with the use of ICT.

8.1 Why is Digital Communication Revolutionary?

Nowadays, there are different models, opportunities for, and types of communication: *asynchronous or synchronous; mono- or bidirectional; one-to-one, one-to-many, or many-to-many; location-dependent or location-independent; immersive or nonimmersive; interactive or noninteractive, with log file and without log file; wired or wireless*. In order to develop more effective communication, we must create new recipes from these different *ingredients*.

Asynchronous and synchronous, mono- and bidirectional

In the recent past—the *electric era* as it was called by Marshall McLuhan—major progress in the field of communications was related to the invention and implementation of new types of communication, such as those mentioned above.

Attempts to ease communication between ships led to the invention of wireless communication. A potential problem with this invention, the *lack of privacy* resulting from the fact that only a standard radio set is required to eavesdrop on

Wireless

Fig. 8.1 Oral communication (Città della Scienza Napoli; photo by the author)

Broadcasting — wireless communications, led to another important innovation: broadcasting! *Broadcasting* provided the opportunity to reach an audience of a size that was previously unforeseeable.

Asynchronous communication — The opportunity to break away from the need for *synchronism* during long-distance communication was provided by voice recorders and later on fax messages, and these technologies were highly beneficial to a wide range of people.

Fax messaging enabled the almost real-time transfer of text and black and white images, as well as the ability to dispatch a message at any time of day (convenient or inconvenient) to the selected recipient.

Location-independent communication — The invention of *email* allowed users to break away from *location-dependent* communication, since it enabled them to access and use mailing services all over the world, thus shortening the operational chain—no more need to collect and distribute faxes, or for assistants to type a reply and fax it.

Enabling personal mass communication — *The Internet era* offers many benefits, including *easy access to broad audience communication,* and *forums* and *blogs* appeared, which are powerful tools.

Mobile communication enabled a kind of virtual ubiquity. Originally intended to be a minor aspect of mobile communication, the utility and popularity of *Mobile communication and SMS* — short message *service (SMS)* messages were initially hugely underestimated as communication tools. As we have seen, they have enabled a new way to work and are an incredibly powerful aid to interpersonal relationships.

Today they are often used as a *private* channel, as opposed to a *public* channel. SMS offers typing and paging features plus emoticons and the time dimension. The employment of text and the time delay enable the use of imagination—the most powerful tool supporting communication.

The increasing number of wireless devices and *always on* terminals has catalysed the creation of new applications and services, and will continue to do so.

However, up to now there has not been a proper way to use technological *Video games* — tools in order to exploit the real advantages of ICT in communication. The only exception to this rule is the *entertainment* and *video game* sector. This sector has found the best way to use technology in order to entertain and to transfer content. Some of the communication techniques commonly used in the computer games market are so efficient that even the *movie image* sector has adopted them.

Once upon a time, the usual added value chain was structured in the following way: *book/script, movie, video game, theme park.* This sequence can now be*: script, video game, movie, book, theme park and various forms of merchandise.* The idea of *contextualising* and *immersing ourselves* in the story using video games seems to be much more effective than the usual approach.

Nevertheless, a closer look to the state of the art in this sector shows *an empty and dead digital world.*

Digital communication — Digital communication is a cornerstone of modern life; email and other Internet services, mobile phones, radio and television, imaging, movies and more are all based on *digital content.*

34 *I Cultural Content and the Information Society*

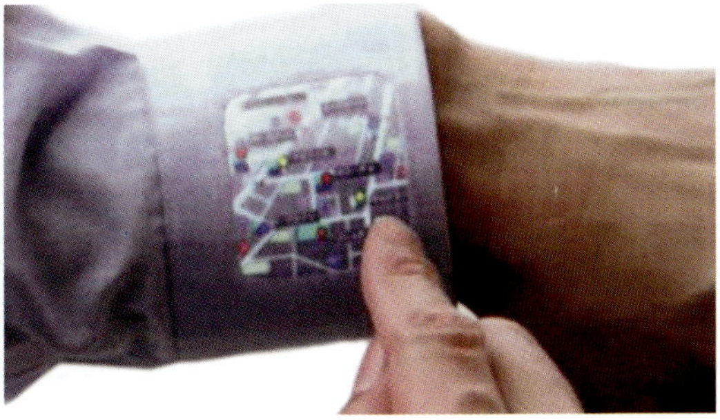

Fig. 8.2 Do.Co.Mo vision of future trends

We even make use of *digital communication* while driving our cars; various devices such as ABS, ESP, and ECM make use of it, as do interfaces between the car and the driver or passengers (cockpit, navigation system, car phone, etc.) and between the car and the rest of the world (e.g. automatic pay toll, automatic parking etc,).

In the world of digital communication, *broadband (BB) communication* is the new frontier. BB promises new added value services and a real revolution for end-users, particularly if delivered through wireless connections. There is not a clear threshold that defines broadband communication; it can be 1 Mbit, 10 Mbits, or more—it is constantly increasing. More simply, BB is just the rate required to access and fully enjoy the requested service.

BB will enable or empower e-health, e-government, e-learning, e-culture, e-commerce, e-work, and last but not least, e-entertainment. We hope that BB will even facilitate e-inclusion, reducing the gap that we earlier termed the *digital divide*.

An interesting, although also worrying, forecast for 2005 was published by a Japanese Bank association in 1999. This forecast was adopted by Masao Nakamura, President and CEO of DoCoMo, in 2001, upon the official disclosure of commercial figures for the *i-mode market*.

He presented an unconventional vision of the near future: that five years on, the vast majority of their customers could be *nonhumans*—machines, computers, or at least animals. Most transactions would be performed directly by computers; for example, our cars would automatically pay highway tolls via telepayment systems or personal transponders that automatically access different resources. Micropayments would be performed by cell-phones which automatically call soda distributors, ladies would talk to their own pets via mini mobile units embedded in their collars, and GPS and microprocessors would be able to activate car ABS and electronic braking systems if there was a risk of a dog being run over while it crossed the road.

Human and nonhuman users

Today RFID-based subscriptions and access codes are used around the world to enable users to enter facilities (underground transport systems, spas and wellness centres, clubs) or to pay for goods and services by simply *showing* an RFID-based card. Mobile phones are offering more and more services due to

RFID

8 *Content, Communication and Tools*   35

their use of standards that ensure interoperability[41]. Triple players are offering more and more entertainment opportunities to their own customers, such as television programmes on the mobile phones.

Within this scenario, integrated solutions that enable information exchange between devices through the use of common interfaces offer incredible opportunities to unleash creativity and aid the start-up of new services. Such devices include smart phones, digital imaging devices, e-books, musical devices and computers.

Software applications that manage text, sound and visual content, and thus support creativity, are becoming the de facto standard; these enable citizens to create their own digital communication objects.

8.2   Memetics and the Internet

Genes and memes

Let us begin this section by discussing communication technology in the context of the theory introduced by Susan J. Blackmore during the 2001 World Wide Web Conference, *The Meme's Eye Web*. The term *meme*[42] is somewhat analogous to the term "gene"; it is the building block of a communication object.

Blackmore argues that *memes* have shaped human nature. By driving the evolution of the machinery that copies them, *memes* have created the enormous human brain, with its specialised capacity for language. More recently, they have driven the invention of writing, printing, mass communication and broadcasting, as well as the Internet. From a *meme's perspective*, the World Wide Web is a vast playground for self-propagation.

Variation and selection

Meme theory is suitable for cultural evolution, including the evolution of knowledge, since both can be modelled using the same basic principles—*variation* and *selection*—that underlie biological evolution. This implies a shift away from *genes*, the units of biological information, to a new type of unit: the *meme*, representing an *atom of cultural information*.

A meme is a cognitive or behavioural pattern that can be transmitted from one individual to another one. Consider young people that wear clothes in an unconventional way or use signs and gestures that show that they belong to a particular community. The basic mechanism is very simple; since the individual who transmitted the meme will continue to carry it, the transmission can be

---

41   In other words, a mobile version of Google Earth or enhanced mobile banking capabilities.

42   *Meme*: an information pattern, held in an individual's memory, which is capable of being copied to another individual's memory. *Memetics*: the theoretical and empirical science that studies the replication, spread and evolution of memes (from Principia Cybernetica Web: http://pespmc1.vub.ac.be/).

36   *I Cultural Content and the Information Society*

interpreted as a replication. A meme carrier, known as a *replicator*, is created when a copy of the meme is made in the memory of another individual.

Replicator

Replication or self-reproduction is the basis for the *memetic* life cycle. This leads to the spread of memes to more and more individuals, such that the meme acts as a replicator, in a similar way to the gene (Dawkins 1976; Moritz 1990).

Following the theory expressed by Dawkins, Susan Blackmore listed the following three characteristics that are required for any successful *replicator*[43]:

- *Copying-fidelity:* the more faithful the copy, the closer the copy will be to the initial pattern after several rounds of copying. If a painting is reproduced by making photocopies of photocopies, the underlying pattern will quickly become unrecognisable.
- *Fecundity:* the faster the rate of copying, the more the *replicator* will spread. An industrial printing press can churn out many more copies of a text than an office copying machine.
- *Longevity:* the longer the replicating pattern survives, the more that it can be copied. A drawing made by etching lines in the sand is likely to be erased before anybody could have photographed or otherwise reproduced it.

8.2.1   More About Memes

Before we tackle technology, and specifically the similarity of the Internet to *memet*ic behaviour, let's have a closer look at the *meme* replication process; the *memetic* life cycle.

The memetic lifecycle consists of four stages that together (just as in genetic science) determine the meme's fitness: *assimilation, retention, expression and transmission.*

Memetic life cycle

In this specific context, assimilation means that a user becomes a meme host, retaining the meme in his/her memory. Then the user incorporates and expresses the meme in his/her own form so that it can be perceived by others.

The transmission phase refers to the transfer of the new message or meme vehicle to other subjects. The cycle then starts again with the assimilation stage, thus closing the replication loop. Each phase includes a selection process that retains the "fittest" memes and eliminates the weaker ones.

We now delve further into the meme life cycle, based on the ideas of F. Heylighen[44].

8.2.1.1 *Assimilation*

Memes must be able to "infect" a new host—to enter its memory. Assume that a meme is presented to a potential new host. Here, "presented" means that

---

43   These three characteristics were defined by R. Dawkins and S. Blackmore.

44   See *Meme Replication: The Memetic Life-Cycle* by F. Heylighen: http://pespmc1. vub.ac.be/MEMEREP.html.

8 Content, Communication and Tools   37

Noticed, understood, accepted

either the individual encounters a meme vehicle, or that he or she discovers it independently by observing external phenomena or by thought, i.e. the recombination of existing cognitive elements. To be assimilated, the presented meme must be *noticed*[45], *understood*[46] and *accepted*[47] by the host.

8.2.1.2 Retention

The second stage of memetic replication involves the retention of the meme in memory. By definition, memes must be retained in memory for a period of time; otherwise they cannot be called memes. The longer the meme stays in memory, the more opportunities it will have to spread further by infecting other hosts[48]. Just like the assimilation process, retention is characterised by strong selection, which means that few memes will survive.

Infecting other hosts

Most of the things that we hear, see or understand during the day are not stored in memory for longer than a few hours. The degree of retention in memory is usually strongly related to how important the idea is to you, and how often it is repeated, either by recurrent perception or by internal rehearsal. All learning paradigms agree that experiences are encoded more strongly into memory by frequent reinforcement.

8.2.1.3 Expression

To be communicated to other individuals, a meme must emerge from its storage as a memory pattern and form a physical shape that can be perceived by others. This process can be termed *expression*. The most obvious form of expression is speech. Other common forms of meme expression are text, pictures, and behaviour. Expression does not require the host to consciously decide to communicate the meme. A meme can be expressed simply by the way that somebody walks or manipulates an object, or through what they are wearing.

Some retained memes will never be expressed. This may occur because the host does not consider the meme to be interesting enough for others to know, they use it unconsciously without it showing up in their behaviour, they do not know how to express it, or they want to keep it secret. On the other hand, the

---

45 This requires that the meme vehicle is sufficiently salient to attract the host's attention.

46 This means that the host recognises the meme as being something that can be represented in his or her cognitive system. The mind is not a blank slate onto which any idea can be impressed. To be understood, a new idea or phenomenon must connect with cognitive structures that are already available to the individual.

47 Finally, a host that has understood a new idea must also be willing to believe it or to take it seriously. For example, although you are likely to understand the proposition that your car was built by little green men from Mars, you are unlikely to accept that proposition without very strong evidence. Therefore, you will generally ignore it, and the meme will not infect you.

48 This is Dawkins' (1976) longevity characteristic for replicators.

host may be convinced that the meme is so important that it must be expressed again and again to everybody he or she meets.

8.2.1.4 Transmission

To reach another individual, an expression needs a physical carrier or medium that is sufficiently stable to *transmit* the expression without too much loss or deformation. Speech, for example, uses sound to transmit an expression, while text will be transmitted through ink on paper or electrical impulses in a wire. The expression will take the form of a physical signal, modulating the carrier into a specific shape from which the original meme can be re-derived. This physical shape can be termed the meme vehicle. Meme vehicles can be books, photographs, artefacts or CD-ROMs for example.

Selection happens at the transmission stage through either the elimination of certain memes, when the vehicle is destroyed or gets corrupted before it is perceived by another individual, or through differential multiplication, when the vehicle is copied many times.

For example, a manuscript may be placed into the shredder or it may be turned into a book that is printed thousands of times. A radio communication may get lost because of noise, or it may be broadcast to millions of listeners. Particularly since the emergence of mass media, including electronic networks, the transmission stage has been the one where the contrast between successful and unsuccessful memes is the greatest, and where selection can have the largest impact.

8.3 The Evolution of the Digital Species

While the technology to create and transfer digital content is available, we haven't found the proper way to exploit these opportunities yet.

Fig. 8.3 Walking eggs (Berengo Fine Arts Murano, Venice; photo by the author)

Fig. 8.4 Early inflatable boat

The use of different media and technology tools seems to be limited to trivial uses—often the reproduction of traditional objects in digital format (just as early cars reproduced traditional coaches and inflatable boats attempted to replicate wooden motor-boats).

For quite a while, multimedia titles were simply paper-based publications that had been ported to a digital format; an approach with little added value.

From writing to printing to radio and television to the virtual and online worlds, the path followed by *communication* has passed from the textual description to the combined use of text and pictures or photographic images, and then to the movie or the so-called *audiovisual* formats that are created by joining together slides and voices or audio/soundtracks. More recently, the mode of communication has changed, and although greater care is taken over the visual part of the content, communication based on the combined use of audio and visual modes is more than doubly effective compared to single-channel communication (i.e. writing) of the same content.

Convergence towards new types of communication enabled by a series of new technologies, including *hypermedia, digital images, virtual reality, telecommunications networks* and others, has created new points of aggregation between software, telecommunications and the entertainment industry, thus forcing us to re-evaluate the market.

Virtual funnel and digital convergence

The *virtual funnel* (usually called *digital convergence*) and the evolution of communication are closely related; *hypermedia, telecommunications* and *virtual reality* are the basic components of this *funnel,* which merges different industrial sectors such as information technology, telecommunications, and entertainment.

This section analyses the historical path of communication in order to identify some biases that have influenced and that are still relevant to communication and its related formats. These are related to the transmission of *complex*

Fig. 8.5 Benz Viktoria, built in 1891 (an early car prototype based on a coach-like design)

structured information, perceptive aspects and the qualities of the new digital products, as well as *ontological aspects*. Some examples are given to aid reader understanding.

New infrastructure and increased bandwidth are some of the drivers of digital convergence. The integration of audio and video with alphanumeric and other digital data offers new opportunities and interaction models.

Digital telephony, instant messaging, short messages, streaming media, multimedia messages and video calls are merely some new ingredients that can be blended into a *newcomm* recipe.

VOIP

The ability to effectively transfer information and knowledge was and still is one of the key factors in the evolution of mankind when viewed from the joint perspectives of anthropology and culture. From the very beginnings of civilization, efforts have been made to improve information management and transfer.

We have moved from verbal communication processes to ideograms, from single instances of messages to multiple instances, inventing alphabets and mechanisms in order to break through the barrier of physical reality and approach metaphysical contents, and from experiences of real objects interacting with our senses to symbolic descriptions of abstract concepts and procedures. In the general arena of multimedia and consumer-oriented applications, some emerging technologies are enabling the creation of new media and formats for communication and reviving overlooked formats. In addition, the interoperability of a wide range of consumer devices, such as photo and video cameras, smart phones, home and car stereos, television sets, palm computers,

Fig. 8.6 *The Three Graces* by Antonio Canova (Hermitage, St. Petersburg); different media: alphabet, grammar, format (photo by the Author)

together with the use of communications- and internet-related applications has unleashed a wave of creativity in terms of both content and the integration of different devices.

So the technologies are available and digital content is easy to acquire and edit. We should be enjoying improved communication based on true multimedia content... however, something is missing... a "proper" format.

Proper format

The evolution of communication in the last centuries is moving toward a mixed model of written/audio and visual communication that focuses, where possible, on visual communication more than on written text or audio. Users prefer to watch more than to read. In this way, we are now rediscovering some old formats for nonlinear communication.

Some examples of these emerging formats are those being adopted by newspapers and magazines, which are more oriented towards the use of images/photos along with a short comment.

So far, we have focussed on moving toward the proper use and exploitation of efficient communication techniques. Convergence toward new communication standards due to the combined action of emerging technologies forces the redefinition of roles in the marketplace, thus creating a new reference node that will include software, telecommunications and entertainment. We have already termed such an association a "virtual funnel", or the convergence of a family of technologies that are able to create and transfer virtual objects. Such melting pots often lead to new applications and services.

It is important to correctly understand this potential because improvements in communication have historically impacted upon everyday life, culture and society. A review of the history of information and communication will help us to understand today's challenges and opportunities.

Fig. 8.7 MediaLab (Dublin, Ireland, photo by the author)

8.4 Historical Background

This chapter summarises some of the most relevant milestones in the history of communication; a short list of bibliographic resources for this field is included at the end of the chapter.

Ancient Greeks

The ancient Greeks believed that verbal communication of relevant events was sufficient; all other forms of communication were nonessential. Philosophers and authors such as Socrates[49] and Homer committed their own art and thoughts to oral tradition, even though the art of writing had already been developed many centuries before by the Sumerians (4000 B.C.)[50], the Mesopo-

---

49 Later on, some philosophers tried to protect their intellectual property rights by creating written versions of their own ideas and keeping them in safe places, such as the naos (the Greek word has an "à") of temples.
50 Some ideograms dating back to 5000 B.C. have recently been discovered in Ram Valley (Jordan).

tamians (4000 B.C.), the Egyptians (3000 B.C.), as well as by the Greeks themselves (1000 B.C.).

A very different situation occurred in the Americas; the Aztecs developed their own form of writing as late as the fifteenth century A.D.

Early symbols appear to be icons that represented objects or concepts; these icons then became ideograms. Later on, ideograms were used to represent not whole objects but merely sounds that could be combined to represent objects

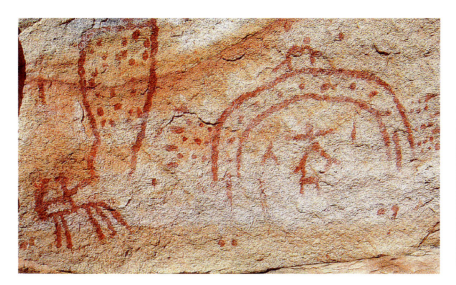

Fig. 8.8 Pictograms

Fig. 8.9a,b
Similar pictograms from different areas and cultures

Fig. 8.10 Hammurabi codex (Musée du Louvre, Paris; photo by the author)

8 Content, Communication and Tools 43

and concepts. This was probably the link between ideograms and phonetic alphabets. Modern languages such as Chinese or Japanese still have some similar features related to ideograms.

At that time, writing was used to convey religious and political acts, and later some archetypal economic documents.

Hieroglyphs formed the basis for other types of writing. The Greeks coined the word "hieroglyph" because this type of writing was mainly used for sacred

Fig. 8.11 a Nicely sculpted hieroglyphic signs on a piece of stone (Karnak, Egypt) **b** (Luxor, Egypt) **c** Detail of the Hwt Ramesses Meryamun (Temple of Ramesses, beloved of Amunin) in Abu Simbel (photo by the author)

Fig. 8.12 The Papyrus of Ani uses a special, more cursive form of hieroglyphic writing

I Cultural Content and the Information Society

inscriptions[51] on temple walls or on public monuments when they arrived in Egypt.

Hieroglyphic writing uses clearly distinguishable pictures to express both sounds and ideas, and was used from the end of prehistory until 396 A.D., when the last hieroglyphic text was written on the walls of the temple of Isis on the island of Philae. Hieroglyphic writing was used in monumental inscriptions on the walls of temples and tombs, but also on furniture, sarcophagi and coffins, and even on papyrus[52].

Fig. 8.13 Demotic script on a replica of the Rosetta stone on display in Magdeburg

Demotic[53] was mostly used in administrative and private texts, but it was also used to tell stories and very occasionally in inscriptions. The last demotic inscription was also found in the temple of Isis on the island of Philae.

The *Chinese language* has a written history of over 3000 years. Today, the standard Chinese language is known as *putonghua* or Mandarin, and a special Romanised phonetic system, known as *pinyin*, has been adopted as part of an effort to promote a standard language. Chinese characters are the symbols used in written Chinese. Modern Chinese characters fall into two categories: those with a phonetic component and those without it. Most of the characters without a phonetic component have developed from pictographs, and these characters are the most relevant to our analysis. Thanks to archaeological relics, we can

Putonghua and pinyin

---

51   Sacred (Ancient Greek *hieros*) inscriptions (Ancient Greek *glypho*).
52   The hieroglyphics were either inscribed or drawn, and they were often painted in many colours. The quality of the writing varied from highly detailed glyphs to mere outlines.
53   Its name comes from the Greek word *demotikos*, meaning "popular".

8 Content, Communication and Tools   45

see their evolution, starting with signs that represented specific objects that are easy to draw.

Fig. 8.14

The above examples represent some common objects/concepts that are very similar to the ancient signs that appeared in different parts of the world.

In order to represent abstract concepts, the Chinese people used their imaginations. For example, the two characters for *up* and *down* are:

Fig. 8.15

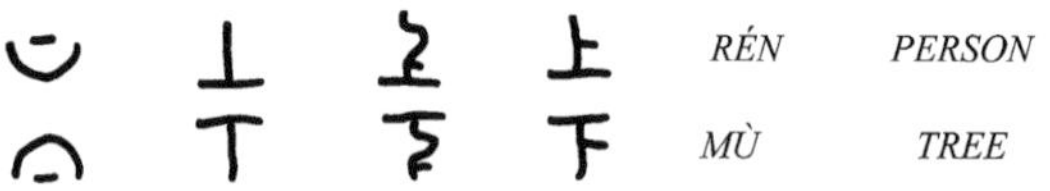

Fig. 8.16 Chinese calligraphy: the so-called "128 strokes" (Yellow Crane Tower located on Snake Hill in Wuhan, Hubei Province, China) (photo by the author)

46 *I Cultural Content and the Information Society*

Fig. 8.17 Advertisement along the streets, Beijing

Combining the two characters, we obtain a new word (kǎ), which means *stuck in the middle*.

Combining two or more simple characters very often results in a new word. This is a very common way of creating new Chinese characters. The meaning of the new word can normally be derived from the original words.

Woodblock printing has a long and distinguished history in China, where printing was invented about 1500 years ago.

人?在数世?通?不同的技?与技巧??生?出越来越多不同格式化的模式.
格式化,技巧与技?在不同的文化,不同的???化莫?.印刷曾是?理内容最后一次真正革命的里程碑.?在由于"数字化?代",我?面?着一次潜在的新革命.数字通?是新一?中最近的一个??,从非?言通?和手??始,然后通?印刷,广播和其他的媒体格式,跨越了?言,符号与?写的障碍.
文化??多?特性的?展,包括"无形"??,在?它?的保存与研究相?新成果成了技?的新挑?,比如:网上各??源的?合利用,跨国家成果与多?言字典,?新与新一代通???的??,?适合不同?言模式与内容??的工具.此外技?的快速更新刺激了?数据的存?. 最后,我??把机会与威??因于所?ε社会的形成与上网与非上网群体之?不断增?的代沟.

Fig. 8.18 An example of Chinese text

The *Japanese language* uses a different approach. Firstly, there are three different sets of signs: *hiragana, katakana* and *kanji. Hiragana* is used to write all Japanese words; these signs look more "round" then the others. *Katakana* signs are used to write foreign words, person and location names and denominations. Each of these two *kana* contains a limited number of signs, 46 each, that correspond mainly to vowels and consonant groups. *Kanji*[54] is the Chinese character set that Japanese people took directly from China.

The *kanji* character set consists of ideograms, which means that each sign has a specific meaning (i.e. ^ means "human"), although Chinese and Japanese people have different pronunciations for the same sign.

Hiragana, katakana and kanji

---

54 Literally "Chinese characters".

8 Content, Communication and Tools

Starting from ideograms, each of which expresses a particular meaning, and progressing to phonetic writing, which compresses communication into a linear format, each object that was originally represented by a single ideogram is associated with a specific sequence of symbols that represents that "item". This sequence of symbols now only has an evocative meaning if reproduced in the right combination.

Signifier, signified and code

In doing this, we introduce a code[55] that links an object to a sequence of symbols. Although the word *dog* does not have any direct link to this four legged animal, there are a small set of words that have meanings that can be directly inferred from their own sounds: onomatopoeia.

Orthography and syntax

From a hierarchical point of view, there are *rules* (codes) for creating *words* (orthography) and *phrases* (syntax)[56], and there are general schemas for *poetry* or *novels*.

Mùltas pèr gentès | et mùlta per aèquora vèctus	*To be, or not to be: that is the question:*
àdvenio hàs miseràs, | fràter, ad ìnferiàs,	*Whether 'tis nobler in the mind to suffer*
ùt te pòstremò | donàrem mùnere mòrtis	*The slings and arrows of outrageous fortune,*
èt mutàm nequì|quam àlloquerèr cinerèm,	*Or to take arms against a sea of troubles,*
quàndoquidèm | fortùna mihì | tete àbstulit ìpsum,	*And by opposing end them? To die: to sleep;*
hèu miser ìndignè | fràter adèmpte mihì.	*No more; and by a sleep to say we end*
Nùnc tamen ìnterea haèc, | priscò quae mòre parèntum	*The heart-ache and the thousand natural shocks*
tràdita sùnt tristì | mùnere ad ìnferiàs,	*That flesh is heir to, 'tis a consummation*
àccipe fràternò | multùm manàntia flètu,	*Devoutly to be wish'd.*
àtque in pèrpetuùm, | fràter, ave àtque valè!	
[Gaio Valerio Catullo, Carme 101]	*[W. Shakespeare, Hamlet, Act Three, scene one]*

---

55 According to Ferdinand De Saussure (1857–1913), a Swiss linguist, signs are composed of two distinct but inseparable parts: the signifier and the signified. The signifier is the materially produced representation. For the dog, the signified is the mental concept to which the signifier refers: the four-legged barking animal in the external world.

56 Phonetics, orthography, orthoepy, morphology and syntax are all components of grammar.

I Cultural Content and the Information Society

Recently, the field of communication has undergone many mutations thanks to the advent of a series of new technologies that have gradually enriched the possible modalities of communication. All of this has had, and still has, a great influence on various disciplines which aim at the combined use of text, graphics and sketches in order to transmit the information in the best way.

Some *emoticons* (symbols that were originally used in emails but are now also commonly used in SMS messages):

Emoticons ☺

Happy :-)	Sad :-(
Very happy :-))	Very sad :-((

8.5 Nonlinear Versus Linear, and Many Media Versus Just One Medium

Understanding Media is the title that Marshall McLuhan gave in 1964 to his work that analysed and described, with remarkable foresight, the consequences of the introducing new communication tools. In this book, McLuhan proposed a new paradigm: *the medium is the message*. This implies that communication techniques are not "information *neutral"* they modify the information while transferring it.

Understanding Media

"The medium is the message"

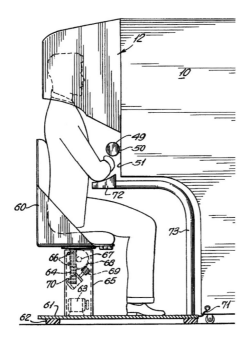

Fig. 8.19 Illustration of Morton Heilig's *Sensorama* device, precursor to later virtual reality systems (1961)

8 Content, Communication and Tools

Electric era Another characteristic of this essay was its reference to the modifications of customs and habits triggered by the increasing pace of life in the *electric era* (as defined by the author).

As we are dealing with both communication and information, we cannot exempt ourselves from considering the most recent communication tools in this context presented by McLuhan due to the significant advances in the digital world.

Current communication tools transfer the message using the most effective *channels* to transmit the information; we therefore have the soundtrack commentary, the movie, the digital animation, and the final frontier in this technological field—the virtual reality, which allows us to actively experience the infinite *universes* of the imaginary.

Fig. 8.20 Linear versus nonlinear: encyclopaedia

All of these tools address the two main perceptive mechanisms, *sight* and *hearing,* but there is also the opportunity to use tools that address other senses, such as those of *olfaction* or touch.

Sensorama In 1962, Morton Helig introduced a machine called *Sensorama* that allowed the user to *experience* a ride through the traffic of New York, using not only three-dimensional images but also congruent smells from the environment being explored.

Fig. 8.21 PHANTOM haptic device made by SensAble Technologies

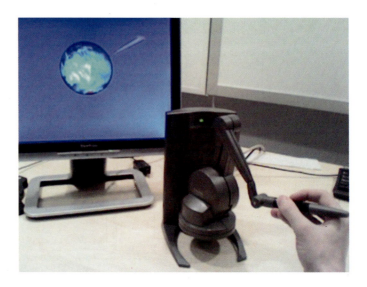

I Cultural Content and the Information Society

In the 1990s, thanks to the spread of virtual reality, experimenters began to explore tactile feedback. This leaves force feedback as the final frontier to address in order to maximise the feeling of *materiality* when exploring virtual worlds.

8.6   Technology: From the Stylus to the Computer

In order to better understand the present, we now consider the past; specifically past revolutions and potentially related bias. After centuries of patient work by scribes and amanuenses, the year 1350 saw the first use of movable metal types, in Korea.

In 1436 in Strasburg, *Johann Gutenberg* invented the manual printing press with movable types, and in 1450 the first widely distributed publication was printed using the Gutenberg method: the Holy Bible[57]. Unfortunately, Gutenberg later went bankrupt, and it took another seventy years to produce a useful book format for the printing process, passing through handmade drawings and miniatures on printed pages to the proper format.

Johann Gutenberg

Fig. 8.22 The "scribe accroupi" found in Saqqara (IV or V dynasty, 2600–2350 B.C.; Musée du Louvre, Paris)

Fig. 8.23 The beginning of the Gutenberg Bible: Volume 1, Old Testament, Epistle of St. Jerome

---

57   It appears that the most popular printed documents at that time were "indulgences".

Manuscripts

Of course the evolution of texts from *manuscripts* to books even included some changes to the format of the text itself, due to the different people being addressed. *Manuscripts* were more like *paintings* or *artefacts* then *books*; clients usually knew the content, relevance and context of the manuscript that they were going to own very well. Books are a very different product, with a different format, that evolved over time from manuscripts due to the needs of the market, with an abstract, a preface, an index and a table of contents plus a brief author bio, since they addressed a different audience.

Nikolaj Kopernik and Galileo Galilei

In 1543, Nikolaj Kopernik (Nicolaus Copernicus) published a new *theory about the celestial bodies,* while in 1600 William Shakespeare published and produced *Hamlet*. In 1609, Galileo Galilei wrote *Sidereus Nuncius*[58] (*Sidereal Messenger*), which announced the discovery of the four satellites of Jupiter. He dedicated Sidereus Nuncius to Cosimo II de' Medici, the fourth Grand Duke of Tuscany, and he named the four moons of Jupiter he had discovered the "Medicean stars". In 1755, Samuel Johnson published the first *dictionary*. In 1847 the *steam rotary machine* was inaugurated by the London Times in order to produce their daily papers.

In 1847, the low productivity of the traditional rotary machine led to the invention of the *high-speed rotary machine by Richard Hoe.*

Otto Mergenthaler

Another step forward in the art of writing was the invention of the fountain pen by Hermann Waterman in 1883. In 1884, Otto Mergenthaler invented the *composition machine* in order to aid printers in their work. In 1889, Thomas Edison developed the first *flexible film*, and in 1896 the invention of *monotype* allowed press characters to be selected from a perforated tape.

Fig. 8.24 Fountain pen (sterling silver) (photo by Francesca Ronchi)

---

58 The optics discipline was founded by Euclid (fourth century B.C. and Claudius Ptolemy (100–178 C.E.). Later on the most important work in pre-modern optics is due to Ibn al. Haytham (965–1039). His work became the basis for the perspectivist tradition of optics in the thirteen century. Eyeglasses became known in the late thirteen century. In 1608 Galileo Galilei discovered a different use of "magnifying glasses" pointing them toward the sky ... the telescope became reality.

Fig. 8.25 The "console" of Hermann Hollerit's Census computer (1890 – courtesy of IBM Foundation)

Over the course of 23 years, starting from 1909, Guglielmo Marconi invented and developed *wireless communication* using a range of wavelengths, from longwaves to microwaves. Radio communication was originally intended to provide a point-to-point private communication system, but its basic lack of privacy led to a completely new form of communication: broadcasting.

In 1920 the first television set and the first motion pictures with both sound and colour were produced. The first analogue processors were created in 1930.

During the summer of 1945, Vannevar Bush introduced the *Memex system* in a famous article entitled *As We May Think*[59], published in the review *Atlantic Monthly*.

Guglielmo Marconi

Fig. 8.26 The basis for patent no. 7777, known as the "Four Sevens" patent, was the tuned circuit developed at the Haven Hotel (picture credit: Comitato Guglielmo Marconi International)

---

[59] Please refer to http://www.w3.org/History/1945/vbush/vbush-all.shtml.

8 Content, Communication and Tools

Fig. 8.27 The wireless laboratory of the yacht Elettra, bristling with the latest technology, allowed Marconi to carry out practical experiments (Franklin Township Public Library Archive)

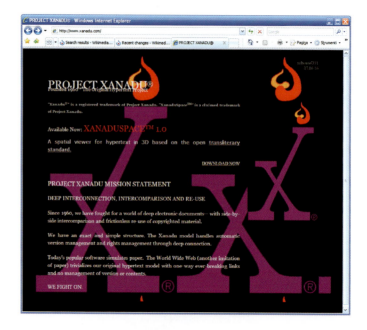

Fig. 8.28 The Xanadu Project home page (Theodor Holm Nelson Oxford Internet Institute and Project Xanadu)

Fig. 8.29 ALTAIR 8800 computer

I Cultural Content and the Information Society

In 1949 the *BIC* pen was created[60], which revolutionised the art of writing. In 1951 the first *commercial television* performance was broadcast by the CBS.
In 1960, Doug Engelbart, father of the mouse, introduced a project called *Augment* at the Stanford Research Institute, which evolved into the *On-Line System* project. Both projects addressed information management. In 1965, Ted Nelson invented the term *hypertext* and established the company Xanadu.

The evolution from ALTAIR (whose history is interlaced with the fortunes of William "Bill" Gates) to APPLE II (created by Steve Jobs) and the SINCLAIR ZX81 (created by Sir Clive Sinclair) in the 1970s took just five years.

Also in the 1970s, the Xerox Corporation gathered together a team of world-class researchers in the information and physical sciences and gave them a mission to create "the architecture of information". The *Xerox Palo Alto Research Center (PARC)* officially opened its doors in Palo Alto, California on July 1, 1970. The first version of *Smalltalk* was deployed in 1972. In 1973 the *Alto* personal computer became operational.

Doug Engelbart: Augment and Online System

Ted Nelson: hypertext

ALTAIR and personal computing

Xerox PARC Alto

Fig. 8.30 Alto computer by Xerox PARC

The Alto featured the world's first *What-You-See-Is-What-You-Get (WYSIWYG)* editor, a mouse for input, a *graphical user interface (GUI)*, and bit-mapped display, and presented menus and icons, provided a link to the local

WYSIWYG and GUI

---

60   László József Bíró invented the ball pen at the end of the 1930s. In 1950 Marcel Bich bought from Bíró the patent for the pen, which soon became the main product of his Bic company.

8 Content, Communication and Tools   55

area network and stored files simultaneously. It represented a revolution in computing; it was the first computer designed for personal data management, since it used an intuitive object-oriented computer/human interface.

The 1970s gave birth to some of the most well known micro- and home computers, including the Sinclair ZX, QL, and Spectrum, various models from Tandy Radio Shack, the Commodore PET, the Apple II and III, the Texas TI 99/4A, the Hewlett Packard 85 and more. While some of these generated a community of software developers, the hardware was the most valuable part of the technical solution, the primary resource, and the software was developed by end-users for each specific platform.

IBM Personal Computer

Later on, in 1981, the first *Personal Computer* was created by a research team working in an IBM laboratory. It was the first large scale de facto standard computer system, and was part of a family of backward-compatible processors (the well-known INTEL 80X86 family). The first page of the history of personal computing had been written.

Standardisation and compatibility enabled the creation of the software market and the proliferation of software houses. As a consequence, the perception of the values of hardware and software started to change and very quickly reversed, so that software assumed pole position.

From that time onward, customers started to look first for applications and then for the proper hardware to run them on.

Fig. 8.31 Apple LISA (1982)

In 1983, after a fleeting glimpse of Apple's *LISA*, the first *Macintosh* was developed, which led to the personal computing revolution.

Hypertext and nonlinear text

Meanwhile, another innovative technology had first appeared approximately thirty-five years earlier, when Vennavar Bush introduced the theoretical structure of *hypertext* in 1945 (Bush 1945). In a mathematical sense, the prefix *hyper*

56   *I Cultural Content and the Information Society*

implies multidimensional extension to a network of independent nodes joined by links traced by the author so as to enable multiple access to information. This technology enabled the creation of *nonlinear texts* and *stories, thus* overcoming the difficulties that had already been faced by some authors who had tried to break up the linear structure of text using smart workarounds in paper publications.

This technology (after some initial attempts to create Internet-like systems using *Mac Hypercard* and *Gopher)* became one of the building blocks of the *World Wide Web.*

One last piece in the jigsaw is provided by *networking*, which multiplies the potential of computers by enabling information from different physical locations to be conveyed to the user.

Further significant events in this evolution have become part of everyday life, covered by the newspapers. However, it is worth mentioning two events of relative importance: the *mass diffusion of personal computing* along with the *affirmation of the Internet and related services,* and the incredible *success of wireless communication.*

8.7 From Standalone Computers to the Internet and Wireless Communication

One of the most significant changes to occur in the field of information technology over the last few decades has been the implementation of real-time communication and information exchange between computers: *networking.*

A computer was originally considered to be Leibniz's[61] "monad", an ultimate atom without windows and doors; a *sealed* entity. Intercommunication processes activated external access to these *monads,* allowing information and data exchange between them and thus multiplying their added value; *networks of computers* possess expanded functionalities and services. A number of different standalone *proprietary* networks were gradually merged into the *network of networks*: the *Internet.*

Monads and networks

The Internet—the de facto implementation of global networking—has revolutionised the worlds of computing and communications like nothing before.

The Internet

Previous inventions, such as the telegraph, the telephone, the radio, and the computer itself, set the stage for this unprecedented integration of capabilities. Even the future evolution of such an innovation is in to a degree unpredictable;

---

61 Gottfried Wilhelm Leibniz (also Leibnitz or von Leibniz) was born on July 1, 1646 (Leipzig, Germany), and died on November 14, 1716 (Hanover, Germany). School/tradition: rationalism. Main interests: metaphysics, epistemology, science, mathematics, theodicy. Notable ideas: calculus, innate knowledge, optimism, monad. See http://en.wikipedia.org/wiki/Gottfried_Leibniz.

Lowering the threshold

will the global network be a mixture of networks (wired, wireless, satellite, sensors, peer-to-peer, private, phone and other appliances)?

The Internet has incredibly facilitated access to mass communication. It combines a worldwide broadcasting capability with a mechanism for information dissemination, which offers us the opportunity to reach a wide audience with minimal effort. Before the Internet, the only way to reach wide audiences was radio and television broadcasting, and before those were invented, mainly printed materials or heralds. In addition, it is a medium that encourages *collaborations* and *interactions* between individuals and their computers almost[62] without regard for geographic location.

The Internet is growing rapidly; the number of hosts worldwide in 1981 was about 213, ten years later it was 617,000, twenty years later in 2001 it had reached 125,888,197, and in January 2006 it was 394,991,609: 1,854,420 times larger than 25 years before!

The Internet was elected as a de facto standard by users soon became the largest and most widely diffused digital telecommunications network on the planet. Access to this network of networks means access to information, and information is considered to be the building block of wealth in the twenty-first century.

Fig. 8.32

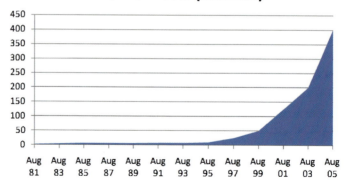

Workstations and UNIX

In the 1980s, the era of Unix and "workstations", around two hundred computers were online—connected into a very experimental network; today there are some four hundred million hosts connected to the Internet. In his novel *1984*, George Orwell created the character of *Big Brother*, and then in 1984 William Gibson gave us another vision of future technologies in *Neuromancer*. Now, in many ways, Gibson's vision of the future describes today's technology.

---

62 Some areas of the globe have greater satellite coverage than others.

8.7.1 When and Where it All Started

"The Internet represents one of the most successful examples of the benefits of sustained investment and commitment to research and development of information infrastructure. Beginning with the early research in packet switching, the government, industry and academia have been partners in evolving and deploying this exciting new technology."

(Leiner et al. 2003).

The history of the Internet involves four distinct aspects:
- The *technological evolution* that began with early research into packet switching and the ARPANET[63]
- The *operations and management* issues associated with a global and complex operational infrastructure[64]
- The *social aspect*, which resulted in a broad community of Internauts that work together to create and evolve the technology
- The *commercialization aspect*, which resulted in the extremely effective transition of research results into a broadly deployed and available information infrastructure.

If we consider basic seeds of the Internet concept in terms of social interactions enabled through networking, we turn first to a series of memos written by J.C.R. Licklider of MIT (in August 1962). The concept expressed was that of a *Galactic Network* that interconnects a set of computers through which everyone could quickly access data and programs from any location. We can easily see how this idea is very close to the concept of the Internet today.

J.C.R. Licklider: Galactic Network

Licklider was the first head (1962) of the computer research program at the *Defense Advanced Research Projects Agency (DARPA[65])*. Within DARPA, Licklider strongly supported the strategic relevance of networks compared with other initiatives, and his views influenced those of his successors: Ivan Sutherland, Bob Taylor, and MIT researcher Lawrence G. Roberts.

DARPA/ARPA

The building block of the whole system is the *packet switching theory* introduced by Leonard Kleinrock at MIT in July 1961[66].

Packet switching theory

---

63 Current research continues to expand the horizons of the infrastructure, in terms of scale, performance, and higher-level functionality.

64 Refer to Internet governance and the temporary resolutions adopted with the introduction of ICANN in the 1990s as well as the Internet Governance Working Group findings.

65 The Advanced Research Projects Agency (ARPA) changed its name to the Defense Advanced Research Projects Agency (DARPA), and then back and forth several times.

66 The first paper and the first book published on packet switching theory were both by Kleinrock (1961; 1964).

8 Content, Communication and Tools

At the time, the main conceptual model applied to networks was *circuit switching*. This is the concept used in telephone and railway networks too. The item to be transferred is almost passive; the channel connecting the source and the destination is created physically using switches and connectors in order to provide a direct path to the destination. The *packet switching* approach, on the other hand, uses an almost static network consisting of usually redundant connections and necessitates close interaction between the information residing in the packet and network control nodes. This approach removes the need for physical switching or connecting; it simply requires logical addresses and logical guidance.

Communications based on *packets* rather than *circuits* were a major step forward in computer networking.

First WAN in 1965 Once reliable communication "pipes" had been established, the next step was to make the computers talk to each other. Some experiments to this end were carried out in the 1960s. In 1965, two computers (the TX-2 at MIT and the Q-32 in California) were connected using a low-speed dial-up telephone line, creating the first *wide-area computer network (WAN)*.

The conclusions drawn from this experiment were that time-sharing systems could work well together while running remote procedures and retrieving data and that *circuit switching networks* are not suitable for this task but the *packet switching* approach was.

ARPANET One year later, in 1996 Lawrence G. Roberts moved to DARPA and began developing the computer network upon which he based the *ARPANET* (Roberts 1967).

In the period of time between 1961 and 1967, three main research groups worked in parallel (none of the groups know about the work being done by the other groups) on the network concept: MIT (1961–1967), RAND (1962–1965) and NPL (1964–1967)[67].

After the publication of the plan for the ARPANET and some merging results and effort between the different research teams, the developmental path for the network ran smoothly until 1972 through a series of improvements[68] that were required to create and complete the operational framework.

Ray Tomlinson: electronic mail (email) The official launch of *ARPANET* was a large, very successful demonstration that was organised and presented by Robert Kahn in 1972 during the *International Computer Communication Conference (ICCC)*. The first *hot* application appeared in March of that year courtesy of Ray Tomlinson[69]: *electronic mail*. Tomlinson wrote the basic email message send and read software, which was

---

67 The word "packet" was appropriated from the work at NPL, and the proposed line speed for the ARPANET was upgraded from 2.4 kbps to 50 kbps.

68 One of the key components developed was the packet switch, known as the Interface Message Processor (IMP), developed by Frank Heart (who worked at Bolt Beranek and Newman, BBN) and Robert Kahn.

69 Who also worked at BBN.

intended to aid cooperation between the distributed research team working on the network project.

In July, Roberts expanded this internal utility, adding listing and selective read, save, forward and reply features. This large, diffuse network application quickly became popular, since it enabled *instant*[70] messaging across the network.

The interconnection of remote computers in the ARPANET enabled document and application interchange, and so the project was quickly deemed a success. The number of connected hosts continued to increase, making the network more and more useful and productive. The system ran continuously until the early 1980s, when the incredible success of these network connections resulted in a number of different *network islands*. This meant that a general agreement between networks was required, and so a more flexible and efficient standard intercommunication protocol was defined.

The proposed protocol was actually a set of specific protocols called *TCP/IP (Transmission Control Protocol/Internet Protocol)*; each network island had to adopt this protocol to make it accessible and interoperable.

TCP/IP

In the meantime, in 1983 ARPANET was subdivided into two main subnetworks: MILNET and ARPANET. This event can be considered to mark the *birth of the Internet*, the network of interconnected networks (*internetwork*), since *ARPANET* subsequently grew into the *Internet*. The Internet was based on the idea that there would be multiple independent networks with rather arbitrary designs, beginning with the ARPANET since it was the pioneering packet switching network, but soon also including packet satellite networks, ground-based packet radio networks and other networks.

The birth of the Internet

The extreme flexibility of the *TCP/IP protocol* enables open architecture networking, including heterogeneous networks within the Internet such as Bitnet, DecNet, Microsoft Network, AppleShare, etc. Within this incredible mixture of different network technologies it is always possible to create a subnetwork using a *bridge*. *Bridges* can filter network messages by seamlessly interpreting different protocols. The turning point of the whole infrastructure was no doubt the invention of the World Wide Web.

These technologies and their applications are now part of our daily life: networking, remote connections, information highways, virtual worlds, cyberspace, instant messaging, VOIP, wireless connections, search engines, 3-D digital world maps, satellite images, and more.

In his recent book entitled *Understanding New Media: Augmented Knowledge and Culture* (Veltman 2004), Prof. Kim H. Veltman included some figures on the Internet explosion:

Understanding New Media

In 2000, it was claimed that only about 1 billion of these pages had been catalogued by standard search engines. By January 2004, Google had indexed

---

70 This was different to today's "instant messaging" applications, like MS Messenger, ICQ or Skype.

8 Content, Communication and Tools • 61

World Wide Web: Tim Berners Lee, Robert Cailliau

over 2 billion pages. That number doubled in February 2004 and as of 1 April 2004 there were 4,285,199,774 indexed pages. In 2000 there were no indexed images. In April 2004 there were 880,000,000 indexed images.

Of course, one of the main drivers for Internet usage was the introduction of the *hypertext transfer protocol (http)*, which led to birth of the *World Wide Web, thanks to the contributions of* Tim Berners-Lee and Robert Cailliau at CERN in 1990 and the success of *Mosaic* (National Center for Supercomputing Applications, NCSA, in 1992), the first web browser.

Following the first two meetings (1991, 1992) of the new community—the World Wide Web community—the third *World Wide Web Conference* held in Darmstadt in 1993 saw the establishment of the general framework, thanks to the active contributions from the local *Technical University* and *Fraunhofer IGD (FhG IGD)*, and the responsibility for management and future developments was assigned (under the acronym *W3C*) to the American association (NCSA) and the French INRIA.

The bottom-up decision mechanism

One of the most important characteristics of the Web community, in the first two or three years of its life, was the bottom-up decision mechanism it employed. Enhancements and extensions were proposed, discussed and implemented mainly by active members of the community of researchers and experts involved in the process.

The Web community at that time was a mixture of ICT experts and scientific content managers. The double role of these *prosumers* was probably one of the key innovative aspects of that community during that period. The subsequent gradual drift from technology developers to general users is a natural process that often occurs with mature technologies. It happened, for instance, in the field of computer graphics, where computer graphics pioneers worked side-by-side with creative people and *special effects (fx)* designers.

Fig. 8.33a,b Mosaic was developed at the National Center for Supercomputing Applications

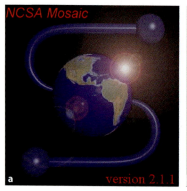 

62 | *I Cultural Content and the Information Society*

Fig. 8.34
One-hundred-dollar computer (photo by the author)

At that early time in the history of the Web, the major players in ICT and telecommunications were looking in from the outside. Then, in 1992, a first implementation of HTTP server for MS Windows NT was made available, and in 1993 a commercial version named *Purveyor*[71] was placed on the market.

HTTP server for MS Windows NT

As usual, the first phase of Web development was characterised by the free circulation of software solutions, and then some commercial products appeared. Some of the most significant of these were undoubtedly the *Netscape* and *Cello* browsers. Updated and enhanced web browsers, their market models were based on licensing and fees.

Windows for Workgroups

Microsoft tackled networking later than Unix, Novell and Apple users. Windows for Workgroups (WFW[72]) was their first attempt to address networking as well as Windows NT.

---

[71] Purveyor was a commercial outcome derived from a beta version of an http server for Windows NT due to a working group named EMWAC (European Microsoft Windows Academic Centre) leaded by the University of Edinburgh, Politecnico di Milano was one of the partners in the project testing and extending the application joining database access and dynamic data exchange.

[72] Windows for Workgroups 3.1 (originally codenamed *Kato*), released in October 1992, supported the NETBEUI and IPX protocols.

8 Content, Communication and Tools

The MS Network: Blackbird

In the middle of the 1990s, MS was still developing an ambitious and advanced project codenamed *Blackbird,* later known as *The Microsoft Network.* This was a huge proprietary commercial version of the WWW that addressed eCommerce and added value service delivery.

During the WWW5 Conference, some of the key players in IT joined the WWW community and started to cooperate by joining various committees. In the autumn of 1995 *Microsoft Explorer* was released and Microsoft's entire suite of web technology products was distributed for free, partially bundled with MS operating systems.

This lead to one of the biggest fights related to the Web: *Explorer vs. Netscape, or Microsoft vs. Netscape.*

Then networking promoted another technological contest: *Java technology* vs. the rest of the world, or *network computers* vs. *personal computers* (but that is another story).

One of the newest challenges, in this current era of digital convergence and quadruple players, after the Windows 95 mass market experience, is to implement the *one-hundred-dollar computer,* in order to bridge the digital divide in developing countries and aid the establishment of a sustainable local economy.

8.8 Digital Convergence and the History of Movies

When dealing with *digital convergence* it seems opportune to consider the evolution of communication techniques, starting with the *seventh muse* (cinema), some of the aspects of which predated similar characteristics of multimedia communication by almost a century.

Linear structure of text and movies

The shift from *texts* to movies is not as great as one might imagine at first; they both share a basic *linear structure*, usually related to the timeline; this was probably one of the key factors that aided the birth of the movie industry. Just as some writers had tried to before them, some movie directors tried to break up the basic linear structure of movies by inventing *flashbacks*, post-production editing, and other tricks, as seen in movies such as *Bolero, Sliding Doors* and more recently *Pulp Fiction.*

1895: the first movie "Locomotive"

1927: Fritz Lang's "Metropolis"

More than a century ago, in 1895, the brothers Auguste and Jean-Louis Lumière terrorized the public by introducing the famous movie *Locomotive*. In 1927, Fritz Lang offered the first cinematographic vision of the future, with the 87-minute epic *Metropolis*. The same year saw the recording of the first soundtrack, by the jazz musician Al Johnson.

1932: the first colour movie

In 1932, the first colour movie, *Silly Symphonies* by Walt Disney, was released. In 1937, the first cartoon, *Snow White,* was shown. 1939 saw the release of The *Wizard of Oz, the* first action film in colour. In the 1960s and early 1970s *Cinemascope* and *Surround* increased the level of movie interaction/emotion.

The first feature movie of the *Star Wars* trilogy was released in 1977, which was full of special effects obtained using computer graphics and later on THX specifications.

Cinemascope and Surround

In 1982, the film *Blade Runner*, directed by Ridley Scott, made use of small-scale urban maquettes that were realistically rendered thanks to the clever use of light and close-ups. 1991 witnessed the huge success of *Terminator 2*, which showcased a new generation of special effects, like 3-D morphing and texture mapping on dynamic models.

After an attempt to make the film *Who Framed Roger Rabbit* the first fully three-dimensional computer-generated cartoon was abandoned due to difficulties in 1988 by Steven Spielberg and Robert Zemeckis (it was made using traditional animation techniques instead), in 1992 Walt Disney produced the first 3-D computer-generated animation: the dance scene in the movie *Beauty and the Beast*.

1992: first 3-D graphics

Fig. 8.35 Typical image from *Metropolis* by Fritz Lang (1927)

Fig. 8.36 Dome Theatre

In 1993, another milestone in the history of the evolution of the cinema arrived with *Jurassic Park,* where digital actors interacted with conventional actors for the first time.

In 1995, one hundred years after the birth of cinema, *Toy Story*, the first feature entirely populated by digital actors, was created by Pixar[73].

Toy Story, the first digital movie

---

73 Thanks to Steve Jobs (CEO of Apple and NeXt Computer, and formerly CEO of Pixar).

8 Content, Communication and Tools

In this short review of the technological evolution of the movies, we have seen that even this form of *communication* has attempted (and still is) to enhance itself by utilising new attributes (colours, soundtrack, cinemascope, 3-D...) and techniques (animations, special effects, 3-D CG) in a continuous *quest* for new ways to express creativity and emotions. In some aspects, the history of cinema is closely linked to those of multimedia and virtual reality. Indeed, we have already mentioned Morton Helig and the Sensorama, which was able to immerse the spectator in a virtual city consisting of images, sounds and smells.

IMAX   *IMAX* theatres (both analogue and digital), THX standards, and digital simulators for individuals, small groups or large audiences are further steps toward new communication standards and formats.

Fig. 8.37 IMAX theatre (photo by the author)

8.9 Information Transmission

How can we take advantage of emerging technologies and new media? How do we create added value applications that exploit the full potential of nonlinear communication? How do we derive a proper format for the effective transfer of information and knowledge?

In order to answer these questions we must investigate learning mechanisms and other issues from the cognitive sciences.

Let's consider the mechanisms utilized by the *human cognitive apparatus*. Cognitive psychology[74] defines two methods of acquiring, elaborating and communicating knowledge.

The human cognitive apparatus

One of these methods is well known to everybody and is associated with learning processes such as reading, interpreting, understanding, reflecting, reasoning, induction, deduction, and involves processing information—being aware and conscious. This method is termed the *symbolic-reconstructive* mechanism, as involves decoding symbols (language) and then mentally "rebuilding" the transmitted concept.

Symbolic-reconstructive

The second method is not as obvious as the first, even though it is familiar to us. It is the *perceptive–motory* method, which involves watching, touching, testing, and then imitating or retesting—in other words "learning by doing". We use this approach when learning a skill for example.

Perceptive-motory

This primary mechanism of perception (visual, tactile, kinaesthetic) is embedded in human beings and some other *animals*. Objects and the environment are perceived by watching them and touching them and, above all, by noting the resulting reactions and behaviour.

This second method is really the primary mechanism from a biological and psychological point of view (*phylogenetic*). It is the method embedded in the human organism, and it is the method by which the child initially experiences and learns until the child artificially develops the *symbolic-reconstructive* method. The perceptive-motory mechanism is without doubt the one that has been around the longest and is the one that becomes the most well-developed over the course of our lifetimes, and in this sense, the most powerful.

How to manage experiential learning

The only limit to this mechanism (although it is an important one) is that we can only apply it to *visible and tangible objects*, and so thus far we have only been able to apply it to objects that exist physically.

Perceptive-motory system limits

I can learn how to ride a bicycle or to rollerskate by attempting to do so; a *symbolic–reconstructive* description of the process is not usually sufficient or convenient. Most well-designed objects—ones that have good "mapping[75]"—are simple and easy-to-use because they make efficient use of the primary

---

74 Relevant contributions in this field come from Prof. Francesco Antinucci (CNR, Rome). This section is mainly based on his work and research.

75 In his work *The Design of Everyday Things*, Donald H. Norman defines *mapping* as "the self-explicative shape or behaviour of an object". Mapping implies that "...you always know which control does what (in the book, I call this a 'natural mapping'). When the designers fail to provide a conceptual model, we will be forced to make up our own...". Furthermore: "A good conceptual model can make the difference between successful and erroneous operation of the many devices in our lives." See Norman (1998).

8 Content, Communication and Tools   67

learning mechanism, the perceptive–motory method. However, the primary mechanism can only be activated, if the object belongs to the physical world. Thanks to the "undo" option, the same trial and error approach entered the world of software, enabling us to use the "learning by doing" method.

But what about nonphysical objects? How do we learn scientific concepts, algebraic or geometric hyperspaces, molecular structures, etc?

How to overcome limits

In this case, we can only use the mechanism of secondary learning, which is not naturally embedded in humans and is much more difficult to use. A deep knowledge of a specific symbolic language is required that we can then use to mentally reconstruct the object and complete the abstraction. How can multimedia and the virtual reality be of benefit to us in all this?

Important role of virtual reality

Interactive virtual reality represents, in this context, the tool that allows us to directly connect the *perceptive-motory* system to nonphysical objects—virtual *digital* objects.

Generalizing the approach

With virtual technology we can materialise a mathematical space—we can touch a molecule and modify its structure, and we can explore a mechanism or the human body from the inside. Using virtual reality, we can expand and generalise the use of the *perceptive-motory* system.

However, this is not the only practical benefit offered by virtual technology. Consider the process of *transmitting knowledge*: if the knowledge consists of a group of concepts with structure (links and relationships), its transmission through conventional media implies a sequential single-channel protocol that involves the disassembly of the structure into nodes, relationships and constraints as well as instructions for recreating the structure when it reaches its destination.

Stream of information, linear format

Consider a typical scenario that corresponds to this way of operating—writing a book. The knowledge related to a specific topic must be transmitted in a way (the writing) that is characterized by a beginning, a development and an end. All of the concepts to be expressed must be taken apart and ordered so that it can be placed in the linear medium called text. It will be then a task care of the reader to reconstruct the acquired data structure mentally.

In contrast, *hypermedia* and *virtual reality* technologies permit the interactive transmission of *structured knowledge* spread across many channels along with the full set of links and relationships.

One example is a pilot's cockpit: a flight handbook will specify a sequence of all of the operations that must be completed and the checks to perform, while a virtual simulator will directly introduce the pilot to the real situation in the cockpit, communicating all the necessary information in parallel.

8.10 Some Concluding Remarks

In this chapter we have explored cultural diversity issues and related initiatives and projects, outlining the relevance of preservation of both tangible/intangible artefacts and digital content. We have also explored the evolution of communication and related tools, outlining both the potential benefits and the lack of proper use of technology to manage and exploit digital content.

Fig. 8.38 ARS Electronica virtual book (photo by the author)

We are currently in a digital *dark age* with respect to lack of content. Without a critical mass of information, technological capacity is a hollow structure.

It is still a challenge to make high-quality content available through digital channels because we have not yet found an appropriate format capable of fully exploiting the added value of digital media. During the evolution of communication from oral traditions to manuscripts to printed books and later on to movies, radio and television broadcasting, a specific format was adopted or re-adopted with each new phase. However, in the era of multimedia we are yet to find a proper format for multiple media channels—we are still *porting* books online.

Creativity must be encouraged and new interactive cultural expressions must be stimulated. "Knowledge is not about circulation of information. It is about adding value to ideas. A Knowledge Society must provide people with opportunities to think in new ways"[76].

Lack of quality content

Creativity and knowledge

---

[76] Suggested by Dr. Shalini Venturelli, (Associate Professor of International Communication Policy, American University), in a lecture on *Knowledge, Civil Society & Culture in the Information Society: Toward a New Model of IT Policy for Developing Countries*, World Bank, Washington, DC, July 2001.

The creation of a fully interactive online culture would transform links between computers into connections between people that could stimulate ideas and new skills. We must create mechanisms that encourage the participation and empowerment of all people in developing and developed countries and allow them autonomy and control.

Then we found the way to shift from the *symbolic-reconstructive* cognitive method to the *perceptive-motory* one and from unstructured serial transmission to structured parallel protocol. How do we take advantage of these interesting possibilities offered by technology?

Reinventing ateliers

One interesting possibility is to use this technology for personal training (in an approach that harks back to the time of *ateliers),* thus making full use of the opportunities offered by multimedia virtual environments. This should not be limited to the reconstruction of *real, feasible, universes*, but also to the creation of *unfeasible universes,* in order to experience new techniques, verify theories, etc. This should be the aim even if, as often happens for new technologies, the initial focus is on imitating existing worlds before finding its own *way*.

In the didactic field it would be extremely interesting to "materialise" some concepts and physical behaviours, such as scientific concepts (functions, integrals, etc) and physical laws (permanent motion, the absence of gravity, etc.).

In order to better exploit the potential associated with technology and media, we must find a proper format; probably not a serial/linear format like the one that has been used for centuries, since the invention of printing. For instance, we could think about reusing old formats that were killed by the rise of the printing press and then building on those in order to create completely new formats.

Nonlinear formats like drawings, graphs and combinations of text and images are some of the reference formats. Video games and interactive installations such as theme parks and technology museums should be considered reference models for enhanced nonlinear communication.

References

1 Digital Content

F. Antinucci (1993) Summa hypermedialis. Sistemi Intelligenti 5

F. Antinucci (2001) La scuola si è rotta—perché cambiano i modi di apprendere. Editori Laterza, Roma

F. Antinucci (2001) Computer per un figlio—giocare, apprendere, creare. Editori Laterza, Roma

F. Antinucci (2002) Il futuro di Internet ovvero "forma" e "business" nell'innovazione tecnologica. Sistemi Intelligenti 2

S. Blackmore (2001) The meme's eye web. WWW10, Hong Kong, 1–5 May 2001 (see http://www10.org/keynoters/speech/susan.html)

M. Colarossi (1997) Où se former au multimédia en Europe? INA, Bry-sur-Marne

Council of Europe (2000) Maximising the educational and cultural potential of new information technologies. Council of Europe Publishing, Paris

Council of Europe (2001a) New information technologies and the young. Council of Europe Publishing, Paris

Council of Europe (2001b) Digital culture in Europe. Council of Europe Publishing, Paris

D. Deutsch (1997) The fabric of reality—La trama della realtà. Einaudi, Torino

W.H. Gates III (1994) The road ahead. Viking Penguin, London

L. Jaeger (2003) La parola crea il mondo. Mente & Cervello magazine, no. 5, Oct. 2003

L. Jeffrey (2001) Vital links for a knowledge culture. Council of Europe Publishing, Paris

B.I. Koerner (2002) The long road to Internet nirvana. Wired, Oct. 2002

C. Majello (1993) L'arte di comunicare. Franco Angeli, Milano

A. Marcolli (1970) Teoria del campo, corso di educazione alla visione. Sansoni editore, Firenze

A. Marcolli (1982) L'immagine-azione comunicazione. Sansoni editore, Firenze

D. Marini et al. (2001) Comunicazione visiva digitale—fondamenti di eidomatica. Addison Wesley, Milano

J. McHugh (2002) Unplugged U. Wired, Oct. 2002

M. McLuhan (1964) Understanding media—Gli strumenti del comunicare. Il Saggiatore, Milano

M. McLuhan (1988) La galassia Gutenberg. Armando, Roma

N. Negroponte (2002) Being wireless. Wired, Oct. 2002

D.A. Norman (1988) The psychology of everyday things. Basic Books, Inc., New York

D.A. Norman (1994) Things that make us smart: Defending human attributes in the age of the machine. Addison Wesley, Reading, MA (ISBN 0-201-58129-9)

D.A. Norman (1998) The design of everyday things. Basic Books, Inc., New York (ISBN-978-0-262-64037-4)

D.A. Norman (2007) The design of future things. Basic Books, Inc., New York

K. Veltman (2000) Cultural and historical metadata: MEMECS (Metadonnées et Mémoire Collective Systématique): http://www.cultivate-int.org/issue1/memecs/

2 e-Society and the Social Divide

A.M. Ronchi (1997) The increasing gap. In: Economic Development in a Global Information Society (Smart Communities Forum), Sept. 1997, Sophia-Antipolis, Nice, France & Rome, Italy

A.M. Ronchi (2003a) On culture in a worldwide Information Society: Cultural diversity, technology and formats. Proc. CIDOC 2003, St. Petersburg, Russia, 1–7 Sept. 2003, pp 165–179 (see http://confifap.cpic.ru/upload/spb2004/reports/doklad_173.doc and http://cidoc2003.adit.ru/eng/default.asp)

A.M. Ronchi (2003b) MEDICI Framework and infopoverty. In: A Regional Workshop on Human Security and Local Initiatives in Development, International Center, Chiang Mai University, Chiang Mai, Thailand, 5–7 Dec. 2003 (see http://coe21-policy.sfc.keio.ac.jp/ja/event/20031205.html)

A.M. Ronchi (2003c) Heritage, identity and education. UNESCO World Summit on Information Society, Geneva, Switzerland, 9–13 Dec. 2003 (see http://www.wsis.org)

A.M. Ronchi (2003d) Digital communication: the long way toward a proper "format". In: Proc. Global Forum: Connecting Business and Communities, Rome, Italy, 6–7 Nov. 2003

A.M. Ronchi, L. Thiesmeyer, A. Quacchia, G. Mihajes, K. Onoda, R. Makkuni (2005) On culture in a world-wide Information Society: toward the knowledge society—the challenge. In: 14th Int. Conf. World Wide Web, Chiba, Japan, 10–14 May 2005 (ISBN:1-59593-051-5; see http://portal.acm.org/citation.cfm?id=1062754&coll=GUIDE&dl=GUIDE&CFID=49211539&CFTOKEN=70338963)

Digital Opportunity Channel: http://www.digitalopportunity.org

Digital Opportunity Trust: http://www.dotrust.org

Local initiatives in development and human security (team leaders: M. Umegaki, L. Thiesmeyer): http://coe21-policy.sfc.keio.ac.jp/en/project/t_umegaki.html

W.J. Pardi (1999) XML in action: Web technology. MS Press, Redmond, WA

O. Sacks (2003) Il caso di Anna H. Mente & Cervello magazine, no. 5, Oct. 2003

3 Quality Content; 4 Digital Content and Creativity

European Academy of Digital Media (EADiM; provides an infrastructure for networking and sharing expertise among the nominees, winners and jurors of EUROPRIX): http://www.eadim.org

International Center for New Media (ICNM; a non-profit organisation seated in Salzburg, Austria, which works in 34 European countries and networks around the world. ICNM runs programs and projects in the field of analysis, support and training for the development of new media content and markets, focusing on best-practice evaluation, promotion, showcasing and education): http://www.icnm.org

Italian eContent Award (inspired by the WSA, this award selects quality e-content and promotes creativity and innovation in new media applications in Italy, nominating the eight best Italian eContent products, and it directs young talent into international contests): http://www.econtentaward.it

A. Rota (2006) Culture and creativity in the context of digital media—a new era for digital media and content: http://www.dmc.keio.ac.jp/en/review/0601_rota1.html

World Summit Award (WSA; a global initiative to select and promote the world's best e-content. It is held in cooperation with the United Nations' World Summit on the Information Society (WSIS) and will be held until 2015. It receives support from numerous national and international non-profit organisations, as well as a substantial contribution from the private industry): http://www.wsis-award.org

5 Cultural Content

Canadian Heritage Information Network (CHIN): http://www.chin.gc.ca

L. Chengsen, P. Galluzzi, A.M. Ronchi et al. (2007) Leonardo in Cina. Giunti Editore, Firenze

Digital Culture (DigiCULT; an IST Support Measure (IST-2001-34898) to establish a regular watch over existing and emerging technologies that can or could be used to optimise the development of, the access to, and the preservation of Europe's rich cultural and scientific heritage within the emerging digital cultural economy): http://www.digicult.info/pages/index.php

Directorate of Culture, Cultural and Natural Heritage (Staff, Structures and partners) http://www.coe.int/t/dg4/cultureheritage/About/governance/default_en.asp

English Heritage: http://www.english-heritage.org.uk

F. Fishnaller et al. (2006) e-Art: Arte, società e democrazia nell'era della rete. Editori Riuniti, Rome

P. Galluzzi, G. Strano et al. (2008) Galileo's telescope: the instrument that changed the world. Giunti Editore, Firenze

Le Portail de la Culture, France: http://www.culture.fr

MEDICI (Multimedia for EDucation and employment through Integrated Cultural Initiatives) Framework (a framework of cooperation established in 1997 by the European Commission): http://www.medicif.org

Ministero per i Beni e le Attività Culturali (MiBAC), Italy: http://www.beniculturali.it

Museum Documentation Association (MDA): http://www.mda.org.uk

NINCH (2001) Guide to good practice in the digital representation and management of cultural heritage materials. National Initiative for a Networked Cultural Heritage, Washington, DC

Réunion des musées nationaux (RMN), France: http://www.rmn.fr

A.M. Ronchi (2004) Digital heritage: cultural heritage and information communication technology. Delewa Editore, Milan

Royal Danish Ministry of Foreign Affairs (2000) The power of culture: The cultural dimension in development. Royal Danish Ministry of Foreign Affairs, Copenhagen, Ch. 3 (see http://www.um.dk/danida/tpoc/index.asp)

UN (2003) UNESCO adopts international convention to safeguard intangible cultural heritage. In: 32nd UNESCO Gen. Conf., Paris, France, 17 Oct. 2003 (see http://portal.unesco.org/en/ev.php-URL_ID=16783&URL_DO=DO_TOPIC&URL_SECTION=201.html)

References 73

6 Digital Communication: the Role of Context

E. Neuhold, C. Niederée, A. Stewart et al. (2004) The role of context for information mediation in digital libraries. Springer, Berlin

7 Cultural Diversity and Cultural Models

D. Ayton-Shenker (1995) The challenge of human rights and cultural diversity (United Nations Background Note): http://www.un.org/rights/dpi1627e.htm

Cultural diversity: a new universal ethic (UNESCO): http://portal.unesco.org/culture/en/ev.php-URL_ID=2450&URL_DO=DO_TOPIC&URL_SECTION=201.html

Cultural diversity in the Treaty (at the European Culture Portal): http://ec.europa.eu/culture/portal/action/diversity/diversity_en.htm

Dublin Core Metadata Initiative: http://dublincore.org

Eternal Gandhi Multimedia Museum: http://www.sacredworld.in

M. MacLean, B.H. Davis (eds.)(1999) Time and bits: Managing digital continuity. Getty Trust Publ., Los Angeles, CA Revealing things (Smithsonian Institution): http://www.si.edu

OCLC (Online Computer Library Center; a non-profit, membership, computer library service and research organisation dedicated to furthering public access to information and reducing the cost of accessing information): http://www.oclc.org/about/default.htm

OCLC PURLS (Persistent Uniform Resource Locators) webpage: http://www.purl.org

Report to G8 on culture in a worldwide Information Society (2001; author: E. Fink): http://www.medicif.org/Activities/Culture/future%20online%20culture%20G-8%20report%20final%204.htm

Revealing things (a Smithsonian Without Walls project, director: J. Gradwhol): http://www.si.edu/ripley/eap/sww.htm

A. M. Ronchi (2005) The bias of printing. In: Proc. of Cultural Heritage Networks Hypermedia, (see http://www.medicif.org)

B. Shneiderman (updated by C. Plaisant, 2008) Treemaps for space-constrained visualization of hierarchies: http://www.cs.umd.edu/hcil/treemap-history

The Crossing Project (a vision of Indian creativity and interactive design combining traditional and modern technology; as computing proliferates in the world, retaining identity becomes an important task in the new millennium): http://www.sacredworld.in

The Environmental Awareness Program (director: J. Gradwhol): http://www.si.edu/ripley/eap/eap.htm

Treemap; Treemaps for space-constrained visualization of hierarchies (author: B. Shneiderman),both available at: http://www.cs.umd.edu/hcil/

8 Content, Communication and Tools

Altair 8800 from Micro Instrumentation Telemetry Systems (MITS, Albuquerque, NM; this is considered by many to be the first mass-produced personal computer, although they were called microcomputers in those days—in 1975): http://oldcomputers.net/altair.html or http://virtualaltair.com/

Apple Lisa (the first commercial computer with a graphical user interface (GUI); prior to the Lisa, all computers were text-based—all commands were typed in via the keyboard): http://www.apple-history.com/?&page=gallery&model=lisa

R. Aunger (ed.)(2000) Darwinizing culture: The status of memetics as a science. Oxford University Press, Oxford

P. Baran (1964) On distributed communications networks. IEEE Trans. Comm. Systems CS-12(1):1–9

Berengo Fine Arts (Murano glass furnace and gallery, Venice): http://www.berengo.com

M.L. Best (1997) Models for interacting populations of memes: Competition and niche behavior. J. Memetics: Evolutionary Models of Information Transmission 1

S. Blackmore (2000) The meme machine. Oxford University Press, Oxford

J.T. Bonner (1980) The evolution of culture in animals. Princeton University Press, Princeton, NJ

R. Boyd, P.J. Richerson (1985) Culture and the evolutionary process. Chicago University Press, Chicago, IL

V. Bush (1945) As we may think. Atlantic Monthly, JulyP. Carbone (ed.)(2002) eLiterature in ePublishing. Associazione Culturale Mimesis, Milano

P. Carbone, P. Ferri (eds.)(1999) Le comunità virtuali. Associazione Culturale Mimesis, Milano

L.L. Cavalli-Sforza, M.W. Feldman (1981) Cultural transmission and evolution: a quantitative approach. Princeton University Press, Princeton, NJ

V.G. Cerf, R.E. Kahn (1974) A protocol for packet network interconnection. IEEE Trans. Comm. Tech. COM-22(5):627–641

A.-M. Christin (2002) A history of writing: From hieroglyph to multimedia. Flammarion, Paris

S. Crocker (1969) Host software. RFC001 Apr-07-1969

V. Csanyi (1991) Evolutionary systems and society: A general theory. Duke University Press, Durham, NC

V. Csanyi (1999) The evolution of complexity. Kluwer, Dordrecht

R. Dawkins (1976) The selfish gene. Oxford University Press, New York

Early cars (Smithsonian): http://www.si.edu/Encyclopedia_SI/nmah/earlycars.htm

Emoticons (chat guide from the BBC): http://www.bbc.co.uk/chatguide/glossary/emoticons.shtml

Encyclopædia Britannica entry for F. De Saussure (1857–1913, who stated that signs are composed of two distinct but inseparable parts: the signifier, and the signified. The signifier is the materially produced representation, e.g. "dog"; the signified is the mental concept to which the signifier refers, i.e. four-legged, barking animal): http://www.britannica.com/eb/article-9065908/Ferdinand-de-Saussure

A. Granelli (2004) Inventori d'Italia. Guerini e Associati, Milano

A. Granelli, F. Traclò (eds.)(2006) Innovazione e cultura. Il Sole 24 Ore, Milano

S. Göbel et al. (2004) Technologies for interactive digital storytelling and entertainment. Springer, Berlin

F. Heylighen (1992) Selfish memes and the evolution of cooperation. J. Ideas 2(4):77–84

F. Heylighen (1998) What makes a meme successful? Selection criteria for cultural evolution. In: Proc. 16th Int. Congr. Cybernetics. Assoc. Int. Cyber., Namur, Belgium, pp. 423–418

History of writing (Historyworld): http://www.historyworld.net/wrldhis/PlainTextHistories. asp?historyid=ab33

Y. Huaqing (1998) La scrittura cinese. Vallardi, Milano

R. Kahn (1972) Communications principles for operating systems. Internal BBN memorandum

R. Khan (guest ed.), K. Uncapher, H. van Trees (assoc. guest eds.)(1978) Proc. IEEE Spec. Issue on Packet Communication Networks 66(11)

L. Kleinrock (1961) Information flow in large communication nets. RLE Quart. Progr. Rep. July 1961

L. Kleinrock (1964) Communication nets: Stochastic message flow and delay. McGraw-Hill, New York

L. Kleinrock (1976) Queueing systems. Vol II: Computer applications. Wiley, New York

B.M. Leiner et al. (2003) A brief history of the Internet. Internet Society, Reston, VA (see http://www.isoc.org/internet/history/brief.shtml)

J.C.R. Licklider, W. Clark (1962) On-line man–computer communication. AFIPS Conf. Proc. 21:113–128

M. McLuhan, B.R. Powers (1999) The global village: Transformations in world life and media in the 21st century. Oxford University Press, Oxford (ISBN 0195079108)

MediaLab MIT: http://www.media.mit.edu

Meme replication: the memetic life-cycle (23 Nov 2001; author: F. Heylighen; from Principia Cybernetica Web): http://pespmc1.vub.ac.be/MEMEREP.html

Mercedes-Benz Museum: http://www.museum-mercedes-benz.com/?lang=en

E. Moritz (1990) Memetic science: I. General introduction. J. Ideas 1:1–23

E. Moritz (1995) Metasystems, memes and cybernetic immortality. In: F. Heylighen, C. Joslyn, V. Turchin (eds.) The quantum of evolution: toward a theory of metasystem transitions. Gordon and Breach, New York (J. Gen. Evolut. Spec. Issue World Futures 45:155–171)

F. Naumann (1907) Das Gehirn der Welt. Süddeutsche Monatshefte 4:759–764 (the notion of "world brain"—Gehirn der Welt—has since been explored using a variety of names, e.g. global brain, global intelligence, global mind, global superbrain, global superorganism, hive mind, mémoire mondiale, noospheric brain (organ of collective human reflection), planetary brain, social brain, super brain, super minds, collective intelligence; see also the Otlet ref. below)

P. Nerozzi Bellman (ed.)(1997) Internet e le muse. Associazione Culturale Mimesis, Milano

P. Otlet (1935) Monde: essaie d'universalisme—connaissance du monde; sentiment du monde; action organisée et plan du monde. Editions du Mundaneum, Brussels

Project Xanadu Mission Statement: http://www.xanadu.com

L. Roberts (1967) Multiple computer networks and intercomputer communication. ACM Gatlinburg Conf., Oct. 1967

L. Roberts, T. Merrill (1966) Toward a cooperative network of time-shared computers. Fall AFIPS Conf., Oct. 1966

S. Ruthfield (1995) The Internet's history and development: http://www.acm.org/crossroads/ xrds2-1/inet-history.html

Sensorama (1962, author: Morton Helig): http://visionary-film.blogspot.com/2007/05/ morton-heilig-sensorama-1962.html

Structuralism and Saussure: http://www.colorado.edu/English/courses/ENGL2012Klages/saussure.html

The Hermitage (St. Petersburg, Russia): http://www.hermitage.ru

The History of Communication: http://inventors.about.com/library/inventors/bl_history_of_communication.htm

Toward a deep electronic literature: The generalization of documents and media (author: T. Holm Nelson): http://xanadu.com/XanaduSpace/xuGzn.htm

Union of International Associations—Virtual Organization (on the laetus in praesens website): http://www.laetusinpraesens.org/docs/otlethyp.php

United States early radio history (author: T.H. White): http://earlyradiohistory.us

K.H. Veltman (2004) Understanding new media: Augmented knowledge and culture. University of Calgary Press, Calgary

Xerox Alto (the first PC to incorporate a "what you see is what you get" (WYSIWYG) editor, a commercial mouse for input, a graphical user interface (GUI), and a bit-mapped display; it also offered menus and icons, a link to a local area network and simultaneous file storage): http://historywired.si.edu/object.cfm?ID=337

Part II The General Technological Framework

9 Native Digital Content

Heading back to the start of the *fil rouge—the common thread*—we find that content in its native format is linked to the use of one or more senses: hearing, sight, touch and smell[1]. The native format used to be analogue, but it has recently become possible to find "native" digital content. This means that the "original" content was created or acquired in digital format, so there is no analogue/physical original. This applies for instance to digital video and audio recordings or "digital art" artefacts.

"native" digital content

Native digital content should not be confused with the so-called "digital original". The term "digital original" used to be applied to a "perfect" digital double of the original physical "object" that is suitable for any use; research, display, etc. This means that the physical original of the digital original is available for future digitisation. In contrast, "native" digital objects are basically the only resource available. The quality, comprehensiveness and preservation of native digital objects are bounded by the digital technology utilised.

Digital originals

We all know that digitisation means "segmentation" into slices, such that the digitised data has defined resolution and quality. Once the standard has been defined (in terms of resolution, palette, frequency sampling, ...), there is no way to accurately recreate the portion of information that is lost. In other terms, when creating native digital objects we must consider the quality, comprehensiveness and long-term preservation of the content, because there is no physical reference object to go back to.

9.1 Data Creation

Native digital content is increasing in quantity and variety. Digital documents, publications, recordings, drawings, sketches, illustrations, pictures, movies, music and more are being produced.

An incredible amount of data has moved from the original analogue format to the digital one; for example, traditional cameras are now almost exclusively used by high-level professionals or are found in collectors markets. Mobile phones and portable multimedia devices can now be customised and tailored

---

1   We are not currently taking taste into account as a main sense used with cultural heritage, even though traditional foods and cuisine form a part of our heritage too.

to our own specific requirements. The same has already happened in the personal movie camera market; Super8 film cameras led to analogue magnetic tape cameras (e.g. VHS, video8) and then to digital tape and digital versatile disk cameras. In the meantime, solid-state *disks* (SmartMedia, Secure Digital, Memory Stick, etc.) have gained a leading position in the marketplace as an innovative and practical "content holder". In the film market, key players are going to stop producing analogue films for the home market. In just a few years the format used to store music shifted from audio cassettes to CD-R/RW. Now, multimedia players that hold gigabytes of data (music, movies, clips, etc.) are so compact that we can lose them in our pockets.

Following the explosion of Mac and post-Win95[2] users, most personal content is now generated, stored, managed and enjoyed in digital format through computers. This upsurge in computer use resulted in a tidal wave of new *objects*, such as playlists, SMS, podcasting, personal websites, communities, blogs, wikis, and more.

In this scenario, interactive installations and the digital preservation of intangible heritage represent some of the most difficult content to manage.

9.2   Native "Nondigital" Content

Most of our heritage was not *born* in digital format; some of it has a physical appearance, some must be performed or played, and some is even more "intangible". Some of this patrimony has already been converted into a digital format, but it must still be harmonised or updated to a new standard from time to time. Since a new standard usually performs better then the old one, we encounter a dilemma if the original artefact is still accessible: should we convert it or start from scratch?

Which is the right choice? There is no "default" answer, but it is often better to start from scratch, if this will not cause any harm, and acquire digital data instead of reusing or modifying existing information.

There is a long tradition of analogue data capture. For example, during analogue audio recording, a plucked string vibrates the air around it. These airwaves in turn vibrate a small membrane in a microphone, and the membrane translates those vibrations into fluctuating electronic voltages. During tape recording, these voltages impart charge to magnetic particles on the tape, and so the sequence of charge on the tape reflects the original sound. The charge is read when the tape is played back, and so the original sound can be reproduced.

---

2   Starting with Win95, the PC market shifted from offices and game players to home users. The "Charlie Chaplin" advertisements for the IBM PC in the 1980s were superceded by those for Win95 ("Start me up" / "Where do you want to go today") in the 1990s.

Moving images are recorded in a similar way, except that instead of the air vibrating a membrane, the light striking an electronic receptor fluctuates, and these fluctuations are changed into voltages.

Sound pressure waves and other analogue signals vary continuously; they change from instant to instant, and as they change between two values, they pass through all of the values in-between. Analogue recordings represent real-world sounds and images that have been translated into continually changing electronic voltages.

This short excursus on analogue data capture was provided in order to clarify the basics of data capture, because in the early phases of the "digital world", analogue formats used to perform better than digital formats, and so those involved in the fields of hi-fi audio, professional photography and movies used to refer to analogue methods and standards.

This is one of the reasons why, some years ago[3], when significant amounts of data were being converted, analogue formats were chosen instead of the early digital ones. For example, early in the 1990s Canadian television converted thousand of videotapes onto analogue video discs.

9.3   Data Acquisition and Digitisation

Even though native digital content is becoming increasingly popular, and so the demand for digitisation is dropping, there are still many items that need to be digitised even if we only consider cultural heritage: monuments and archaeological sites, codices, statues, paintings, historical records, etc.

Each data stream that is collected as the representation of a virtual environment contributes to contextualising and creating an "experience", as some tend to say. Experiences appear to be personal assets that should be acquired and preserved.

If the data we are going to use are not in digital form natively, we need to acquire these data and convert them into a digital format.

We know that "to digitise" means to break the analogue continuum into predefined *slices*, which inevitably results in the loss of some of the original information. Digitisation is performed in different ways with different equipment for different classes of data: images, sounds, 3-D objects, and others. We might use image scanners, sound and voice recorders, camcorders, 3-D solid scanners, etc., as equipment. But how do we deal with different classes of data: sounds, images, smells, taste, touch... and behaviour.

Digitisation

Analogue and digital data are fundamentally different: whereas analogue information is generally smooth and continuous, digital information consists of discrete chunks; and whereas analogue information bears a direct and nonarbitrary relationship to what it represents, digital information is captured using

Analogue and digital data

---

3   In the 1990s, and subsequently too.

Fig. 9.1 Contemporary work of art in Paris (photo by the author)

formal codes that have only an arbitrary and indirect relationship to the source.

Thus, while an analogue image, for instance, consists of continuously varying colours and shading, a digital image consists of a set of individual dots or pixels, each recording the colour intensity and other information at a given point.

Due to the digital structure of data, the *continuum* is broken into slices—a best approximation to the given analogue value—and then coded as a sequence of digits (bits). This ensures that there is no degradation of quality between the original digital dataset and any copy. The bit streams representing the information can be transferred correctly, so the information at the destination is equal to the original. While the bit stream may sometimes be corrupted, in this case the error is highlighted and sometimes automatically corrected for by control bits.

Although the specific kind of information stored varies from medium to medium (sound waves, light intensities, colours), this basic difference remains constant.

"Digitisation", the conversion from analogue to digital, thus requires that the *continuous* analogue information be sampled, measured, and then recorded in digital format. There are several basic factors which govern this process and which determine the quality of the resulting digital data.

Density of the data sampled: the resolution

Density of the data sampled: the resolution. The first of these is the density of the data captured from the analogue original; in effect, how often the original is sampled per unit of time (in the case of video and audio) or area (in the case of images and video).

For digital audio, the higher the sampling rate, the smoother the transitions between the individual packets of sound, to the point where, with modern digital audio, these transitions cannot be detected by the human ear.

A low sampling rate results in *clipping*—the audio equivalent of "rough animation". For digital images, the higher the sampling rate (i.e. the resolution), the smoother and less "pixelated" the image appears, and the more it can be magnified before its granularity becomes visible.

Amount of information recorded at each sampling. The second factor is the amount of information that is recorded during each sampling. Individual pixels in an image may contain very little information; at their most minimal, each may comprise just one binary digit to express "on" versus "off" or "black" and "white". On the other hand, each pixel may consist of 32 bits[4] (2^{32} choices) in order to express millions of possible colours. A large sample size may be used, in digital images for instance, to capture nuances, finer shadings of difference between values.

It may also be used to express a wider total range, for instance in digital audio, where a higher frequency response means that the recording can capture a greater range of frequencies, with higher highs and lower lows.

File size versus quality. Sampling frequency (or resolution) and sample size (frequency response, bit depth) both involve a trade-off between data quality and file size. It is clear that as the sampling frequency is increased, the amount of information captured at each sampling increases, and so the file size increases too, and file becomes the more costly to create, transmit, store, and preserve.

File size versus quality

Decisions about digital data capture are thus not simply a matter of achieving the highest possible quality, but rather of determining the level of quality that will adequately represent the original given your needs. Obtaining the perfect balance between "technical quality" and "perceived quality" is usually key to producing successful applications. Sometimes a 256-colour image will perform better than a 16,000-colour image if the palette is properly optimised.

Adequate reproduction of the original

9.3.1   Text

Although it may seem odd to discuss *digital text* in this context, there are some important although indirect parallels between the principles described above and those that govern digital text capture.

When capturing "digital text", it is commonly understood that we do not sample the original in the same way that we sample audio or images. However, the process of text capture does involve making choices about the level of granularity of the resulting digital representation.

---

4   More bits are usually allocated per pixel in order to pre-load dynamic images.

Fig. 9.2 Formatted text in a desktop publishing application

Fig. 9.3 Ancient books and codices

When capturing a twentieth-century printed text, for instance, a range of different "data densities" are possible: a simple transcription of the actual letters and spaces printed on the page; a higher-order transcription which also represents the nature of textual units such as paragraphs and headings; or an even more dense transcription which also adds inferential information such as keywords or metrical data.

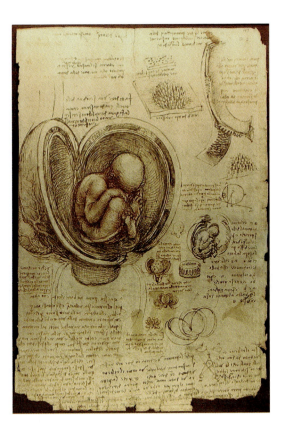

Fig. 9.4 Ancient manuscripts: *Studies of Embryos* by Leonardo da Vinci (pen over red chalk; 1510–1513; photo by Luc Viatour)

Other possibilities arise for texts that are structured on different levels of internal granularity. In the case of a mediaeval manuscript, one might create a transcription that captures the graphemes, the individual characters of the text, but does not distinguish between different forms of the same letter (for instance, short and long). Or one might capture these different letter forms, or even distinguish between swashed and unswashed characters. One might also choose to capture variations in spacing between letters, lines of text, and text components, or variations in letter size, or changes in handwriting, or any one of a number of possibly meaningful distinctions.

These distinctions, and the choice of whether or not to capture them, are the equivalent of sampling rates and bit-depth: they govern the amount of information which the digital file records about the analogue source, and the resulting level of nuance that can be obtained when reusing and processing the digital file.

9.3.2 Sound

There are at least three main categories of sound data that are acquired: voice, electronic musical instruments, music and compound sounds.

Fig. 9.5
Multimedia player (photo by Francesca Ronchi)

Electronic musical instruments may offer a MIDI interface as well as computer-generated sounds. The MIDI format relies on a standard language that encodes sounds, rhythms and musical properties into a digital file. Electronic instruments might create MIDI output files when played, as might a musical application running on a computer. Later on the file can be replayed using a MIDI player.

Quality and fidelity in the MIDI format is linked to the technical specifications of the standard. In contrast, voice and compound sounds may be digitised using different quality standards.

Analogue-to-digital converter   Digital recording involves converting the analogue wave into a stream of numbers and recording the numbers instead of the wave. The conversion to a digital format is achieved using a device called an *analogue-to-digital converter* (ADC). To play back the music, the stream of numbers is converted back to an analogue wave by a *digital-to-analogue converter* (DAC). This process results in a recording with very high fidelity[5] and perfect reproduction every time you play it back, no matter how many times it has been played[6].

---

5   In other words, very high similarity between the original signal and the reproduced signal.
6   In other words, the recording sounds the same every time you play it, no matter how many times it has been played.

II The General Technological Framework

When a sound wave is sampled using an analogue-to-digital converter, two variables must be controlled. The first is the *sampling rate*, which controls how many times the sound is sampled per second. The second is the *sampling precision*, which controls how many different gradations[7] are possible when sampling.

The fidelity of the reproduced wave can never be as accurate as the analogue original; the difference between the analogue signal value and the closest digital value to it is known as the *quantization error*. This error is reduced by increasing both the sampling rate and the sampling precision. As the sampling rate and the level of quantization increase, so does the perceived sound quality. Again, this is a matter of human perception or "perceived quality".

Quantization error

In digital sampling, the fluctuating voltages are sampled or measured at a specific rate[8]. The sample value is equal to the signal amplitude at the instant of sampling. The frequency response of the digital audio file is slightly less than half the sampling rate (accordingly to the Nyquist Theorem). Because of sampling, the digital signal is segmented into steps that define the overall frequency response of the signal.

A signal sampled at 48 kHz has a wider frequency response than one sampled at 44.1 kHz. These samples are represented by bits (zeros and ones) that can be processed and recorded. The more bits that a sample contains, the better the picture or sound quality (e.g. 10-bit is better than 8-bit). A good digital signal will have a high number of samples (high sampling rate) and a high number of bits (quantization).

Digital-to-digital processing is a lossless process that produces perfect copies (clones), because the digital information can be copied with absolute exactness, unlike analogue voltages. A high bit-depth will also result in an enhanced dynamic range and lower quantization noise.

Ideally, each sampled amplitude value must be exactly equal to the true signal amplitude at the instant of sampling. ADCs do not achieve this level of perfection. Normally, a fixed number of bits (binary digits) are used to represent a sampled value. Therefore, the infinite set of values possible in an analogue signal are not available for the sampled values. In fact, if there are R bits in each sample, exactly 2^R sample values are possible. For high-fidelity applications, such as archival copies of analogue recordings, 24 bits per sample (or "24-bit resolution") should be used. As before, the difference between the analogue signal and the closest value that the digital sample can take is the *quantization error*. Since this can be regarded as a noise that is added to an otherwise perfect sample value, this is also often called *quantization noise*. 24-Bit digital audio has a negligible level of quantization noise.

Speeches are usually recorded using two main quality standards: high-compression low-quality (e.g. DSP 8,000 kHz, 1 bit, mono, 1 kbps), high-quality

---

7 The amount of data captured during each sampling. Sometimes the lowest and highest frequencies are cut out during sampling, yielding a less realistic "sound".

8 For example 48,000 times a second (48 kHz).

(e.g. PCM 44,100 kHz, 16-bit stereo). There is a wide choice of digital formats for compound sounds.

The size per second of an audio file depends on the digital sampling frequency, the number of bits used for sampling (sampling quality) and the number of channels: mono or stereo.

CD-quality uncompressed stereo audio files may require around 150 kilobytes per second, whilst a mono 16-bit 22-kHz file uses only 45 kB per second.

It is a good idea to compress audio files using *audio codecs* (coder/decoder) in order to save disk space and to enable better file transfer across the Internet.

A wide variety of specialised audio codecs are available thanks to the research activities of different laboratories and special interest groups (SIGs). Some of these are designed specifically for the human voice, while others address compound sounds and sound sampling issues.

Following the basic distinction between voice and compound sounds (e.g. music), commonly used voice codecs include the DSP Group's TrueSpeech or Microsoft's Groupe Spécial Mobile (GSM) 6.10.

The DSP codec was designed to perform better at low/medium bit rates. (Tech. Spec.: 8,000 kHz, 1 bit, mono, 1 kbps; see Table 9.1.)

GSM 6.10 was designed to offer an efficient compression rate (2:1 in real time) for voice tracks; it offers a medium/high bit rate. It is slower than DSP and not suitable for music (the quality is too poor), but its real-time decompression makes it suitable for use with modems and networks. GSM high audio compression cannot be performed in real time. (Tech. Spec.: 8,000 kHz, mono, 1 kbps, 11,025 kHz, mono, 2 kbps, 22,050 kHz, mono, 4 kbps, 44,100 kHz, mono, 8 kbps).

MP3 — Among the music codecs, the most well known is undoubtedly MP3 (MPEG Layer 3), developed by the Fraunhofer Institut (FhG). The MP3 codec is designed to create high-quality (CD-quality) music files that are up to 25% of the original size. It offers a high bit frequency and reduced CPU usage. Please refer to the table below for further information.

Table 9.1

Tech Spec			
8 kbps	8,000 kHz	Mono	0 kbps
16 kbps	8,000 kHz	Mono	1 kbps
8 kbps	11,025 kHz	Mono	0 kbps
16 kbps	11,025 kHz	Mono	1 kbps
18 kbps	11.025 kHz	Mono	2 kbps
20 kbps	11.025 kHz	Mono	2 kbps
24 kbps	11.025 kHz	Mono	2 kbps

Table 9.1 (*continued*)

Tech Spec			
32 kbps	11.025 kHz	Mono	3 kbps
8 kbps	12,000 kHz	Mono	0 kbps
16 kbps	12.000 kHz	Mono	1 kbps
18 kbps	12,000 kHz	Mono	2 kbps
20 kbps	12,000 kHz	Mono	2 kbps
16 kbps	16.000 kHz	Mono	1 kbps
18 kbps	16,000 kHz	Mono	2 kbps
20 kbps	16,000 kHz	Mono	2 kbps
24 kbps	16,000 kHz	Mono	2 kbps
32 kbps	16,000 kHz	Mono	3 kbps
24 kbps	22,050 kHz	Mono	2 kbps
32 kbps	22,050 kHz	Mono	3 kbps
24 kbps	24,000 kHz	Mono	2 kbps
32 kbps	24,000 kHz	Mono	3 kbps
18 kbps	8,000 kHz	Stereo	2 kbps
20 kbps	8,000 kHz	Stereo	2 kbps
24 kbps	8,000 kHz	Stereo	2 kbps
32 kbps	8,000 kHz	Stereo	3 kbps
18 kbps	11.025 kHz	Stereo	2 kbps
20 kbps	11,025 kHz	Stereo	2 kbps
24 kbps	11,025 kHz	Stereo	2 kbps
32 kbps	11.025 kHz	Stereo	3 kbps
18 kbps	12,000 kHz	Stereo	2 kbps
20 kbps	12,000 kHz	Stereo	2 kbps
24 kbps	12,000 kHz	Stereo	2 kbps
32 kbps	12,000 kHz	Stereo	3 kbps
32 kbps	16,000 kHz	Stereo	3 kbps

Table 9.1 (*continued*)

Tech Spec			
48 kbps	16,000 kHz	Stereo	5 kbps
56 kbps	16,000 kHz	Stereo	6 kbps
48 kbps	22,050 kHz	Stereo	5 kbps
56 kbps	22,050 kHz	Stereo	6 kbps
48 kbps	24,000 kHz	Stereo	5 kbps
56 kbps	24,000 kHz	Stereo	6 kbps

9.3.3 Images

Two-dimensional graphical content can be acquired in two different formats: vector and raster.

Vector　　*Vector graphics* are often created manually from technical sketches or using vector graphics applications. Sometimes vector images are produced automatically, for example by specific instruments such as digital high-accuracy measurement systems that collect sequences of nodes. A third way in which they are created is by the conversion of raster images back into the vector format.

Raster　　*Raster graphics* can be acquired directly from physical objects via photo/video cameras or by scanning pre-existing images.

Digital image capture involves dividing the image into a grid of tiny regions, each of which is represented by a digital value that records colour information. The *resolution* of the image indicates how densely packed these regions are and is the most familiar measure of image quality (DPI, dots per inch). However, in addition to the resolution it is also important to consider the *bit depth* (e.g. 1, 8, 16, 32), which is the amount of information recorded for each region and hence the possible range of tonal values. Scanners record tonal values in digital images in one of three general ways: black and white, greyscale, and colour.

In black and white image capture, each pixel in the digital image is either "black" or "white" (on or off). In 8-bit greyscale capture, where each sample is expressed using eight bits of information (yielding 256 possible values), the tonal values of the original are recorded with a much larger palette that includes not only black and white, but also 254 intermediate shades of grey. In 24-bit colour scanning, the tonal values of the original are reproduced from combinations of red, green, and blue (RGB); such colour palettes can represent up to 16.7 million colours.

Digital cameras are usually characterised by some of the same technical specifications as analogue cameras, such as focal length, lens luminosity, optical zoom range, etc. However, they are also characterised by specifications related to their digital nature, such as number of CCDs, acquisition speed, resolution, sensitivity, data formats, etc.

These days, the resolution and palette size are not major constraints on the everyday use of digital cameras. Acquisition speed and sensitivity are more significant parameters because they can influence the resulting image. Acquisition speed can be considered to be the period of time between one shot and the next, and thus includes the reaction time, the acquisition time, the compression time and the time taken to store the image. Sometimes the delay between pressing the button and the acquisition of the picture is so large that even a pedestrian crossing the scene will move too quickly to be captured. Sequences or bracketing[9] are influenced by acquisition speed.

Digital cameras usually offer different standard file formats for storing the data, such as RAW, JPG, TIFF[10] or QuickTime with audio. Video cameras can output files in the JPEG, QuickTime Motion, MPEG or AVI formats.

If we have pre-existing images we can use a *raster scanner* to process them. *Raster scanners* In this case, set of sensors captures an array of pixels with the required resolution and palette (there can be 24 or more bits per pixel). Scanners can differ in shape (e.g. drum-shaped, flat, barcode readers, etc.), size (e.g. A5, A4,... A0) and resolution (e.g. 300, 600, 1200, 2400,... dpi), and can utilise different techniques (e.g. direct light or reflected light).

Aside from barcode readers, which are useful in various fields (e.g. taking *Laser scanners* inventories, identifying customers), flatbed scanners are one of the most popular scanner shapes. The sensor scans the document by moving across the surface of the document in columns and rows, step-by-step. After scanning a raster file is outputted. Raster files can be very big, even hundreds of megabytes in size (if an A4 image is scanned with a bit depth of 24 bit and a resolution of 96 dpi, the resulting raster file will be 2.56MB; if we use 1200 dpi instead, $9924 \times 14040 \times 24 = 3.26$ GB).

Physical originals may be placed on the flat screen and illuminated directly by a laser beam (for opaque documents) or placed in a specific adapter and illuminated by a uniform lighting system in the background (this approach is applied to e.g. transparency films).

---

9   Bracketing: each time a scene is photographed three shots are actually taken: one using the automatic exposure setting of the camera, another which is overexposed, and another which is underexposed.

10   Please refer to the relevant section for further details.

9.3.4 3-D Models

A number of technologies and a great deal of experience can be applied to the reconstruction and digitisation phase. These technologies include 3-D scanners (for small and large objects), digital cameras, processes and equipment for converting video recordings of 3-D objects into 3-D models, 3-D reconstruction using photogrammetry techniques, and a number of geometric modelling and animation systems.

Three-dimensional vector graphics are often created manually via 3-D technical modelling or vector graphics applications. Sometimes vector images are produced automatically, e.g. by specific instruments such as digital high-accuracy 3-D scanning systems, by acquiring "clouds of points".

A rather complex operation called *triangulation* is then used to convert these "clouds of points" into triangles and polygons, creating meshes. Three-dimensional models can even be created by calibrating photographic images of 3-D objects and accurately measuring them. This method is particularly suitable for buildings and large *objects*.

Fig. 9.6 Milan city centre: a 3D model (by HMG Laboratory – 1989)

Three-dimensional data acquisition

9.3.4.1 Laser Scanning

Three-dimensional data acquisition via laser scanning technology can be performed using two different approaches: the *time of flight* approach, or with instruments that use CCD cameras where distance measurement is based on the *principle of triangulation*. Both of these depend, of course, on the ratio of the size of the object of interest to the laser's wavelength (the smallest detail to be scanned must be several times this wavelength), but as a rule of thumb time-of-flight models are more suitable for large but distant objects, such as monuments, and telemetric scanners are more suitable for obtaining highly accurate descriptions of small objects. This is because, as usual, the size of the telemetric base is directly linked to the potential accuracy of the measurements.

3-D scanners record the three-dimensional coordinates of numerous points on an object's surface in a relatively short period of time. To accomplish this, a laser beam is projected onto the object's surface. The scanning effect is achieved using one or two mirrors, which allow the deflection angle of the beam to be changed in small increments. In addition, the entire instrument and/or object may be rotated to achieve complete three-dimensional point coverage. It is important to record the angular settings with a high degree of accuracy, since both the angles and the base distance are required in order to calculate the 3-D coordinates of each point.

Both of these will provide a description of the geometry of the target in terms of the density of the cloud of points. Each point is characterised by spatial coordinates (x,y,z) from a common point of origin, the position of laser scanner.

Fig. 9.7 **a** Rendered view of the 3D model of the Crypt of Santa Cristina in Carpignano Salentino, Italy; **b** The same rendered view but the colour has been removed and the 3D model is artificially shaded (V. Valzano, J.-A. Beraldin, A. Bandiera (2002) Carpiniana: virtual representation of the Crypt of Santa Cristina in Carpignano Salentino (CD-ROM). Coordinamento SIBA University of Lecce, Italy, ISBN 8883050061)

Fig. 9.8 3D model of the metope *Perseus and Medusa*, point cloud view (V. Valzano, A. Bandiera, J.-A. Beraldin (2006) The metopes of Selinunte (CD-ROM). Coordinamento SIBA University of Lecce, Italy, ISBN 8883050398)

Fig. 9.9 *Pietà Bandini* by Michelangelo Buonarroti (Museo del Duomo Florence; photo by the author)

Usually each 3-D dataset requires more than one scan, mainly because of occlusions[11], so we need to change the relative positions of the scanner and the target object or to make use of a mirror if some parts of the target cannot be seen directly. Sometimes this is not enough and the final model has some holes that need to be patched manually.

In order to be able to reconstruct the three-dimensional patchwork with high accuracy, some overlapping reference points (marks) are needed. Textures and colours are often captured separately using cameras, reference points and a reference colour palette.

9.3.4.2 Time of Flight

This family of scanners[12] use a laser diode that sends a pulsed laser beam to the scanned object. The pulse of light is diffusely reflected by the surface of the target object and part of the light returns to the receiver. The time that the light needs to travel from the laser diode to the scanned object surface and back is measured and the distance from the scanner to the target object is calculated using an assumed speed of light.

---

11 The rear side of the object is not visible because it is occluded (hidden from view) by the front side. Occlusions are sometimes hard to solve because of the shape of the object.

12 Otherwise known as "ranging" scanners.

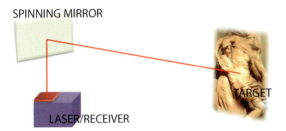

Fig. 9.10 Time of flight

Ranging scanners works better over long distances than instruments that work by triangulation, but they are much less accurate at close range. Their accuracy ranges from a few millimetres to two or three centimetres, depending to some extent on the distance between the object and the scanner (the object distance).

9.3.4.3 Triangulation

The family of scanners that use a simple triangulation principle project a light spot or stripe onto the target object's surface, and the position of the spot on the object is then recorded by one or more CCD cameras.

The angle of the light beam as it leaves the scanner is recorded internally and the fixed baselength between the laser source and camera is known from calibration. The distance from the scanner to the target is geometrically determined from the recorded angle and the baselength.

The accuracy depends on both the baselength[13] and the distance from the scanner to the target. For a fixed baselength, the standard deviation of the distance measurement will increase in proportion to the square of the distance. To provide a rough idea, the deviation when working at very close range (2–3 m) is less than 1 mm.

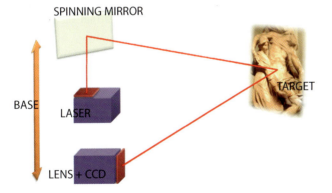

Fig. 9.11 Triangulation

---

13 The telemetric base—the distance between the light emitter and the light receiver, the base of the triangle that has its apex at the scanned point of the target object.

Triangulation can even be applied to stereo images taken by a couple of digital cameras mounted at opposite ends of the telemetric base. Image-matching techniques can be used to compute the 3-D coordinates of large numbers of target object surface points. In this case we must know the exact position and angle of the two cameras, the focal length of the lens and the distortion mask of the lens (the digital filter).

This technique is very well known and is used in photogrammetry. It is often necessary to refer to visual features in order to be able to find matching points, so a geometrical pattern is projected onto the object in order to increase the number of available points.

9.3.4.4 Processing 3-D Clouds of Points

At the end of the process, both methods will provide a cloud of 3-D points that varies in density with the shape of the object. If we look at this dataset in a 3-D viewer, we will recognise the shape of the object but it will be impossible to convert it into a realistic model.

We must convert the cloud of points into a structured mesh of triangles or polygons. This process is one of the hardest parts of 3-D laser scanning. Processing procedures should include the identification and elimination of inaccurate points or noise, the merging of different clouds taken from different locations in order to complete the scan, and last but not least, finding the best logic to connect the 3-D points to create triangles.

If the goal is a photorealistic reconstruction of the target, we will then need to add textures and colours in order to accurately render the model and achieve a photorealistic appearance.

Textures can be obtained via digital cameras in the scanning device or from external digital imaging systems. In both cases, special care must be taken to acquire realistic colours (e.g. using a reference palette) and to obtain accurate geometric representations of the "skins" that will applied onto the mesh. The second aspect is often neglected and textures taken from curved surfaces are used as parallel projections and vice versa.

Let's now consider some of the laser scanners that have been used in the field of culture and museums.

9.3.4.5 Laser Camera
(Remote Access and Display of 3-D Colour Images)

In the 1990s the National Research Council of Canada (NRC), in collaboration with the Canadian Conservation Institute (CCI), developed and patented a laser scanner imaging system for the rapid and high-resolution three-dimensional digital recording of museum and cultural objects in colour. This technology enables high-quality 3-D images of museum objects to be recorded and displayed in detail with excellent colour reproduction. The objects can be interactively rotated and viewed from any angle and magnified or reduced in scale. Using stereo viewing equipment, the objects can be examined in stereo with a realistic perception of depth. The compact data file size facilitates convenient data transmission to remote virtual museum and educational sites using standard communications links.

This system enables accurate high-resolution archival quality digital records of the shape, colour and dimensions of important objects to be created, which will be compatible with the higher definition displays and communications systems of the future. Consequently, the collections will not have to be re-recorded as these new technologies become available. Once recorded, the image data can be used for a wide variety of museum activities, including research, scholarship, conservation, publication, reproduction, insurance and repatriation applications. Museums will be able to generate revenue from royalties through the use of images for display and reproduction. To reduce the increasingly high costs of insurance and shipping associated with loaning objects for exhibitions, museums will be able to prepare *virtual museum exhibitions* to display their collections to much larger audiences. It is also anticipated that this application will result in increased revenues from cultural tourism. After viewing them online, people will want to physically visit the museum to see the actual objects.

A similar application has been developed by the ISPG (Image and Sound Processing Group) of the Electronic and Information Department of Politecnico di Milano. One of the first tests of this application was the digital 3-D reconstruction of the *Teatro Romano* of Aosta. This *Laser Camera* application was appointed the best practice in digitisation during the G7 summit held in Midrand (South Africa) in May 1996.

9.3.4.6 VASARI Scanner

Around the same time, VASARI led to European leadership in the field of very high quality imaging for museums. The main results can be summarised as follows:

- Two working scanning prototypes installed at the National Gallery in London and at the Dörner Institute in Munich. The VASARI scanning system is able to capture images at a resolution over 20 pixels per millimetre. Both of these prototypes were used by the two museums. Later on another prototype was placed in the Uffizi Laboratory.
- Real colour data-capture and advanced developments in colorimetry and colour difference measurements that can be used in various fields outside of the museum sector (including accurate colour displays and textiles).
- Advanced imaging software such as mosaicing of high-resolution images, and painting deterioration measurements. These software packages associated with high-definition VASARI data capture could be adapted and applied outside of the museum sector.
- Two computer-aided learning (CAL) applications developed by SIDAC (on a CD-ROM) and Birkbeck College (under Windows 3). In addition, substantial infrastructure investments have been made; for example, a new picture-processing laboratory has been created at Birkbeck College.

Fig. 9.12 An example of a 3D scanner: the Leica ScanStation

9.3.4.7 Cyberware 3-D Scanner

Early Cyberware 3-D scanner products were used to scan 3-D objects up to 30 cm in diameter and 30 cm in height. The device was optimised for scanning people but could be used to scan other 3-D objects if they complied with certain criteria concerning reflectivity and colour.

The first 3-D digitiser with colour capabilities, Cyberware's Model 3030 delivered industry-leading performance for a variety of applications. In less than a minute, it scanned an object at high resolution and presented the resulting 3-D image on a graphics workstation, complete with true-to-life colour. The availability of colour information for 3-D digitisation provided nearly all of the information that a graphics application needs to fully describe an object.

In addition to enhancing realism in graphic models, colour denotes boundaries that are not obvious from shape alone. Colour indicates surface texture and reflectance. Also, by marking an object's surface before digitisation, colour can be used to transfer ideas from the object to the graphic model. In some specialised applications, colour can reveal characteristics such as skin discolouration, the grain of a piece of wood, or the locations of fasteners. Working in the infrared region, a customized colour subsystem can even detect surface temperature.

The scanner extends the resolution of the colour texture map by a factor of sixteen. The texture map contains more than enough detail for almost any type of rendering, animation or analysis. Details as small as individual hairs and the fine print on packaging are discernable. The digitised colour texture map is valuable in anthropometry, animation, and industrial design. The device scans four million RGB pixels in order to produce a 2000×2000-pixel image. A pitch of 165 pixels per inch is realized. This compares with the 250,000 pixels and 40 pixels per inch pitch of the 3030 RGB scanner.

When the scanner is used for the typical application of scanning the human head, a complete scan can be accomplished in under 20 s. An invisible infrared laser of wavelength 780 nm is used in place of the usual orange–red 632-nm laser. The same safety classification is attained. The high geometrical resolution of the standard product line is retained.

A self-contained light source illuminates the surface with cold white light. Cold light is light with the infrared portion of the spectrum removed using special mirrors. This and a special filter on the geometry camera prevents the white light from interfering with the process of measuring geometry. Similarly, the laser is infrared and the colour video camera is fitted with a filter that blocks infrared light. This enables both colour digitisation and geometry digitisation to be performed simultaneously.

10 Datasets and Formats

10.1 Data Types

The present chapter aims to provide a comprehensive review of the more popular datasets and formats. It describes, in particular, the properties and inherent advantages of various de facto data standards.

10.1.1 Sound

We can distinguish two main classes of audio content: music and speech. Taking into account quality and properties, we can differentiate basic quality recordings and high fidelity, hi-fi stereo, hi-fi 3-D, holophonic and surround recordings with or without special audio filters such as Dolby Digital effects.

High-fidelity music

Digital sound fidelity is based mainly on the size of the digital sample, expressed in kHz and bits[14], such as the 44 kHz, 16 bit samples used in audio CDs.

Once you have defined the quality you can choose an appropriate digital format, such as WAV, CCITT A Law or MPEG Layer 3. When dealing with music it is sometimes possible to use another digital format called MIDI, which is used to store the direct output from electronic instruments. This is a completely different archive format to the others; instead of digitising the combined effects of sounds (a "melting pot" approach), MIDI stores a sequence of alphanumeric codes associated with each sound, which makes it possible to modify the music stored by editing the sounds from specific instruments.

More recently, cutting-edge sound reproduction technologies have focused on methods of generating 3-D or surround sound effects without the need for the 5+1 or 6+1 stereo kits usually required.

Speech digitisation is easier and requires fewer resources. MPEG layer 3 digital recorders are suitable for creating durable recordings and, using specific software tools, it is even possible to translate the speech into ASCII code (i.e. we can convert speech into text).

Speech

---

14 For example 8.000 kHz, 8-bit mono or 48.000 kHz, 16-bit stereo, among others.

A final remark about audio content. Sound is still largely under-utilised in multimedia applications. It is not considered to be a "full" medium that actively participates in the process of *communication.* Nevertheless, we all know that it can enhance message transfer, just as happens, for instance, in the movies.[15]

10.1.2 Haptic

A range of different effects and feedbacks are usually grouped under the umbrella term *haptic*. When we encounter virtual 3-D objects, we can simply pass through them (like ghosts), feel their presence as a basic tactile feedback, feel their surfaces in a full tactile/thermal experience, and even receive "force feedback". This sequence represents an increasing level of complexity in the simulation of physical behaviour.

Exoskeletons

The basic tactile experience is usually recreated by placing tiny balloons under the fingers; these are automatically inflated when required. The feeling of the presence of a surface can be reproduced by an array of needles that are activated electromagnetically. Very complex haptic feedback (i.e. force feedback) can be implemented by wearing a heavy exoskeleton that progressively blocks arm movements.

Tactile and force feedback is still relatively rare in multimedia applications and services; however, there are some relevant case studies in the field of simulation and interactive virtual reality.

Haptic interfaces are still uncommon even though some devices that contain them, especially those related to computer games, have already been on the market for some time, such as Sony's *PlayStation DualShock2* controller, joysticks that simulate vibrations and force feedback from the cloche of a helicopter and the steering wheel of a Formula One racing car, or a mouse with six degrees of freedom that is used for solid modelling. Amongst the devices aimed at the professional market, there is a wide range of "pens", such as the SenseAble *Phantom*. We should also mention the gesture recognition device from Nintendo: the *PowerGlove*.

Some interesting and innovative applications that use haptic interfaces are also applied in order to manipulate artefacts and archaeological objects or as enhanced interfaces for blind users.

Fig. 10.1 Nintendo PowerGlove (photo by the author)

---

15 An excellent example is "Memories of Venice and the traces of a city" by Massimo Catalfo, Italy.

10.1.3 Motion Capture

This technology was initially developed as an ancillary application in the field of virtual reality. Motion capture involves recording real motion using a series of sensors tracked by a real-time 3-D system. One of the most popular ways in which this technology is applied is to *animate* digital puppets and actors in association with the performance of a real actor.

Virtual actor

An important set of research programs have been carried out over the last two decades in support of the entertainment industry, and these have led to new special effects, virtual actors, 3-D cartoons, virtual autonomous actors, and even virtual sets. In less than twenty years we have seen a virtual Bruce Lee in *The Crow*, 3-D keyframing of the ball scene in *Beauty and the Beast*, the crowd on the deck of the *Titanic*, and the extensive use of this technology to create *Polar Express* and *Shark Tale*.

Fiat Lux

In the field of virtual sets, important results are expected from image-based rendering applications such as Paul Debevec's short film *Fiat Lux*[16] and its *sequel*.

10.1.4 Smell

When dealing with smell we must consider both input and output procedures. On the input side, "artificial noses" are very relevant in various sectors, such as poisonous gas detection, brandy selection, among others. On the output side, the idea of adding smell effects as an "output" has been occasionally used in the past, such as in the *Sensorama* experience created by Morton Helig. However, it is difficult to deal with smell and taste, especially on the output side, since these related senses are linked to chemical transformations rather than physical signals and receptors.

Sensorama

10.1.5 Taste

In addition to the remarks about taste in the previous paragraph, it is important to note that this sense results from the combined and interrelated actions of different receptors installed in different regions of our tongue, and many factors can contribute to the final taste perceived.

This technology does not seem to be related, at the moment, to digitisation as applied to the field of culture.

---

16 Paul Debevec from the University of Southern California, Institute for Creative Technologies Graphics Laboratory. See http://www.debevec.org.

10.1.6 Behaviour

Such a characteristic represents the new frontier of digital simulation and virtual environments. We do not want to simply replicate pure objects and persons; the next step is to replicate the behaviours of machines, humans, animals and more. The inclusion of behaviour enriches simulations and improves interactions and experiences.

We can give a digital object its own natural behaviour or even an unrealistic one. This aspect was explored in the early stages of virtual reality experimentation. Researchers tried to add unrealistic behaviour to objects: negative gravity, zero friction, and even modified force feedbacks. Sometimes this is the starting point for computer game design.

10.1.7 Graphics: Visual Simulation and 3-D Models

This domain includes various representations of the real world, including still images, dynamic images and 3-D models.

When dealing with images we need to be aware of the two types of graphic files, vector and raster, and how they work with each other.

Vector graphics   *Vector images* are collections of two-dimensional primitives (vectors, arcs, circles, etc.). Vector graphics describe shapes mathematically using a language that must be interpreted. Vector files rely on a language (for example Post-Script) to describe how to draw a graphic. It's very simple to convert vector graphics into raster graphics; the vector information is processed as if it is to be printed and then the output is saved as a raster graphic. As a result, vector files aren't tied to a particular resolution; we can generate raster images of any size from vector files.

The corresponding datasets are usually small and easy to manage (to scale, modify, etc.). Technical drawings and sketches are usually created in this way. A number of graphic/illustration tools are also based on vector graphics due to their lightness and scalability.

Raster graphics   *Raster*[17] *images* are arrays of dots (pixels, i.e. picture elements) aligned in rows and columns, so the size of the image is predetermined and can only be changed (reduced) by resizing or resampling.

Vector to raster   *Format conversion* of vector to raster images is a very common processing task. If we consider how graphics are usually displayed, it soon becomes clear why this is this case. Both CRT and LCD monitors display images as arrays of

---

17   This explanation is correct for raster files; however, technically speaking, the term *bitmap* actually describes a bilevel, black-and-white raster graphic. While "bitmap" is a term commonly used to describe both raster and bitmap files, in order to be technically accurate we'll use raster instead.

104   *II The General Technological Framework*

dots (the raster structure) and laser printers (xxx dpi, i.e. raster structure) also print arrays of dots.

The main task involved in such a conversion is to find the best approximation to each vector from the available sequence of pixels. The conversion is performed in real-time automatically, where "automatically" means by hard-coded algorithms, taking into account the size of the array, the shapes of the pixels and the palette of colours available.

If the conversion involves colour images, an additional *anti-aliasing* algorithm might be used in order to improve the conversion. Anti-aliasing algorithms use a range of colours to smooth approximations to curved lines when converting them into arrays of pixels, this improving the perceived quality of the image (see the related images).

Anti-aliasing

Unfortunately, the opposite conversion—of a raster graphic into a vector graphic—isn't as easy. The conversion of a vector image into a raster format results in the loss of a significant amount of (mainly contextual) information. An array of dots doesn't retain information about the relationships between the dots and the basic shape described by a collection of dots.

Raster to vector conversion

In order to recreate this missing information, it is necessary to interpret the patterns of pixels as shapes and then figure out how to write the instructions for drawing them. Some tracing programs, "vectorizers", can convert raster graphics into vector graphics, but the results are less than perfect—sometimes even bizarre!

To make things even more confusing, the last ten to fifteen years have seen an increase in the interoperability of graphic formats, enabling for instance the creation of *ad hoc* text and *lettering* that can be embedded into technical drawings. This led to the idea of creating "overlays" that embed raster graphics in a vector graphics file. Because a vector graphics file is a description of how to draw an image, a raster graphic can be inserted into it by including the raster information in the vector graphic. Basically, you create a shape and give it a complicated filling: the raster graphics file. For example, saving a Photoshop file as an EPS embeds a raster graphic inside a vector graphic.

However, you can never embed a vector graphic in a raster graphic because a raster graphic does not contain vector information. The only way to combine a vector graphic with a raster graphic is to convert the vector image into raster information first and then consolidate the two.

Fig. 10.2 a No anti-aliasing; **b** Anti-aliasing; **c** Enlargement: whole-pixel aliasing

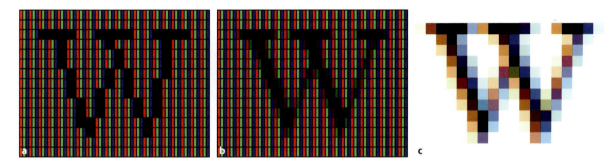

10 Datasets and Formats   105

10.1.8 From Still Images to Dynamic Imagery

There are a great many methods and tools that can be used to "break through the ice" of *frozen* (still) images. These range from creating a short sequence of still images to animating some components of the scene to producing a true full motion movie.

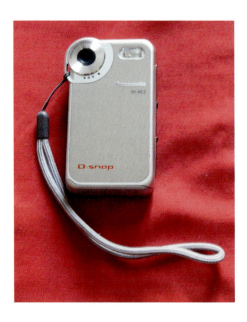

Fig. 10.3 Multimedia digital recorder (photo by the author)

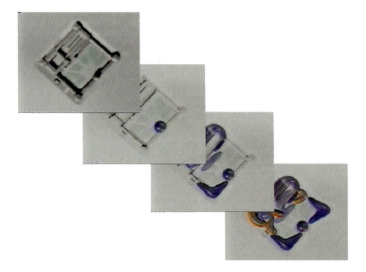

Fig. 10.4 Dynamic imaging of a key framing sequence from the map of a castle to a schema.

On the Internet we can display (using cross-fading) a timed sequence of still images; animated gifs can produce the effect of short movies. Macromedia *Flash* or SMILE webpages enable very sophisticated presentations. Most "intros" are created in this way.

Special attention must be paid to movie files. Nowadays there is a range of everyday devices that are able to create movie files: mobile phones, web cameras, digital cameras, video cameras, etc.

All of these can create standard video files such as MPEG 2, MPEG 4, AVI, MOV, DIVX, etc., and all of them can transfer their files directly to a computer thanks to wired connections (e.g. Firewire), memory cards, DVDs or wireless connections. Once we shoot some footage we can immediately make it available online!

Fig. 10.5 a Panoramic image (courtesy of JRC, Ispra, Italy); **b** A panoramic shot from Mt. Ainslie; **c** Panoramic shot of Venezia, Italy; the Doge's Palace is directly in front, along with the Campanile that overlooks Piazza san Marco (photo by Sébastien Bertrand); **d** Northern view of Schönbrunn Palace (photo by Aconcagua)

Movie Map Most photo cameras are equipped with a special option that enables the creation of a so-called *QuickTime VR*[18] representation, such as *PhotoBubbles* by OmniView or Real *Vista*. All these evolved from the *Movie Map* used many years ago to provide a virtual tour of Aspen. The *Movie Map* technology was developed in the 1980s. Three video disks were the image bank of *Movie Map*; touching the display up, down, left, or right caused the scene to move forward, backward, left or right, and the technology allowed a virtual tour of Aspen using the same visual reference points as we use in reality.

10.2 Image Compression

Lossy versus lossless One of the potential benefits of digital formats is the opportunity to shrink data files using compression methods. Raster images can be compressed using *lossy* or *lossless* algorithms. Compression involves changing the format in which the data in the original dataset (representing rows, columns and colours) is stored *Joint Photographic Experts Group (JPEG)* in order to save disk space or improve performance. The Joint Photographic Experts Group (JPEG) developed a very well known and popular algorithm that can compress raster images by a factor of as much as ten! Obviously there is a price to be paid for doing this, in terms of overall image quality.

There are currently two types of compression schemes that are used to shrink large graphics files: lossless and lossy.

Lossless compression *Lossless* compression is the most common of the two, and although there are several varieties of it, all lossless compression algorithms work in the same way. While an uncompressed image encodes the value of each and every pixel in an image, lossless compression looks for areas where the pixels all have the same value, and encodes these areas. This gives only a moderate compression ratio but it ensures that when the file is decompressed it will look identical to the original file.

Lossy *Lossy* file compression, a relatively new compression scheme which is currently only applied to the JPEG file format, actually results in the loss of some of the information in the file. However, this disadvantage is compensated by the fact that lossy compression achieves compression rates that are ten or more times greater than those obtained in lossless compression.

Furthermore, even though the compression scheme loses information, there is little or no degradation of the image when it is decompressed. How can this be? It works on the principle that graphic images can represent many more colours than the human eye can perceive or printers can print. In other words, the information lost during compression is related to colours that are beyond the range of human vision. Lossy compression works well for high-quality, 24-bit or higher photographic images, but it is not intended for computer-created graphic files, where any image information loss can corrupt the file.

---

18 *QuickTime* and *QuickTime VR* are products from Apple Inc.

10.3 Archiving Tools and Standards

When you prepare a graphic or a document that you'll distribute to others, how much thought do you give to the file format? Do you know which file format is best for a particular application? If you send a file in the wrong format, some data loss may occur or the recipient may not be able to use the file at all.

Only a few years ago, you probably created and printed a project using only one application. Now, it's common to create an illustration with one application, add some highly formatted text using another ad hoc, and then to print the document via yet another application. Therefore, in order to freely exchange information between applications, you must know which file formats are currently supported by your applications. This is especially true when you're working with graphic files.

Two or three years ago, a Mac user would never have heard of a PCX or BMP file, and a PC user wouldn't know a MacPaint file from a PICT file. Nowadays more applications are becoming cross-platform, and so desktop publishers need to familiarise themselves with graphic file formats that were previously platform-specific.

Keeping all graphic file formats compatible with one platform is a difficult enough task, but for two or more platforms it's close to impossible. Fortunately technology marches on, and in that spirit we're presenting some of the most commonly used graphic file formats on both the Mac and Windows platforms. In this section, we'll first review the basics of image file formats, and then we'll outline each of the most popular image file types.

10.4 Colours and Palettes

How many colours are in the colour palette of a 1-bit image? How many are in that of an 8-bit image? Can you display a 24-bit image on an 8-bit monitor?

If these questions confuse you, you're not alone. To most designers and Playstation and Nintendo players, the naming conventions of 1-, 2-, 4-, 8-, 24-, and 32-bit graphics are only loosely understood—more means better. However, as Table 10.1 shows, the naming convention is easily understood and based on simple mathematics.

Bit Depth	Colors Available
1-bit	black and white
4-bit	16 colours
8-bit	256 colours
16-bit	thousands of colours
24-bit	millions of colours

Table 10.1 Bit depth

Bit depth The bit depth of an image determines the colour value that can be assigned to each pixel in the image. For instance, a 1-bit image assigns each pixel a black or white value, a 4-bit image assigns each pixel one of 16 colour values, and so on. The only exception is that a 32-bit image is usually a 24-bit image with additional information encoded in the remaining eight bits; an *alpha channel*[19] *for example.*

As for the answers to our introductory questions: there are two colours (black and white) in a 1-bit image and 256 colours in an 8-bit image; a 24-bit image, though dithered, will appear on an 8-bit monitor display.

10.5 The Most Popular Graphics File Formats

BMP, JPEG, TIFF BMP, JPEG, TIFF, ...; which file format should we use?

The correct choice largely depends on the application in which you intend to use the image. Let's review the most popular image file formats to see which works best in which situation (see Table 10.2).

TIFF *TIFF.* Versatility and compatibility make the TIFF image format the optimum choice for almost any project, although the TIFF format is rarely seen on the Web because it offers poor compression. However, TIFF files can store up to 24-bit images with no loss, making them better than JPEG files for archiving images when space is not critical.

This format works on both the Mac and PC platforms, supports almost any picture bit depth, and allows various forms of compression. It is usually welcome in desktop publishing and printing.

PSD *PSD.* This is the native *Photoshop* file format created by Adobe. In this format, you can save multiple alpha channels and paths along with your primary image. You can't import this format directly into most desktop publishing applications; it is usually necessary to merge the different layers into one layer.

PNG *PNG.* Its high compression rate is unsurpassed among lossless formats (lossy JPEG is better for photos). The PNG format is a recent one that aims to solve some of the problems of GIF compression. Although PNG is lossless like GIF it supports more colours and more flexible transparency. PNG is, however, not widely supported yet.

JPEG *JPEG*[20]. The JPEG format uses lossy compression to highly compress images with many colours. The compression works best with continuous-tone

---

19 The *alpha channel* concept was introduced by A.R. Smith in the late 1970s in order to specify pixel transparency. The alpha channel contains a value ranging from 0 to 1. A value of 0 means that the pixel does not have any coverage information and is fully transparent, while a value of 1 means that the pixel is fully opaque.

20 Even though JPEG is relatively new, a related format has already been developed. JFIF is a new TIFF subformat that embeds a JPEG image into a TIFF file. The JFIF file format has yet to become popular because it's much more complex without offering more capabilities.

II The General Technological Framework

Format	Mac	PC	Raster	Vector	1-Bit	2-Bit	4-Bit	8-Bit	16-Bit	24-Bit	32-Bit	Comp
TIFF	X	X	X		X	X	X	X	X	X	X	Yes
PSD	X	X	X		X	X	X	X	X	X	X	No
PNG	X	X	X		X	X	X	X	X	X	X	Yes
JPEG	X	X	X							X	X	Yes
TGA	X	X	X					X	X	X	X	Yes
PCX	X	X	X		X	X	X	X		X		No
BMP	X	X	X		X		X	X		X		No
WMF		X		X								No
CGM		X		X								No
DXF		X		X								No
HP GL X		X		X								No
EPS	X	X		X								No

Table 10.2 Format = extension, Mac & PC available platforms, Raster or Vector data, 1.32 bit is the pixel coding depth, Comp stands for compression

images—images where the change between adjacent pixels is small but not zero. JPEG images generally store 16 or 24 bits of colour and thus are best for 16- or 24-bit images. Due to the noticeable loss of quality during the compression process, JPEGs should be used only where image file size is important, primarily on webpages.

TGA. Targa was the most common format in the video industry. This file format is also used by high-end paint and ray-tracing programs. The TGA format has many variations and supports several types of compression. This file format is used to display AT&T *Truevision* images and is sometimes supported by DOS applications.

PCX. PCX is a straightforward raster file that was originally available only on the PC. However, PCX is migrating to the Macintosh as more mainstream programs become cross-platform. Aldus *PageMaker*, Adobe *Photoshop*, and *QuarkXPress* for the Macintosh support the PCX file format.

BMP. The BMP file format is available in almost all Windows-based graphics applications, although it's primarily used in Windows application development. This format supports black and white, 16-, 256- and true-colour images.

WMF. A Windows Metafile has its good and bad points. Metafiles—which consist of a list of calls to the Microsoft Windows graphics drawing library—are both small and flexible, but unless the program that created them is running, they're difficult to display properly.

CGM   *CGM*. Computer Graphics Metafile is a very flexible vector format that can also save raster information. Unfortunately, it's so flexible that very few applications can use all of the types available.

DXF   *DXF*. AutoCAD DXF is an AutoCAD file format that has become the standard for exchanging CAD drawings. Due to the many enhancements of AutoCAD and 3D Studio this format has several versions. However, because the vector information is ASCII-encoded, the files can become very large and thus require a lot of memory to read.

HP GLx   *HP GLx*. The Hewlett-Packard Graphic Language is a HP plotter language that's often used as an exchange format for graphics. The "x" stands for the version.

EPS   *EPS*. The Encapsulated PostScript format is a vector file that uses the PostScript page description language to draw its image. This format can also contain raster information, even though it's not a raster format. EPS files generally contain a raster graphic as a screen preview—Mac EPS files use a PICT, while PC EPS files use a TIFF graphic. EPS is the only format that supports transparent white in bitmap mode.

RAW   *RAW*. The RAW input file format, produced directly by digital cameras, contains the sequences of "raw" bits captured by the CCD or CMOS of the camera. Adobe *Photoshop* produces an output RAW format, a flexible interchange high-quality image format that is available as a "save as" file format.

10.5.1   Suggestions

Suggestions   JPEG usually performs better with 16- or 24-bit scanned photographs or computer-generated high-palette images.

The GIF format performs better with black and white, text on plain background, cartoons and monochromatic images.

Preferably use TIFF or EPS for publishing.

11 Data Visualisation and Display Technologies

Data visualisation encompasses an interesting set of methods and techniques that are suited to different goals. Based on the idea that "a graphical representation is far better than a huge set of alphanumeric data", a number of different representations were created. These include common graphs such as diagrams, histograms, pie charts as well as three-dimensional graphs such as surfaces, colour maps, isosurfaces, and even four-dimensional graphs that use coloured surfaces and isosurfaces or animations.

In order to display the usual fourth coordinate in such graphics, time, animations or three-dimensional scenes with a time control were introduced.

A very interesting application was developed by ART+COM[21], which introduced the *Invisible Shape* concept. The basic idea was to convert an abstract object (a movie in this case) into a sequence of virtual geometric and georeferenced objects (stills from the movie) that could then be organised into a 3-D model and manipulated.

Invisible Shape by ART+COM

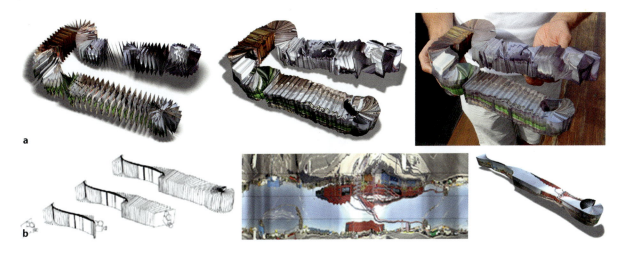

Fig. 11.1a,b *Invisible Shape of Things Past* (by Joachim Sauter and Dirk Lüsebrink, ART+COM, Berlin, Germany, 1995)

---

21   Please refer to the ART+COM website: http://www.artcom.de.

11.1 From Two-Dimensional to Three (and Higher)-Dimensional Views

Most conventional images offer a two-dimensional projection of a three-dimensional scene, with the exception of some techniques such as *dotted images*[22] (where the viewer must focus beyond the picture to get the 3-D effect) or stereo viewers.

Stereo pictures were invented in the first half of the nineteenth century by Wheatstone, at almost the same time that Nicéphore Niépce (and later on Daguerre) invented photography.

Stereo viewer

Stereo viewers were very popular in the first half of the last century. They are based on the idea of simultaneously showing slightly different images of a scene to each eye, which reflects how each of our eyes will see the same scene slightly differently. Special twin cameras were used at the time.

The basic viewer includes two sliding frames to host the film frames, two wide-angle magnifying lenses, and a handle to hold the viewer. When we look through the lens, each eye sees its own picture. Our brain "merges" the two images (as usual for binocular vision) into one three-dimensional scene, leading to an illusion of reality. Of course, there are some benefits of this illusion, such as enhanced realism, a better comprehension of the structure of the scene, and, where applicable, a far better ability to interact with objects.

Fig. 11.2 Stereographic camera: Le Rêve, France, 1904 (photo by Jean-Jacques Milan)

---

22 Random dot stereograms (RDS) and pattern shaped stereograms (PSS).

Fig. 11.3 *Le Verascope* stereo viewer (photo by the author)

Later on, when three-dimensional computer graphics became feasible, the same idea of stereo imaging led to the development of various techniques.

Let's start with stereo pairs, the first step in the evolution of stereo visualisation. Stereo pairs must be generated or acquired from two points of view separated by the intraocular distance. The directions of sight for the two points of view must be parallel and at the same height. The directions of sight must not converge or the images will be distorted by perspective and the final result will be useless.

Stereo pairs

Stereo pairs can be used without any additional device by simply tracking a pencil moving toward the pair of images while trying to focus on the two images.

Following this idea, a kind of cover that was to be superimposed on the display was released some years ago, which offered two magnifying lenses and a frame that separated the two images displayed on the screen.

In 1891, thanks to Louis Arthur Ducos, a special technique enabling three-dimensional visualisation using a single image was released. The basic idea was to merge the stereo pairs into the same image by using two different colours (e.g. red and blue) to represent the left and right images. By looking at the single image through glasses fitted with filters that filter different colours to each eye, it is possible to obtain an illusion of a three-dimensional image. Such a tech-

Anaglyph nique, usually called anaglyph[23], works best with black and white images, even if it was and still is often used with colour images. Of course, the colour palette is strongly reduced in this case because of the dominant filtering colour. Nevertheless, this appears to be one of the easiest and least expensive ways to offer three-dimensional scenes to large audiences (e.g. at the movies).

3-D viewing with polarizing filters In a similar way, the stereo pairs can be merged not into the same print but on the same projection screen using cross-polarised light. This should be light polarised in the vertical plane for the right eye and light polarised in the horizontal plane for the left eye.

By wearing glasses fitted with cross-polarization filters, the unwanted image is then filtered out, resulting in a stereoscopic image. This method works better with coloured images, and the glasses required are very cheap and easy to use.

Additional methods that are used to convey the appropriate image from the stereo pair to the appropriate eye have also been developed, although these involve using more expensive and intrusive devices.

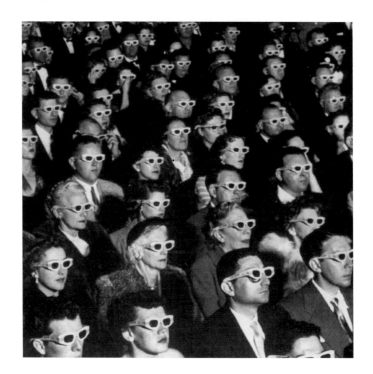

Fig. 11.4 Watching *Bwana Devil* in 3D at the Paramount Theatre (photo by J.R. Eyerman, 1952)

Fig. 11.5 A pair of CrystalEyes liquid crystal shutter glasses

---

23 Stereograms are similar to anaglyphs but they use patterns of dots to code stereo pairs (random dot stereograms or RDS and pattern shaped stereograms or PSS), where users view the image by trying to focus beyond the scene.

Fig. 11.6
3D display of Dresden (photo by the author)

Shutter glasses represent one of the basic methods of conveying the correct image to each eye. A relatively high frequency monitor (e.g. 120 frames per second) displays the two images from the pair (e.g. 60 frames each), and a sync signal (e.g. transferred through an infrared interface) synchronizes the displayed image with the appropriate shutter on the glasses, blinding the opposite eye.

Shutter glasses

The glasses use voltage-activated liquid crystal shutters in order to blind the appropriate eye when the "wrong" image is displayed. Other than this, the merging of images by the brain etc. is the same as for the stereoscopic techniques mentioned previously.

Other methods may use one or two separate displays or printed representations, but they are still ultimately based on the same principle as before. So we have panoramic screens, video tables, 3-D sets. The two basic reference points are the required output (printed or projected) and, in the case of projection, the number of simultaneous users (one, a few, many).

Unintrusive 3-D viewers

Among these, we should briefly outline an interesting application that uses a single display and does not require that any device be worn in order to enjoy three-dimensional animated images: the so-called *Dresden display*[24].

This works by coding the stereo pairs into two sub-frames of a monitor. Looking at the display, we see a set of even and odd columns of pixels. The first

---

24 Presented at CeBIT in 2002.

11 Data Visualisation and Display Technologies   117

image is sent to the even columns and the second to the odd ones, meaning that the stereo pairs have effectively been cut into thin strips.

A plastic lens with columns of prisms that alternately deflect the even and odd columns of pixels towards the right and left eyes, in order to recreate the 3-D effect. In addition, by adding a sensor (e.g. an infrared sensor) to provide a rough idea of the user's position with respect to the screen, we can optimise the deflections of the two images for the specific viewpoint.

Speaking of three-dimensional representations, holograms are another potential way to break through the barrier of two-dimensionality[25].

11.2   Computer Graphics and Virtual Reality

Ivan Sutherland's Sketchpad

In the last thirty years the field of computer graphics has been revolutionised, starting from Ivan Sutherland's *Sketchpad* in 1962 and reaching its current apex in desktop interactive virtual reality.

Three-dimensional computer graphics has evolved from Boolean operations on elementary solids (Platonic solids) to surfaces, Bézier and Coon's surfaces, *meta balls*, parametric and implicit surfaces, and others. These approaches were developed in specific application fields in order to satisfy user requirements.

How do we shape a double curvature surface using 3-D modelling of elementary solids? How can we take advantage of computer graphics in mechanical design without using a parametric approach? Or create virtual characters and animation without appropriate tools?

Just like in two-dimensional graphics, in today's 3-D modelling routines we can mix together objects created using different approaches in the same scene.

Rendering and photorealism

The subsequent step, computer-based rendering (either photorealistic or nonphotorealistic) has evolved even more, from the early "wire frame" representations of 3D scenes through to Lambert flat shading, Gouraud and Phong algorithms, ray-tracing and radiosity methods to image-based rendering and more. These different methods and algorithms are usually grouped together under the catch-all term of *global illumination algorithms*, which provide the focus for one of the most active special interest groups working under the flag of SIGGRAPH[26].

In addition, a number of enhancements have surfaced recently, including particles, flames, morphing, bump mapping, procedural mapping, fur rendering, and lip syncing.

---

25   Refer to the *Virtual Cockpit* or the use of lasers to "write" 3-D shapes onto the retina (both of which were developed by Tom Furness).

26   SIGGRAPH is the ACM Special Interest Group in Computer Graphics. See http://www.siggraph.org and http://www.acm.org.

II The General Technological Framework

In the 1990s the main focus of computer graphics research moved from the defence (including "Star Wars") sector to the entertainment industry. There has also been movement from the special effects (fx) sector towards experimentation with virtual actors and virtual sets.

The main field of investigation in computer graphics are currently natural effects modelling, virtual clothing, virtual fur, and realistic human animation, based on reverse cinematic, synchronisation, chroma key and image-based rendering.

A subset of the virtual actor field of investigation is tackling the world of *artificial life* and *virtual creatures*. These include virtual entities equipped with autonomous behaviour based on a set of simple rules. Such actors do not obey key framing rules, they act autonomously, just like the crowd on the deck of the Titanic in the movie or the army of Uruk-hai in *The Lord of the Rings: The Two Towers* movie.

11.3   Evolution of Virtual Reality

The evolution of virtual reality is often misinterpreted because of the fact that the general public only found out about this technology fairly recently, through a "media blitz" early in the 1990s. This blitz has generated the general impression that VR was born at NASA in 1984, and the virtual reality is a solely technological triumph. In fact, this technology originated more than a decade before that, and we must underline the important contributions that artists have made to the development of this technology.

When *Myron W. Krueger* coined the term *artificial reality* in the middle of the 1970s, he was referring to both the *Videoplace* technology and the head-mounted display technology that enables three-dimensional vision, created by *Ivan Sutherland*.

Artificial reality

These two technologies represented two different paths toward the same goal: total body immersion in computer-generated environments that is convincing that it is just like a "real" experience.

Flight simulators, which have long been used to train aircraft pilots, were one of the first interactive virtual reality applications. In such a system, mechanical actuators are used to move the cabin in order to simulate six degrees of freedom (movements and accelerations). The pilot is immersed in a realistic simulation of a flight experience. This has two main advantages: reduced costs and dangers compared to actually flying, and (even more relevant) the opportunity to experience a wide range of critical events over a short period of time, sometimes directly taken from a real "black box" (a flight recorder)—events that nobody would want to experience in the real world.

Terms like *virtual worlds*, *virtual environment*, and *virtual workstation* have been coined in order to describe similar advanced research projects.

Virtual reality

In 1989, *Jaron Lanier*, the general manager of VPL Research, a Californian society that has focussed on "virtual technologies" from its inception, coined the term *virtual reality* in order to group together all virtual experiences.

Data gloves and head-mounted displays

The term "virtual reality" mainly refers to three-dimensional worlds that are typically experienced through the use of special VR appliances such as *data gloves* and *head-mounted displays* [27].

In the 1980s, along with the spread of Unix and workstations, a new vision of technological development arose in the field of literature: William Gibson's seminal work Neuromancer (published in 1984, coincidentally the same year in which Orwell's famous novel about the future, which introduced the concept of Big Brother, was set). In this book, Gibson popularised the term *cyberspace*, which referred to a single artificial reality that could be experienced simultaneously by thousands of persons all over the world. This novel revolutionised science fiction because it introduced a credible vision of the near future that was extrapolated from the present; the novel is set in the early twenty-first century in a world where a vast number of computers are interconnected in a universal network. This gigantic network of computers generates its own world where space and time is completely redefined and data surfing is enabled thanks to an advanced virtual reality interface that is directly connected to the human central nervous system. The cyber surfer therefore lives in a virtual space populated by virtual representations of the data hosted by the computers he visits.

Cyberspace

Let's now have a close look on the facts and the events that led to the birth of virtual reality.

Information scientists were not the first to consider realistic artificial experiences. In the mid-1960s the movie industry started to experiment with new formats and technologies that were intended to generate more spectator interaction. Such systems included *Cinerama* and the *Cinemascope.*

Sensorama

In 1956 *N. Heilig* invented *Sensorama,* a machine that was very similar to some that we encounter today in gaming centres. The user sits down, places their head in a stereoscopic viewer box and grabs a handlebar. The seat and the handlebar start to vibrate in concert with the scenes of a three-dimensional movie showing a tour along the crowded streets of Manhattan. Artificial wind blows on the user's face and the arms at a realistic speed that is synchronised with the movie, and the user smells car exhausts and even a delicious pizza at appropriate points in the movie.

This was the first attempt to immerse a spectator into a multisensorial experience. Of course, since there was no interaction with the "artificial world", this was not a virtual reality experience in a conventional sense; however, it was undoubtedly one of the ancestors of modern virtual experiences and prophetic of future trends in this sense. Unfortunately, the *Sensorama* didn't succeed commercially. This is a pity, because its success would probably have sped-up the incorporation of artificial realities and multisensorial experiences into video and computer games.

---

27 Data gloves, one of the enhancements developed and tuned by Jaron Lainer, is an innovative physical interface shaped like a glove that includes fibre optics, mechanical transducers or bending resistors, which are used to translate gestures into commands that control both virtual walkthroughs and virtual object manipulation.

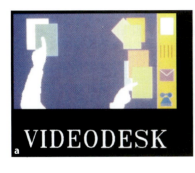 

Fig. 11.7a,b
Videodesk and Videoplace (by Myron Krueger)

At the end of the 1960s *Myron Krueger*, after working on various projects such as *Glowflow, Metaplay, Psychic Space*, created and experimented with artificial interactive environments (which today would be defined as being "not intrusive"). He created an environmental technology called *Videoplace*, which was environmental in the sense that the artificial system surrounded participant and responded to their actions. *Videoplace* was a relatively flexible and user-friendly technology since it could be experienced without the user having to wear special instruments. However, there was concurrently also a line of research into the technology of sensors and displays that were designed to be worn, and were therefore relatively cumbersome (today termed "intrusive").

In 1969, at the University of Utah, *Ivan Sutherland*, the father of computer graphics, created what he called the "ultimate display", a *head-mounted display* that was able to generate and manage two stereoscopic images and thus generate a three-dimensional scene in real time.

Videoplace

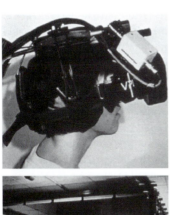 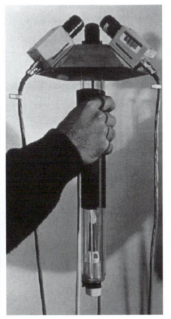

Fig. 11.8
Early experiences in the field of head-mounted displays (by Ivan Sutherland)

11 Data Visualisation and Display Technologies 121

The two images were displayed on two tiny monitors (one for each eye), which were mounted on equipment suspended from the ceiling of the lab and connected to the head of the observer. This was the first example of a virtual reality helmet and its appearance inspired its nickname: *Sword of Damocles*.

Sword of Damocles

Turning the head while wearing the device caused the three-dimensional scene viewed by the user to change. The head movements were detected by sensors connected to the computer that generated the scene.

In 1976 *P.J. Kilpatrick*, who collaborated with the University of North Carolina, connected radioisotope manipulators to a somewhat stylised graphical world. The system created by *Kilpatrick*, *Grope II*, created a virtual simulation of the mechanical arm in a stereoscopic viewer. By 1978, the concept of force feedback was realised in North Carolina.

At the end of the 1970s, a number of coordinated projects in the field of virtual reality were activated at MIT (Massachusetts Institute of Technologies).

Put-That-There

One of these, named *Put-That-There*, was based on a three-dimensional tracking system coupled to a rudimental voice-controlled interface. The user simply pointed a finger wearing a magnetic transducer (enabling 3-D tracking) toward a target object on a screen, and then stated voice commands—for example: "move that..." (user points at the destination) "...there"!

In 1983 an interesting high-end application of virtual reality appeared on the scene due to research performed under the leadership of *Tom Furness III*.

Starting in 1966, he began to develop and test (at the Wright Patterson Air Force Base) an incredible array of methods and technologies aimed at transferring information to and communicating with a pilot engaged in combat, including methods that the pilot could use to set and activate weapons whilst being subjected to high g-forces.

Virtual cockpit

He eventually came up with the idea of transferring information to the pilot by graphically projecting all of the information onto a "virtual screen" outside the cabin. The technology needed to realize this *virtual cockpit* was developed during the 1970s, and a prototype of the cockpit was realized in 1981. Nowadays a similar system is available in the Chevrolet Corvette (2003 model); the information is projected onto a virtual display beyond the windscreen.

In such systems, a "virtual hemisphere" located in front of the pilot depicts a digital terrain model (DTM) of the landscape below the aircraft, as well as the airspace around it, including missiles and other friendly and enemy aircraft. The pilot receives further information by simply pointing a finger at an item in the display and asking "what is this?". In this graphical representation, enemy missiles are reproduced, as is enemy-controlled airspace (CAS), and the pilot can simply turn his/her head to view a graphical representation of how many missiles are left on each wing of the aircraft.

This technology remained top-secret until 1983, when was made publicly available.

Later on *Furness* moved to the University of Washington and dedicated himself to the study, development and fine-tuning of a new technology based on the idea of drawing three-dimensional images directly onto the retina of the user's eye with a laser beam.[28]

The subsequent evolution of virtual reality is closely associated with NASA, the national aerospace agency in the US.

In 1984 *Michael McGreevy* from NASA started to become interested in the work of *Furness*. Having been informed that the cost of the helmet for *the virtual cockpit* was a million dollars, he, together with an entrepreneur and a budget of only twenty thousand dollars, decided to demonstrate that the flat screen monitor from a pocket television could do the same job. They constructed a helmet that used two liquid crystal displays to supply the stereoscopic images, special fibre optics to generate the illusion that the images were further away than they really were (2.5 cm), and a magnetic position sensor that determines the direction of sight.

In the meantime, *Scott Fischer* moved from MIT to NASA, and under his direction the size of the helmet viewer was reduced significantly, and became known as "Krueger glasses with stereo viewers".

At this stage of our historical excursion we should interject some comments about helmets and stereo-glasses. Even today, accordingly to in-depth studies from American research centres, users should not use such devices for over thirty minutes at a time. The main reason for this is that the eyes have to constantly focus at the same distance (approximately 1 or 2 cm—very close to the eye) when the viewer is worn. The fact that the focus must remain constant and that the user is immersed in an unreal environment can unbalance the user at a psychological level.

As a consequence of this, as an example, it is recommended that the user should not drive a car after experiencing an extended VR while wearing the helmet.

Fig. 11.9 VPL Data Suite (photo by Dave Pape, 1999)

Limits on stereo viewing

Fig. 11.10 *ImmersaDesk2* at the Foundation of the Hellenic World, a cultural/history museum in Athens (photo by Dave Pape, 2001)

---

28 Human Interface Technology Laboratory – University of Washington, Seattle, url http://www.hitl.washington.edu.

11 Data Visualisation and Display Technologies   123

Fig. 11.11 a *Cave Automatic Virtual Environment* at EVL, University of Illinois, Chicago (photo by Dave Pape, 2001); **b** Fakespace BOOM (courtesy of NASA)

A final important fact is that, according to some studies, only 20% of the general population is able to see in "3-D", and in any case our vision while doing so is subject to optical illusions at distances of less than a few metres.

Our perception of three dimensions is made possible by our binocular vision: our eyes, which are approximately 7 cm apart, perceive the same scene from two different points of view.

The human brain is able to extract a great deal of information from the small differences between the images seen by each eye; among them, the exact spatial positions of objects. Because of the relatively small distance between the eyes, object widths are appraised with greater precision than object depths or heights, which always seem to be greater than they actually are. Moreover, the reduced *telemetric base* available strongly limits the visual cone and the distance at which we can estimate the third dimension.

An exact knowledge of the mechanisms of visual perception is indispensable if we are to be able to effectively "deceive" our senses. It is well known, for example, that "classical" perspective is not be perceived linearly with scenic depth; it tends to approach axonometric projection for elements that are close to the observer. Another important aspect is the different perception we have between the acute field of vision (approximately 70°) and the peripheral field (approximately 220°).

Resuming our excursion through the technological evolution of this field, *Scott Fischer* commissioned VPL Research to develop a high-resolution glove that was sensitive to folding (the *Data Glove*).

Later on, NASA introduced a magnetic position and orientation sensor that enabled the bending of each finger to be linked to a particular point in three-dimensional space. This ability enabled the data glove to be used to point to and manipulate objects in a three-dimensional artificial reality.

The laboratories at NASA developed many advanced projects using this glove. Indeed, *Warren Robinett* established glove use conventions that are still in use today[29].

---

29 Gestures, positions of fingers, and other conventions involving actions and motion (closed fist = grab, index finger pointing forward = forward motion, etc.).

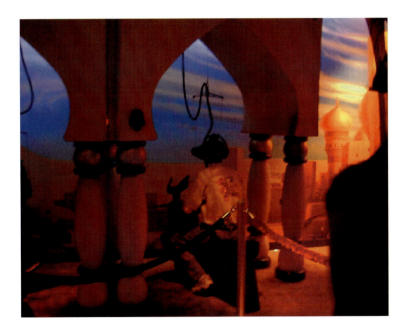

Fig. 11.12 *Aladdin Adventure* at DisneyQuest (photo by the author)

The most well-known person in this field is *Jaron Lanier*, the founder of VPL Research, who was the first to move beyond NASA demonstrations and use the powerful Silicon Graphics (SGI) workstations.

It is worth noting that both the *Data Glove* and the *EyePhones* created at that time by VPL Research were, and still are, used in research laboratories.

From 1989 onwards virtual reality underwent constant and frantic development, from the *total body suit* (*data suit*), to new types of helmet, including Virtual Research's *Eye Gen III*, a CRT-based helmet, *Sym Eye* goggles, and CAE Electronics' "million dollars" helmet[30].

In parallel with these technological feats, we have the performance of Monica Flaischmann from ART+COM[31] during CEBIT in 1989; the VR systems of W-Industries and Division Dimension; Sense8 and Autodesk's *World Toolkit (both software products)*; and, in terms of hardware, *FakeSpace's Boom* and the University of North Carolina's *CAVE*[32]—all in the 1990s.

In order to understand the relevance of this sector, consider the attention paid by the media to this emerging technology.

Some journalists link this technological development to the fall of the Berlin Wall and thus the end of the Cold War. This event may have caused highly specialised technology that was originally used for defence-related applications to enter the public domain.

Fig 11.13 SimEye XL100A

---

30 The same one used in the movie *Blue Thunder*.
31 ART+COM Berlin: http://www.artcom.de.
32 Tom De Fanti and Carolina Cruiz Neira at the University of North Carolina.

11 Data Visualisation and Display Technologies

The blossoming of industrial activities in this area, such as those pursued by VPL Research, was accompanied by a renewed enthusiasm towards research in this area from groups at the most famous American universities, such as Kilpatrick's group at the University of North Carolina, and Tom Furness' group at the University of Washington, which began a new set of experiments in this field.

It should be remembered that, after being neglected for twenty years by academic researchers, virtual reality became a field of research "by definition" as soon as this technology was applied to the field of entertainment. This coincidence emphasises a strange irony: applied research in the field of entertainment is economically more profitable than that performed in the defence sector.

When toys companies such as Mattel, Nintendo, Sega and later Sony entered the field of virtual reality, interest in this new technology started to accelerate.

It is worth noting that computer games and video games based on virtual reality have been sold for quite some time in the US. Recent trends in the entertainment sector have targeted the application of virtual reality to theme parks and science and technology centres, a segment of the market that is growing rapidly in a number of European countries.

As a conclusion to our review of the evolution of VR, we should note that in the past few years, changes in the political approach to defence (DoD) in the United States have provoked a significant movement of human resources from defence research to companies traditionally associated with entertainment, including Warner Brothers, Walt Disney MGM and Sony Dreamworks.

The outstanding *Aladdin* application created by Disney and hosted for a short time at the Epcot theme park before being moved to Disney Quest is a meaningful example here. Twelve Silicon Graphics Onyx Reality Engine II servers provide the incredible graphics engine of this real-time adventure that can be experienced by four people at the same time using "gator-vision" viewers mounted on "rock lobster" helmets.

The Disney Vision experiment was a very interesting test because, for the first time (at least in the United States), technological competence in VR was coupled to the expressive (and impressive) artistic abilities of the cartoon designers. This combination is potentially interesting if we consider the significant immersive potential of high-quality texture mapping.

VRML Furthermore, fulfilling Gibson's dream of cyberspace, video games such as DOOM have popularised networked virtual reality software, such as those based on the markup language called VRML (Virtual Reality Modelling/ Markup Language).

VRML was introduced by Mark Pesce during SIGGRAPH '93. His demonstration started with a short movie showing a building; then he displayed a picture of the same building, before finally showing a VRML interactive model of it. The latter representation was far smaller than the previous two in terms of storage size. The paper, entitled *VRML Equinox*, announced the birth of this new technology.

The synergy between the Internet and virtual reality is undoubtedly interesting from the point of view of pure surfing and limited interaction applications;

Fig. 11.14 a Intrusive: haptic interfaces: anthropomorphic (courtesy of PERCRO, Scuola Superiore Sant' Anna, Pisa, Italy); b Intrusive: head-mounted display and datagloves (courtesy of NASA); c Nonintrusive: xFace Games, Jakob Leitner, FH-Hagenberg (photo by the author)

this requires that *a web browser* that is able to process the VRML format is available and that it is possible to transmit a codified navigable model written in this language via the network.

This technology reached a reasonable stage of development because once the user has preloaded what is required (3-D model with texture, and even submodels and incremental textures), navigation simply means updating the viewpoint. Most subsequent applications that use VR technology can be classified as "virtual walkthroughs"; they involve almost no interaction with the objects in the virtual scene and therefore represent a very limited use of the potential of VR[33].

Virtual reality has always been a fascinating realm, whether fully interactive or static, and whether or not the virtual world generated is photorealistic. The appearance of some early applications late in the 1980s generated both curiosity and concern. Some suggested that virtual reality was a gateway to the world of dreams (*dreamland*). Virtual reality: a new appealing drug or a powerful tool that leads to a number of useful solutions/applications?

Of course, as often happens for emerging technologies, early approaches were not easily accessible to potential end-users. On the one hand, the overall cost of the bare technology (hardware and software) combined with the cost of application development was a significant barrier for quite a long time.

---

33 Although there are some interesting applications using haptic interfaces and enhanced interactions (see the next section).

11 Data Visualisation and Display Technologies

In addition, the overall quality of the experience was not good enough at that time to enable its use in some potential fields of application (i.e. culture, fashion, etc.). Nevertheless, a number of artists, interested by definition in new media exploration and in unusual modes of expression, tested and experimented with virtual reality from the very start.

Indeed, one of the first virtual reality experiences made available in Europe was an interactive visit to the Alexander Platz metro stop in Berlin, as created by Monica Fleischmann (ART+COM in 1989).

Virtual reality has also inspired many other artists, such as painters, sculptors and movie directors (Brett Leonard, *The Lawnmower Man*; Josef Rusnak, *The Thirteenth Floor*; Andy and Larry Wachowski, *The Matrix* and its sequels).

Blurring the line between virtual reality, art and entertainment, we should also mention some computer games such as *Final Fantasy*, as derived from the drawings of Akihiko Yoshida.

However, in some cases, when the door to interactive virtual reality was opened, all that was found was a long, dark corridor: it was simply too early.

11.3.1 VR Technology

The world of virtual technology is wide-ranging and does not have well-defined borders. As is often the case in new disciplines, particularly those in the field of computer science, the boundaries of this technology are difficult to define; they constantly change as subsets of the field move from being innovations to becoming everyday tools. We can refer here, for instance, to artificial intelligence and to its "domain" during its earliest years, which included *Computer Vision* and *Fuzzy Logic*.

In the field of virtual reality there is still some dispute over whether VR needs to be "immersive" and "intrusive"; *computer-augmented reality* is still considered close to the limit of this technology, and in addition a number of VR applications are very closely linked to the multimedia field; therefore, in order to avoid postulating an improbable definition of interactive VR, we refer to a taxonomy that covers the full panorama of the objects and methods typical of the virtual domain.

Fig. 11.15 a,b Virtual reality parachute trainer. Students wear the VR glasses while suspended in a parachute harness, and then learn to control their movements through a series of computer-simulated scenarios; **c** Nonimmersive: a typical personal computer workspace (photo by Dave Pape)

Intrusive versus nonintrusive

We must first define "intrusive" and "nonintrusive", which are terms that distinguish virtual experiences that require the use of particular wearable equipment (helmets, data suits, gloves) from experiences generated by high-tech environments equipped with sensors, display walls and other devices that does not need to be worn. This delineation has led to the use of the term "virtual reality" to indicate intrusive experiences (as opposed to "artificial reality").

Immersive versus nonimmersive

Another delineation, and one that is undoubtedly more arduous, is that between *immersive* environments and *nonimmersive* ones. This type of classification is complicated by the fact that different levels of immersivity are required by different applications, and that the ability of each player to be "immersed" in a particular virtual environment differs. There are those of us that become so deeply involved in a story that they cry when something bad (or even good!) happens, while there are others that cannot "switch off" from reality even when they are using the most realistic and immersive virtual environment.

After all, 3-D viewers, 3-D audio, force feedback and other such technologies are all useless if the subject does not want to be immersed, while a simple display might be immersive enough for a particularly receptive subject. This aspect is easy for anyone that has become engrossed in a book or a TV show to understand.

Essential requirements for immersivity are undoubtedly the ability to freely interact with the scene and the ability of the system to provide real-time feedback (we call this IVR, or interactive virtual reality).

During the early developmental stages of this technology interactivity was bounded by the limited performance of both the hardware and the software used. In particular, 3-D stereo viewing provided a major bottleneck in such systems.

Fig. 11.16
An interactive "virtual shop" on show in the window (photo by the author)

The generation of computer graphics, especially 3-D computer graphics, is not just a number-crunching process; it is a resource-constrained process in general. The graphic pipeline must be perfectly tuned in order to ensure high-quality real-time graphics.

Each time we interact or simply move the viewpoint in the virtual universe, by turning our heads for instance, the virtual reality system has to recalculate and render the entire scene. If we want the scenes to change smoothly, we need at least eighteen or more frames to be created per second, and if we want to enjoy three-dimensional effects (stereo effects), the system must do this twice, once for each eye.

Fig. 11.17 F1 GP Simulator (photo by the author)

Fig. 11.18 Panoram Technologies GVR-120: a large, curved screen projection system displaying three channels of stereoscopic computer video (photo by Dave Pape, 1999)

The human brain, the most important component of the human vision system, interprets stereo pairs in real time in order to provide us with meaningful information. On the one hand it merges stereo pairs to generate a three-dimensional view, and on the other it is in charge of capturing sequences of pictures at up to seven or eight frames per second and merging sequences of pictures captured at approximately fourteen or fifteen frames per second or higher into full-motion movies. There is no chance of adapting to inputs that have frame rates in-between these, and so we suffer from a kind of motion sickness when we encounter them. This was exactly the range in which early IVR systems and (later on) PC-based systems were able to perform.

We should at this point make a distinction between *input* and *output* devices.

Input devices. These include simple navigation devices (e.g. a mouse) as well as those that track movement using specific positional sensors. Sensors can even be placed in virtual objects in order to react to our stimuli.

Common navigation peripherals possess two to six degrees of freedom, while position sensors usually offer six degrees of freedom using different technologies and thus different reaction times, accuracies and operational ranges.

If deep interaction with the virtual world is our goal, another family of devices is required. Such devices range from the common keyboard to objects created ad hoc (e.g. *SpaceBall*, *Magellan*) and physical or virtual replicas of real control devices such as those used to simulate F1 racing cars or jet fighter cockpits. The three main functions already mentioned (*navigation, tracking and interaction*) are often performed using a single device, such as the data glove, which is equipped with a position sensor and interprets a language based on gestures (e.g. W. Robinett's conventional gesture language).

Output devices. These include different types of displays, from helmets (HMD or head-mounted display) that may or may not generate three-dimensional effects (stereo view), to panoramic screens (e.g. the *Visionarium*).

Output devices may use hydraulic and mechanical actuators to produce movement and acceleration, as in flight simulators and adventure rides in theme parks.

Other I/O devices specifically designed for virtual reality applications include force and tactile feedback devices, smell simulators and artificial noses, and thermal feedback devices. Of particular relevance in this context, considering their popularity, are the devices dedicated to the entertainment and computer games market, such as six degree of freedom controls, force feedback controls, stereo glasses, and others.

11.4 Enhanced Reality

Enhanced reality (also termed *enriched reality*) can be thought of as a version of the real world that has been enriched with computer-generated information. There are two main approaches to producing enhanced reality: the first provides a direct view of the real world but with digital information superimposed, while the second acquires the "shape" of the real world (in two or three dimensions), merging the real world with other data to produce a comprehensive output image.

The second approach is usually easier to achieve than the first because the merged world that results is more accurate and stable. This because the merging process involves finding the same features in the two-dimensional images and overlapping them accurately before the combined scene is outputted.

Both enhanced reality and virtual reality have ignited the imaginations of moviemakers, as can be seen by watching *Blue Thunder* and *Firefox*. Both of the helmets featured in these films superimpose digital information onto the real world and are typical devices used in ER. One of the most well known of these helmets was the "one-million-dollar" display by Kaiser Optics.

In the 1990s one of the most popular solutions for obtaining enhanced reality was based on Virtual IO goggles, an inexpensive device that offered good virtual reality and enhanced reality performance. More recently, Carl Zeiss began to sell a set of goggles. Such devices have been used for various applications, such as for technical assistance and repair, in location-dependent information systems, and for physical item retrieval.

There are also solutions that are used by car mechanics to aid with disassembling and reassembling parts of the engine.

Fig. 11.19a,b ARCHEOGUIDE: an enhanced reality-based system for personalized tours at cultural heritage sites (see http://archeoguide.intranet.gr)

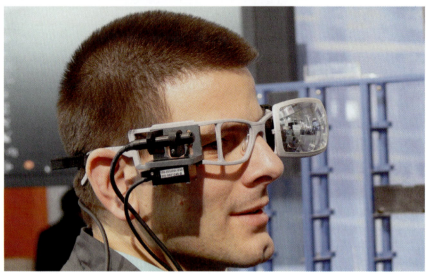

Fig. 11.20 Enhanced reality goggles by Carl Zeiss (photo by the author)

Fig. 11.21
Video conference 3D desk
(photo by the author)

11.5 Telepresence and Robots

Telepresence is, to some extent, a result of virtual reality applications. One of the most well known of these applications of virtual reality is in navigation and interaction systems for machines exploring remote and inhospitable environments, such as the surface of the planet Mars or the depths of an abyss or volcano[34]. This is telepresence.

Telepresence is also a suitable approach to use when exploring very tiny or huge environments; we move our "avatar" around a remote location using a real/virtual representation of that location, and we can interact with the environment via mechanical or other physical interfaces. A branch of this technology has been applied to surgery and health applications, enabling less invasive therapies to be performed, such as laparoscopy and telesurgery[35].

One of the symbols of technological development has been, and perhaps still is, the "automaton". The eighteenth century saw the creation of dozens of automata, many of which were shaped like animals, such as birds, while some others had a human appearance. The first steam machines were created during this period. In the past century the term *robot*[36] has become a popular term for

---

34 For example the NASA robot named Dante (1990).
35 Relevant research studies were carried out by Col. Satawa (US Army).
36 Derived from the Russian term for work, *robota* (работа), which underlines the ultimate goal of automaton creation.

11 Data Visualisation and Display Technologies   *133*

human-shaped automata. Such robots are characterised by strength and power beyond human capabilities: the "perfect workers". These workers must obey a specific code consisting of three laws:

Law I

A robot may not injure a human being or, through inaction, allow a human being to come to harm.

Law II

A robot must obey orders given it by human being except where such orders would conflict with the first law.

Law III

A robot must protect its own existence as long as this protection does not conflict with the first or second law.

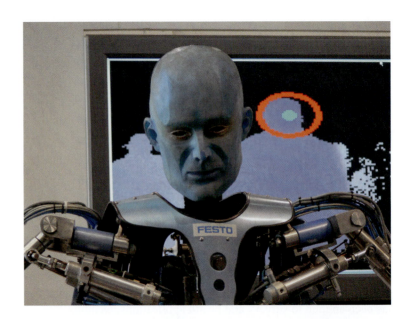

Fig. 11.22 Mirror: it moves, copying the human in front of it (photo by the author)

Fig. 11.23 a Semi-autonomous "spider"; **b** Detail of the "spider" (photos by the author)

134 | *II* The General Technological Framework

This is the legal framework for robots created by one of the most popular scientists and writers in this field, *Isaac Asimov*.

In Western countries at least, robots have subsequently largely evolved into arm or kart shapes instead of human shapes and have been used for hard and dangerous tasks as well as highly accurate and precise tasks in outer space for example.

The anthropomorphic robot reappeared in Japan during the Tsukuba Expo in 1983 and more recently in work done by Sony and Honda. A few years ago, Sony presented a prototype of a dog-shaped automaton, *AIBO*. AIBO was not intended to be the latest and greatest expensive children's toy to replace Tamagotchi; as the Japanese meaning of its name implies, it was supposed to provide a perfect companion, and was designed to entertain people by acting in an almost autonomous way.

More recently Sony decided, after of several generations of these dog-like automatons, to stop producing them and make prototypes of AIBO that are still under development public. Among these is a prototype that was able to learn through trial-and-error; this "dog" is able to lean how to stand and walk in an autonomous way. A Sony project codenamed the SDR-4X Small Biped Entertainment Robot, launched on March 2002, led to the development of *QRIO* an anthropomorphic robot that is able to stand, walk and even dance in sync with its own "brothers".

Fig. 11.24 I robot (photo by the author)

Fig. 11.25 SONY AIBO© (photo by the author)

11 Data Visualisation and Display Technologies   135

Fig. 11.26 Shelby© (photo by Francesca Ronchi)

Fig. 11.27 SONY© SDR-4X Small Biped Entertainment Robot

AIBO and QRIO were superceded in 2003 by Honda's ASIMO, an anthropomorphic robot that is able to chat with its "brothers" and perform some tasks such as walking in public spaces, climbing stairs and even dancing in sync with its own brothers.

Looking at the sector that bridges high technology and entertainment, we often find innovative materials and products, popular devices that are economic versions of cutting-edge technologies intended for the consumer market.

The reader may also recall the first vector displays that Vectrex commercialised twenty-five years ago in order to display future universes, the liquid crystal shutter stereoscopic googles produced by Sega and the *PowerGlove* by Nintendo, all of which enabled the use of virtual reality on a reduced budget.

In this context we should also mention hi-tech "objects" such as the *Furby*, *Gizmo* and *Shelby*, all of which show how it is possible to recreate high-end technological devices at minimal cost. Indeed, in a recent interview offered to the *Wireless* newspaper, Caleb Chung, fifty-year-old creator of the Furby, Gizmo and Shelby, an advanced technology expert and a successful sitcom character in the US, said, "How is it possible to take advantage of a three-million-dollar robot arm if your budget is five dollars?" Chung accepted similar challenges during the creation of the Furby and during projects like Microsoft's *Barney* or Nickelodeon's *Zog Logs Playsets*.

The solution, said Chung, is to use low-cost motors, sensors and batteries. TOY, the company that Chung co-owns, is redefining how high-tech content is used in low-cost products.

Fig. 11.28 Light version of the enhanced reality goggles from Carl Zeiss (photo by the author)

Most high-tech companies are investing in basic research, but none of them have invested in toys up to now.

TOY has recently introduced a patented mechanism that uses a single motor to activate and control dozens of independent functions simultaneously, such as to rotate the eyes, to fold the ears, and to move the arms. All this and it costs less than a dollar! According to Caleb Chung, "this is like breaking the laws of physics"!

Fig. 11.29 Pleo Dynosaur created by Caleb Chung

11 Data Visualisation and Display Technologies

12 Interaction Design

What is *interaction design*? Some authors define it as "the design of interactive products that are able to support humans in their own working activities and in everyday life".

Consider how many interactive products we deal with in a typical day: mobile phones, computers, personal organisers, remote controls, soft drink machines, coffee machines, ATMs, railway and bus ticket machines, the Web, photocopiers, alarm watches, digital cameras, camcorders, printers, media centres, iPods, VCRs, car navigation systems, calculators, video games... the list is endless!

Now consider how usable they are. How many of these products are actually easy and enjoyable to use? All of them, several, or simply one or two? This list is probably pretty short. Why is this the case?

Interaction design involves defining the behaviours of artefacts, environments, and systems. Although human—computer interactions were required for

Fig. 12.1
Personal computer: workplace with an extended set of I/O devices
(photo by the author)

the previous generation of computer applications, interaction design involves much more than just analysing human—computer interactions.

Two well-known interactive devices that cause many of us problems are the photocopier, when it doesn't copy in the way that we would like it to (lighter, darker, etc.), and the VCR, when it records a different programme from the one we wanted it to (or even nothing at all!).

Why do these issues crop up time and time again? Is there any chance of improving the situation; of fixing major problems?

A number of applications that require user interactions in order to carry out their tasks were not designed with the users in mind—it can often seem that designers have never tried to use their own products.

They are systems that are typically created and "engineered" to perform routine functions. While they may work effectively from an engineering perspective, it is often up to the user to make the extra effort to bridge the gap in man/machine communication.

The aim of interaction design

The aim of interaction design is to close this gap by bringing usability into the design process. This means developing interactive products that are easy, effective, and enjoyable to use from the users' perspective.

Interaction design is undoubtedly a discipline that has gained in prominence with the incredible rise in popularity of the World Wide Web and wireless communication. Interaction design involves cognitive, social and emotive aspects, and proposed solutions are taken from various fields, ranging from psychology to computer science.

Fig. 12.2 Relax & Interactivity for creative people (photo by the author)

When a software solution is intended to satisfy an identified need, interaction design defines which product should be built and how it should behave, down to the last tiny detail. The process involves focussing on:
- Understanding interactions
- Understanding potential users
- Having a clear idea about how interfaces may influence users
- Identifying user's needs and requirements
- Applying a user-centred design process
- Design, prototyping and digital mock-ups
- Evaluating and assessing the results.

It also involves using an evaluation schema, tracking users, interviewing experts and users, and finally testing and user profile modelling.

Interaction design aims to discover users' goals, and is therefore concerned with:
- Defining how the forms of products relate to their behaviour and use
- Anticipating how the use of products will mediate human relationships and affect human understanding
- Exploring the dialogue between products, people, and contexts (physical, cultural, historical).

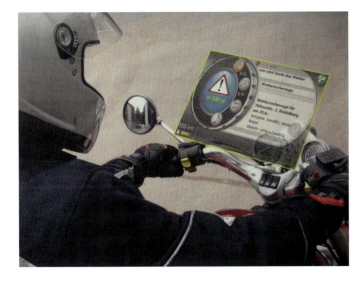

Fig. 12.3 Experimental virtual cockpit for motorbikes (photo by the author)

12.1 Interaction Design and Affective Aspects

An interesting aim of interaction design is to develop interactive systems that elicit positive responses from users, such as feeling at ease, being comfortable, and enjoying the experience of using them.

More recently, in accord with the trend towards emotional experiences, designers have become interested in how to design interactive products that elicit specific kinds of emotional responses in users, motivating them to learn, play, be creative, and be social.

In addition, in a similar way to how architecture and design traditionally relates to the business sector[37], there is currently much interest in how to design websites that people can trust—that make them feel comfortable about divulging personal information or making a purchase.

Affective aspects This newly emerging area of interaction design is based on the concept of *affective aspects*. Later on we will meet this concept again when we discuss theme parks and tourism. When following such principles, the designer will attempt to ensure not only that the experience of the product will be remembered by the user, but also that the experience is extended as much as possible in time and space, with the ultimate aim being continuous feed.

We will now look at how and why the designs of computer systems (e.g. Palm, PowerBook, Vaio) can cause certain kinds of emotional responses in users. We begin by looking in general at expressive interfaces, examining the effect of an interface's appearance on users and how it influences the usability (e.g. for the iPod).

12.2 Tyrannical or User-Friendly Technology?

I can recall being present at SIGGRAPH '99, when Caleb Chung gave a talk in his role as a member of a panel on user interfaces. He started his presentation by showing some high-tech devices with dull interfaces, and then asking whether the designers of these dull interfaces considered the actual, everyday use of such devices.

Why is it that many designers do not seem to take their target users and the way in which their devices interact with our everyday life into account?

Tyrannical technology Based on this, we can distinguish between two main approaches to technological innovation. The first is termed *tyrannical technology*, and corresponds to the view that technology imposes its own vision of the world on the target user. This is the approach that forces humans to operate according to the needs of the machine or product: to browse long lists of items in tables, to remember

---

37 Simply consider the architecture associated with banks and insurance companies, or the shapes of their headed paper and publications—so rigorous and so consistent.

II The General Technological Framework

complex and meaningless sequences of codes, to adapt themselves to use complicated interfaces.

Such an approach was or is prevalent in the first version of the online White Pages, when programming a VCR, when setting up telephone switchboards, and when using setup options on the first generations of mobile phones and to change the ringtone ("it is really easy, simply press CODE 1,7,3,2 Send in sequence"). Even a "relative" of a well-known family of user-friendly interfaces, Pocket Windows, had some problems with its early versions because its implementation on pocket PCs made it almost impossible to write a note or browse the schedule whilst speaking on the telephone; paper and pencil were still a useful alternative.

Other examples include everyday devices such as car navigators or communicators, only few of which are actually equipped with touchscreen displays. Some of them do not even offer a real or virtual numeric pad—it is necessary to rotate a *knob* in order to compose the required phone number (1,2,3,... 0, Cancel).

Indeed, it is only very recently, due to the increasing popularity of "on-board computers", that we have been able to read exactly how far the fuel left in the fuel tank can take us, rather than having to guess based on the level of the fuel tank (¾, ½, ¼).

Of course thanks to the amount of technology embedded in cars these days (*engine status, fuel, ABS, ESP, DHC, GPS, GPRS, maps, databases of services and other relevant issues*) we can make use of a number of useful services; however, these subsystems are only rarely integrated.

The opposite approach is termed *user-centred*; in this case, the product design is based upon user needs and requirements.

User-centred

Therefore, during product development, we must gain some understanding of not only what is required of the product, but where these requirements come from. *User-centred design* is a new design philosophy that proposes that users should be consulted throughout the development cycle. But who are the users? And even if we know who they are, will they know what they want or need? For an innovative product, users are unlikely to be able to envision what is possible, so where do these ideas come from?

At the corporate level, this means that sales and marketing experts must be involved in the decision-making process as well as designers. In addition, product development will require psychologists skilled in human/computer interactions and test laboratories that can check whether the product fulfils the requirements of the end-user when used in the "real world". Very often users interpret the functionality of the product in a very personal way, resulting in unexpected actions.

An interaction design project may aim to replace or update an established system, or it may aim to develop a totally new product with no obvious precedent. There may be an initial set of requirements, or the project may involve producing a set of requirements from scratch. Whatever the initial situation, and whatever the aim of the project, the user's needs, requirements, aspirations, and expectations must be discussed, refined, clarified, and probably reassessed.

Fig. 12.4 Design evaluation...

This requires, amongst other things, an understanding of the users and their capabilities, their current tasks and goals, the conditions under which the product will be used, and constraints on the product's performance.

The approach described above, although apparently more time- and resource-consuming than the other approach, will yield products that will integrate easily and quickly into the user's everyday life. They will be used appropriately due to their own good design.

Such products do not force us to learn additional information; they offer a clear vision of how they work. These may be doors and handles that operate correctly, taps that mix to give the required water warmth, and panels of switches that clearly indicate which switches activate which appliances (avoiding the need for guesswork).

They also include well-designed software applications that execute their own added-value tasks without involving the user in technological problems, allowing them to focus their attention on the application itself.

In my opinion, this corresponds to the "information at your fingertips" approach to software design proposed in 1990 by Bill Gates: *"the opportunity to focus on our own task assisted by a friendly and transparent (to the user) technology."*

12.3 Expected Product Life and Life Cycles

The life cycles of technological products tend to consist of well-defined phases.

At the beginning of the cycle the product is taken up by the technological audience (experts and those who have a special interest in the corresponding product field), who want to get their hands on the "gizmo" and try it out, even if this means investing time and resources into debugging[38] the product. They are essentially alpha- or beta-testers; forerunners. Such users do not care about reliability and usability, and even productivity is not crucial to them.

Later on, if/when the device reaches maturity, the customer profile changes. The product attracts many more new customers, who adopt the device even when they have to devote some time and energy to adapt to it, because they believe that the increased performance and productivity resulting from the adoption of the product will more than compensate. This is the stage in the lifecycle, for example, that computer-based drafting and solid modelling has now reached, after two decades of development.

---

38 The origin of the term *debug* is often attributed to the extraction of a moth that flew into the relays of an early computer (Mark II), causing it to shut down, as reported on 9th September 1947 by scientist Grace Hopper.

Fig. 12.5 On board infotainment (photo by the author)

Once this phase is over, when the technology has proved its practical worth, it is made available to the mass market. Generic customers do not tend to debate the functionality and reliability of the product; they are more interested in its style, its design, its use as a status symbol, being part of a particular user community, etc.

Consider small music players or mobile phones. Consumers expect them to be able to reproduce hi-fi stereo music or make phone calls, so they tend to focus on the design, the size, the appeal of the product. The device becomes part of the large consumer market, where a device is often replaced by the consumer even when the old device still functions properly simply because the consumer likes the new device more. Such products do not usually find their way onto the second-hand market; their lives are over and there is no reason, even an economic one, to keep them alive.

It is hard to create a second-hand market for old devices, since newer ones are (usually) more aesthetically appealing, perform better and cost less than the predecessor. In addition, or as a consequence, support for the old device is dropped by the manufacturer, and technical help for it becomes incredibly expensive; it is already a vintage product! Therefore, inheriting a vintage hi-tech product is usually not a stroke of good fortune!

Second-hand market

This aspect, which is typical of ICT, is important because it is becoming applicable to more and more areas of our lives, and it results in deep modifications to our way of life.

In the automotive sector, for instance, the increasing number of ICT components being incorporated into cars makes them safer and more reliable and easy to use, while it also turns them into consumer goods with many similar aspects to mobile phones and digital cameras.

12 Interaction Design

When the technological device exceeds its shelf life, it becomes completely useless for all practical purposes, and so its value is immediately erased.

Over the last few decades we have observed small- and large-scale changes in the market due to the introduction of new technologies—consider, for example, the music sector at both the consumer and professional levels.

Personal computers have become a melting pot for music: from audio sets to synthetic sounds and digital editing, and from classical musical instruments to more modern ones. Musical instruments like synthesisers (i.e. old electronic instruments) and classical musical instruments can now be replicated by a personal computer. This has produced a revolution in terms of the musician/instrument relationship, unleashing creativity and new opportunities (e.g. "one-man orchestras").

The world of "high-fidelity" music reproduction was once ruled by a few well-known and market-leading companies. These companies produced highly refined valve-based power amplifiers that outputted a few dozen watts of round sound, as well as preamplifiers with golden switches, loudspeakers as large as refrigerators, at prices comparable with that of a small car.

The photography market is also changing, in a similar way to that already seen in the wristwatch market. Selected sectors like these have developed a double market where the high end of the market is devoted to the evolution of traditional technologies whereas the consumer market is concerned with new technological digital devices that are more suitable for the mass market.

Now let us consider the world of personal computers and related applications. Throughout the 1980s we suffered from a lack of hardware performance and limited software. Consider the early releases of *Office Automation Suite* or drafting software. How long we were seated powerless in front of our 286 PC waiting for a segment or the for the display list to be regenerated on our display?

Later on, after various generations of 486 PCs, we had almost reached *Valhalla*—overall performances were almost good! In the *rush towards interactivity,* the goal of creating two-dimensional sketches (which had been attained) was substituted for the target of three-dimensional modelling, photo-realistic rendering and animation: resulting in a new push for ever-greater performance!

Once reasonably good overall performances are obtained for such applications, what is the next step in the evolution of software products? How do we keep the market alive?

Fig. 12.6 a McIntosh C26 pre-amplifier (1970 – photo by the author); **b** Leica M4 (1967)

Looking at the past, one application that has reached its goal of good performance is *word processing*. This application, which is based on the functional model of a typewriter to some degree, initially followed two parallel development paths: the natural evolution of the original device (the typewriter) in terms of updating and upgrading, as well as the development of the same service on a general purpose device like the personal computer.

However, even though it had the advantages of a the familiar shape and very well known functionality, the original device was eventually comprehensively beaten in terms of market share by the more complex and less popular (at that time) personal computer. After a short period of development, the PC was able to offer more powerful, sophisticated and useful options.

In this way, we moved from an ability to write, amend and manage texts before printing them to more relevant options: the ability to save and retrieve documents, to specify the font, style, body, formatting and page template used. The number of options available increased so rapidly and to such a degree that users got lost in the jungle of menu and submenu choices!

12.4   Sustainable Development of Menus and Options

The enrichment of menus and functions alluded to above could not proceed unchecked because it confused some users while other users began to question why it was necessary to host, for example, the Cyrillic alphabet or functions for creating hand-written letter headers on their PCs when they never used these functions.

Сто лет мы с вами знакомы

Such issues were solved by using modular application design, which enabled software components to be loaded and unloaded, as well as menu personalisation features and options to hide menus. This is a similar approach to that applied to TV and VCR remote controls, where covers are used to hide groups of buttons that control rarely used commands and options, meaning that only five or six buttons are usually available: those to change channels, play, stop, pause, rewind, and fast-forward.

As soon as computational power increases the focus of innovation moves onto "smartness" – applications are starting to customise menus by themselves and to predict the needs of the user (for instance, suggesting best practices, amending spelling and grammar mistakes in real time, accepting voice commands and dictation).

User-centred design has resulted in an emphasis on the machine adapting itself to the user in general, but especially to the implicit and explicit requirements of any specific user. User profiles and adaptive components have jumped from research laboratories into the marketplace.

The evolutionary path of the user-centred approach resulted in early examples of *fake* user profiling, such as the airline lounge message of "Welcome John

Smith!" that is issued upon swiping a *frequent flyer* card across the door handle, and then in *real* user profiling by credit card companies in order to tightly monitor the lifestyle and behaviour of the card holder, as well as the incredible evolution of search engines and eCommerce-targeted services that are able to offer to the registered customer not only the requested items but also a full range of related products and services, an approach that even beats methods and techniques that have been used in supermarkets and malls for a long time.

Evolution How can we expect this field to evolve in the future? On the application side, the trend is towards even more effective compatibility and application integration, improving productivity and user-friendliness. The virtuality and mobility of the working place are already issues—the migration from the Information Society to the Knowledge Society an absolute necessity.

It is over ten years since we first started to hear about the evolution of web services, the semantic web, Web 2.0, a new generation of electronic services based on ontologies that enable complex services such as "search for the least expensive Y-class flight ticket to Stockholm, flying late in the morning of 2nd September, as well as an available 3-star hotel that is close to the city hall, ...". This is one of the many services promised by the "ontological and semantic revolution", and we can look forward to trying them.

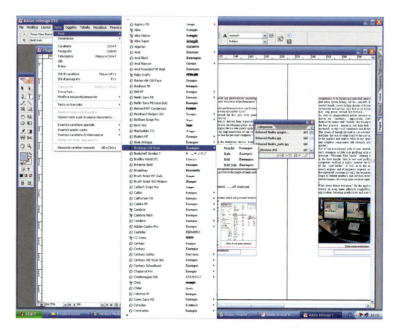

Fig. 12.7 Menu and submenu choices

Fig. 12.8 Multiscreen workstation (photo by the author)

12.5 Accessibility

Accessibility issues came to the fore at the end of the 1990s, supported by technological issues related to the potential social role of the Internet. *If the Internet has a "social" role, then, in order to avoid any "divide", it must be accessible by anyone, anywhere, and at any time.* In the present section we do not take into account accessibility from the physical or economic point of view. According to accessibility guidelines, we should make web content more accessible to all types of users and devices, such as different web browsers, voice browsers, palm computers, smart phones, media centres, interactive television, car computers, etc.

One of the reference organisations in this field is the W3C WAI (Web Accessibility Initiative) group[39], so we refer to them for our definition of accessibility.

For those unfamiliar with accessibility issues pertaining to web page design, consider that many users may be operating in contexts very different from your own:

- They may not be able to see, hear, move, or may not be able to process some types of information easily or at all
- They may have difficulty reading or comprehending text
- They may not have or be able to use a keyboard or mouse
- They may have a text-only screen, a small screen, or a slow Internet connection

---

[39] Another such organisation is the ACM SIGAccess.

- They may not speak or understand fluently the language in which the document is written
- They may be in a situation where their eyes, ears, or hands are busy or interfered with (e.g. driving to work, working in a loud environment, etc.)
- They may have an early version of a browser, a different browser entirely, a voice browser, or a different operating system.

The guidelines proposed by W3C WAI are articulated in 14 guidelines. Each of them includes:
- The guideline number
- The statement of the guideline
- Guideline navigation links
- The rationale behind the guideline and some groups of users who benefit from it
- A list of checkpoint definitions.

In order to correctly apply the guidelines, each checkpoint has a set of definitions:
- The checkpoint number
- The statement of the checkpoint
- The priority of the checkpoint; Priority 1 checkpoints are highlighted through the use of style sheets
- Optional informative notes, clarifying examples, and cross-references to related guidelines or checkpoints
- A link to a section of the *Techniques Document* where implementations and examples of the checkpoint are discussed.

In addition, a list of priorities is provided in order to scale the results and related efforts. Each checkpoint has a priority level that is assigned by the Working Group based on the checkpoint's impact on accessibility.

Priority 1. A web content developer must satisfy this checkpoint. Otherwise, one or more groups will find it impossible to access information in the document. Satisfying this checkpoint is a basic requirement for some groups to be able to use web documents.

Priority 2. A web content developer should satisfy this checkpoint. Otherwise, one or more groups will find it difficult to access information in the document. Satisfying this checkpoint will remove significant barriers to accessing web documents.

Priority 3. A web content developer may address this checkpoint. Otherwise, one or more groups will find it somewhat difficult to access information in the document. Satisfying this checkpoint will improve access to web documents. Some checkpoints specify a priority level that may change under certain (indicated) conditions.

There are *three different levels of conformance* to this document, represented by A, AA, or AAA:

- Conformance Level "A": all Priority 1 checkpoints are satisfied
- Conformance Level "AA": all Priority 1 and 2 checkpoints are satisfied
- Conformance Level "AAA": all Priority 1, 2, and 3 checkpoints are satisfied.

The complete list of WAI guidelines (please refer to the original document available online at http://www.w3c.org):
- *Guideline 1.* Provide equivalent alternatives to auditory and visual content
- *Guideline 2.* Don't rely on colour alone
- *Guideline 3.* Use markup and style sheets and do so properly
- *Guideline 4.* Clarify natural language usage
- *Guideline 5.* Create tables that transform gracefully[40]
- *Guideline 6.* Ensure that pages featuring new technologies transform gracefully
- *Guideline 7.* Ensure user control of time-sensitive content changes
- *Guideline 8.* Ensure direct accessibility of embedded user interfaces
- *Guideline 9.* Design for device-independence
- *Guideline 10.* Use interim solutions
- *Guideline 11.* Use W3C technologies and guidelines
- *Guideline 12.* Provide context and orientation information
- *Guideline 13.* Provide clear navigation mechanisms
- *Guideline 14.* Ensure that documents are clear and simple.

A complete guideline and a list of checkpoints and priorities associated with it are now provided for illustration purposes. (Note that the following guideline excerpt was taken from a webpage containing many hyperlinks; these are indicated below through the use of italics.)

Guideline 1. Provide equivalent alternatives to auditory and visual content

Provide content that, when presented to the user, conveys essentially the same function or purpose as auditory or visual content.

Although some people cannot use images, movies, sounds, applets, etc. directly, they may still use pages that include *equivalent* information to the visual or auditory content. The equivalent information must serve the same purpose as the visual or auditory content. Thus, a text equivalent for an image of an upward arrow that links to a table of contents could be "Go to table of contents". In some cases, an equivalent should also describe the appearance of

---

40 Pages that transform gracefully remain accessible despite any of the constraints described in the introduction, including physical, sensory, and cognitive disabilities, work constraints, and technological barriers.

visual content (e.g., for complex charts, billboards, or diagrams) or the sound of auditory content (e.g., for audio samples used in education).

This guideline emphasizes the importance of providing *text equivalents* of non-text content (images, pre-recorded audio, video). The power of text equivalents lies in their capacity to be rendered in ways that are accessible to people from various disability groups using a variety of technologies. Text can be readily output to speech synthesizers and *braille displays*, and can be presented visually (in a variety of sizes) on computer displays and paper. Synthesized speech is critical for individuals who are blind and for many people with the reading difficulties that often accompany cognitive disabilities, learning disabilities, and deafness. Braille is essential for individuals who are both deaf and blind, as well as many individuals whose only sensory disability is blindness. Text displayed visually benefits users who are deaf as well as the majority of Web users.

Providing non-text equivalents (e.g., pictures, videos, and pre-recorded audio) of text is also beneficial to some users, especially nonreaders or people who have difficulty reading. In movies or visual presentations, visual action such as body language or other visual cues may not be accompanied by enough audio information to convey the same information. Unless verbal descriptions of this visual information are provided, people who cannot see (or look at) the visual content will not be able to perceive it.

Checkpoints (W3C Recomendations Excerpt)

1.1. Provide a text equivalent for every non-text element (e.g., via "alt", "longdesc", or in element content). This includes: images, graphical representations of text (including symbols), image map regions, animations (e.g., animated GIFs), applets and programmatic objects, ASCII art, frames, scripts, images used as list bullets, spacers, graphical buttons, sounds (played with or without user interaction), standalone audio files, audio tracks of video, and video. [Priority 1]

For example, in HTML:
- Use "alt" for the IMG, INPUT, and APPLET elements, or provide a text equivalent in the content of the OBJECT and APPLET elements
- For complex content (e.g. a chart) where the "alt" text does not provide a complete text equivalent, provide an additional description using, for example, "longdesc" with IMG or FRAME, a link inside an OBJECT element, or a *description link*
- For image maps, either use the "alt" attribute with AREA, or use the MAP element with A elements (and other text) as content.

Refer also to *checkpoint 9.1* and *checkpoint 13.10*.
Techniques for checkpoint 1.1

1.2 Provide redundant text links for each active region of a server-side image map. [Priority 1]

Refer also to *checkpoint 1.5* and *checkpoint 9.1*.

Techniques for checkpoint 1.2

1.3 *Until user agents* can automatically read aloud the text equivalent of a visual track, provide an auditory description of the important information of the visual track of a multimedia presentation. [Priority 1]

Synchronize the *auditory description* with the audio track as per *checkpoint 1.4*. Refer to *checkpoint 1.1* for information about textual equivalents for visual information.

Techniques for checkpoint 1.3

1.4 For any time-based multimedia presentation (e.g., a movie or animation), synchronize equivalent alternatives (e.g., captions or auditory descriptions of the visual track) with the presentation. [Priority 1]

Techniques for checkpoint 1.4

1.5 *Until user agents* render text equivalents for client-side image map links, provide redundant text links for each active region of a client-side image map. [Priority 3]

Refer also to *checkpoint 1.2* and *checkpoint 9.1*.

Techniques for checkpoint 1.5.

…

12.6   Usability

The Web's presence has heightened awareness of usability, but unfortunately all too often software designers assume that if they and their colleagues can use their products and find them attractive, others will too. Furthermore, they prefer to avoid evaluation because it adds development time and costs money. So why is evaluation important? Because without evaluation, designers cannot be sure that their software is usable and is what users want. But exactly what do we mean by evaluation? There are many definitions and many different evaluation techniques, some of which involve users directly while others call indirectly on an understanding of users' needs and psychology. In this book we define evaluation as the process of systematically collecting data that tells us what it is like for a particular user or group of users to use a product for a particular task in a certain type of environment.

When evaluating the needs and requirements of users we must avoid the usual approach: *We know exactly what users need, even if they do not agree with our analysis! We are right!*

13 Computer Games, Edutainment and Theme Parks

Game-playing dates back to the very origins of mankind. Archaeologists have found dolls and game sets at many ancient sites around the world, from China to Egypt to the Americas. Games are therefore also part of our heritage and a powerful medium for reaching out to people.

13.1 Information Technology and the Young

Television is the most traditional and consolidated medium. Nevertheless there are some variations in levels of use based on age and economic resources (for instance, children and boys from low-income families spend more time watching television).

Fig. 13.1 Puppets from the Han Tombs in Xi Yan (photo by the author)

The percentage of young people that have their own television set or even a personal videocassette recorder or DVD player has grown constantly over the years. Boys are more interested in personal computers than girls and very often have their own personal computers connected to the Internet in their rooms. Young people mainly use personal computers to play video games. The total amount of time dedicated to video-game-playing on personal computers is far more then other applications, even when compared with game consoles.

The report *New Information Technologies and the Young*[41] identified the extent of provision and access to technologies, the ways in which young people use them, and some of the opportunities and difficulties associated with each form of communication and expression. The report provides a comprehensive picture of young people as users and consumers of new technologies, but especially in terms of their creative activity, such as their use of digital audio and video, website creation, and distributing visual, musical or literary work across the Internet.

The fact that a great deal of software development is carried out at local level provides more job opportunities for young people, since this market sector is dominated by young people because they are characterised by competences and ambitions typical of the software development sector, and this promotes culture and creativity.

Across Europe, the six main activities related to the Internet are educational content searching, email messaging, use of chat rooms, online entertainment, online gaming/gambling and shopping.

It is not completely clear whether computer-based activity and particularly Internet browsing will decrease the amount of time devoted to traditional work. According to a recent report from the UK, network activities eat into the time normally reserved for other entertainment activities and even active work.

13.2 Computer Games and Digital Cultures

The first International Conference on Computer Games and Digital Cultures (CGDG) was held in Tampere, Finland in June 2002. The event was organised by the Hypermedia Laboratory of Tampere University along with the University of Turku, the IT University of Copenhagen, UIAH Medialab of Helsinki, and some partners from the digital content industry[42].

---

41 The project New Information Technologies and the Young was launched by Screen Digest—General Direction Office IV of the Council of Europe. A final report on the project was published; see Council of Europe (2001).

42 In 2003 the First Digital Games Research Association (DiGRA) International Conference was held at Utrecht University (The Netherlands). More recently (24–28 September 2007), the Third Digital Games Research Association International Conference was held at the University of Tokyo's Hongo campus in Tokyo, Japan.

This event was a follow-up to a series of international meetings and workshops devoted to computer games inaugurated in Copenhagen in 2001 by Computer Games and Digital Textualities. The MILIA[43] (held in Cannes, France) and Imagina (held in Monte Carlo) events have been around for a long time and are still key events in this field.

Another relevant event devoted to new technologies, education and edutainment applications is usually held in the US—the ASTC (Association of Science and Technology Centres) Annual Conference[44]—where, together with the traditional "hands on" approach, we can find thematic educational games.

Association of Science and Technology Centres

These events and others associated with the entertainment and games sector provide clear evidence of the relevance of this sector.

Consoles, media centres, digital wristwatches, palmtops and mobile phones are just some of the devices that now support video games—one of the engines of IT, and now even of ICT.[45] One of the emerging gaming sectors is termed *serious games*. The core markets for serious games are the military, government, healthcare, corporate training and education, although the traditional gaming sector still plays a major role.

Serious games

The Serious Games Initiative[46] focuses on the use of games to explore management and leadership challenges facing the public sector. Part of its overall charter is to help forge productive links between the electronic game industry and projects involving the use of games in education, training, health, and public policy.

Ignoring the defence sector[47] (which includes war games) and the "adult" market, entertainment is one of the main engines for the digital market.

The explosion of opportunities to communicate afforded by the popularities of the Internet and mobile telephony has enabled the development of multiplayer games on mobile phones (e.g. multiplayer role-playing games), and *massively multiplayer games* are now on the horizon of mobile telephony.

Massively multiplayer games

Finally, we should also mention *peer-to-peer* communication. Although this is sometimes associated with the illegal exchange of copyrighted files, it has

---

43 MILIA (http://www.miptv.com/) is hosted by MIPTV; Imagina Montearlo: http://www.imagina.mc.

44 ASTC Annual Conference: http://www.astc.org/conference/index.htm.

45 Online gaming represents a significant proportion of this market. A number of mobile phone-based role-playing games are also emerging, even location-based versions.

46 Serious Games Initiative: http://www.seriousgames.org/index2.html; Serious Games Summit: http://www.seriousgamessummit.com/.

47 At the end of the "Star Wars" project a number of researchers moved from the defence sector to the entertainment sector, bringing with them knowledge of a number of advanced technologies, such as virtual reality, computer vision, artificial intelligence and artificial life (creatures), which they then used the field of entertainment.

opened the door to innovative services and approaches to interpersonal communication.

13.3 Games

The "game" has always represented a vital component of human life, since it allows us to unleash energy and creativity beyond the boundaries of current conventions. Obviously each game has its own rules, which are usually well-defined and consistent. These rules represent, as we will see, essential reference points for creative people[48].

The world of games
The "gaming universe" can be analysed according to many different taxonomies: games played alone, in small groups and in teams; educational or neutral games; games requiring the use of specific devices, high-tech games and games based on simple objects or symbols; games based on rules and behaviours; games that depend on physical fitness and games that do not; games that require the physical presence of the other players or not; games that require specific knowledge or ability; simulations or purely abstract games; games based on chance or skill; games that have a winner those that do not[49]; as well as others.

There is a key aspect to gaming: the ability to interact, to be an "actor" in the action. Just how physical these interactions are depends on the game, but it is (almost) always present to some degree[50]. Here, we will focus mainly on those games based on advanced technologies, particularly computer games.

Computer games originated in laboratories, but were quickly ported to arcades and bars in the form of customised gaming platforms. The next evolutionary step was to create gaming platforms for the home, like the classic PET, the VIC 20, the Commodore 64, and the TI99, resulting in a home software market.

From that time onwards, arcades, bars and, a short time later, theme parks took up the challenge of offering highly immersive games characterised by high complexity, making it impossible to release a domestic version of such games.

Note that computer games are not limited to video games. In this domain we can also find innovative products and technologies, devices based on concentrated versions of cutting edge technologies that are simply scaled down to make them less expensive to consumers. We have already mentioned how, over thirty-five years ago, Vectrex enabled players to fly through future "uni-

---

48 Consider, for example, the rules and character creation associated with role-playing games such as *Dungeons & Dragons*.

49 The reader may remember the games of tic-tac-toe (each of which ended with no winner) played between the protagonist David Lightman and the computer Joshua in the movie *WarGames* (1983, directed by John Badham).

50 There are some exceptions. An example is provided by the Japanese game called *Pacinko*. Players do not interact at all with the games machine; they simply place balls in it.

Fig. 13.2 Tennis game on a plasma display (photo by the author)

Fig. 13.3 Interactive gaming table for pubs (Peyote, Austria, photo by the author)

verses", fighting against enemy spaceships, as well as the stereo goggles based on liquid crystal shutters produced by Sega and the *PowerGlove* by Nintendo. These devices provided a path to low-cost interactive virtual reality for many computer buffs.

While on this subject, we should also recall some "objects" that fall somewhere between computer games and toys such as Furby, Gizmo, Shelby and more recently Pleo, which provide astonishing examples of how it is possible to reproduce high-profile technological devices at minimal cost.

13.4 Interactivity and Immersivity

Fig. 13.4 *Force Feedback by Percro (Scuola Normale Superiore Sant'Anna, Pisa, Italy)*

Computer games technologies have often anticipated (with some reasonable limitations and differences of course) innovative technologies.

Because of the obvious limits on platforms and configurations, computer game developers have always had to use the resources at their disposal as efficiently as possible, taking advantage of "bugs" in our perceptive system and other tricks in order to improve performance "virtually".

Consequently, texture was used instead of 3-D models, spots of colour instead of sharp images, pictures were rendered at various resolutions, pre-rendered scenes were created with predefined direct shadows and effects of generated shadows, and the level of detail (LoD) was varied depending on the location of the display and the speed of camera movement within the scene, etc.

One of the most relevant characteristics of computer games is the *interaction* involved. Most games make it possible to play against the machine, resulting in the development of interactions between the player and the game itself.

A well as interaction, there is another fundamental aspect of games that we should take into account: *immersivity*. Immersivity is the level of sensory and emotional involvement that captures the user and links them to the application. This involvement is strongly subjective; due to a number of factors related to the person and the context, some users become "immersed" in a digital story-telling adventure or when simply reading a novel, while others maintain absolute separation even when they are handling the controls of an fighter jet flight simulator.

The "side effects" of immersivity have led critics to suggest that video games should be considered to be a new drug, a potential trigger for epileptic fits, and that they encourage violence and other asocial behaviour.

Single-player versus group adventures

In principle, it does not matter how similar the hardware we use to immerse ourselves in the simulation is to the equipment used to perform the action in "real life". While ergonomic aspects are appreciated by players, it is possible to become immersed in a flight simulation even when it only uses the keyboard and a small LCD screen. As we will see for theme parks, adequate training, a realistic "location" and some other tricks make immersion easier to achieve.

In addition we can split adventures into two main categories: single-player and group adventures. Such groups can range from few players in the small cabin of a simulator or a theatre filled with eight hundred players.

13.5 Abstract Games

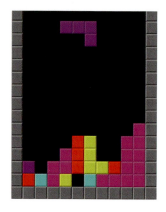

Fig. 13.5 *Tetris (originally designed and programmed by Alexey Pajitnov in June 1985)*

Amongst the several taxonomies applicable to computer games, we can make one simple distinction between *simulations* (which recreate real or imaginary universes virtually), such as flight simulators or SimCity, and *abstract games*, which are based on abstract entities, such as Nim, Filetto or Tetris.

Games based on *abstraction*, which are less popular than games based on simulation, are often derived from logic problems or more simply tests of abilities (reflexes, shape and colour recognition, etc.). This type of game, which does not have to replicate the physical world in some way, is not directly bound by the evolution of computational performance, unlike simulation games. The quality of an abstract game is not influenced by factors that influence the quality of a simulation, such as how much the simulation resembles what it simulates, or how well it performs during direct interactions.

A classic example of an *abstract* game is *Mastermind*, which initially appeared in a physical form that utilised coloured pegs. It was later "virtualised" so that it could be played on computers. In analogy with popular books, this game has been "translated" into many different computer languages, including FORTRAN.

13.6 Simulations

Computer-mediated storytelling has always been about what you do, right here and now, while you are sitting at the keyboard. That's where the story comes from. It's not about what somebody else did, once upon a time, in a land far, far away.

Dennis G. Jerz

The first digital stories were *Adventure* and other *interactive stories* that were "told" via a textual interface. In such stories, a simple situation was generated involving characters, a location, and some details concerning the location, such as:

You are in a dismal swamp
Obvious exits: North, South, East, West, Up
You can also see: cypress tree—evil smelling mud—swamp gas—floating patch of oily slime—chiggers

(From *Adventureland* by Scott Adams[51], written in 1979). Based on this descriptive text, the user is then asked to specify what the character representing the user should do next (by writing it at the command line on the display). The user's answer generally consists of a simple command written in natural language, such as:

climb the cypress

The response from the game would then be "you are now in the top of a tall cypress tree". Obviously the player could, for example, state "take the cypress", an action that the game does not recognise. The game could also provide hints or paths that help the player to reach the end of the story. This was great fun at the time!

---

51 Try a demo of the game at http://www.malinche.net/demos/adventureland.html.

Fig. 13.6 a Asteroids (a video arcade game released in 1979 by Atari Inc.); **b,c** Space Invaders (developed by Toshihiro Nishikado in 1978 and produced by Taito)

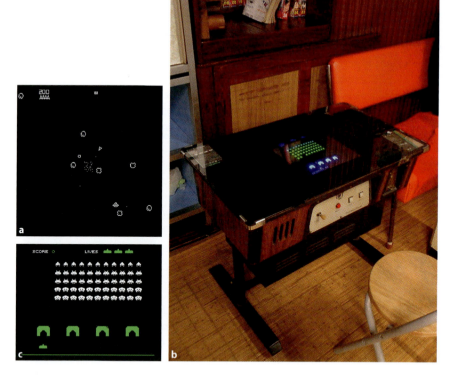

Our imaginations and fantasies were highly stimulated by such digital stories, in a very similar way to what happens when we read novels and books. Such adventures allowed the player to shape the "plot", increasing their degree of immersion in the game.

These early simulations based on a purely textual interface gradually evolved into more and more realistic representations of locations and atmospheres that made extensive use of graphics. This evolution moved from the use of still images (as used in physical stories too), to animations inside static pages, to the first simulations with two- and three-dimensional navigation (e.g. *Asteroids* and *Space Invaders*).

Spacewar, a game with computer graphics released in 1962, introduced meaningful simulation effects; for example, gravitational effects were realistically simulated, as were the explosions of the targets. Just like one of the best science fiction special effects, the game included "hyperspace jumps" that allowed small spaceships to disappear from a dangerous area and reappear somewhere else in cyberspace.

13.7 Simulators, Dark Rides and Other Nonlinear Formats

As they have evolved, video games have exerted their own demands on the development of hardware and software, resulting in not only better computational resources but also more sophisticated peripherals, from audio cards and video adapters to more and more sophisticated navigation and interaction devices (from jet fighter controls to the data glove and helmet to haptic devices and force feedback).

The simulation of natural behaviour has long been a field that has attracted great interest. Indeed, several of the programme sessions, courses, round tables and research papers presented at ACM SIGGRAPH[52] are devoted to natural phenomena simulation.

Natural phenomena simulation

A number of simulations are presented in graphical form, including fluid dynamics, realistic movements of virtual actors, dynamic effects, fluid and particle diffusion, vegetation growth, and the behaviour of crowds of virtual actors. From a scientific point of view, these simulations have been applied to well-known physical principles, genetic algorithms, behavioural laws, neural networks, artificial intelligence, and computer vision.

In 1987, a groundbreaking animation was produced by the Symbolics Graphics Division: *Stanley and Stella in Breaking the Ice*. *Stanley and Stella*, with its flocks of birds and fishes, was one of the first applications of Craig Reynolds' *boids* behavioural animation model. Since 1987 there have been many other applications of the *boids* model in the realm of behavioural animation. S-Graphics running on Symbolics hardware became almost ubiquitous in film and broadcast animation in the late 1980s and early 1990s.

Stanley and Stella in Breaking The Ice

The 1992 Tim Burton film *Batman Returns* was the first to contain computer-generated *flocks* and *swarms*. It contained computer-simulated bat swarms and flocks of penguins, which were created with modified versions of the original *boids* software developed at Symbolics. Andy Kopra produced the realistic imagery of bat swarms, while Andrea Losch and Paul Ashdown created the animation of an *army* of penguins marching through the streets of Gotham City.

Fig. 13.7a–c Stanley and Stella in Breaking The Ice (1987). Stanley and Stella was one of the first applications of Craig Reynolds' (SMBX Alum 1982–1991) "boids" behavioral animation model

---

52 Special Interest Group in Computer Graphics: http://www.siggraph.org.

13 Computer Games, Edutainment and Theme Parks   163

Go Fish!   Around the same time we saw *Go Fish!* and other amazing research work from Demetri Terzopulos, which eventually led to the animated onslaught of the *Uruk-hai* in the movie *The Lord of the Rings: The Two Towers*.

These technologies have been utilised many times, even when creating blockbuster computer games, in order to make the battles in war games or the chases and shootings in action games more realistic and interactive.

The technologies used in computer games are therefore advanced and sophisticated enough to make researchers working in this field comparable in many ways to employees of the American Department of Defense (DoD). Both of these groups of workers are interested in setting up new and sophisticated simulators of conflict situations or training systems for the army.

Simulation: added value   The added value of simulators usually derives from their ability to offer, over a very short period of time, a huge range of situations that one person would only very rarely be able to experience in a lifetime. These simulations can be constantly updated with new situations, which is often the case for flight simulators for example. The simulations can then focus on realism or artificially emphasised behaviours.

Arcade simulators   Arcade simulators, on the other hand, do not aim to replicate the real world exactly; instead, they emphasise the effects of the simulation in order to generate strong emotional experiences.

The simulators used for entertainment are descendents of military ones, with one basic difference: those used in the defence and manufacturing sectors emulate reality in order to check how the user will react and behave in certain situations, while those used in entertainment generally do not react in a realistic way and in real time, but produce amplified and predefined scenarios.

Fig. 13.8 The "real/external" aspect of a simulator (photo by Dave Pape)

Fig. 13.9 Simulation of a volcanic eruption (Vesuvius, Naples; courtesy of CINECA, Bologna)

Therefore, a software engineer is needed along with an expert in multimedia communication to design the reactions of a simulator used for entertainment (in terms of the accelerations, vibrations and movements as well as the sounds, images, smells, smoke, etc.).

The popularity of virtual reality arcade games (Virtuality SU, Sega, etc.) has driven this industry. The mechanical part of a simulator can have different shapes, dimensions and offer different numbers of *degrees of freedom* (DOF). The *degrees of freedom* indicate the number of directions and angles in which the simulator is able to move, up to a maximum of six (three axes and three angles).

Most simulators offer three degrees of freedom; they can be tilted, rotated and raised using hydraulic or pneumatic *actuators*. A few of them offer six degrees of freedom. Another difference in terms of performance relates to how much they can move in each direction, even if, in entertainment, *acceleration* is more relevant than *absolute motion*.

From a perception point of view, we tend to associate displacement with acceleration, as the acceleration grows, so does the feeling of displacement.

Let us now summarise different types of simulator.

Single users. These include 3-D goggles, HMD helmets, large screens or a small cabin with large screen, stereo or 3-D audio via headphones or loudspeakers (5+1 or more); movements are often limited to the basic movements associated with the specific simulation (e.g. arcade: riding bikes or motorbikes, sky, snowboards and more).

Single users

Small groups (approx 2–25 people). This encompasses cabins with large screens instead of windows and glasses, if needed. Audio stereo or 3-D is provided by loudspeakers if a multilanguage service is not required; actuators

Small groups

produce movements and other mechanical effects (vibrations, explosions, etc.) in coordination with images and sounds (e.g. *Disney Quest* in Orlando, FL, USA).

Mass experience

Mass experience. Such experiences include simulation theatres with panoramic screens or *IMAX* theatres, sometimes equipped with active groups of seats or active single seats (e.g. *Terminator 3D* at MGM Studios, Orlando, FL, USA), and 3-D audio (very often following THX specifications).

360° panoramic effect

One slightly different type of simulation theatre is the *360° theatre*. In this case, the full panoramic effect may be produced by a special "periscope-like" optic (as used in, e.g., Museum of Transportation in Luzern, Switzerland) or an alternate sequence of screens and synchronised projectors (e.g. the *Wonderful China* experience in Disney World, Orlando, FL, USA).

In 360° theatres, people attending the show do not have a specific seats with certain orientations because of the *omnidirectional* view on the scene, so no seats are available. A set of pipes shaped as "back holders" is usually used, however, in order to stop people from losing their balance as they look at things moving quickly across the scene.

Dome

A special version of the panoramic theatre is the *dome*. This type of theatre is a mixture of the previous two. The dome completely fills up the *field of vision* of each spectator, who is usually seated on an *active* seat. In this case, active means that it is able to move, vibrate, blow, touch and more (e.g. the *Back to the Future* ride at Universal Studios, Orlando, FL, USA or the *Time Elevator Experience* in Rome).

Cabins

Cabins are usually designed to hold only a limited number of spectators so that they can be shipped and installed without any specific problems. They can be installed on trailers that are moved by trucks; these trailers are fully equipped with a ticket office, power plants and various services. They can easily move from village square to village square, offering a wide range of high-quality experiences to different audiences. Such simulators can be set up to provide an *ad hoc* experience for a specific event or location.

Theatres

Theatres can offer *mass experiences* when required, but the dynamic impression provided by such a theatre is based on just few degrees of freedom.

We all know that some events are best experienced in large groups (e.g. football matches, rock music concerts, etc.) because the presence of a large number of spectators—their behaviour, their looks, gestures, screams—are fundamental ingredients of the experience.

Domes tend to offer better immersivity but less spectator room compared with theatres. The ability to effectively simulate movements, shocks and other immersive effects can be increased in domes by using active seats or customised *cabins*. Such cabins may look like a car or a small submarine moving across a scene composed of images projected onto the dome as a visual panorama (e.g. cars, spaceships, or submarines in the cases of *Back to the Future*: *The Ride* in MGM Studios, Orlando, FL, USA, or *Abyss* in SeaWorld, Orlando, FL, USA).

Dark rides

Dark rides are special adventures hosted by interactive *moving* theatres that involve a kind of automatic interactive story told via technological devices and by dynamically immersing the *viewer* in a sequence of different scenes. The *viewer* is usually seated in a moving car or on a platform. The car moves following a predefined path, passing through different scenes accompanied by different story-telling actions. Of course, there is also the reverse scenario, where the people are seated in the theatre and a revolving scene presents *animatronics*[53].

Dark rides usually begin with a short briefing that *immerses* the viewers in the *story* told by the ride as they are queuing up to enter the attraction. At the end of the experience, on the way out, it is common to have to pass through shops with merchandise themed on the ride. If some interaction is needed during the ride, a special briefing session is added to the initial one, together with a specific "safety" briefing.

A complete sequence of *briefings* would therefore involve a first briefing on general topics related to the experience (given while people are queuing outside the theatre); a second briefing describes what is currently happening in the ride (via live video); last but not least is a briefing on how to use the equipment associated with the ride, interaction methods, and safety and emergency instructions. One of the early European examples of "dark ride" in natural science museums was created in the "Parc Oceanique Cousteau" located at the Forum Des Halles in Paris (mid-1980s).

Briefings

Moving back to the general topic of this chapter, theme parks, people often say that "you pay the entrance ticket to a theme park in order to start queuing". There is undoubtedly an element of truth to this; The ratio of the amount of time spent by customers queuing to the time devoted to actually experiencing the attractions is often pretty big: two hours queuing to five minutes experiencing, that's entertainment!

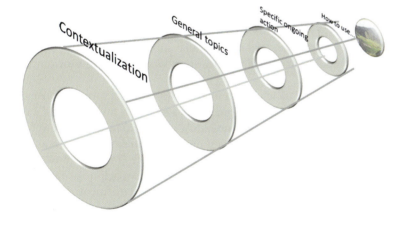

Fig. 13.10 Multilayered briefing

---

53   Disney revolving theatre.

13 Computer Games, Edutainment and Theme Parks   167

Due to the structure of the attraction, with a regular flow of people, the timing of the experience can be accurately estimated and allocated so as to maximise its effects. Therefore, the potential number of visitors is easy to estimate, which is an important aspect sometimes. A similar approach is often applied in museums that lend out digital audio guides with just a single button, *play*. These guides suggest the best path and timing to use during the museum visit.

All of these *attractions* are relatively novel and flexible communication formats, and they are capable of communicating in very effective and immersive ways. They are usually immersive experiences with different levels of interaction, enabling nonlinear communication channels. They are widely used today, even for didactic purposes, in *theme parks and science centres*.

The ability to transfer information in the form of a direct "hands on" experience, thus breaking the rigid linear sequential format offered by books and lectures, provides teachers with an extremely powerful instrument. When this is combined with a series of *tricks* that have been cultivated in the field of entertainment in order to enhance the experience, thus ensuring positive feedback from visitors, we find that we have a perfect recipe for a teaching tool.

Methods of communication and experiences developed in the field of games and theme parks have been found to be the most efficient and performant communication methods; indeed, the movie industry has recently realised that games immerse and involve the viewer in the action far more efficiently than movies do, and so games are playing an increasingly prominent role in the promotional phases of new movies.

Relevance of the context

Returning to the general topic of simulation, it is commonly believed that camera movements can be used to simulate cabin movements; in truth, this only happens in military simulators. In the field of entertainment, *we are not looking for realism—we are looking for pure emotions*. The simulation device must be therefore programmed in a way that supplies an illusion of the action, emphasising motions and accelerations, since visitors want to experience emotions and thrills.

Designed to get the viewer lost...

We have noted that the ability to immerse oneself in a scene depends on the individual. In order to reach the goal of providing an involving and exciting experience to the audience, we must keep the attention of the viewer as far from the real world as possible, even if the action quickly moves from a spaceship battle to a boat cruise down the Nile during the Golden Age of the Pharaohs. Appropriate architecture and interior design can help to achieve this, by providing a lack of reference points and a *neutral* environment.

Additional care is needed during two specific stages of the adventure: the *beginning* and the *end* of the simulation. These two specific moments are key points to the success of the experience. Something must happen to move the focus of the viewer; for instance from the "real world" to the beginning of the simulation. This is why flashing lights, smoke, loud sounds and other such distractions are employed during these phases.

168 *II The General Technological Framework*

Fig. 13.11 SONY PlayStation 2©: noninvasive interface for an interactive boxing game (photo by Francesca Ronchi)

Let's add some basic info about the way to program a simulator. We need to take advantage of application software that synchronises the images with the movements of the simulator. Such software are often *wave-shape editors* (similar to those used in the music industry), which make sure that the movements of the simulator along each axis are fluid.

In this case, programming involves literally *carving* the wave rather than writing code. During the production process, one or more versions of the movie are run in the cabin while someone sitting in it attempts to move the cabin in sync with the movie via a joystick controlling the actuators of the simulator. These movements are fed as input data into the computer, yielding a preliminary motion track. Each motion must then be optimised and emphasised.

This where the wave shape editor comes in; it is needed to refine and tune the movements in order to make them smooth, amusing, electrifying and to stop them from generating motion sickness.

13.8 A Brief History of Computer Games

The world of computer games has long been an important playground for software developers, due to the ability to define clear rules and the free creativity associated with games.

Some of the key computer game manufacturers have long and fascinating histories. For example, in 1889 Fusajiro Yamauchi established the Marufuku Company in Japan; this company was dedicated to the production and distribution of *Hanafuda*—Japanese playing cards. In 1907, the Marufuku Company extended its production to the Western playing cards. The company then changed its name in 1951 and became *The Nintendo Playing Card Company*. *Nintendo* means "leave luck to heaven" in Japanese.

Nintendo

Also, in 1945, on the other side of the Pacific, working in a garage, Harold Matson and Elliot Handler begin to produce frames for pictures and, in an attempt to reuse spare pieces of wood, they begin to produce furniture for doll houses under the brand name Mattel[54] (a combination of parts of their surnames).

Mattel

Then, in 1949, Ralph Baer[55], a student at the *American Television Institute of Technologies* (ATIT) in Chicago, designed a television[56] set that was intended to be the best television set in the world, since it incorporated other forms of entertainment, such as games.

However, Baer's design for a video game was not approved by the management of the company, and it took another 18 years for him to create one. During this period, a researcher named Willy Higinbotham created the first interactive tennis game using an oscilloscope, and another researcher, Steve Russell, created a basic interactive game called *Spacewar!* that ran on a Digital Pdp-1 mainframe.

Nolan Bushnell then recreated *Spacewar!* as *Computer Space*, which advantageously ran on a much cheaper hardware platform than the Pdp-1. Later, a company started by Bushnell (Atari) produced seminal games such as *Asteroids* (1979) and *Asteroids 64*, *Space Invaders, Centipede, Frogger*, as well as the first video game to gain public popularity, *Pong*—a refinement of the game produced by Willie Higinbotham.

Atari

Sega

Interestingly, the history of video games contains an American company with a Japanese name, Atari[57], created by the Americans Nolan Bushnell and Ted Dabney, as well as a Japanese company, *Sega*, created by the American David Rosen in the 1950s to initially import (from the USA) artworks, and then instant portrait picture boxes, and then video arcade machines after they bought a company manufacturing jukeboxes.[58]

---

54 In the 1980s Mattel introduced the *Intellivision* home games console, which took advantage of the success of the Atari VCS. Intellivision offered better instructions and a cheaper price than Atari's VCS ($299).

55 Considered the inventor of the video game (see http://www.pong-story.com/rhbaer. htm).

56 For Loral Electronics.

57 Nolan Bushnell—the visionary that foresaw a mass market for video games—and his friend Ted Dabney founded a company, *Syzygy*, in order to produce *Space Computer* (distributed through Nutting Associates Inc.). In the 1972 they changed the name of their company to *Atari*, which is a term (equivalent to "check") associated with the Japanese chess game *GO*, of which Bushnell was a big fan.

58 In the middle of the 1990s, a veteran of the Korean War, David Rosen, decided to create a gaming application based on an automatic photographic booth because the entertainment market in Japan was expanding rapidly. The company he created was named Rosen Enterprises Ltd. In 1964 Rosen decided to merge its company with that of Nihon Goraku Bussan ("Service Games"). The resulting company was named Sega Enterprises, Ltd. Sega is a contraction of the words "SErvice GAmes".

II The General Technological Framework

In 1976 Atari introduced a new game for its games platform, *Breakout*. This game was created by its fortieth employee, Steve Jobs, and his friend Steve Wozniak. A year later they created *Apple Computer* while Bushnell sold *Atari* to *Warner Communications,* while retaining his role as general manager.

Apple Computer

1978 saw the release of one of the most popular games ever, *Space Invaders*. Space Invaders was the first video game to have a great impact on the games market, since it was played not only on arcade machines in bars and pubs but also at home, on the famous Atari 2600 or *VCS (Video Computer System)*.

Another interesting characteristic of computer games originated in this period too, due to the copyright polices applied by Atari. Atari did not recognise the personal rights of employees as the authors of the games; instead, it decided to protect the intellectual property as a company asset.

This approach led to the creation of the first virtual *Easter egg*—a special characteristic or message hidden inside a game by the author. Warren Robinett, the creator of the game *Adventure*, included a secret room that contained his name in luminous letters in the colours of the rainbow. In order to enter the room, the player must find a special grey pixel hidden somewhere within the game and bring it back to the start. In the space of a decade Easter eggs became the norm in both computer games and the most popular computer science applications.

Easter eggs

One of the most famous Easter eggs is the live duel fought between the *icons* of Microsoft *Word* and Corel *WordPerfect*, which was triggered by creating an empty macro named SPIFF in Word and then clicking on the credits of Word itself or on the complete list of the team that developed Windows 95 (simply by clicking on the credits of this software).

SPIFF

In the history of video games, there is one computer game that is better known than any other. Created at the end of the 1970s by Toru Iwatani, *Pac-Man* [59] *was based on an ancient Japanese folk tale.*

Pac-Man

The basic idea behind the game was to move the Pac-Man around a maze using four keys (forward, backward, left, right) in order to make it eat as many "dots" and other "eatable" items as possible whilst avoiding the ghosts that are trying to kill it.

Pac-Man rapidly become an iconic symbol, appearing in reviews, newspapers, on T-shirts, and more. Thanks to its great success, Pac-Man was ported to many platforms. I remember that early in the 1980s the source code for a version written in Pascal was for the Hewlett Packard 9816S, a small workstation used for scientific tasks.

---

59 *Pac-Man*, marketed by NAMCO, was the most popular arcade game of all time. It has sold over 300,000 units around the world, even ignoring all of the counterfeit Pac-Man products that have been sold. More than 100,000 of these were sold in the United States alone. The game was originally called *Puck Man*, but it was soon renamed Pac-Man after the company realised that vandals could easily modify the letter "P" to an "F"!

The concept of a sequel

Fig. 13.12 Pac-Man® (by NAMCO, 1980)

Fig. 13.13 SONY® magnetic tape factory

In addition, Pac-Man was one of the first video games to spawn a sequel (in fact many: Ms. Pac-Man, Pac-Man Plus, Super Pac-Man, Mr. & Mrs. Pac-Man, Baby Pac-Man, Jr. Pac-Man, Professor Pac-Man, Pac & Pal, Pac-Land, Pac-Mania, Pac-Attack, Pac-Man 2, Pac-Intimate, Pac-Man VR, Pac-Man Ghost Zones…).

Innovation can even come from consolidated companies with great historical traditions. Magnavox[60], the company that produced the first video game console, is a company owned by Philips. A number of companies that are over a hundred years old, like Nintendo, have therefore been given a new lease of life by the domestic video games market.

And then we come to Sony[61], the company founded by Akio Morita and Masaru Ibuka. The company initially dealt with magnetic tapes, but the real turning point in the history of Sony was its acquisition, for $25,000, of the rights to produce the transistor outside the US and then apply it as a revolutionary basic component of the first consumer electronics product: *the portable battery-operated radio*.

From that time onward the name Sony became synonymous with portable radio. Later on, Sony also became the first company to sell a portable audio cassette player (the *Walkman*), and a portable CD player (the *Discman*). However, it entered the MP3 player market at a relatively late stage.

More recently, Sony entered the mobile phone and mobile entertainment market, where the company benefits from both its technological know-how as well as the entertainment divisions of the firm, including Sony Music, Sony Entertainment and Dreamworks.

Sony, Microsoft and Nintendo are currently the key players in the computer games market, due to the popularity of consoles like *PlayStation* and the *X-Box* as well as mobile consoles like the *PlayStation Portable (PSP)*, *Game Boy Advance* and the revolutionary *WII*.

---

60 In 1971 Magnavox acquired Baer's television technology from Sanders Associates and began to develop the *Odyssey* device, a plug-in device that transformed the TV into a video game console.

61 History of Sony: http://www.sony.net/Fun/SH/. Initially called Tokyo Telecommunications Engineering Company, the name of the company was changed to *Sony* in the 1950s. "Sony" is a deformation of the Latin term "sonus".

Fig. 13.14 Nintendo *WII* (photo by the author)

13.9 The History of Computer Games Viewed From an Application Perspective

One of the first games to appear on computer screens[62] was chess, an optimal exercise in the "art of programming" (Knuth 1968), featuring well-defined rules, a wide variety of strategies, and an equally large archive of solutions.

This game also already has its own standard alphanumeric syntax that is commonly used by chess players. This helped software developers to find a consolidated solution based on alphanumeric interfaces before the advent of graphical interfaces. Indeed, this game is still used as an aid when developing refined applications.

Close to the end of the 1970s, *simulation games* based on a pure textual interface were introduced and became popular. These represented an interesting combination of adventure novels with video games. Titles included *Adventure, Dwarf's Mines*, and *Zork*: *"You are in a large square room with tall ceilings. On the south wall is an enormous mirror which fills the entire wall. There are exits on the other three sides of the room."* Zork was an interactive novel. It unleashed the imagination of the player, creating a personal experience of living through the adventure. It was one of a number of such games created by Scott Adams, who in 1979 also devised *Adventureland,* another textual game,

Adventureland by Scott Adams

---

62 Early on, computer displays were not very popular and so the first games of computer chess we played using printouts.

13 Computer Games, Edutainment and Theme Parks   173

The origins of textual games

which opened up this market and established *Adventure International*, a company that greatly influenced the world of computer games in the early 1980s.

Textual games originated the middle of 1970s, when Will Crowther, a computer programmer and keen speleologist who had just divorced, created a virtual cave exploration based on a textual interface for his daughters.

This application, called *Colossal Cave Adventure* (often shortened to *Adventure*), offered a guided tour of a cave. The guide was able to introduce different phases of the tour via a natural written language interface. The system was able to accept two-word sentences as inputs (i.e. very close to natural language).

Crowther's daughters' were really impressed and passionate about the game. One of the most exciting features of it was the ability to talk with the computer in almost natural language, be understood, and then receive a reply back from the computer.

Some time later, a student from Stanford, Don Woods, found the preliminary version of this game on a University mainframe. Don enhanced both the content and the functionality of the game and put it onto the ARPANET (a forerunner of the Internet).

Scott Adams was among the people that found this game on the network. It inspired him to write *Adventureland*, the first commercial video game (as far as we know). The code had to be very compact in order to run on the minimal computer resources available at that time.

Indeed it was not until the end of the 1970s that microcomputing pioneers created the first microcomputers, which were based on eight-bit chips equipped with four or eight kilobytes of random access memory (RAM), a TV video adapter, plus an analogue mass storage system based on compact audio cassettes.

Fig. 13.15 Commodore *PET* (photo by the author)

As we have already seen, one of the first computer games to take advantage of a graphical interface was *Pong*, followed by several generations of *Space Invaders*[63].

Following work done by *Sinclair* and *PET,* some games with better graphics were made available for the *TI99* (1981) and the *Commodore 64* (1982). These games made use of hardware *video RAM* (VRAM) and software *sprites*.

At this point we should again mention the incredibly popular *Pac-Man* (1980) game from this period, and the revolutionary game *Tetris,* released in 1988 (designed in 1985).

Since their conception, computer game creation has been a programming exercise, concerning input/output functions, natural language interfaces, and algorithm and data structure efficiency.

In more recent times the graphical interface has become increasingly relevant, and artificial intelligence[64] has assumed an enhanced role in the implementation of strategies and rules.

Thanks to the universality of video games they were some of the first software applications developed, distributed and sold in the marketplace. The video game interface was also one of the first de facto standards in information technology, from the definitions of the function keys (F1, F2...) to the use of specific keys such as ESC, J, K, I, M, Enter and others.

The great potential of this market was apparent from the moment that the first video games were developed by home computer programmers and distributed within their communities as *source code*[65]. In a short period of time they became commercial products[66], and were sometimes manufactured by small companies in which the average age of the management did not exceed 24 years old.

---

63   In 1982 General Consumer Electronics (GCE) produced and distributed the *Vectrex*, the first and also only home video console based on vector graphics (it included a nine-inch monitor), in Italy. The *Vectrex* was bundled with the game *Minestorm* (a beautiful clone of *Asteroids*) and analogue joystick controllers with four keys.

64   Sophisticated technologies can often find useful application in games; consider, for example, artificial intelligence, game theory, artificial life, virtual truth, genetic algorithms, neural networks, computer graphics etc.

65   Very often written in assembler, although sometimes in PASCAL.

66   One of the first commercial video games that was intended for home computers was *Tombstone City* (1981) for the TI99/4A, which was distributed in assembler source code. This game made use of some of the special features of the platform: video RAM memory, software sprites and a speech synthesizer.

13 Computer Games, Edutainment and Theme Parks

13.10 Other Kinds of Entertainment

Let us now consider alternative forms of entertainment to games. We will begin by considering cinema.

Cinema originated a little over a hundred years ago, and can be described as the art of projecting a series of static images onto a screen in such a way as to create the illusion of movement. This approach is an ingenious way of introducing a sense of time into imagery (note that this had been attempted before; for example, consider the sequences of static images employed in many frescoes and by ballad singers).

Cinema quickly gained popularity due to the natural *linearity* of *movies* (i.e. moving pictures) and thus the natural tendency to convert linear stories, such as literary works, into movies. Since then, some artists have attempted to break up the usual linear flow of time in their books or movies using various tricks or devices (e.g. flashbacks, parallel storylines) with varying degrees of success.

Today we have *digital multiscreen theatres, DVD* and *home theatre*. How has this changed our approach to cinema? According to experts, there are at least two ways to enjoy visual experiences: *privately* and *in a group*. Some types of visual performance are best enjoyed as *group experiences*: sports events, pop concerts, horror films… Others are more applicable to *single* or *small homogeneous groups*. Therefore, large multiscreens will be able to offer sport events and pop concerts, while authored movies may be preferably watched in home theatres.

Private viewing versus group viewing

Another recent development in the movie industry is its increasingly close links to the games industry. Movies that spawn games and games that spawn movies are commonplace.

Fig. 13.16 Dante Symphony, Ravenna Festival (visual director: Paolo Micciché)

For a long time the Hollywood *industrial pipeline* accustomed us to watching a movie, then reading a book based on the movie, buying merchandise linked to the movie, and playing a game derived from the movie. Today, an increasing number of simulation games allow us to see sequences from the film from different viewpoints, as dictated by the player. In the future, such computer games could/will provide companions to or even replace some action movies. However, thus far attempts to transfer famous video games to movies have not been as successful as one might have hoped. Watching the movies of *Tomb Rider*, *Final Fantasy* and *Resident Evil* often triggers an impulse in the player/audience to move a nonexistent joystick and shoot!

13.11 Creative Activities

Digital technology has dramatically increased the opportunities for *creative people* to express themselves, by either offering new forms of expression or drastically reducing the production costs associated with existing ones.

Significant examples include music and video composition, where production costs have plummeted, allowing young talent to realise their own productions. In addition, in the field of computer games, the use of easy access[67] technologies has allowed talented people that are not particularly skilled in computer science to express themselves.

Digital technologies, especially the Internet, have completely overturned the concept of commercial and distribution goods, since *any product that can assume the digital format can be cloned*[68] *an essentially unlimited number of times at almost no cost.*

Key aspects of the digital format

This aspect also means that we must reconsider some ontological aspects. An interesting comparison can be made with the introduction of the printing press, which allowed written content to be reproduced a great number of times at minimal cost in comparison to the previous approach to copying content, based on hand-written copies, by reducing the content to sequences of lines of text[69].

---

67 For example Macromedia *Flash*.

68 *Cloning* is perfect reproduction without any·loss of quality. This aspect has deep ontological repercussions; digital objects represent a completely new class of objects. The concept of ownership of the original becomes meaningless—in the digital world access means ownership.

69 As observed by Prof. Francisco Antinucci, in such a context the manuscripts produced by amanuenses should not be considered to be books; they are more like paintings created by an artist. A person that was well informed about the content of the manuscript of interest commissioned an amanuensis to recreate it. The copy was usually personalised and refined to order.

What happened subsequently is well known: text prevailed over other communication formats, influencing most information transmission to be linear in format. Today *digital objects* can easily be cloned and transmitted instantaneously over long distances, making new ways of accessing information feasible. This has made access to information much easier than most would have thought possible up to a few years ago.

While some may worry about the incredible availability of information and ability to communicate provided by technology, the way that it greatly encourages the self-expression and creativity of young people is surely one of its remarkable benefits. The network provides *a great melting pot* of common interest groups and forums, enabled by content sharing services. Many such groups are born and die every day; the network is constantly changing.

13.12 Smart Phones

Lately there has been an interesting convergence between the *portable game console market* and the *smart phone market*. Nokia and Sony Ericsson have produced a generation of portable devices with audio and video functionality that are able to satisfy the requirements of players who habitually use handheld game consoles to play quality games at market prices. The smart phone is now considered the ideal device for popularising paid *content* delivery via the TLC market model.

A market that seemed dominated by Palm devices up until a few years ago is now driven by smart phones. This has been achieved by distributing large numbers of smart phones that are comparable (in terms of functionality) to handheld PCs. In addition, it is very easy to promote new products using the *telephone market model*. Paid content delivery through mobile phones represents a new business opportunity. Services that can be provided include information, music, television on demand and video entertainment, together with high-quality games.

Mobile content is already a driver in the mobile communications market; telecom operators are competing to provide better contents and services. Some key players are in a position to offer a number of integrated services since they own a range of different entertainment-related assets[70].

---

[70] For example, beyond its mobile phones, can offer music and movie services because it owns other companies from these markets.

II The General Technological Framework

Fig. 13.17 *Classical Spectacular*, featuring state-of-the-art lasers and lighting designed by Durham Marenghi (photo by Wing-Chi Poon)

13.13 Theme Parks and High-Tech Shows

Theme parks are one of the key players in the so-called "spare-time economy". Among the most well known (and oldest) are the Disney Parks, inspired (according to Walt Disney, their founder) by Tivoli Park in Copenhagen (Denmark). Today there are a number of similar or derived experiences that can be subdivided into *theme parks*, *media centres* and *technology and science centres*.

Media centres are a newer concept than theme parks. They enable visitors to try out new media and related technologies. This concept developed from the idea of *facility sharing*, particularly of expensive or group/mass-oriented applications.

Media centres

Technology and science centres were conceived by Frank Oppenheimer, who *wanted* a place where people that were not directly involved in working with science and technology could experiment with the principles of physics and other sciences in a "hands on" manner. In 1998 Oppenheimer inaugurated the *Exploratorium* in San Francisco (CA, USA), which was the first science centre to use this approach.

Technology and science centres

Today's key phrase is the "live experience". Operators want the experiences delivered by parks to be remembered and extended as much as possible in time and space, with the ultimate aim being "continuous feeding" of the user, resulting in a *virtuous circle*. In other words, the user might want to extend the experience and is thus motivated to undergo the experience again to gather more information, or is encouraged to try other similar experiences.

Light/laser and music shows represent another interesting sector. Such shows should be performed in both closed and open environments. The ancestors of these include the *Son et Lumiére* shows, such as the traditional one in Luxor (Egypt) or the magnificent one performed in the Grand Place in Brussels.

As an extension of the concept, each summer there is an international festival that celebrates the best show of pyrotechnical art—*Art Pyrotechnique*[71] in Cannes (France). These shows are a mixture of fireworks, lasers and music.

---

[71] The Festival de l'Art Pyrotechnique takes place in July and August in Cannes (France).

Indoor shows are very popular in high-tech theatres such as the ones included in science centres. For example, the *Pacific Science Centre* in Seattle offers laser shows based on contemporary music, such as the *Smashing Pumpkins Laser Show*.

Fig. 13.18 Live event at CeBIT, Hannover (photo by the author)

Fig. 13.19 Classical Laser Show

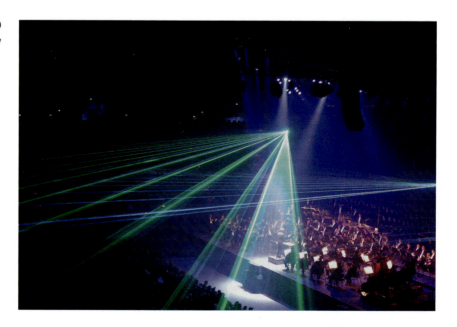

180 *II The General Technological Framework*

14 Customer Relationship Management

Customer relationship management (CRM) is a very well known and successful customer management strategy that is commonly used by enterprises but is usually neglected by museums and *memory institutions*, even though it is applicable to the cultural sector and the potential benefits of doing so are significant.

The CRM approach helps organisations to be more competitive, to maximise profits, reduce duplication of effort, effectively store information and make it accessible to every employee, and present a consolidated profile to customers, partners and visitors.

A CRM solution includes the methodologies, technology and capabilities that support an enterprise in managing customer relationships. A significant part of this task is directly related to developing the information and communications technology that will enable organisations to gather a greater amount of information on their customers, including their behaviour and ways to contact them, as well as providing efficient methods and tools to manage this information.

Therefore, the general idea of CRM is to enable organisations to better manage their customers through the introduction of reliable systems, processes and procedures. When this approach is applied, the organisation will gather a greater amount of information about customers and business contacts than ever before. This structured and detailed information will help in targeting products and services and developing new products and markets.

Customer relationship management is a corporate-level strategy which focuses on creating and maintaining lasting relationships with its customers. Although there are several commercial CRM software packages on the market that support the implementation of the CRM strategy, CRM ultimately requires a change in an organisation's philosophy, resulting in an emphasis on the customer, rather than just a change in the technology used by the organisation.

A successful CRM strategy cannot be implemented overnight. Changes must occur at all levels, including policies and processes, front-of-house customer service, employee training, marketing, systems and information management; all aspects of the business must be reshaped to be customer-driven.

A successful CRM strategy will not happen overnight

Without an appropriate CRM solution, customers may have a fragmented and even contradictory view of the organisation, increasing the possibility of inefficiencies arising due to the limited or inappropriate use of customer information or other vital resources.

A "good" CRM

To be effective, the CRM process needs to be integrated end-to-end across marketing, sales, and customer service. A good CRM program needs to:

- Identify customer success factors
- Create a customer-based culture
- Adopt customer-based measures
- Develop an end-to-end process to serve customers
- Recommend what questions to ask to help a customer solve a problem
- Recommend what to tell a customer with a complaint about a purchase
- Track all aspects of selling to customers and prospects as well as customer support.

The full set of information directly or indirectly gathered from customers must be carefully considered because it represents a relevant, unique and important company asset that is able to provide real benefit to the business.

15 Smart Labels, Smart Tags and RFID

Smart labels and smart tags are often mentioned in the field of cultural applications. Amongst such smart tags and labels, *radiofrequency identification* (RFID) tags are the most popular. RFID-based systems were originally (in the 1960s) developed by large manufacturers and retailers that wanted a way to track their inventories through supply chains.

Uniquely identifying specific objects offers clear benefits in terms of identification, classification, counting, organisation, and many other desirable activities; even tracking and discovering stolen objects.

From a technological perspective, there are two types of RFID tags: *active* and *passive*.

Active and passive tags

Active tags provide an identification number and possibly some additional information, such as the transportation history of the tagged object. They usually require power. *Passive tags* provide only an identification number, which is emitted when the tags are irradiated with radio waves from a specialised reader.

The electric field radiated by the reader antenna *supplies electrical power* to the tag and *establishes an asymmetric communication link* between the reader and the tag. Once the tag has harvested all of the power it needs from the reader's emanations, it starts to communicate (the ID code) by modulating the reflected electric field.

The ability to harvest electric power from external emitters/illuminators makes passive RFID particularly appealing. They don't require batteries, wired power supplies, or dedicated radio transmitters, so they can be very small and very cheap, providing a relevant building block for any mass application based on the unique identification of different items.

There are already pilot RFID applications in museums and archaeological sites. Today's RFID technology promises orders of magnitude greater efficiency and accuracy than was possible with previous identification technologies.

When considering identification technologies suited to mass application, most of us will immediately think of bar codes, the most diffuse and easy-to-manage identification system. Nevertheless, even though *passive RFID* systems are often cited as competition for *bar code systems,* we should underline the fact that *passive RFID* tags are much more than replacements for bar codes.

Fig. 15.1 RFID passive tag (photo by the author)

The basic features of passive tags, such as wireless communication, makes them more flexible for tracking items because they can be read without the need for line-of-sight communication and from much further away, and they can also hold significant amounts of data (which can be written by readers if required), enabling each tag to carry its own database. In addition they can easily be embedded in objects without marring their appearance—a particularly relevant feature when dealing with artefacts.

Recent generations of some tags also include sensing capabilities that make it possible to monitor environmental information. Such a feature is very relevant to the field of immovable heritage monitoring, for environmental purposes and for security reasons.

Wireless networks of sensors

One interesting and well-known application of RFID sensors is termed the *wireless sensor network (WSN)*. Such networks are very useful for monitoring environmental information, including physical parameters and security measures.

Fig. 15.2 Use of a handheld barcode reader in archives (photo by the author)

Fig. 15.3 RFID reader for drugs (photo by the author)

16 Standards and Protocols for Interoperability

<interoperability>
ability of a system (such as a weapons system) to work with or use the parts or equipment of another system

Merriam–Webster dictionary

<interoperability> (computer science)
meaning the ability of the user of one member of a group of disparate systems (all having the same functionality) to work with any of the systems of the group with equal ease ...

Encyclopædia Britannica

Interoperability is currently one of the most popular buzzwords used in the ICT industry. This focus on interoperability and *interworkability* has arisen due to the spread of the Internet and the increasing need to get different applications to "talk" to one another. Without a way to exchange information, high-tech systems literally can't communicate with each other, and if they can't communicate, they can't work—interoperate—with each other.

The need to exchange data between different applications has long been a common requirement in several key sectors, such as research, banking, computer-aided design, etc. Information systems often *speak* different languages or dialects. This happens not only when the products that need to communicate come from different suppliers, but even among different generations or variants of the same product.

Different languages and dialects

Offline information exchange between different CAD[72] systems was, for instance, a key issue in the *space* and *automotive* sectors. While an interoperability problem might be due to a minor incompatibility, its impact on a system can be dramatic, and the task of getting all the relevant parties to participate in solving the interoperability problem can often turn into a nightmare.

The availability of *intercommunication* has enabled incredible new scenarios based on information linking and exchange. *Interoperability* is both the exchange of information and its utilisation.

---

72 Computer-aided design.

Within a given company, there are usually many different systems that all talk different languages. At the same time, companies are spending huge amounts of money buying and testing new systems that need to be able to interoperate with their existing infrastructures.

There are therefore compelling reasons to create information technology products that can be guaranteed to interoperate (e.g. digital signature, digital certificates, etc.). This can only be achieved if all of these products conform to the same, publicly available, standards (*open standards*).

16.1 More on Interoperability

Interoperability can be regarded as an ongoing process of ensuring that the systems, procedures and culture of an organisation are managed in such a way as to maximise the opportunities for the exchange and reuse of information. It influences the long-term accessibility to information.

There are many forms of interoperability, including:

- *Technical interoperability*: the development of communication, transport, storage and representation standards
- *Semantic interoperability*: the use of different terms to describe similar concepts can cause problems in communication, program execution and data transfer
- *Political/human interoperability*: the decision to make resources more widely available also has implications for organisations, their staff and end-users
- *Intercommunity interoperability*: there is an increasing need to access to information from a wide range of sources and communities
- *International interoperability*: when working with other countries there are variations in standards, communication problems, language barriers, differences in communication styles and a lack of common ground.

17 Data Tags and the Semantic Web

Tagging is a very common practice in information technology. Every time information must be transferred between different data structures it is a good idea to *tag* (i.e. label) the information in order to make sure that the destination understands the context of the information and therefore categorises it correctly (in the same way as done by the source).

More recently, tagging has become a widespread activity. The spread of the World Wide Web and the increasing interest in HTML and languages and dialects derived from it has encouraged the use of tags.

17.1 Markup Languages and Data Tagging

A *markup language* is a structured set of tags that are embedded within text in order to label specific parts of it. The reason for doing this is to provide useful information about these parts of the text.

The tagged text in a document is usually called the *source code*, or simply the *code* for that document. Specific attributes (e.g. "bold", "italic", etc.) can be switched on and off using tags.

While some markup languages, such as *Microsoft RTF*, are human-readable, easy-to-understand languages, generally speaking they are not human-readable. Of course, this could be a potential disadvantage if we use a markup language to preserve content and services[73].

RTF

Markup languages can be *specific* or *generalised*. Specific languages are used for specific applications or devices (e.g. XBRL extensible business reporting language, XMP extensible metadata platform by Adobe Inc.), while generalised ones describe the structure and the meaning of the text in the document without specifying how the text should be used. This means that the language is generic enough to be useful for a range of applications. Documents written in a generalised markup language are usually easy to port from application to application.

Specific versus generalised markup languages

Once a document has been *coded* the only other item required is a processor or *renderer* that is able to read and interpret the code. Renderers are usually included in browsers, word processors and other specific appliances.

The renderer

---

[73] For further details, please refer to Sect. 19.5 Long Term Preservation of Digital Archives

From a historical point of view *markup languages* were born in the world of the printed word; even the term "markup" is a concatenation of the words *mark* and *up,* clearly referencing the traditional way of managing a document that is to be formatted and printed.

"Marking up", which refer to the act of tagging digital documents, is performed for two main reasons: to define and modify the look and format of bare text, and to structure the document before it is outputted to some medium, such as a printer or a webpage.

Generalized Markup Language (GML)

Generalized markup language was first introduced by Dr. C.F. Goldfarb and two of his colleagues, who proposed a method of describing text that was not specific to a particular application or device.

Two general rules were introduced:
- The markup should describe the structure of the document and not its formatting or style characteristics
- The syntax of the markup should be strictly enforced so that the code can easily be read by a software program or by a human.

These rules resulted in the development by IBM of the *Document Composition Facility Generalized Markup Language* (*DCF GML,* or *GML* for short).

Standardized Generalized Markup Language (SGML)

Then, building on GML, the *Standardized Generalized Markup Language (SGML)* was developed by the *International Standard Organisation* (ISO[74]) in 1986. SGML is an enhanced version of GML with more features. For example, it:
- Identifies the character set to be used within the document (e.g. ISO 646, ISO 8859)
- Provides a way to identify the objects (entities[75]) used within the document. Entities are very useful when some items of text or data appear more than once in the document
- Provides a way to incorporate external data into the document.

Hypertext Markup Language (HTML)

Hypertext Markup Language (HTML) is an application of SGML; that is, HTML was created using the SGML standard and its methods. Of course, the two languages are different; for instance, there are no closing tags in SGML and one of the main differences between SGML and HTML is the lack of any reference or tag specifying the look and format of the document in SGML.

SGML addresses document structure and meaning. Tags in an SGML document can be created on the fly because the language is extensible. For example,

---

[74] The International Standards Organisation (ISO) was founded in 1947 and represents some 130 countries (see http://www.iso.ch).

[75] By declaring the entity once in the document, any changes to the declaration will result in all of the instances of the entity present in the document being updated simultaneously.

II The General Technological Framework

if I needed to create an SGML document containing bibliography references, I could create tags for *author, title, publisher, year of publication, ISBN, etc.*

Since HTML is an application of SGML that is devoted to formatting and publishing documents on the World Wide Web, it is not extensible (in other words we cannot create another language from HTML). Extensions must instead be defined and standardised universally to ensure that they can be decoded and understood by browsers and renderers[76].

Recently, another relative of SGML has gained prominence: *XML* (Extensible Markup Language). Its extensibility means that XML is much more closely related to SGML than to HTML. XML can be considered to be a subset of SGML; it qualifies as a *metalanguage,* meaning that other markup languages or vocabularies can be developed from it.

eXtensible Markup Language (XML)

17.2   Content, Structure, Format and Reference

The following sections will review the history of data and tagging, the need for *metadata (data about data, which is* crucial to the implementation of distributed datasets), and the origins of RDF and XML. We will illustrate the evolution from compound documents to separate documents containing pure text, logical structure, formatting rules, hyperlinks and why we need ontologies and semantics.

The reason for tagging text documents is closely related to the layers of logic and the functions associated with the document (pure text, logic structure, formatting and links).

Content is one of the first components. It usually consists of text and graphical components. The *sentence* is the largest grammatical text structure (ignoring poetry and other fields in which there are additional rules for linking together words and sentences into larger structures or *templates*). Once we have sentences of text it is useful to have a way of structuring them in order to make the full text more readable and comprehensible.

Structure

These *structures* can be hierarchical, such as volumes, chapters, paragraphs, subparagraphs, etc. However, it is also important to specify the formatting (*fonts, sizes, attributes and positions, indents, justifications)* of text and images in order to make them as readable as possible.

Format

Last but not least, when creating *hypermedia*, we might want to add some *hyperlinks between documents or different parts of the same document.*

Hyperlinks

Before the advent of electronic publishing, the draft copy of a paper-based manuscript or typed document would be reviewed, edited and annotated or marked up by hand. The draft would then undergo more revisions and amend-

The traditional workflow

---

76   This happened very early on in the history of HTML to enable it to display pictures (GIF, JPEG, etc.) and tables, perform justification, etc. ...

ments, sometimes leading to the complete retyping of the whole manuscript in order to create carbon copies of it for review or distribution purposes.

After this long and tedious process a list of specifications that assigned formatting and style preferences for various parts of the document would be included as handwritten notes.

The next step would then be a typeset proof of the formatted and laid out document, leading to the final approval to print. The typesetter then set the text (i.e. the fonts, margins, styles, and justification) based on the annotations and markup, and performed copy-fitting calculations to make sure that the printed page was readable.

This was the usual workflow before the digital revolution. Now, however, a number of the steps based on manual work are no longer needed. Most of the revisions is usually made before the draft is even printed.

Since the development of the first *word processor* or formatting tool, the way to perform this task has been based on digitally marking up the content. Initially the markup tags were mixed with the content and were visible, whereas *WYSISYG* the final result of the reformatting was not. Then *WYSISYG* (what you see is *(what you see is* what you get) software was developed, that made the tags invisible and the *what you get)* layout visible.

XHTML (Extensible Hypertext Markup Language) is a general-purpose markup language that is designed to represent documents used for a wide range of purposes on the World Wide Web. In order to achieve this goal it does not attempt to be all things to all people by providing every possible markup idiom, but instead it supplies a generally useful set of elements.

17.3 Data and Metadata

Metadata are usually described as data about data, or information about other information. Why do we need this additional information?

One application that requires the creation of a so-called *metadata layer* is the integration of several databanks in order to offer a set of added value services that require the collaborative use of the information stored in the databanks.

In an extension to this scenario, it may be necessary to integrate the data from various services provided by different organisations. In order to integrate the information provided by the different organisations and so obtain the added value services, we need to place a *metadata* layer on top of the databanks which redirects user queries appropriately and thus enables the requested information to be retrieved.

190 *II The General Technological Framework*

17.4 Semantic Web

The "semantic" vision of the Web was introduced by Tim Berners-Lee in 1998 on the occasion of the WWW conference held in Brisbane, Australia. Following the definition given by the *World Wide Web Consortium*[77]:

The Semantic Web provides a common framework that allows data to be shared and reused across application, enterprise, and community boundaries. It is a collaborative effort led by W3C with participation from a large number of researchers and industrial partners. It is based on the Resource Description Framework (RDF), which integrates a variety of applications using XML for syntax and uniform resource identifiers (URIs) for naming.

The *WWW* is a web of information and data—a *world of information*— containing spreadsheets, text documents, pictures, databases and other data. However, even though the Web is a huge mine of information, if I ask for two data sources on the Web to work together (i.e. interact) to give me an answer to a query—to find the best combination of train schedule and bus service, say— there is almost no chance that they will be able to do so. The reason for this is answered by the W3C in a discussion of what is known as the *Semantic Web*:

"Why not? Because we don't have a web of data. Because data is controlled by applications, and each application keeps it to itself.

The Semantic Web is about two things. It is about common formats for inter- change of data, where on the original Web we only had interchange of docu- ments. Also it is about language for recording how the data relates to real world objects. That allows a person, or a machine, to start off in one database, and then move through an unending set of databases which are connected not by wires but by being about the same thing."

Common formats and a language that specifies how data relates to real objects

17.4.1 Semantic Objects, Webpages and Search Engines

The *Semantic Web* is a project that intends to create a *universal medium for information exchange* by placing documents with computer-processable mean- ing (semantics) on the World Wide Web.

Currently under the direction of the Web's creator, Tim Berners-Lee of the W3C, the Semantic Web extends the Web through the use of standards, markup languages and related processing tools. At present, the World Wide Web is based primarily on documents written in *HTML*, a markup language that is used to code text interspersed with multimedia objects such as images and interactive forms.

---

[77] The World Wide Web Consortium (W3C): http://www.w3c.org.

HTML, as it is generally deployed, has limited ability to classify the blocks of text on a page, apart from the roles they play in a typical document's organization and in the desired visual layout.

RDF and OWL The Semantic Web addresses this shortcoming, using the descriptive technologies of the *Resource Description Framework* (RDF), the *Web Ontology Language* (OWL), and the data-centric, customisable *Extensible Markup Language* (XML). These technologies are combined to provide descriptions that supplement or replace the content of web documents.

XHTML Thus, content may manifest itself as descriptive data stored in Web-accessible databases, or as markup within documents, particularly those written in *Extensible HTML* (XHTML) interspersed with XML, or, more often, purely in XML, with layout/rendering cues stored separately.

The machine-readable descriptions enable content managers to add meaning to the content, thereby facilitating automated information gathering and research by computers.

The Semantic Web comprises the standards and tools of *XML, XML Schema, RDF, RDF Schema and OWL*.

The *OWL Web Ontology Language Overview* describes the function and relationship of each of these components of the Semantic Web. *XML* provides a surface syntax for structured documents, but imposes no semantic constraints on the meaning of these documents. *XML Schema* is a language for restricting the structures of XML documents.

RDF is a simple data model that defines objects ("resources") and how they are related. An RDF-based model can be represented in XML syntax. *RDF Schema* is a vocabulary for describing the properties and classes of RDF resources, along with the semantics for the generalization-hierarchies of these properties and classes.

OWL adds more vocabulary for describing properties and classes: among others, relations between classes (e.g. disjointedness), cardinality (e.g. "exactly one"), equality, richer typing of properties, characteristics of properties (e.g. symmetry), and enumerated classes.

How to enhance the usability and usefulness of the Web The intent is to enhance the usability and usefulness of the Web and its interconnected resources by:

- *Marking documents up with semantic information* (an extension of the HTML <meta> tags used in today's web pages to supply information for web search engines using web crawlers). This could be machine-readable information about the human-readable content of the document (such as the creator, title, description, etc., of the document) or it could be pure metadata representing a set of facts (such as resources and services elsewhere in the site). It should be noted that anything that can be identified with a *uniform resource identifier* (URI) can be described, so the Semantic Web can rationalise animals, people, places, ideas, etc.

- *Using common metadata vocabularies* (ontologies) and maps between vocabularies that allow document creators to work out how to mark up their documents so that agents can use the information in the supplied metadata (so that the author of a webpage won't be confused with the author of a book that is the subject of a book review).

- *Using automated agents* to perform tasks for users of the Semantic Web using this metadata.
- *Using web-based services* (often with agents of their own) to supply information specifically to agents (for example, a trust service that an agent could contact if some online store has a history of poor service or spamming).
- *Using semantic search engines* that are capable of retrieving information by interpreting the associated metadata.

17.5   Advanced Online Services

More than fifteen years after its birth, the World Wide Web is now undergoing a transformation—it is evolving. A new generation of web services are enhancing the utility of the Web, "updating" it: creating a *Web 2.0*. One of the main characteristics of Web 2.0 is an increased level of *interaction* between users and the Web and amongst users themselves.

Web 2.0 and interaction

A short list of services usually considered to be part of Web 2.0 might be:
- Blogs
- Wikis
- RSS/Atom feeds
- Semantic objects, webpages, search engines
- Social bookmarking
- Web conferencing.

17.5.1   Blogs

A *blog* is a website where entries are made in *journal style* and displayed in a reverse chronological order.

Blogs often provide commentary or news about a particular subject, such as food, politics, or local news, while others function as more personal online diaries. A typical *blog* combines text, images, and links to other blogs, webpages, and other media related to the topic of the blog.

Most blogs are primarily textual, although some focus on photographs (*photoblogs*), videos (*vlogs*), music (*MP3 blogs*), or general audio (*podcasting*), and are part of a wider network of what are usually called *social media*.

Social media

A variety of systems are used to create and maintain blogs. There are web applications dedicated to blog creation and management, which eliminate the need for bloggers (users that create and manage blogs) to be experienced programmers. Since they have web interfaces, such systems allow travellers to blog from anywhere in the world via the Internet, and they allow users to create blogs without having to maintain their own server. These systems provide tools that allow users to maintain their blogs without the need to be online while composing or editing *posts* (i.e. "journal entries", which might consist of passages of text or other media or both, and often include links to other resources on the Web).

Blog creation tools and blog hosting are also provided by some web hosting companies, Internet service providers, online publications and Internet portals.

17 Data Tags and the Semantic Web   193

Some advanced users have developed custom *blogging* systems from scratch using server-side software, and often implement membership management and password-protected areas.

A blog post typically consists of the following:

- *Title:* the main title, or headline, of the post
- *Body:* main content of the post
- *Permalink:* the URL of the full, individual article
- *Post date:* date and time the post was published.

A blog post optionally includes the following:

- *Comments and polling/rating:* comments and polls allow blog readers (and bloggers) to discuss posts or provide feedback about them (to rate them or point out errors, for example)
- *Categories (tags):* a list of words or terms that quickly establish what the entry is about (i.e. keywords); these are useful when searching for posts about a particular topic
- *Trackback and/or pingback:* links to other sites/blogs that refer to this post.

17.5.2 Wikis

The *wiki* is another type of enabling technology that was first introduced by the WWW community a few years ago. It is a type of website that allows visitors to easily add, remove and generally edit some or all of its content, sometimes without the need for registration. This ease of interaction and operation makes the *wiki* an effective tool for collaborative authoring. The term *wiki* can also refer to the collaborative software used to create and maintain the wiki (i.e. the *wiki engine*).

Users of the wiki do not need to know the HTML language. Furthermore, most wikis record the changes made to them, so that at any time a page can be reverted to any of its previous states if required.

The wiki system may also include various tools that provide users with an easy way to monitor the constantly changing state of the *wiki,* as well as a place to discuss and resolve disagreements over *wiki* content.

The nature of a wiki means that its content can sometimes be misleading, as users can accidentally or intentionally add incorrect information to it. Many public *wikis* will allow completely unrestricted access; anyone can contribute to the site without having to be a registered user of the wiki. This contrasts with the approach adopted by various other types of interactive websites, such as Internet forums or chat sites, where users must register and "log on" if they want to post (and sometimes to view posts too). The open approach adopted by wikis therefore encourages new users to participate and contribute.

Wiki pages are written collectively in a simple markup language using a web browser. These pages are usually highly interconnected via hyperlinks. Therefore, in effect, a *wiki* is actually a very simple, easy-to-use user-maintained database. The information in the database can be added to, edited, or searched for.

Fig. 17.1 *Wikipedia* online encyclopaedia

Recent wiki engines allow "WYSIWYG" editing, usually by means of JavaScript or an ActiveX control that translates editing commands entered via a graphical interface, such as "make this text bold", into the corresponding HTML tags.

In those implementations, the markup for the HTML version of the edited page is generated and submitted to the server transparently, and the user is shielded from the technical details. Simple *wikis* allow only basic text formatting, whereas more complex ones provide support for tables, images, formulae, and even interactive elements such as polls and games.

17.5.3 RSS/Atom Feeds

A *web feed* is a data format used to provide users with frequently updated content. Content distributors syndicate a web feed, thereby allowing users to subscribe to it. Making a collection of *web feeds* accessible in one spot is known as *aggregation*.

In the typical *web feeds* scenario, a content provider publishes a feed link on their site to which end-users can register by running the corresponding *aggregator program* (also called a feed reader or a news reader) on their own machines; this is usually achieved by simply dragging the link from the web browser to the aggregator.

When instructed, the aggregator asks all of the servers in its feed list if they have new content; if so, the aggregator either makes a note of the new content or downloads it. Aggregators can be scheduled to check for new content periodically. It is common to find web feeds on major websites and they are often found on many smaller ones too.

RSS (Really Simple Syndication) is a simple XML-based web feed system that allows users to subscribe to their favourite websites. Using RSS, webmas-

RSS (Really Simple Syndication)

ters can put their content into a standardised format, which can be viewed and organised through *RSS-aware* software or automatically conveyed as new content on another website.

RSS-aware programs are available for various operating systems. *Client-side readers* and *aggregators* are typically constructed as standalone programs or extensions to existing programs such as web browsers.

Web-based feed readers and news aggregators require no software installation and make the user's "feeds" available on any computer with web access. Some aggregators combine existing web feeds into new feeds, for example by taking all items from several eCulture feeds and combining them into a new eCulture feed. There are also search engines for content published via web feeds.

RSS and HTML
The most serious compatibility problem is with HTML markup, because RSS originally did not filter out HTML markup from feeds. As a result, publishers began placing HTML markup into the titles and descriptions of items in their RSS feeds. This behavior has become widely expected of readers, to the point of becoming a *de facto* standard, although there is still some inconsistency in how software handles this markup, particularly in titles. The RSS 2.0 specification was later updated to include examples of entity-encoded HTML, although all prior plain text usages remain valid too.

In response to such issues with RSS (and because the development of RSS 2.0 was delayed), a third group began a new syndication specification, Atom, in June 2003. Their work was later adopted by the Internet Engineering Task *Atom format* Force (IETF), leading to the publication of a specification (RFC 4287) for the *Atom Format* in 2005.

Work on the *Atom Publishing Protocol*, a standards-based protocol for posting to publishing tools, is ongoing. The relative benefits of Atom over the two versions of RSS are that it relies on standard XML features, by specifying a payload container that can handle many different kinds of content unambiguously, and that its specification is maintained by a recognised standards organization.

17.5.4 Social Bookmarking

Social bookmarking is a web-based service, where shared lists of user-created Internet bookmarks are displayed. Such services generally organise their content using semantic tags, which allows users to easily locate, classify, rank, and share Internet resources through the inferences drawn upon grouping and analysing tags.

In a *social bookmarking system*, users store lists of useful Internet resources. These lists are often publicly accessible, and other people with similar interests can view the links by category, tags, or even randomly. Some *social bookmarking* systems allow for privacy on a per-bookmark basis.

They also categorize their resources through the use of informally assigned, user-defined keywords or tags. Most *social bookmarking* services allow users to search for bookmarks that are associated with given *tags* and *rank* the resources by the number of users which have bookmarked them.

II The General Technological Framework

Fig. 17.2 *del.icio.us*: social bookmarking

Many *social bookmarking* services also incorporate algorithms that draw inferences from the tag keywords that are assigned to resources by examining the clustering of particular keywords and the relations between keywords.

This system has several advantages over traditional automated resource location and classification software, such as search engine spiders.

All tag-based classification of Internet resources (such as websites) is done by *human beings*, who understand the content of the resource, as opposed to software, which algorithmically attempts to determine the meaning of a resource. This provides for semantically classified tags, which are hard to find with contemporary search engines.

Additionally, as people bookmark resources that they find useful, the most useful resources that bookmarked by the most users. Thus, such a system can *rank* a resource based on its perceived utility. This is arguably a more useful *metric* for end-users than other systems that rank resources based on the number of external links pointing to it.

Since the classification and ranking of resources is a continuously evolving process, many social bookmarking services allow users to subscribe to *syndication feeds* (see the "RSS/Atom Feeds" section above) based on tags or collections of tag terms. This allows subscribers to be made aware of new resources for a given topic as they are noted, tagged, and classified by other users.

17 Data Tags and the Semantic Web

17.5.5 Web Conferencing and VoIP

Web conferencing refers to group meetings or live presentations that are held over the Internet. In the early years of the Internet, the terms *web conferencing* and *computer conferencing* were often used to describe group discussions conducted on a message board (via posted text messages), but nowadays the term is mainly used in relation to *live* or *synchronous* meetings, while discussions on message boards are called *forums*, *message boards*, or *bulletin boards*.

The last ten years have seen the introduction of many different web conferencing tools, some of them more aimed at telecooperation, others at telecommunication in a broader sense. Starting from audio/video and data *peer-to-peer* connections based on ISDN lines, which represented the only way to interact until early in the 1990s, the next step was to take advantage of Internet technology to get better conferencing services.

Some early examples of such software intended for PC platforms were Intel *Pro-share* and Microsoft *Netmeeting*.

In a web conference, each participant uses his/her own computer, and is connected to other participants via the Internet. The characteristic feature of a web conference is *screen sharing*, whereby conference participants see whatever is on the presenter's screen. Usually this is accompanied by voice and video communication obtained by traditional telephone conferencing or through the use of the *Voice over IP (VoIP)* and *webcam technologies*, although sometimes web-based text messaging is used instead of voice-based conferencing.

Other typical features of a web conference include:
- Slide presentations (often created *through* Microsoft *PowerPoint*)
- Application and data sharing, in which participants can cooperatively manipulate a spreadsheet on the presenter's computer
- Web co-browsing
- Annotation (allowing the presenter to highlight or mark items on the display)
- Instant text messaging
- Private and public blackboards
- File sharing
- Polls and surveys.

VoIP and telephony   More recently, a significant innovation was developed from this set of technologies, *VoIP telephony*. This has revolutionised telecommunication since it enables a suite of popular services (*mobile phone telephony, video conferencing, file exchange, instant messaging, SMS and voicemail*) to use the Internet as their communications network. It is also possible to dial up traditional phones (both *wired* and *wireless) using VoIP telephony,* and to buy a *dial-in* number on the traditional phone network, based at a preferred location[78]. Thanks to *wire-*

---

[78] For example, a user could ask for a fixed-line dial-in phone number based in Washington, DC in the US, since this is the users main address; this number can then be called from the traditional telecom network as well as by other VOIP users.

198   **II** *The General Technological Framework*

less connectivity to the Internet (e.g. WiFi) and smart phones, *VoIP telephony* can even be conducted outdoors.

17.6 Advanced W3C Design and Evaluation

Thanks to the incredible success and the spread of the World Wide Web, a number of different devices are connected to the Web in a variety of different ways, and it is used by many different groups of people (e.g. elderly people). As a consequence, the World Wide Web Consortium (W3C) has assigned a number of working groups to work on developing standards and standard compliance evaluation criteria.

The next section provides some guidelines and suggestions regarding web design evaluation; the most common options, functionalities and features are listed.

17.6.1 Text Version

Text only versions of a website should only be used as a last resort. Indeed, the *W3C* does not recommend the provision of text only websites; their guidelines say that this approach should only be considered as a last resort.

Providing an alternate text only version of a website can actually reinforce the sense of exclusion that people with disabilities already feel. However, it is important that at least the homepage of a website is accessible as plain text.

Other W3C recommendations regarding text accessibility include:
- Extend the use of CSS and of relative fonts, giving people the ability to change text size with the AAA functionality
- Avoid using text characters to simulate graphics
- Use the clearest and simplest language
- Explain acronyms and abbreviations
- Sound an alert when the user changes language versions; if speech or Braille outputs are being used, the user will then be informed of the change.
- Provide an automated text-based site map as an alternative means of navigation.

17.6.2 AAA Button

As mentioned above, we can allow the relative font size of the text to be changed by including an AAA button functionality in the toolbar.[79]

---

79 Please refer to Section 12.5 Accessibility

17.6.3 Bookmark This Page

This feature, if placed in the upper area of every page of the website, will automatically appear to registered users. When a page is bookmarked, the title of the page is displayed in a dedicated area on the homepage for faster navigation.

17.6.4 Most Visited Pages

This function should be made available only to registered users. It is displayed under the header of the website and presents a hierarchical list of the most visited pages.

17.6.5 Sitemap

This functionality is presented as an icon in the header. The *content management system* automatically updates the text-based map whenever content is added.

17.6.6 Print This Page/Document

The *print this page* icon is displayed on every page. When the icon is pressed the page is reformatted to fit well onto the printed page.

17.6.7 Send to a Friend

This icon should appear on the right-hand side, near to single documents, articles, projects or links.

18 Ambient Intelligence

A number of buzzwords, such as "pervasive computing", "disappearing computers", "ubiquitous computing", "reactive environments" and even "active museums" are related to the same concept, *ambient intelligence.*

According to the *ISTAG*[80] *vision statement, an environment with ambient intelligence (AmI)* contains *intelligent interfaces* that are supported by computing and networking technology embedded in everyday objects such as furniture, clothes, vehicles, roads and smart materials; even particles of decorative substances like paint.

AmI implies a seamless environment of computing, advanced networking technology and specific interfaces that are designed to enhance our everyday lives. This environment should be aware of the specific characteristics of human presence and personalities; adapt to the needs of users; be capable of responding intelligently to spoken or gestured indications of desire; and even provide systems that are capable of engaging in intelligent dialogue.

In some ways, AmI is the result of combining the *nonintrusive* approach to technology introduced by Myron Kruger, Mark Weiser's[81] *ubiquitous computing*[82] principles, and extending the old *domotic* concept.

Ambient intelligence should also be *unobtrusive*—interactions should be relaxing and enjoyable for the citizen, and not involve a steep learning curve. ISTAG does not think it necessary to define the term *ambient intelligence* more strictly than "a set of properties of an environment that we are in the process of creating". However, it is important to appreciate that AmI remains an *emerging property,* and that future environment that are created with it in mind should treat AmI as an *imagined concept*, not as a set of specific requirements.

Subsequent reports have expanded the AmI vision but have not significantly altered it. The 2002 ISTAG Report *Strategic Orientations & Priorities for IST*

Evolution of the AmI vision

---

80 Information Society Technology Advisory Group, an advisory group working for the IST programme of the European Commission.

81 Mark Weiser's website homepage: http://www.ubiq.com/weiser/.

82 Mark Weiser's *Ubiquitous Computing* webpage: http://www.ubiq.com/hypertext/weiser/UbiHome.html.

in FP6 introduced the concept of *AmI space*: seamless interoperation between different environments, such as the home, vehicles, public space, etc.

There has also been the important recognition that, to be accepted, "AmI needs to be driven by humanistic concerns, not technologically determined ones", and that it should be "controllable by ordinary people".

While AmI should not be promoted as a universal panacea for social problems, it certainly represents a new paradigm for how people can work and live together, and it provides radically new opportunities for both individual fulfilment and social discourse.

We should not underplay the radical social transformations that are likely to result from the implementation of the AmI vision. AmI enables and facilitates participation by the individual in society, in a variety of social and business communities, and in the administration and management of all aspects of their lives, from entertainment to governance.

19 Long-Term Preservation of Digital Archives

In the last few decades we have witnessed two related processes: the increasingly visible inclusion of electronic devices in our everyday lives, and the *rush to digital formats*. Institutions, organisations and private companies have begun to convert their own archives into digital formats.

The general public has also started to convert personal data into digital formats: documents, music, movies, drawings and photos have been converted from their original formats into *bitstreams* in digital media.

People used to believe (and many still do) that digital formats were the *ultimate formats* for storing information *indefinitely*. The idea that texts, images and artefacts can be perpetuated by converting them into *digital* form is popular and widely supported/sponsored.

As a result, a significant amount of our future heritage, our legacy to future generations, relies on digital technology. But is digital technology really suitable for long-term preservation? And are electronic devices, which are required in order to experience information stored in digital formats, durable enough to guarantee future access to this information? If not, what can we do to overcome this problem?

19.1 Graffiti From the Digital Era

The rapid evolution of technology makes the preservation of digital content a challenge. Considering the huge amount of data to be filed, the amount of time permitted to accomplish this task, and the length of time that such information needs to be stored, it is important to address the issue of the long-term conservation of digital information—a problem that has largely been underestimated up to now.

We need to consider two aspects: technological obsolescence and the *temporary nature* of p*ermanent storage systems*.

The "internal clock" of ICT beats much more rapidly than that of cultural heritage. Digital formats undergo relatively rapid turnover, periodically suddenly becoming obsolete and disappearing. An extraordinarily long-lived digital solution, such as the PC/DOS combination that was popular for over twenty years, is relatively short-lived compared to the time that much of our heritage has spent "sleeping" in state-owned archives.

Computer systems are aging; the media on which information is stored are disintegrating; magnetic diskettes can be stored and used without problems for thousands of hours, but this is not long enough to be considered *permanent* from the point of view of long-term heritage storage.

Given this issue, what are the long-term implications of relying on current digital technology to preserve our cultural memory?

The long-term preservation of digital archives is an issue that affects not only cultural heritage but also e-government and social services.

Electronic devices are constantly being made redundant because newer, updated versions of them enter the market, and so manufacturers stop supporting the older devices. This means that it becomes more and more difficult to obtain replacement components for the older devices. Ultimately, the only real options left to the user are to update the device, if possible, or to have a look at the vintage market, if there is one for this device.

In May 2004, a panel on the Long-Term Preservation of Digital Content was convened in New York during the World Wide Web Conference[83]. In September 2006, during an event held in Asolo, a set of recommendations regarding this topic was issued. The present section provides background on the critical issues and concerns related to long-term preservation of digital information.

Fig. 19.1 A PC after a fire (photo by the author)

---

[83] Please refer to report on the Long-Term Preservation of Digital Content panel available at http://www.medicif.org.

19.2 Already Lost... and To Be Lost

The past contains much lost heritage that we can now only imagine: the *Battaglia di Anghiari* fresco by Leonardo da Vinci, the *Alexandria Library*, the lost *plays of Aeschylus,* or the original contents of the *Palimpsests* and the *Egyptian Papyri*. Could we lose much of our recent heritage too, after it has been sucked into a "digital black hole"?

Will future generations, even those of the near future, be able to access the content produced by this generation? Will they be able to play our electronic music, experience computer art, browse our multimedia archives or play our archaic video games?

Rolls Royce recently celebrated its first century of production by organising a huge parade of vintage cars from the early twentieth century. Will future generations be able to enjoy similar parades celebrating two or three centuries of Rolls Royce production?

Drawbacks of the everyday use of ICT

These future parades will probably involve the same cars—those from the early twentieth century—as used in the recent parade, because while there are still people that are able to build a carburettor from the 1920s, nobody can refurbish or rebuild the PNP transistors or early ICs found in more recent Rolls Royces.

In a similar way, I could speculate about the fate of my electronic Leica R4 in the near future, given that it became difficult to operate my mechanical Leicaflex SL2 when its PX625 batteries vanished from the market. And what are the chances that preamplifiers such as the glorious McIntosh C28 will survive the extinction of thermoionic valves?

ICT and its *fragility* are deeply entwined with our everyday lives. We rarely stop to consider this fragility until malfunctions, viruses, blackouts or "millennium bugs" occur. Will future generations have the opportunity to enjoy todays exhibits at Ars Electronica? Or the impressive recent products from MIT Media-Lab?

Digital fragility

Similar considerations can impact on our perception of the value of objects and their everyday use. Of course, we cannot preserve everything; there are products and content that will not necessarily reach future generations. Sometimes this will simply affect the economic value of the object; for instance, "pre-owned" electronic wristwatches are usually less expensive then the mechanical ones.

Impact on the perceived economic value

Perhaps we should devote some time to choosing what should be destroyed/recycled. This approach mirrors one of the ways that the advent of digital cameras has changed photography; whereas we used to take 36 photos and save, say, 30 acceptable ones, today we shoot 360 digital photos and select 10 acceptable ones. But what should we do with the 350 photos left?

However, we do need to leave some *objects* to future generations; we cannot leave a "black hole" as our legacy. Consider the family photo album. We still have photos from the end of the nineteenth century, but we risk passing on nothing from the early twenty-first century to future generations: leaving them a photo album with lots of blank pages...

The "digital black hole"

19 Long-Term Preservation of Digital Archives

The ability of a culture to survive into the future depends on the richness and acuity of its members' sense of history.

Society, of course, has always shown a great deal of interest in preserving materials that document issues, concerns, ideas, creativity, art, discourse and events. Even if we simply focus, for the moment, on basic digital content such as text, we cannot guarantee that textual records stored in digital electronic form will always be accessible.

As already outlined, although the loss of data due to the deterioration of storage media is an important consideration, the main issue is that software and hardware technologies rapidly become obsolescent.

Computers and microchips age very quickly; this is the basis for the market model for ICT-based products. Companies cannot afford long life cycles; customers must provide them with financial support by updating their equipment periodically; as Nathan Myhrvold said, "software is like a gas that expands to fill the room" (i.e. computer resources).

Sometimes technological advances are so significant that backward compatibility becomes impossible or irrelevant.

Decades ago hardware was so valuable that major efforts were made to reuse devices from generation to generation: punching machines, printers, tape units etc. were adapted to new mainframes. Software drivers were written ad hoc and applications were redesigned or adapted to suit.

We now face the opposite problem; according to Moore's Law the cost of hardware will continue to drop, while the software and content are the assets that must be preserved.

Storage media degradation

Storage media are subject to *degradation*; they are not designed to survive for long periods of time (the kinds of timescales associated with archives and cultural heritage). Magnetic technology does not guarantee long-term access to stored information; tapes and disks lose their properties and are sensitive to environmental conditions such as heat, humidity, magnetic fields, static electricity, dust, fire, etc.

In addition, they become obsolete as the devices capable of reading them become outdated and are mothballed. Even though they were once cutting-edge formats, today it is very difficult to obtain equipment that will read a 9600 bpi magnetic tape, an 8″ floppy disk or even a 5¼″ one. The same can be said for early RLL or IDE hard disks. Old formats and standards are essentially shelved in favour of newer formats and standards.

Obsolescence of software standards

This even happens for *software standards*, because ways of coding information and the quality of the information stored are constantly improving. This situation holds for both electronic records converted from analogue forms (paper, film, video, sound, etc.), and records that were originally created in electronic form (*born digital*).

For digital content that is derived from an analogue source, the analogue source (provided it is still available) can be digitised again to new and improved standards and formats, so this issue is not a big problem. On the other hand, content that originated in digital form must be preserved based on the original record.

206   *II The General Technological Framework*

Until recently, documents were generally *paper-* or *microfilm*-based. Microfilm technology was popular because of its efficiency, usability, robustness and we now recognise that it is almost hardware-independent. A few decades ago people started to convert microfilm archives into digital archives. This conversion required significant resources to digitise the documents and sometimes convert them into formatted text, as well as to store vector versions of drawings and sketches.

Almost twenty years ago, scanners with raster vector conversion were bestsellers and companies started to convert their huge archives from paper and microfilm formats to digital ones.

This rush to digital formats was driven by powerful incentives, including the ability to make perfect copies of the "digital originals", publish them on a wide range of media, and significantly accelerated distribution and dissemination since the Internet could be utilised.

The publication of content on the Internet allowed people to reformat and convert the content into alternate forms, to easily locate it, search through it and retrieve it, and to process it with automated and semi-automated tools.

More recently some organisations have started to perform the opposite process: using microfilm machines to process digital data into microfiches.

However, today's data storage methods include digital storage, and more and more organizations are storing more and more of their information digitally. Yet, surprisingly little attention is given to the preservation of digital information over long periods.

19.3   Historical Background of Initiatives

In December 1994, two US-based organisations, the *Commission on Preservation and Access* and *The Research Libraries Group,* created the *Task Force on Digital Archiving*.

The purpose of the Task Force was to investigate ways of ensuring "continued access indefinitely into the future of records stored in digital electronic form".

Composed of individuals drawn from industry, museums, archives and libraries, publishers, scholarly societies and the government, the Task Force was charged specifically to:

- Frame the key problems (organisational, technological, legal, economic etc.) that need to be resolved for technology refreshing to be considered an acceptable approach to ensuring continuing access to electronic digital records indefinitely into the future
- Define the critical issues that inhibit resolution of each identified problem
- For each issue, recommend actions to remove the issue from the list
- Consider alternatives to technology refreshing
- Make other generic recommendations as appropriate.

The Task Force issued a draft report in August 1995. An extended comment period followed, during which a wide variety of interested parties located both in the United States and abroad contributed numerous helpful and thoughtful suggestions for improving the draft report, many of which were incorporated into the final report issued in May 1996.

During the *International Conference on ICT for Cultural Heritage (CULT-H)*, held in Vienna in 1999, a specific session and exhibit was devoted to media aging and information preservation. Panels with disintegrated magnetic tapes, dusty computers and *melted* floppy disks highlighted the physical side of the problem.

Studies and research were then carried; in 2002, during the *International Conference on Digital Libraries,* sponsored by the *Association for Computing Machinery (ACM),* a *panel on digital preservation* was held.

Levels of abstraction   Reagan Moore from the San Diego Supercomputer Centre introduced the *levels of abstraction* that are needed to create infrastructure-independent representations of data, information, and knowledge; in addition, a prototype *persistent digital archive* was presented. The persistent archive infrastructure was developed for use by the *National Archives and Records Administration (NARA)* and other federal agencies.

NARA's *Vision for the Electronic Records Archives* states:

The Electronic Records Archives will authentically preserve and provide access to any kind of electronic record, free from dependency on any specific hardware or software, enabling NARA to carry out its mission into the future.

William Underwood reported on the lessons learned in the preservation of digital records created on personal computers, and more specifically the digital records created on personal computers during the administration of President George Bush (1988–1992).

19.4   Digital Fragility: Problems and Issues

The general problem can be structured and analysed. At the top of a theoretical taxonomy we need two main branches:
- *Aging and disappearance of hardware/firmware and software*
- *Content preservation.*

The aging and disappearance of hardware/firmware and software is mainly (but not only) related to the preservation of devices and computer-controlled functions. This includes car components, electronic devices such as cameras, videos, hi-fi stereos, most interactive installations for computer art, and even machinery usually designed to last a long time (i.e. those that used to be controlled by relays but now incorporate microchips).

American National Research   A good overview of this problem was provided by a 1995 report from the
Council report 1995   American National Research Council: "The fact that most electronic hardware is expected to function for no more than 10 to 20 years raises very serious problems for long-term (more than 20 years) archival preservation. Even if the operating system and documentation problems are somehow dealt with, what is

208   *II The General Technological Framework*

the archivist to do when the machine manufacturer declares the hardware obsolete or simply goes out of business? Will there be an IBM or Sony in the year 2200? If they still exist, will they maintain a 1980–1990 vintage machine? Moreover, it must be realized that no archival organization can realistically hope to maintain such hardware itself. Integrated circuits, thin film heads, and laser diodes cannot be repaired today, nor can they be readily fabricated, except in multimillion-dollar factories."

The other side of the coin from hardware preservation is *merely content preservation*. An increasing number of institutions, organisations and companies are storing more and more of their organisational information and content digitally. Furthermore, according to Moore's Law, progress in computer technology is constantly making new generations of systems that are more powerful and more cost-effective available. These advantages mean that the new generation is quickly adopted, often resulting in the loss of some backward compatibility. As the older technologies are replaced by newer generations of hardware and software, new data formats (PICT, GIF, TIFF, BMP, JPG...) are introduced. Over time, we lose our knowledge of how the previous generations of systems stored and accessed documents; simply consider two of the vector graphics file formats that have been used over the last two decades, IGES and VRML.

Within many organizations around the world today, digital documents that are official records must be categorised and managed in accordance with approved record schedules that differ from country to country, but basically all ensure that data is retained for at least a minimum period of time. These records must be retained and be accessible throughout their life cycle in accordance with the same laws and standards that govern paper records. *Approved record schedules*

These life cycles are usually over 90 years for medical records, ten years for basic technical documentation and accounting, 75 years for copyrights, and a "potentially unlimited" amount of time for historical records and state archives.

In the United States, for instance, in the case of government documents the law dictates that an official government record must be classified into one of 26 retention periods set forth by the Archivist of the United States. These retention periods range from 30 days to permanent storage, and include time periods of 30 years, 50 years, and 75 years. In addition there are special requirements, such as archives of copyrighted information created in order to preserve content until copyright expiration and public consumption; in Europe, this corresponds to more then 75 years of storage.

Let's now consider another point of view, just as the optimist sees a half-full glass, the pessimist sees a half-empty one, and the engineer sees an oversized container! *Consider a half-full glass...*

Storing content in digital format does not only present problems and potential danger; one of the positive aspects of storing digital objects is the ability to clone them, which solves the eternal conflict between preservation and access. Also, due to *de facto* standards and almost platform independency, Internet technology has improved the potential lifespan of its own content.

Digital content: different levels of complexity

In order to approach the issue of the long-term preservation of pure content, we can list the different levels of complexity and function that need to be preserved. Content and functionalities to be preserved could range from:

- *Plain text* (for a long time the basis for interoperability and long-term formats)
- *Text with specific formats and functions* (such as camera-ready pages, spreadsheets, database import/export formats)
- *Multi/hypermedia content* (images, movies, sounds in different formats, links, refs)
- *Technical sketches, 3-D models* (vector graphics, interactive scenarios)
- *Content deeply merged with specific applications* (archives, databases, video games, custom applications)
- *Interactive installations for computer art, virtual enhanced reality applications, etc.*
- *Future applications involving greater interaction with users and heterogeneous distributed data structures.*

Of course, each level of content complexity requires a different amount of effort to preserve or restore. Obviously plain text is easy to maintain, while videogames usually require the emulation or preservation of the original platform (the speed of the emulator may have to be reduced to replicate the original performance of the game).

19.5 The Rationale Behind Preservation

The digital and electronic assets that need to be preserved range from high-level and mission-critical information and applications to objects from everyday life. This task of preservation will involve both highly skilled *ad hoc* organisations and citizens, the former saving military or census records and the latter saving their photos, music, and documents.

The big mis understanding

The idea that once you have managed to convert your original into a digital format you're home and dry does not reflect reality; once the digital data have been obtained, it is necessary to consider a different conservation strategy.

One of the first things to consider is that content has its own life cycle. Even though the *paperless* office uses more paper than ever before, and low-cost storage technology has created terabytes of "digital garbage", we must take into account what is relevant and what it is not; not only because preservation will cost some resources but also because irrelevant data will simply increase the *entropy*.

Another relevant aspect of preservation is the *data refresh rate,* which is related to the concepts of fixed (written once) and dynamic (rewritten or continuously updated) information.

II The General Technological Framework

The *life cycle* of the data will even influence the way in which it is created[84] and will generate an accounting record for the resources to be preserved. *Since prevention is better then cure,* if we define *preservation strategies* we are halfway to the solution. Considering the nature of the problem and related potential strategies, some interventions are:

- *Refreshing.* In order to avoid the physical decay of data in magnetic storage media, information is simply refreshed every so often. There are specific software applications that can implement such a process. If the storage media is "write only", or a significant proportion of the lifespan of the magnetic medium has elapsed, the system will move the data to a *fresh* storage medium.
- *Printing/microfilming.* Sometimes the last resort is to keep the data in a safe between one generation and the next. Unfortunately some digital data cannot be converted to paper or microfilm formats. In this case, technology does not help because it is constantly delivering new generations of *digital objects* that are different to established ones. How can we revert back from a digital signature to paper format, or do so for a cooperative document created on the fly? How can we permanently store wikis or blogs? How can we manage interactive electronic art installations?
- *Multiple instances (copies).* This is analogous to the human approach to survival: we simply replicate ourselves as much as possible (refer to the *Meme's Eye Web*[85]).

Now we come to the more difficult approaches; the ones that are considered when the objects to be preserved are more complex than plain text or simple documents. When choosing between them it is important to consider from both current and long-term perspectives:

- *System preservation.* This is the hard way to keep vintage technologies such as the Apollo DN300 or PDP11 alive. It is a very expensive approach and it is very difficult to guarantee preservation for a reasonable period of time. This approach may involve buying used equipment in order to cannibalise it for parts.
- *Emulation.* This approach appears to be one of the most attractive because we might envisage a "universal emulator" that enables every vintage application to run on the latest computers without the need to preserve the original system. In terms of very common applications and single computer system emulation, video games like Pac-Man are usually preserved in this way. Of

---

84 In terms of quality, quantity, technology, format, etc.

85 In *The Meme's Eye Web*, Susan J. Blackmore argues that memes have shaped human nature. By driving the evolution of the machinery that copies them, memes have created the enormous human brain with its specialised capacity for language. See Blackmore (2001).

course, emulators could be shared by groups of applications that originally ran on the same platform. However, problems arise if the application needs to interact with some specific software configuration or hardware device[86].

- *Migration.* This is an alternative to both the preservation and emulation of vintage systems. The idea here is to migrate/move the digital information and/or application to a new system. Migration is a very useful approach and it is widely used in the software industry to move applications and database systems from one *system generation* to the next. One of the key points is to start migrating before the knowledge related to the application is lost. When dealing with personal information managed by desktop applications, internal data formats and functionalities are not known by the owner of the information, so it is necessary to rely on third parties for migration, who have no direct evidence of how much knowledge is lost. In this case it could helpful to keep an additional copy of the content coded according to different standards (i.e. Internet technology standards). *Open source* software could potentially be used here due to availability of the source code, but it is only really relevant to users that are very skilled in software engineering, and so it is not applicable to most content producers. The *forward migration* of digital objects to a new system generation is time-consuming and costly; in addition, if we consider one of the *basic philosophical rules of conserva tion*[87]—minimize harm—migration breaks this rule because it involves data modification. This modification will degrade the information if the new format does not incorporate all of the features of the original format. For instance, tests where data have been put through multiple migration cycles until they are eventually migrated back to their original formats have shown that the original data sometimes do not match the migrated data, even though they are in the same format.

The basic philosophical rule of conservation: minimise harm

- *Standardisation.* This is migration from the original proprietary formats to standard formats (i.e. Internet technology formats). If we are going to create long-lasting digital content we must start by defining the standards that we are going to use, taking into account how stable they are and whether they support forward migration. Standardisation is advantageous because knowledge of the standard data formats used should always be available even support for the standard diminishes at a later date. Standardisation addresses two of the challenges associated with migration: the *loss of information due to the loss of knowledge about it, and the degradation of the content due to multiple migrations.* But how do we choose the best standard for organisational preservation, and how does a future user determine the standard that was used to preserve the information? A possible and reasonable solution is to use a format that incorporates metadata (e.g. XML), which will provide a

Standardisation and its challenges

---

86 For example, if it requires the use of Sega *Goggles* or Nintendo *PowerGlove*.
87 Viewing conservation as a continuous process of taking care of things.

212 ∎ *II The General Technological Framework*

rich description of the standard used by the original owners of the information. This process is usually called *encapsulation*:

- *Encapsulation.* Here the digital object is preserved for future use by *wrapping it in* a *human readable skin*. The wrapper contains simple information that both supports organisational preservation and documents the preserved object, allowing future users to decode and access it. Because there is no unique and optimal solution, encapsulation has two main challenges. The first is the need to generate encapsulated digital data directly from applications. Since current applications are not able to produce such data, a *plug-in* or *postprocessor* must be developed and added to existing applications. The second challenge is the potential storage overhead arising from the addition of the wrapper; each record needs to be enriched with descriptive data. We could combine the use of *data standards* with *encapsulated* records, saving a significant amount of storage, but how long will these published standards be available for?

Migration and encapsulation are related to some degree, but while migration attempts to solve the problem in advance when detailed information about both the data and the systems used are available, encapsulation represents a potentially self-sufficient package of information and data that we can deliver to future generations in the hope that we have included enough information to enable them to manage and read the digital objects they receive from us.

Therefore, there is no unique or optimal solution to the problem of preservation; the best approach is to get an expert or consultant to identify the proper strategy and its physical implementation. As ironically stated by Jeff Rothenberg in *Avoiding Technological Quicksand* (Rothenberg 1999), "*Digital documents last forever, or five years, whichever comes first*".

Digital documents last forever, or five years, whichever comes first

19.6 Economy and Infrastructure

The preservation problem involves several other aspects in addition to the bare technological ones: there are *administrative, procedural, organisational, legal, IPR and policy issues* surrounding the long-term preservation of digital content. This increased complexity tends to be due to the different natures of digital and traditional physical documents.

At least one aspect should be investigated before settling on a particular preservation approach: the overall *cost of preservation*. This involves considering the best way to ensure future access to information during the design phase of the long-term dataset. This approach may involve collecting feedback about the way that technology and standards are chosen and even the way that datasets are formed. Once the dataset is created, in addition to infrastructure costs, running costs may include: additional room on storage devices to archive copies and/or documentation and metadata, software applications that manage data refreshing, and costs related to porting or emulation.

19 *Long-Term Preservation of Digital Archives*

19.7 Some Closing Remarks

The long-term preservation of digital content is a big challenge in the era of the Information Society; important digital information is in danger of being lost forever. The technologies required by particular types of digital content become obsolete; application versions and files formats frequently change, making data inaccessible. Even when content is coded in the simplest format, such as ASCII code, the degradation and obsolescence of storage media can result in its disappearance.

Online information sources such as webpages and databases become more difficult to find as the web(s) in which they are located become more complex and diverse (due to an increasing number of hyperlinks, cross-references as well as types of web application and even webs themselves).

A number of global studies and projects have been and are being carried out into digital preservation; for instance the work carried out by the *Taskforce on Archiving of Digital Information* (94–96) on the mandate of *The Commission on Preservation and Access and The Research Libraries Group Inc.*, as well as the *OASIS Open Archival Information System* project, *CAMiLEON* emulation and the *VERS Victorian Electronic Record Strategy*. Along with the *ERA* initiative launched by NARA, *Interpares I, II* and *III* are some of the most well known projects in this field.

In addition, a comprehensive vision of electronic record management is provided by the *US Department of Defence* standard entitled the *Design Criteria Standard for Electronic Records Management Software Applications* (*dod 5015.2 STD*)[88].

Finally, it is very important that research into digital preservation is carried out by strong interdisciplinary groups, since this should guarantee that an effective approach to a problem that concerns the foundations of the *digital era* is defined.

Perhaps the only chance of avoiding the "technological quicksand" (Rothenberg 1999) is to find the *"digital Rosetta Stone" (Heminger and Robertson 2000)* in the digital desert.

---

[88] Available at http://jitc.fhu.disa.mil/recmgt/standards.html.

19.7.1 Integrated Conclusions of the International Expert Meeting Held in Asolo[89]

The papers presented at the symposium *Conservare il Digitale*, held in Asolo on September 29, 2006, demonstrate the need for further reflection, the results of which will be submitted to national and international authorities and to the institutions and organizations involved in digital preservation. This reflection must start from some points of principle that all experts attending this international event share. They are expressed in the following agreed upon statements.

Importance and timeliness of the topic: We confirm and emphasize the significance and timeliness of the abovementioned topic, which directly concerns the arts, the sciences, administration and governance.

Information needs: We express the need for experts on this and allied areas of knowledge to be actively involved in outreach activities aimed at promoting awareness of the challenges presented by the long term preservation of digital entities among the institutions and organizations whose materials are potentially endangered either by lack of adequate strategies or by lack of understanding of the issues involved.

Complexity of the issue: We note the complexity of the issue of digital preservation, which directly affects many sectors: culture (i.e. history, liberal, visual & performing arts, cultural heritage, archives, etc), citizenry, public administration, justice, economy, research, privacy, security, etc. This issue is also global and pervasive, being strictly related to a wide variety of other issues, such as copyright, certification of documents and authors, the concept of "original", accessibility of original formats, creation and conservation of annotations, metadata, historic "traceability" of accesses and users, etc.

Technological neutrality of the approach: We firmly believe that the approach chosen to address the issue of digital preservation must not be based on or guided by technological advances, requirements or interests but on the functional needs and legal requirements of the organisations that create, maintain or preserve the material. We agree that the range of practical solutions is ample and varied, and the choice of the one or the other has to depend in part on available resources and specific contextual conditions, but, whatever the adopted solution, it must descend from the preservation principles internationally shared by the experts in this area of knowledge.

---

[89] This subsection contains the text from the final report submitted to the participants of the International Expert Meeting "Conservare il digitale", held in Asolo on 29 September 2006. The report, entitled *Long-Term Digital Preservation: An International Focus* (see http://www.ndk.cz/dokumenty/asolo_memorandum.pdf/ download), was created in order to provide some guidelines and suggestions on this topic.

Preservation principles: We believe that the principles that should guide the design of an organizational preservation strategy relate to the protection of the identity and integrity of the digital entities from the moment of their creation, through their maintenance, use and continuing preservation; the selection of the appropriate metadata sets to attach to the digital entities at various stages of their life-cycle; the use of the open source software to bring forward the material from creation to preservation; the choice of the trusted custodian who will be responsible and accountable for the on-going authentic re-production of the digital entities to be preserved; and of course the right of future generations to have full access to the authentic record of their past.

Research: Technology will continue to evolve at an increasingly fast pace and in unpredictable directions. Any solution found to the issue of preservation of the entities produced by one technology will likely be inadequate for those produced by a subsequent one. We consider it vital for all the professionals whose sphere of competence focuses on long term preservation to be constantly involved in research that is on the leading edge in the development of new theory and methods, in the study of the social, ethical and legal implication of each proposed approach, in the assessment of costs, risks and benefits of each choice, and in the adoption of new methods of inquiry and different perspectives.

Dissemination of existing knowledge: In order to support already existent and forthcoming preservation initiatives and to test various strategies in a variety of contexts, we consider essential to undertake activities directed to the dissemination of research findings and products, their implementation and the resulting best practices in various interested sectors ranging from private business to public administration.

Suggested initiative: We propose the creation of an international network of organizations and groups that is open to all interested parties and has the function of promoting potential synergies. The network would be structured in teams dedicated to specific topics (e.g. cost of long term preservation), and would organize yearly conferences.

Asolo, 29 September 2006

The subscribers

Chen Bitan (Cyber-Ark Software – Tel Aviv – Israel); Rossella Bonora (DocArea Project – Province of Bologna – Italy); Giorgetta Bonfiglio Dosio (University of Padua – Italy); Elettra Cappadozzi (C.N.I.P.A. – Italy); Paola Carucci (Manager of Historical Archives of the President of the Republic – Rome – Italy); Luciana Duranti (School of Library, Archival and Information Studies of The University of British Columbia – Canada); Giustiniana Migliardi o'Riordan (Archives curator of Veneto – Italy); Mariella Guercio (University of Urbino – Italy); Nitya Karmakar (University of Western Sydney,

Sydney, Australia); Guenther Kolar (Ludwig Boltzmann Institute Media.Art. Research & Ars Electronica Futurelab – Linz, Austria); Mathias Jehn (German National Library – Frankfurt on Main – Germany); April Miller (The World Bank – Washington – US); Stefano Pigliapoco (University of Macerata – Italy); Mario Pò (Management ULSS8 Asolo – Italy); Micaela Procaccia (Ministry for the cultural assets and archives – Directors General's Office for Archives – Italy); Giangiulio Radivo (Delegated Diocese of Rome near Vatican Radio – Vatican State); Alfredo M. Ronchi (MEDICI Framework – Politecnico di Milano – Italy); Seamus Ross (Humanities Advanced Technology and Information Institute (HATII) – University of Glasgow – UK); Irmgard Schuler (Vatican Library – Vatican State); Kim Henry Veltman (Scientific Manager of Maastricht McLuhan Institute – The Netherlands); Loreno Zandri (City of Pesaro – Urbino – Italy).

Fig. 19.2 The International Meeting in Asolo (photo by the author)

20 The Future:
the Weave of the Digital Fabric

Some years ago the first *World Summit on the Information Society (WSIS)*, a global forum devoted to shaping the impact of information and communications technology on society, was held. Representatives of different actors (governments, companies, civil society) from around the world contributed to the WSIS.

During the WSIS some remarks were made about technological developments in the field of ICT and how they were greatly influencing our habits and interpersonal relationships, as well as how they provided the opportunity for development (personally and from the point of view of society). *What technological trends should we expect for the future? Is there any evidence that may provide us with hints about the way that we can expect technology to evolve in the future?*

20.1 Predicting the Future

In 1937 the League of Nations commissioned an international group of leading scientists to consider the evolution of technology over the next fifty years. The subsequent report contained some predictions that actually came true, but it is interesting to note the technologies that were not predicted, including *radar, jet propulsion, television, antibiotics, nuclear energy* and even the *Pill*.

It has been said that *"prediction is difficult, especially if it involves the future!"* [90] We can, however, reach into the past and consider what earlier generations thought the future would look like, and then compare their predictions with how technology actually did evolve.

How did our grandparents imagine that technology would develop in the future? Looking back, which were the most significant "clues" to technological progress?

If we consider articles, books and movies from the past, we find that at least three aspects of future technologies are emphasised: the presence of objects with incredible features (or at least features that were unattainable at the time

---

[90] Quote from Neils Bohr, who won the Nobel Prize in Physics.

that the movie etc. was released), the simplification of daily activities, and finally (often the most interesting aspect of the future to novelists and movie directors) the negative aspects of technological development, the dangers posed by *hardware and machinery*.[91]

Sometimes our predictions for the future come true, at least to some degree, and sometimes they do not (consider, for example, the evergreen prediction that by the 1970s/1980s/1990s... everyone would be using flying cars, just like those depicted in the film *The Fifth Element* by Luc Besson).

20.2   Institutes for the Future

I once attended a presentation by a technology forecaster—a "future guru" —Paul Saffo, the director of and a high-level researcher at the *Institute for the Future*[92], a "think tank" based in Silicon Valley that attempts to predict trends in various sectors.

Initially I thought of another "researcher of the future" (from the movie *Back to the Future*), but Saffo did not have flowing white hair or a wild expression, so no time travelling (at least for the moment!). Instead he presented a talk analysing technological potentials and current trends that could be used to predict the progress of technology over the next ten or so years.

The scenario proposed for this first decade of the new millennium was that of businessmen that are permanently flying around the world and permanently connected to the global telecommunications network while doing so. These businessmen are continually racking up frequent flyer *bonus miles* and credit card *rewards* from travelling, which then enable them to travel to places that they really do not want to visit—a vicious circle!

Another interesting interpretation of the future of technology comes from Susan J. Blackmore[93], in a discourse that, among many other topics, encompasses viruses, religions and amanuenses. She believes that the Internet functions as a *replicator* that is able to perpetuate content, just as nature makes species that are destined to survive more prolific.

Consider the already mentioned, interesting and somewhat alarming forecast for 2005 published by the Japanese Banks Association in 1999. The forecast

---

91   In the world of cinema, we often encounter dark visions of a technological future, including *Metropolis* by Fritz Lang, *Modern Times* starring Charlie Chaplin, *2001: A Space Odyssey* by Stanley Kubrick, *Tron* from *Disney*, *The Lawnmower Man* by Brett Leonard, *Johnny Mnemonic* by Robert Longo (based on the work of William Gibson), *The Thirteenth Floor* by Josef Rusnak, *The Matrix* by Andy and Larry Wachowski, *Enemy of the State* by Tony Scott, *Nirvana* by Gabriele Salvatores, *Minority Report* by Steven Spielberg, and the off-the-wall *Brazil* by Terry Gilliam.

92   Further information is available at: http://www.iftf.org.

93   Please refer to Sect. 8.2. Susan J. Blackmore, University of the West of England, Bristol: http://www.www10.org/keynoters/speech/susan/Memes.html.

was delivered by the general manager of DoCoMo, Masao Nakamura, in 2000 while presenting the commercial response to their i-mode system.

The study forecasted that in 2005 the vast majority of the clients of banks and telecommunications would not be human. Most transactions would be carried out between *machines*, while in some cases one of the actors would be an animal.

The study predicted highway telepayment systems, prepaid cards (evolutions of the credit system) that are able to communicate directly with the current accounts of the suppliers, and wearable devices for kids, elderly people and animals that are able to converse with cars, warning the driver or triggering the engine control unit or ABS system if danger is imminent, as well as the attendance of virtual *videopresences* at ceremonies and job meetings, as made possible by three-dimensional holographic images.

Predictions in the field of technology are sometimes or usually based on hints that do not represent true trends.

References

9 Native Digital Content

F. Antinucci (1993) Summa hypermedialis. Sistemi Intelligenti 5

F. Antinucci (2001a) La scuola si è rotta—perché cambiano i modi di apprendere. Editori Laterza, Roma

F. Antinucci (2001b) Computer per un figlio—giocare, apprendere, creare. Editori Laterza, Roma

F. Antinucci (2002) Il futuro di Internet ovvero "forma" e "business" nell'innovazione tecnologica. Sistemi Intelligenti 2

Digital Natives project (while we often consider digital natives to be the generation "born digital", not all young people are digital natives; digital natives share a common global culture that is defined not by age, strictly, but by certain attributes and experiences related to how they interact with information technologies, information itself, one another, and other people and institutions): http://www.digitalnative.org

A. Granelli, L. de Biase (2004) Inventori d'Italia. Dall'eredità del passato la chiave per l'innovazione. Guerini e Associati, Milano

L. Jaeger (2003) La parola crea il mondo. Mente & Cervello magazine, no. 5, Oct. 2003

B.I. Koerner (2002) The long road to Internet nirvana. Wired, Oct. 2002

A. Marcolli (1982) L'immagine-azione comunicazione. Sansoni editore, Firenze

J. McHugh (2002) Unplugged U. Wired, Oct. 2002

M. McLuhan (1964) Understanding media—Gli strumenti del comunicare. Il Saggiatore, Milano

M. McLuhan (1988) La galassia Gutenberg. Armando, Roma

N. Negroponte (2002) Being wireless. Wired, Oct. 2002

10 Data Sets and Formats

Data formats (on Google): http://www.google.com/Top/Computers/Data_Formats

Data formats and standards (on Webopedia): http://www.webopedia.com/Data/Data_Formats

International Organisation for Standardisation (ISO): http://www.iso.org/iso/home.htm

W. Kester (ed.) Engineering Staff of Analog Devices, Inc. (2004) Data conversion handbook. Elsevier, Amsterdam

MPEG reference website: http://www.mpeg.org

W3C Web Application Formats Working Group (chartered to develop languages for client-side web application development): http://www.w3.org/2006/appformats

11 Data Visualisation and Display Technologies

AIBO: http://support.sony-europe.com/aibo

BARCO: http://www.barco.com

BOOM 3C (Fakespace Labs): http://www-cdr.stanford.edu/html/DesignSpace/sponsors/boom.html

P. Bourke (1999–2003) Calculating stereo pairs; Creating correct stereo pairs from any ray-tracer; Creating stereoscopic images that are easy on the eyes: http://local.wasp.uwa.edu.au/~pbourke/projection/stereorender

Caleb Chung and Ugobe: http://www.ugobe.com

CAVE (at Ars Electronica Center—Museum of the Future): http://www.aec.at/en/center/project.asp?iProjectID=11197

CAVE (CAVE Automatic Virtual Environment): http://inkido.indiana.edu/a100/handouts/cave_out.html

C. Cruz-Neira, D.J. Sandin, T.A. DeFanti (1993) Surround-screen projection-based virtual reality: The design and implementation of the CAVE. Comput. Graph. (Proc. SIGGRAPH'93), pp. 135–142

Electronic Visualization Laboratory: http://evlweb.eecs.uic.edu/index2.php

Fakespace: http://www.fakespace.com

M.W. Krueger (1990) Videoplace (at Prix Ars Electronica): http://www.aec.at/en/archives/prix_archive/prix_projekt.asp?iProjectID=2473

M. Lucente (1997) Interactive three-dimensional holographic displays: seeing the future in depth. Comput. Graph. (Proc. SIGGRAPH'97) 31(2):63–67

Rockwell Collins: http://www.rockwellcollins.com/optronics

A.M. Ronchi (1994) Virtualità reale. Boll. D'Inform. Centr. Ricerche Inform. I Beni Cultur. Pisa IV(1):7–31 (especially pp. 26–27)

A.M. Ronchi (1997) Real virtuality: use of hypermedia and VR in the field of education and cultural heritage. In: IEEE Int. Symp. Ind. Electron. ISIE 97, Guimaraes, Portugal, 7–11 July 1997 (see http://ieeexplore.ieee.org/iel4/5230/14218/00651770.pdf?arnumber=651770)

SeeReal Technologies S.A: http://www.seereal.com

Stereoscopic displays (author: H. Hua): http://www.optics.arizona.edu/opti588/reading/Stereoscopic_displays_Hua_rev.pdf

I.E. Sutherland (1965) The ultimate display. Proc. IFIP'65 2:506–508 (see http://www.informatik.umu.se/~jworth/The%20Ultimate%20Display.pdf)

The invisible shape of things past (1995, ART+COM project): http://www.artcom.de/index.php?option=com_acprojects&page=6&id=26&Itemid=144&details=0&lang=en

Views and viewers (stereographs and ways to view them): http://stereographer.com/viewers.html

VRLogic (head-mounted displays): http://www.vrlogic.com/html/head_mounted_displays.html

12 Interaction Design

B. Moggridge (2007) Designing interactions. MIT Press, Cambridge, MA (ISBN 0-262-13474-8)

J. Nielsen (1993) Usability engineering. Academic, Boston, MA (ISBN 0-12-518405-0)

D.A. Norman (1988) The psychology of everyday things. Basic Books, Inc., New York

D.A. Norman (1994) Things that make us smart: Defending human attributes in the age of the machine. Addison Wesley, Reading, MA (ISBN 0-201-58129-9)

D.A. Norman (1998) The design of everyday things. Basic Books, Inc., New York (ISBN-978-0-262-64037-4)

D.A. Norman (2007) The design of future things. Basic Books, Inc., New York

J. Raskin (2000) The humane interface. New directions for designing interactive systems. Addison-Wesley, Boston, MA (ISBN 0-201-37937-6)

B. Shneiderman, C. Plaisant (2004) Designing the user interface: Strategies for effective human–computer interaction, 4th edn. Addison-Wesley, Boston, MA (ISBN 0-321-19786-0)

13 Computer Games, Edutainment and Theme Parks

Computer Games and Digital Cultures Conference: http://www.gamesconference.org or http://www.digra2007.jp

Corso Game Design at Polo Universitario di Crema: http://www.crema.unimi.it

Council of Europe (2001) New information technologies and the young. Council of Europe Publishing, Paris

J.C. Herz (1997) Joystick nation: How computer games ate our quarters, won our hearts and rewired our minds. Little, Brown, Boston, MA

History of SONY from 1946 onwards: http://www.sony.net/Fun/SH/index.html

History of video games: http://www.gamespot.com/features/index.html or http://www.gamespot.com/features/all/historyof/index.html

International Association for Digital Games Research (DiGRA; the association for academics and professionals who research digital games and associated phenomena): http://www.digra.org

S.L. Kent (1997) Super Mario nation: the video game turns twenty-five this year, and it has packed a whole lot of history into a mere quarter-century. Am. Heritage 48(5) Sept. 1997 (see http://www.americanheritage.com/articles/magazine/ah/1997/5/1997_5_65.shtml)

P. Kuittinen (1997) History of home videogames: http://users.tkk.fi/~eye/videogames

Magnavox ODYSSEY (1974; the first home videogame): http://www.magnavox.com/index.cfm?event=about

Milton Bradley (now owned by Hasbro): http://www.hasbro.com

J.H. Murray (1997) Hamlet on the holodeck: The future of narrative in cyberspace. Free Press, New York

K. Philipkoski (2000) There's a PC in my salt shaker. Wired 19.02.2000 (see http://www.wired.com/science/discoveries/news/2000/02/34464)

Planet Dreamcast (Sega's Dreamcast has come and gone, but this site remains as a reminder of its greatness): http://www.planetdreamcast.com

Ralph Baer interview: http://www.gooddealgames.com/interviews/int_baer.html

W. Shao, D. Terzopoulos (2006) Populating reconstructed archaeological sites with autonomous virtual humans (in Proc. 6th Int. Conf. on Intelligent Virtual Agents, Los Angeles, CA, Aug. 2006). In: J. Gratch et al. (eds.) Intelligent virtual agents (Lecture Notes in Artificial Intelligence, vol. 4133). Springer, Berlin, pp. 420–433

M. Taddei, E. Zanon et al. (2003) DDD Giochi; Disegno e Design Digitale, no. 8 (Oct–Dec 2003): http://www.mediadigitali.polimi.it/ddd/numero/archivio.htm

The Dot Eaters (videogame history): http://www.thedoteaters.com

The history of RHBC (Ralph H. Baer Consultants): http://www.ralphbaer.com

The Pong Story: http://www.pong-story.com

Videotopia (historical videogame exhibits): http://www.videotopia.com

Welcome to PONG-story! (site dedicated to Ralph H. Baer, inventor of the videogame; author: D. Winter): http://www.pong-story.com

14 Customer Relationship Management (CRM)

Customer Relationship Management Association: http://crmassociation.org

Customer Relationship Management (by Gartner Group): http://www.gartner.com/it/products/research/asset_129491_2395.jsp

Definitions of customer relationship management on the Web (via Google): http://www.google.com/search?hl=en&defl=en&q=define:Customer+Relationship+Management&sa=X&oi=glossary_definition&ct=title

Microsoft Dynamics for customer relationship management: http://www.microsoft.com/dynamics/businessneeds/customerrelationshipmanagement.mspx

Oracle Customer Relationship Management: http://www.oracle.com/applications/customer-relationship-management.html

Webopedia definition of CRM: http://www.webopedia.com/TERM/C/CRM.html

15 Smart Labels, Smart Tags and RFID

S. Ashley (2004) Penny-wise smart labels—if smart tags cost only one cent apiece, they would be everywhere. Sci. Am. Aug. 2004 (see http://www.sciam.com/article.cfm?id=penny-wise-smart-labels)

M.J. Back, J. Cohen (2000) Page detection using embedded tags. In: Proc. 13th Annu. ACM Symp. User Interface Software and Technology, San Diego, CA, 5–8 Nov. 2000 (see http://portal.acm.org/ft_gateway.cfm?id=354441&type=pdf&coll=ACM&dl=ACM&CFID=12147632&CFTOKEN=20438114)

M.A. Bonuccelli, F. Lonetti, F. Martelli (2007) Exploiting ID knowledge for tag identification in RFID networks. In: Proc. 4th ACM Workshop on Performance Evaluation of Wireless Ad Hoc, Sensor, and Ubiquitous Networks, Chania, Crete, Greece, 22 Oct. 2007 (see http://portal.acm.org/ft_gateway.cfm?id=1298210&type=pdf&coll=ACM&dl=ACM&CFID=12147157&CFTOKEN=98652913)

M. Brandel (2003) RFID: Smart tags, high costs—RFID technology is hot, but the costs and complexity mean that ROI for suppliers is a long way off. Computerworld 15 Dec. 2003 (see http://www.computerworld.com/softwaretopics/erp/story/0,10801,88130,00.html)

D.E. Culler, H. Mulder (2004) Smart sensors to network the world. Sci. Am. June 2004 (see http://www.sciam.com/article.cfm?id=smart-sensors-to-network)

S. Hsi, H. Fait (2005) RFID enhances visitors' museum experience at the Exploratorium. Commun. ACM 48(9) Sept. 2005 (see http://portal.acm.org/ft_gateway.cfm?id=1082021 &type=pdf&coll=ACM&dl=ACM&CFID=12147632&CFTOKEN=20438114)

M. Ohkubo, K. Suzuki, S. Kinoshita (2005) RFID privacy issues and technical challenges. Commun. ACM 48(9) Sept. 2005 (see http://portal.acm.org/ft_gateway.cfm?id=1082022 &type=pdf&coll=ACM&dl=ACM&CFID=12147632&CFTOKEN=20438114)

F. Stajano (2005) RFID is X-ray vision. Commun. ACM 48(9) Sept. 2005 (see http://portal. acm.org/ft_gateway.cfm?id=1082015&type=pdf&coll=ACM&dl=ACM&CFID=121476 32&CFTOKEN=20438114)

E. Toye, R. Sharp, A. Madhavapeddy, D. Scott, E. Upton, A. Blackwell (2007) Interacting with mobile services: an evaluation of camera-phones and visual tags. Pers. Ubiq. Comput. 11(2) Jan. 2007 (see http://portal.acm.org/ft_gateway.cfm?id=1229066&type=pdf&c oll=ACM&dl=ACM&CFID=12147632&CFTOKEN=20438114)

16 Standards and Protocols for Interoperability;

17 Data Tags and the Semantic Web

C. Anderson (2004) The long tail (Change This 14 Dec. 2004): http://www.changethis. com/10.longtail

Y. Benkler (2005) Sharing nicely: On shareable goods and emergence of sharing as a modality of economic production (excerpt). Yale Law J. 114:273

S.D. Berkowitz (1982) An introduction to structural analysis: The network approach to social research. Butterworth, Toronto

T. Berners-Lee, M. Fischetti (1999) Weaving the Web: The original design and ultimate destiny of the World Wide Web. Harper, San Francisco, CA (ISBN 0062515861)

T. Berners-Lee, J. Hendler, O. Lassila (2001) The Semantic Web—A new form of web content that is meaningful to computers will unleash a revolution of new possibilities. Sci. Am. May 2001 (see http://www.sciam.com/article.cfm?articleID=00048144-10D2-1C70-84A9809EC588EF21)

R.L. Breiger (2004) The analysis of social networks. In: M. Hardy, A. Bryman (eds.) Handbook of data analysis. Sage Publications, London

Broku University Department of Sociology: http://www.brocku.ca/sociology

Censis (a social study and research institute that was founded in 1964 and became a legally recognised foundation in 1973 through Presidential Decree; it enjoys the support and participation of several large public and private institutions, is located in Rome, and the staff consists of approximately 30 researchers and 15 research assistants): http://www.censis.it

Centro Nazionale per l'Informatica nella Pubblica Amministrazione (CNIPA; National ICT Center for Public Administration): http://www.cnipa.gov.it/site/it-IT

W.W. Cohen (2002) A flexible learning system for wrapping tables and lists in HTML documents. In: Proc. World Wide Web 2002 Conf., Honolulu, Hawaii, May 2002 (see http:// www2002.org/presentations/hurst.pdf or http://delivery.acm.org/10.1145/520000/511477/ p232-cohen.pdf?key1=511477&key2=7232330021&coll=GUIDE&dl=GUIDE&CFID=1 2193329&CFTOKEN=95944715)

Creative Commons: http://creativecommons.org

D. De Kerckhove (1993) Brainframes. Mente, tecnologia, mercato. Baskerville, Bologna

D. De Kerckhove (2001) L'architettura dell'intelligenza. Testo & Immagine, Torino

Del.icio.us (social bookmarking): http://del.icio.us

Dion Hinchcliffe's Web 2.0 blog: http://web2.wsj2.com

Epistematica.org (dedicated to the research and development activities of Epistematica srl in the field of the technology of the symbolic representation of knowledge and automatic reasoning): http://www.epistematica.org/

Extensible Markup Language (XML): http://www.w3.org/XML

Extensible Markup Language (XML) 1.0 (W3C Recommendation, 16 August 2006): http://www.w3.org/TR/REC-xml

Facebook (a social utility that connects you with the people around you): http://www.facebook.com

Flickr: http://www.flickr.com

H. Geser (2004) Towards a sociological theory of the mobile phone (University of Zürich website): http://socio.ch/mobile/t_geser1.htm

G. Gesar et al. (2003) Toward a semantic web for heritage resources. DigiCULT Thematic Issue 3, May 2003 (see http://www.digicult.info/downloads/ti3_high.pdf)

Giant global graph (2007, timbl's blog): http://dig.csail.mit.edu/breadcrumbs/blog/4

Go 2 Web 20: http://www.go2web20.net/

Google: http://www.google.com

A. Granelli (2006) Il sé digitale. Guerini e Associati, Milano

G. Granieri (2005) Blog generation. Laterza, Roma

G. Granieri (2006) La società digitale. Laterza, Roma

M. Hatala, G. Richards (2003) eduSource: Interoperable network of learning object repositories. In: Proc. World Wide Web 2003 Conf., Budapest, Hungary, May 2003 (see http://www2003.org/cdrom/papers/poster/p336/p336-hatala.html)

H. Hewitt (2006) Blog: Understanding the information reformation that's changing your world. Thomas Nelson Inc., Nashville, TN (ISBN 078528804X)

S. Hoermann et al. (2003) Representation of knowledge as support for authors of reusable educational content. In: Proc. World Wide Web 2003 Conf., Budapest, Hungary, May 2003

Is One Laptop Per Child really a solution? (Article on Technology Business website): http://www.we.excelalways.net/techbiz

LastFM: http://www.lastfm.it

P. Lévy (1996) L'intelligenza collettiva. Per un'antropologia del cyberspazio. Feltrinelli, Milano

P. Lévy (1997) Il virtuale. Raffaello Cortina Editore, Milano

Linked in: http://www.linkedin.com

M. McLuhan (1995) Gli strumenti del comunicare. Il Saggiatore, Milano

M. McLuhan (2001) La Galassia Gutenberg. Nascita dell'uomo tipografico. Armando, Roma

M. McLuhan, E. McLuhan (1994) La legge dei media. La nuova scienza. Edizioni Lavoro, Roma

M. Miller (2007) Absolute beginner's guide to computer basics. Que, Indianapolis, IN

Ofcom (the independent regulator and competition authority for the UK communications industry, responsible for television, radio, telecommunications and wireless communications services): http://www.ofcom.org.uk

T. O'Reilly (2005) What is Web 2.0—Design patterns and business models for the next generation of software: http://www.oreillynet.com/pub/a/oreilly/tim/news/2005/09/30/what-is-web-20.html

S.B. Palmer (2001) The Semantic Web: An introduction: http://infomesh.net/2001/swintro

H. Rheingold (2002) Smart mobs. The next social revolution. Perseus, Cambridge

S. Ross, M. Donnelly, M. Dobreva (2003) New technologies for the cultural and scientific heritage sector. DigiCULT Technol. Watch Rep. 1, Feb. 2003 (see http://www.digicult.info/downloads/twr_2_2004_final_low.pdf)

B. Simon et al. (2003) Building interoperability among learning content management systems. In: Proc. World Wide Web 2003 Conf., Budapest, Hungary, May 2003 (see http://users.softlab.ece.ntua.gr/~retal/papers/conferences/www2003/Interoperability_poster.pdf)

SmartMobs—The next social revolution (mobile communication, pervasive computing, wireless networks, collective action): http://www.smartmobs.com

Social Science Information System (based at the University of Amsterdam): http://www.pscw.uva.nl/sociosite/topics/sociologists.html#MEAD

W.R. Stanek (2002) XML pocket consultant. Microsoft Press, Redmond, WA (ISBN 9780735611832)

L. Suryanarayana et al. (2002) Profiles for the situated web. In: Proc. World Wide Web 2002 Conf., Honolulu, Hawaii, May 2002 (see http://www2002.org/CDROM/refereed/214)

The Communications Regulatory Authority (Agcom) Italy: http://www.agcom.it

The International Standard Organisation (ISO; founded in 1947 and now represents some 130 countries): http://www.iso.ch

Twitter: http://twitter.com

Web 2.0—How to design guide: http://www.webdesignfromscratch.com/web-2.0-design-style-guide.cfm

Web 2.0 'neglecting good design' (May 2007, BBC News): http://news.bbc.co.uk/2/hi/technology/6653119.stm

E. Wenger, N. White, J.D. Smith (2005) Technology for communities: http://technology-forcommunities.com

WidSets (free service that sends favourite web content straight to a mobile phone): http://www.widsets.com

Wikipedia (The Free Encyclopedia): http://www.wikipedia.org

Wired magazine: http://www.wired.com

World Wide Web Consortium (W3C): http://www.w3c.org

xml.org (online community advancing the use of open standards): http://www.xml.org

YouTube: http://www.youtube.com

18 Ambient Intelligence

ISTAG (2001) Scenarios for ambient intelligence in 2010, final report. IPTS, Seville

ISTAG (2002) Strategic orientations and priorities for IST in FP6 (ISTAG Report). IPTS, Seville

Mark Weiser's homepage: http://www.ubiq.com/weiser

Mark Weiser's ubiquitous computing webpage: http://www.ubiq.com/hypertext/weiser/UbiHome.html

D. Merrill, P. Maes (2005) Invisible media: Attention-sensitive informational augmentation for physical objects. Proc. 7th Int. Conf. on Ubiquitous Computing, Tokyo, Japan 11–14 Sept. 2005 (see http://ambient.media.mit.edu/assets/_pubs/dmerrill_maes_ubicomp2005.pdf)

H. Rheingold (1994) PARC is back! Wired Feb. 1994, pp. 91–95 (see http://www.wired.com/wired/archive/2.02/parc_pr.html)

G. Riva, F. Vatalaro, F. Davide, M. Alcañiz (2005) Ambient intelligence: The evolution of technology, communication and cognition. Towards the future of human–computer interaction. IOS Press, Amsterdam

M. Weiser (1994) The world is not a desktop. Interactions Jan. 1994, pp. 7–8

M. Weiser (1993) Some computer science problems in ubiquitous computing. Commun. ACM July 1993

M. Weiser (1991) The computer for the 21st century. Sci. Am. Ubicomp Paper Sept. 1991 (see http://www.ubiq.com/hypertext/weiser/SciAmDraft3.html)

M. Weiser, J. Seely Brown (1995) Designing calm technology. Xerox PARC 21 Dec. 1995 (see http://www.ubiq.com/weiser/calmtech/calmtech.htm)

M. Weiser, J. Seely Brown (1996) The coming age of calm technology. Xerox PARC 5 Oct. 1996 (see http://www.ubiq.com/hypertext/weiser/acmfuture2endnote.htm)

19 Long-Term Preservation of Digital Archives

D. Bearman (1999) Reality and chimeras in the preservation of electronic records. D-Lib Mag. 5(4) (see http://www.dlib.org/dlib/april99/bearman/bearman-notes.html)

D. Bearman, K. Sochats (1996) Metadata requirements for evidence. University of Pittsburgh, PA (see http://web.archive.org/web/20000819132426/www.sis.pitt.edu/~nhprc/BACartic.html)

Consultative Committee for Space Data Systems (2001) Reference model for an open archival information system (OAIS). CCSDS, Reston, VA (see http://public.ccsds.org/publications/archive/650x0b1.pdf or http://public.ccsds.org/publications/RefModel.aspx)

L. Duranti, K. Eastwood (2002) The preservation of the integrity of electronic records. Kluwer, Dordrecht (see http://www.interpares.org/UBCProject/index.htm)

EC (2002) DigiCULT Report: Technological landscapes for tomorrow's cultural economy: Unlocking the value of cultural heritage. Office for Official Publications of the European Communities, Luxembourg (ISBN 92-828-6265-8; see http://www.salzburgresearch.at/fbi/digicult)

Ernst & Young (1996) Keeping electronic records forever: Records management; Vision development. Public Record Office Victoria, North Melbourne (see http://www.prov.vic.gov.au/vers/pdf/kerf.pdf)

Ernst & Young/CSIRO (1998) Victorian electronic record strategy (final report). Public Record Office Victoria, North Melbourne, ISBN 0-7311-5520-3 (see http://www.prov.vic.gov.au/vers/pdf/final.pdf)

Ernst & Young/CSIRO/Public Record Office Victoria (2007) Management of electronic records, Public Record Office Standard (PROS) 99/007. Public Record Office Victoria, North Melbourne (see http://www.prov.vic.gov.au/vers/standard)

Functional requirements for evidence in recordkeeping. School of Information Sciences, University of Pittsburgh, PA (see http://www.archimuse.com/papers/nhprc)

S. Granger (2000) Emulation as a digital preservation strategy. D-Lib Magazine, October 2000 (see http://www.dlib.org/dlib/october00/granger/10granger.html)

M. Guercio (2004) La conservazione a lungo termine dei documenti elettronici: normativa italiana e progetti internazionali. In: Proc. 3 Conf. Organizz. Arch. Univ. Italiane, Padova, Italy, 5–6 April 2001 (see http://www.unipd.it/archivio/conferenze/3conferenza/3%20 Conf%20-%20Mariella%20Guercio.pdf)

M. Hedstrom (1997) Research issues in migration and long-term preservation. Arch. Mus. Informatics 11(3–4):287– 292 (http://www.springerlink.com/content/w4624u883j075261)

A.R. Heminger, S.B. Robertson (2000) The digital Rosetta Stone: a model for maintaining long-term access to static digital documents. Commun. Assoc. Inform. Syst. 3:2

B. Lavoie (2000) Meeting the challenges of digital preservation: The OAIS reference model. OCLC Newslett. Jan./Feb. 2000:26–30

D. Levy (1998) Heroic measures: Reflections on the possibility and purpose of digital preservation. In: Proc. 3rd ACM Conf. on Digital Libraries, Pittsburgh, PA, 23–26 June 1998, pp 152–161

R.A. Lorie (2001) Long-term preservation of digital information. In: Proc. 1st ACM/IEEE-CS Joint Conf. on Digital Libraries, Roanoke, VA, January 2001, pp 346–352

C. Lynch (1999) Canonicalization: A fundamental tool to facilitate preservation and management of digital information. D-Lib Mag. Sept. 1999 (see http://www.dlib.org/dlib/september99/09lynch.html)

National Archives of Australia (1995) Keeping electronic records (policy for electronic record-keeping in the Commonwealth Government). National Archives of Australia, Canberra (see http://www.naa.gov.au/images/digital-recordkeeping-guidelines_tcm2-920.pdf)

National Archives of Australia (1999) Recordkeeping Metadata Standard for Commonwealth Agencies, version 1.0. National Archives of Australia, Canberra (see http://www.naa.gov.au/images/rkms_pt1_2_tcm2-1036.pdf)

National Archives of Australia and Office for Government Online (1999) The Australian Government Locator Service (AGLS) Manual for Users, Version 1.1. National Archives of Australia and Office for Government Online, Canberra (see http://www.naa.gov.au/records-management/create-capture-describe/describe/AGLS/index.aspx or http://www.naa.gov.au/records-management/publications/AGLS-Element.aspx)

National Archives Washington and San Diego Supercomputer Center: http://www.npaci.edu

National Library of Australia (1999b) Preservation metadata for digital collections. National Library of Australia, Canberra (see http://www.nla.gov.au/preserve/pmeta.html)

National Research Council (1995) Study on the long-term retention of selected scientific and technical records of the Federal Government Working Papers. National Academy Press, Washington, DC

Networked European Deposit Library (2000) Metadata for long term preservation. NEDLIB, The Hague, The Netherlands (see http://nedlib.kb.nl/results/NEDLIBmetadata.pdf)

OAIS standard: http://public.ccsds.org/publications/archive/650x0b1.pdf

OCLC/RLG Working Group on Preservation Metadata (2001) A recommendation for content information. OCLC, Dublin, OH (see http://www.oclc.org/research/projects/pmwg/pm_framework.pdf)

V. Reich, D.S.H. Rosenthal (2001) LOCKSS: A permanent web publishing and access system. D-Lib Mag. June 2001 (see http://www.dlib.org/dlib/june01/reich/06reich.html)

Research Library Group (1998) RLG REACH element set for shared description of museum objects. RLG/OCLC, Dublin, OH (see http://www.oclc.org/programs/ourwork/past/museumresources/reach.htm)

Resource Description Framework (RDF) model and syntax specification: http://www.w3.org/RDF

RLG-OCLC Working Group (2001) Attributes of a trusted digital repository: Meeting the needs of research resources (report; draft for public comment). OCLC, Dublin, OH (see http://www.oclc.org/programs/ourwork/past/trustedrep/attributes01.pdf)

A.M. Ronchi (2004) From Hammurabi Codex to Rosetta Stone. Long term preservation of digital archives. Proc. CIDOC 2004, St. Petersburg, Russia (see: http://confifap.cpic.ru/upload/spb2004/reports/dokladEn_172.doc)

J. Rothenberg (1995) Ensuring the longevity of digital documents. Sci. Am. 272(1):24–29

J. Rothenberg (1999) Avoiding technological quicksand: Finding a viable technical foundation for digital preservation. Council on Library and Information Resources, Washington, DC (ISBN 1-887334-63-7; see http://www.clir.org/pubs/reports)

T. Shepard, D. MacCarn (1998) The Universal Preservation Format: Background and fundamentals. In: Sixth DELOS Workshop: Preservation of Digital Information, Tomar, Portugal, 17–19 June 1998 (see http:/www.ercim.org/publication/ws-proceedings/DELOS6/upf.pdf)

Standards Australia (1996) Australian standard on records management, AS4390-1996. Standards Australia, Homebush, NSW (ISBN 0-7337-0306-2)

State Records NSW (1995) Documenting the future (policy and strategies for electronic recordkeeping in the New South Wales public sector). State Records NSW, Kingswood (ISBN 07310-5038-X; see http://www.records.nsw.gov.au/recordkeeping/policy_on_electronic_recordkeeping_6879.asp or http://www.records.nsw.gov.au/recordkeeping/docs%5CPolicy%20on%20Electronic%20Recordkeeping.pdf)

Task Force on Archiving of Digital Information (1996) Preserving digital information (report). Commission on Preservation and Access and The Research Libraries Group, Inc., Washington, DC (see http://www.oclc.org/programs/ourwork/past/digpresstudy/final-report.pdf)

US Department of Defense Standard 5015.2 (Design Criteria Standard For Electronic Records Management Software Applications): http://jitc.fhu.disa.mil/recmgt

A. Waugh, R. Wilkinson, B. Hills, J. Dell'oro (2000) Preserving digital information forever. In ACM 2000 digital libraries: proceedings of the fifth ACM Conference on Digital Libraries, June 2-7, 2000, San Antonio, Texas, New York: Association for Computing Machinery, 175-184. http://portal.acm.org/citation.cfm?id=1456476

S. Weibel, J. Kunze, C. Lagoze, M. Wolfe (1998) Dublin Core metadata for resource discovery (RFC 2413): ftp://ftp.isi.edu/in-notes/rfc2413.txt

P. Wheatley (2001) Migration: a CAMiLEON discussion paper (Ariadne 29): http://www.ariadne.ac.uk/issue29/camileon

F. Yergeau (1998) UTF-8, a transformation format of ISO 10646 (RFC 2279): http://www.ietf.org/rfc/rfc2279.txt

20 The Future: the Weave of the Digital Fabric

Agcom (2007) Il sistema delle comunicazioni (relazione annuale). Agcom, Rome

M. Bangemann et al. (2003) Europe and the global information society ("Bangemann Report"; Recommendations to the European Council): http://ec.europa.eu/archives/ISPO/infosoc/backg/bangeman.html and http://www.medicif.org/Dig_library/ECdocs/reports/Bangemann.htm

G. Bertrand (Coord.), A. Michalski, L.R. Pench (1999) Scenarios Europe 2010: Five possible futures for Europe (European Commission working paper): http://ec.europa.eu/comm/cdp/scenario/scenarios_en.pdf

Confindustria Servizi Innovativi e Tecnologici (2008) e-Content 2008—3° rapporto sul mercato dei contenuti digitali in Italia. Rome (http://www.confindustriasi.it/news-376.html)

D. Deutsch (1997) The fabric of reality: The science of parallel universes and its implications—La trama della realtà. Einaudi, Torino

EC i2010 Annual Reports: http://ec.europa.eu/information_society/eeurope/i2010/key_documents/index_en.htm

e-Europe 2005: http://ec.europa.eu/information_society/eeurope/2005/index_en.htm

eEurope—An Information Society for all (launched by the European Commission on 8 Dec. 1999): http://portal.etsi.org/eEurope

EITO (European Information Technology Observatory) Annual Reports 2004–2007: http://www.eito.com/start.html

FEDERCOMIN (2005) Evoluzione dell'innovazione in Italia secondo i parametri eEurope 2005—Internet. Accesso e utilizzo. FEDERCOMIN, Rome (see http://www.federcomin.it/sviluppo/Produzio.nsf/7c1dcc3598966887c125696e0034e51e/3855b3f24ca63d85c12570c100456fcb/$FILE/oss3_cap01_intro.pdf

FEDERCOMIN (2006) e-Content 2006—2° rapporto sul mercato dei contenuti digitali in Italia. FEDERCOMIN, Rome (see http://www.confindustriasi.it/news-156.html)

Information and communications technologies—OECD key ICT indicators: http://www.oecd.org/document/23/0,3343,en_2649_34223_33987543_1_1_1_1,00.html

ISTAG (2001) Scenarios for ambient intelligence in 2010: Final report. IPTS, Seville (see ftp://ftp.cordis.europa.eu/pub/ist/docs/istagscenarios2010.pdf)

ITU (2006) digital.life (report). ITU, Geneva (see http://www.itu.int/dms_pub/itu-s/opb/pol/S-POL-IR.DL-2-2006-R1-SUM-PDF-E.pdf)

L. Jeffrey (2001) Vital links for a knowledge culture: public access to new information and communication technologies. Council of Europe Publishing, Paris (see http://book.coe.int/EN/ficheouvrage.php?PAGEID=36&lang=EN&produit_aliasid=518)

J.H. Murray (1997) Hamlet on the holodeck: The future of narrative in cyberspace. Free Press, New York

UNESCO (2007) Ethical implications of emerging technologies: A survey (Geneva Net Dialogue). UNESCO, Paris (see http://unesdoc.unesco.org/images/0014/001499/149992E.pdf)

Part III   Exploitation, Applications and Services

21 Content, Communication and Tools

In the previous parts, we considered the general framework of ICT, problems and issues associated with it and some of the technologies that are currently available. We now turn our attention to communication processes and the potential benefits and disadvantages of using ICT in the field of culture. Our discussion will encompass digitisation, archiving and management tools, exploitation and added value services.

We will start with a general overview of this subject, taking into account content, standards, sustainability, economic models, data acquisition, digital preservation, comparisons between classification schemes, interoperability, large datasets, navigation tools and metaphors, experiencing cultural content, information policies, intellectual property rights (IPR) and privacy and lastly education and training.

Fig. 21.1 Chinese tourists looking at the last supper poster (photo by the Author)

21.1 Culture, ICT and Emerging Technologies

Information and communications technology is transforming the way that we work and live. Its social and economical impacts provide a key opportunity to make advances every field of knowledge.

Another significant development in recent years has been the growing awareness of the importance of cultural heritage, and the need to exploit and manage it: the number of visitors to museums, historical monuments and archaeological sites grows day by day.

Heritage in Europe
As already expressed in many other publications, Europe evidently has a wealth of cultural heritage—artworks and "cultural treasures"—expressed in various forms, from graffiti to frescos to architecture, created over the centuries by people from various cultures, and epitomising various styles (Greek, Renaissance...).

21.2 Which Role?

Information and communications technologies provide powerful facilitatory tools, but they will never supersede content and skills. Experts in applying ICT
Technology trained approach
to culture must avoid the *technology trained approach*, which can be summarised as "once you have developed a new technology, try to find or invent a problem that can be efficiently solved by that technology".

As usually happens, technology is becoming *invisible*; the emphasis has shifted from continuously enriching options and tools on menu bars to a "background intelligence" approach that is aimed at helping the end-user in everyday tasks.

Tangible added value
Last but not least, ICT must provide a real, *tangible* added value to cultural applications, so it is not enough to create nice gadgets or visually impressive presentations.

There are many fields in which ICT tools and methods could contribute to the cultural agenda. Some of them are listed below, along with basic recommendations.

21.3 Cultural Content

How do we develop a critical mass of digital cultural content? As we approach an era in which it will be possible to hide substantial computing power and wireless networking capacity within everyday objects, we will also find it necessary to recreate and redefine *content* in order to exploit new opportunities.

Intangible heritage
Cultural content is not necessary related to physical objects; *intangible heritage* should benefit significantly from new technologies. The preservation and exploitation of *intangible heritage* is one of the most important cultural issues today. Various institutions have launched their own projects and actions in this field; for example, UNESCO recently established the Intangible Heritage Task Force.

238 ⋮ *III Exploitation, Applications and Services*

The creation of a fully interactive *online culture* would transform links between computers into connections among people that should stimulate ideas and new skills.

Recommendations: We must select, collect and distribute high-quality content. In addition we must create mechanisms that encourage the participation and empowerment of all people in developing and developed countries and allow them autonomy and control.

21.4   Standards and Good Practices

Although many institutions have begun to digitise collections, many (even in the industrialised nations) have not. Larger institutions typically find the funding to implement complex and costly digitisation projects, while smaller institutions, that have fewer resources and no standards or models to guide them, risk costly mistakes. New standards for formulating and managing data as well as migrating data to new platforms must therefore be developed. This will require significant investment, which in turn demands that the standards and terminology developed ensure the long-term viability of electronic information and an ability to search across databases.

Recommendations: Develop standards for creating and managing digital collections and "guides to good practices" for creating cultural content. Good practices are needed to help smaller institutions and developing nations avoid "reinventing the wheel". Create incentives for using de facto standards and build a portal for international data standards, good practices and policy frameworks to promote and encourage harmonization of cultural content.

21.5   Sustainability and Economic Models

One of the most critical aspects in this sector is sustainability. This is not limited to "anthropic risk"; it is more strongly linked to economic sustainability. One of the major weaknesses of project proposals is usually the business and market model: defining who is going to pay, and even who is going to manage the service on a mid/long-term perspective. A study currently underway for the European Commission is intended to provide memory institutions with information on how to address new ICT challenges. Results so far indicate that cultural institutions can earn revenue from ICT when they market their cultural resources to media companies (in a business-to-business fashion) or produce their own value added products and services (in a business-to-customers model).

Recommendations: Promote institutional awareness of new economic models. For cultural institutions, coming to terms with the Internet paradigm will be an important factor in keeping up with the dynamics and expectations for users in the Knowledge Society.

21.6 Data Acquisition and Digital Preservation

The objective of digital preservation of cultural heritage is to address new ways of representing, analysing, manipulating and managing different kinds of digital cultural objects from different media sources, with special attention given to surrogates of fragile physical objects or sites damaged by humans or environmental conditions. It provides new and important ways to manage multivariate data in a dynamic way at various levels (museum, city, region, by country or author, etc.).

Recommendations: Applications should focus on the sustainable development of valuable digital repositories in libraries, museums and archives. Preliminary studies should address the technical and organisational problems surrounding the viability of scaleable digital repositories, e.g. through test bed creation for long-term preservation and content management in distributed heterogeneous collections. Particular attention should be paid to long-term accessibility, both by citizens and for scientific analysis, and to quality, affordability and acceptability.

21.7 Comparing Classification Schemes

The ability to compare classification schemes is an issue that is directly connected to the requirements listed above. Take, for example, an object listed under a specific chapter in the Marburg archives, but which appears under a different chapter in another archive since a different classification scheme is used. How can we link the two data?

Recommendations: We strongly recommend the development of multilingual thesauri that can be shared by organisations within each specific sector of applications.

21.8 Data Structure and Interoperability

In general, the filing process (ignoring how it is achieved) is key to cultural heritage management. For ICT tools, the creation of appropriate data structure and format definitions is crucial to ensuring added value, good performance and high interoperability.

Recommendations: Use standardised reference, description and content models and de facto technological standards.

21.9 Maintenance of Large Databanks

Permanent supports Considering the huge amount of data to be filed, we need to objectively tackle a problem that has been greatly underestimated so far: the maintenance of digital information for long periods of time. There are two aspects to consider: technological obsolescence of hardware and software, and the temporary nature of so-called "permanent" storage systems. ICT evolves over timeframes that are much shorter than that associated with the storage of cultural heritage.

Recommendations: Hardware and software obsolescence requires the use of main and de facto standards along with the creation of rich text or XML backup datasets that can be used to migrate the data toward new standards. The aging of media issue necessitates that we carefully consider the lifetimes of various media and do not rely on so-called "permanent" media. There are methods and solutions that can be used to refresh data and guarantee data integrity.

21.10 Navigation Tools, Interfaces and Metaphors

Navigation tools are undoubtedly interchangeable, considering the rapid obsolescence of interface solutions and the evolution of the abilities and tastes of users themselves, but the navigation tools associated with an application are still usually key to its success. The ability to freely and directly access information through semantic and knowledge maps, map trees and virtual interfaces have certainly contributed in a profound way to the success of the World Wide Web since they circumvent the need to directly use the (more complex) query form of a databank. Non-Western societies may require design innovations in this area. For example, the current Internet is mainly a scrolling medium, and is based on a "Western" textual tradition. However, online culture for developing regions will have to represent both oral traditions and the movements through space and time that characterise local life practices.

Recommendations: Foster new design concepts and interfaces that allow wider access and use of the technology. Encourage the development of multilingual capabilities, and create new modes of mapping and indexing information and new conceptual search capabilities beyond the Semantic Web. Develop new authoring and interactivity tools.

21.11 Experiencing Cultural Heritage

The communication process associated with cultural heritage possesses a reasonable degree of complexity, but ICT undoubtedly enhances the enjoyment of cultural heritage, since it allows us, for example, to offer personalised explorative and cognitive routes based on user profiles and the recommendations of communications or cognitive science experts.

According to psychologists, we can classify objects into two main categories: objects that are used for practical purposes and objects that are used to communicate. Artefacts are basically communication objects. Objects that are used for practical purposes can also be communication objects (according to industrial design), but when they are no longer in practical use they can be considered to be solely communication objects (artefacts).

Since they are communication objects, artefacts must "speak", and even sometimes transmit different messages to different people.

21 Content, Communication and Tools

Fig. 21.2
On-site reconstruction of the floor of a Roman bath in Armenia (photo by the author)

We can present a work of art and propose an interpretation for it that has been established in advance, or try to offer visitors all the elements required for them to evaluate the work of art autonomously. Some of the main difficulties inherent in communicating cultural heritage arise from the fact that the work of art often belongs to a different historical cultural context and is probably not situated in the same scene that is was originally, and so it is difficult to interpret the meaning of the artefact when viewed out of context. This usually happens in archaeological or ethnographic museums.

Recommendations: Multimedia techniques and virtual reality extensions should help the user to interpret or reconstruct the original shape, function and location of the cultural artefact, or it can recreate the original context and environment. Virtual reality representations of historic monuments and evidence of their historical evolution have become powerful tools for museum exhibits.

Open-air in situ museums and exhibits provide a novel approach to cultural education. The creation of digital artefacts will help to both preserve the originals and to make inaccessible or lost heritage available and exploitable.

21.12 Information Policies: Frameworks and Intellectual Property Rights

In order to foster global cooperation, particularly with respect to access to cultural information across boundaries, governments must develop information policies. Most industrialised nations have created or are creating such policies, and must now work with developing countries to establish policy frameworks. The global Information Society mandates a better understanding of the value of open communication, access, and the educational use of content.

Recommendations: Promote the adoption of clear, publicly available national and international information policy frameworks. Encourage proactive intellectual property rights that emphasise the public good.

21.13 Monument Conservation

ICT should provide innovative methodologies, technologies and products for the diagnosis, risk evaluation, protection, conservation, maintenance, restoration, sustainable management and enhancement of, accessibility to, and functions that allow the reuse of European cultural heritage. There is currently a trend to move from heavy restoration to a planned continuous conservation approach, following the motto "prevention is better than cure". This approach leads to smaller costs but more quality.

Recommendations: Promote and support by different means the development of new ICT tools for monument conservation; create and exploit a virtual network of European competence centres; create and feed a digital library addressed at monument conservation. Establish an information and best practice sharing mechanism focusing on ICT and new technologies for built heritage.

21.14 Education and Training

The end-goal of economic promotion is to create appropriate conditions for the development of new economic activities that enhance the enjoyment of cultural heritage and create new employment opportunities in associated sectors. One strategic issue for the application of the ICT and emerging technologies market to the cultural heritage sector is the availability of appropriately trained professionals.

To meet this challenge, cultural institutions will require additional personnel with skills in managing and producing digital content and services. Because the number of qualified IT personnel is limited, the cultural sector will have to compete for employees with other industry sectors and actively support ICT training for their existing staff. Information processing and "knowledge work" will become more and more vital to the missions of cultural and memory institutions.

Recommendations: Support the hiring and training of qualified staff, and develop training programs for technicians and managers. Particular attention should be given to identifying appropriate profiles and defining suitable study curricula at various levels. In particular, humanistic and classical study curricula must be considered in order to promote the use of ICT for innovative research in these areas. The development of training programs at various levels (local, regional, national, international and also institutional) is essential. A European network of educational and training centres should be established to facilitate the exchange of both students and professors.

22 Exploitation, Applications and Services

The three main activities usually associated with cultural heritage are *conservation*, *research* and *exploitation*. Museums, cultural institutions and organisations are committed to these goals. Conservation is considered to be the most important goal that enables future generations to enjoy our common heritage. Huge conservation efforts are therefore constantly being planned and implemented, which can sometimes cause conservation to overshadow the other two goals.

Conservation, research and exploitation

Of course, research is the key to obtaining information and background on and hints regarding future works. Nevertheless, financial resources realistically limit research activity. However, a number of research projects aimed at the local level and at the European level have been launched over the last ten or fifteen years. The Fifth and Sixth Framework Programmes have been deeply involved at European level. Information and communications technology is one of the main catalysts for this new interest in culture and cultural heritage; in fact, a number of different European Commission Frameworks have launched specific bids[1] that support the application of ICT and new emerging technologies to culture. There is widespread understanding that ICT[2] could play a positive role in the preservation and promotion of cultural assets.

Exploitation and education are sometimes overlooked because they can conflict with the aims of conservation and they are not strictly related to either conservation or research. Nevertheless, these are among the most important activities since they address one of the basic needs of humankind: to increase knowledge and enrich culture. This activity is therefore complementary to the other two because protection, care and research cannot exist without knowledge.

Protection, research and knowledge

---

1   Ranging from basic research up to market validation projects (IST, Culture 2000, eTEN, eContent+, Media, etc.).
2   As well as new emerging technologies (e.g. the *BioBrush* project, where microorganisms are used to clean archaeological remains).

Fig. 22.1 Museum duties

A number of activities have recently been launched in the field of culture[3], some of which are general frameworks or cultural policies, while others target specific goals such as cultural identity preservation, freedom of cultural expression, exploitation of minor cultural assets, development of market models, etc.

One of the first acts of the new millennium aimed at addressing these aspects was the expert meeting in Lund organised by the European Commission.

Lund Principles

On 4 April 2001, under the Swedish EU Presidency, the European Commission organised an expert meeting with representatives from all Member States in Lund. The conclusions and recommendations of this meeting are known as the *Lund Principles*[4] and were further developed in the Lund Action Plan, which establishes an agenda for actions to be carried out by Member States and the Commission.

The main conclusions of the meeting at Lund were for Member States:
- To establish an evolving forum of coordination
- To support the development of a European view of digitisation policies and programmes
- To develop mechanisms to promote good practice and skills development
- To collaborate in order to make the digitised cultural and scientific heritage of Europe visible and accessible.

---

3   The enlargement of European Union and the enrichment of its cultural roots is a powerful motivation for enhanced cultural policies.
4   See: http://www.cordis.lu/ist/digicult/lund-principles.htm.

III Exploitation, Applications and Services

22.1 Accessing European Cultural Heritage

As is widely known, the cultural wealth of Europe, which is derived from all of the different populations who have existed on this continent over many centuries, is unique and extremely rich in terms of the quality and quantity of art objects of all kinds, from graffiti or frescoes to architectural and urban works through to works of craftsmanship.

At a first glance it may appear strange that this incredible wealth could cause the problems that notoriously afflict the field of cultural assets in Europe in general and Italy in particular.

The lack of adequate locations for exhibitions, the high cost/benefits ratio encountered when making spaces open to the public, the lack of infrastructure, costs linked to the restoration and maintenance of cultural works, and other aspects linked to the main issues associated with the management of cultural assets, such as their preservation, exposure to the public, and didactics, are just some of the problems that could be solved through the use of advanced technologies. *Drawbacks*

In addition, there are a number of situations in which these technologies appear to be the ideal solution. Simply take into account, for example the considerable number of artworks locked in storage rooms or otherwise inaccessible to the public (because they are hosted in privately owned buildings for instance[5]).

Global networking and the World Wide Web offers an incredible chance to pursue this goal. The support usually offered by ICT to cultural heritage involves enhancing the visibility of the collections hosted by the European museums, broadcasting cultural knowledge and enhancing cultural exchange between European nations, and particularly providing access to European culture to countries outside Europe.

Investing in the use of advanced technologies in the cultural heritage domain should aid access to Europe's cultural heritage as well as our understanding, preservation and economic promotion of it.

Relatively recent studies[6] have indicated that while about 28% of Europeans are interested in accessing art online, the potential number of North American and Japanese visitors is far greater. *Potential users*

When dealing with access to different collections, it seems appropriate to add some comments on the evolution of distributed database searches. A number of restrictions on database access will be removed through technological advances. These include the ability to search multiple databases (as opposed to websites) other than those associated with specific projects (e.g. Aquarelle).

---

5 Sometimes even historical buildings (e.g. monuments) owned by institutions.

6 Such as Eurobarometer 1997 (see http://ec.europa.eu/public_opinion/index_en.htm) and EITO 1999–2005 (see http://www.eito.org/start.html).

22 Exploitation, Applications and Services

This may not be desirable for all databases (e.g. those that charge for access or contain highly specialised contents).

Resource descriptions for detailed content such as that provided by museums will allow users to identify suitable databases for queries. Technological advances are enabling websites to exploit cultural content fully by making use of new presentation and communication technologies, as described above.

Moreover, the detection and analysis of data held in various cultural databases will require not only appropriate database access software, but also that target data (e.g. that held by museums and galleries) is stored in a standard or predictable format. Such issues are largely resolved by using XML and standard DTDs (e.g. CIDOC CRM, CIMI). It is expected that this level of access will be required both by students and researchers as well as basic users looking for specific gallery exhibits (e.g. a particular painting).

Metadata The application of tagging based on specific ontologies and data schemas plus the creation of datasets containing "metadata" (data about each entry in the cultural databank) will greatly enhance database searches.

23 Prioritisation in Digitalisation

The path from the "originals" to the dissemination and exploitation of cultural content through ICT usually starts with the creation of so-called *digital originals* via digitisation.

Digital originals

The development of a European view of digitisation policies and programmes seems to be one of the key points on the agenda every time that the application of ICT to culture is discussed.

Let us start this chapter with an excerpt from the final report from Working Group 4 of the Memorandum of Understanding on Multimedia Access to Europe's Cultural Heritage (1996):

"Historical" digitisation policies and programmes

Until today there has been no common—open, modular, interoperable—digital platform for museums, galleries, libraries and other institutions essential to culture.

Thus far the WG have only found proprietary solutions, with no clear perspectives on European/global communications (interactivity, virtual reconstruction, etc.), no access for a very wide public, no prospects of realising services and products without *"ensuring that there is a substantial European cultural content to the services and products in the Information Society"* (Peter Johnston's foreword to the MoU publication, 28 June 1996).

The WG has already initiated a survey to find out which media museums have used for documentation and presentation of their collections, and which digital media in particular. We have come to the conclusion that only museums can decide about [what] their priorities in digitisation should be—thus, the development of consensus and common strategy is essential to maximising synergy within European networks of particular types of museums and between different types of museums. This means that without developing consensus and common strategy it is difficult to come up with guidelines of any precision relating to which parts of the collections should be given priority in the period leading up 2000.

Conclusion: A number of European pilot projects should be started with the goal of developing consensus and common strategy relating to a network of co-operation on priority for digitisation.

These were the findings of the working group way back in 1996. So what happened in response to these findings? Many resources were devoted to the digitisation of artefacts and archives.

Such investments in digitisation must be carefully planned due to the huge number of artefacts in some collections, the risk of damaging or destroying the original artefact during the digitisation, and last but not least, the evolution of technological performance and standards. All of these factors shape digitisation policies. Copyright issues can also emerge.

Text Digitisation may be limited to textual documents that are acquired in both an editable format and as graphical images, such as those found in paper-based documents and in archives. Highly automated and cost-effective solutions that achieve this goal are commercially available nowadays. The choice is basically to use an in-house solution or to outsource the service. OCR conversion to text file format enables full-text searches and indexing, as well as in-depth searches and metadata creation.

Images The digital imaging of frescos, paintings and images can also be achieved using commercial solutions, although the increased complexity of the task (compared to paper document digitisation) usually requires some expertise in the specific sector.

High-resolution colour scanners or digital cameras can be used, and multi-spectral imaging modes such as X-ray or infrared might be required in order to visualise invisible shapes.

3-D objects The 3-D digitisation of small and large objects is becoming an increasingly popular technique. It usually provides significant added value and ranges from experimental studies into the "thickness" of the colour on a canvas to the accurate reconstruction of an historical building in 3-D to "mint fingerprints" on ancient coins through to the virtual restoration of fragile objects.

Three-dimensional datasets are usually acquired as clouds of points and then converted in multi-facetted models requiring huge amounts of storage space. This activity is usually outsourced to specific laboratories that can provide a ready-to-use dataset that is sometimes already decorated with accurate textures.

Fig. 23.1 Sinar camera with a digital back

24 Cataloguing Standards and Archiving Tools

One of the main problems with applying ICT to cultural heritage concerns the selection of appropriate filing systems and data structures. The filing process, no matter how it is realised, is generally a key process in cultural heritage management. Data filing is a somewhat complicated task; it requires positive and fruitful cooperation between computer scientists and humanists. Of course, the fact that huge data sets are produced that must be managed all over a long period of time generates some problems, as does the requirement that the data retrieval process is sufficiently efficient.

Some of the goals of cataloguing and data filing are:

Goals of cataloguing and data filing

- To gain a structured view of cultural assets
- To ensure good management of the filed patrimony
- To realise a proper documentation service.

Of course, all this of requires that significant financial resources (mainly qualified human resources) are available. Some difficulties associated with cataloguing and data filing include the tricky task of harvesting only high-quality data, and (related to the first two points to some extent) ensuring that the task is completed in a reasonable period of time. Because of these reasons, the cataloguing/filing procedure is sometimes dropped after a pilot phase because of a lack of resources or an unsustainable cost/benefits ratio. This means that changes in human resources result in a loss of continuity and knowledge about specific topics.

When searching for potential solutions, it is important to define not only the reference database, but also the granularity and homogeneity of the information to be gathered. In addition, some basic rules for managing inhomogeneity must be devised.

The consistent use of standards is another useful strategy for preserving museum data, because it recognises the shortcomings and costs of making the information dependent on a particular hardware and software combination and provides a blueprint for migrating data.

Last but not least, most of the key tasks in the cataloguing/filing process must be performed by humans; relatively few of the activities associated with the process can be performed automatically. In addition, when dealing with cultural heritage, we need to employ qualified experts and skilled operators.

24.1 Historical Background of Cataloguing

The idea of creating a comprehensive catalogue of artefacts is a very attractive one that has stimulated many meetings and conferences, at both national and international level. It took a long period of discussion about data homogeneity and integration before the standardisation of computer-based alphanumeric and graphical data management could begin to be studied.

Global information system fundamentals

At the end of the 1960s, during a meeting at the Metropolitan Museum of Art in New York, the fundamentals of a global information system were defined. The idea was to create an integrated encyclopaedic knowledge system.

At European level, the idea of creating a centralised "unique catalogue" prevailed. This approach entails some problems, such as:

Unique catalogue

- The need to carefully consider the types of information technology resources available and their costs.
- A common inventory model must be defined a priori.
- The complexity of the workflow due to the web of relationships between the central authority, regional authorities, local authorities and even private organisations. Each of these can gather information about artefacts, which must then be transferred to the upper level of the workflow in order to update the information.

In order to implement this mechanism at a national level, a set of handbooks and guidelines have been published by special interest groups managed by central authorities. Such guidelines do not force the adoption of predefined standards and methods; they simply suggest the use of some best practices and standards when filling in paper forms, leaving sufficient freedom to choose terms and syntax.

ICCD

The most well known and relevant catalogues were created in the 1970s. In Italy the Ministry of Culture created a set of institutes (Cataloguing and Documentation, Restoration, etc.). The Istituto Centrale per il Catalogo e la Documentazione—ICCD (Central Institute for Cataloguing and Documentation) began to build the kernel of the general catalogue.

Inventare General des Monumentes et Richesses Artistique

In France the Inventare General des Monumentes et Richesses Artistique was created. A number of additional initiatives targeting the local and private levels also made contributions.

Canadian Heritage Information Network (CHIN)

Some countries decided to invest directly in information technology-based catalogues. This happened in Canada with the National Inventory Programme [subsequently renamed the Canadian Heritage Information Network (CHIN)], and in Great Britain with the Information Retrieval Group of Museum Association (IRGMA) [subsequently renamed the Museum Documentation Association (MDA)[7]].

Museum Documentation Association (MDA)

---

7   Museum Documentation Association: http://www.mda.org.uk/.

252   **III** *Exploitation, Applications and Services*

CHIN[8] was one of the first (possibly even *the* first) institution to experiment with using networks and related technologies in the field of cultural heritage.

In the 1970s the arrival of low-cost computers led to the creation of number of projects and initiatives that aimed to establish the use of IT in museums. A large number of local institutions, museums and art galleries developed solutions tailored to their own needs, with little regard paid to data standardisation and interoperability. On the other hand, libraries also began to invest in information technology, but they targeted the creation of a distributed catalogue.

The advantages of the distributed scheme created by libraries resulted in positive experiences and the scheme yielded concrete (useful and valuable) results.

The proliferation of applications and proprietary standards triggered by the availability of low-cost computer systems led to the development of applications that did not consider:

Standards

- Potential and real end-users
- That institutions need to manage the information
- That researchers from many different disciplines need to access the information.

In addition, there was usually only a limited degree of integration of the skills of technicians with those of art historians/humanists.

In the 1980s enhancements in database management systems technology led to the need to agree on data standards in order to ease both data entry and retrieval. But what are the building blocks of a data standard? A standard comprises rules and conventions that define:

- How information should be structured
- Data forms that respect standard grammar and syntax
- Appropriate terms (i.e. a vocabulary)
- Appropriate communication protocols.

Standards are relevant to all of the main phases of data management:

- Gathering/harvesting
- Organisation
- Retrieval
- The definition of strict rules for managing inhomogeneous data.

While the roles played by institutions in managing the general inventories may differ from country to country, their main functions are usually to unify and exploit methods by:

- Defining general cataloguing methods
- Defining data standards for each specific sector (e.g. archaeological items, photographic images, anthropological items, intangible heritage, etc.)

---

8   Canadian Heritage Information Network (CHIN): http://www.chin.gc.ca/English/index.html.

- Organising proper tools for data checking and validation (sometimes even archiving tools and data entry tools)
- Creating and managing the central catalogue
- Participating in national or international research/development projects (e.g. multilinguistic thesauri).

If we do not utilise standards, we will encounter issues such as:
- Problems when attempting to access information in specific databases
- The need to rearrange information when transferring it between different databases
- Doubt over whether the full set of information archived is being accessed.

Examples of the cataloguing standards used include those defined by the Italian ICCD[9]:
- Archaeological relics
- Artefacts
- Contemporary artworks
- Engravings and dies
- Photographs
- Scientific heritage
- Demo-anthropological assets
- Intangible heritage
- Musical instruments and organs
- Numismatics and coins
- Immovable heritage
    - Architecture
    - Gardens and parks
    - Urban/extraurban
    - Monuments and archaeological units
- Town planning and territory
    - Archaeological sites
    - Municipal territory
    - Historical centres
- Archives
    - Author/biography
- Events
    - Thefts.

In addition to these standards, there are others related to:
- Information technology (digital imaging and data transfer)
- Imaging (photographic documentation, annexed into cataloguing forms)
- Aerial photography (instructions for the use of).

---

9   Please refer to http://www.iccd.beniculturali.it.

24.2 Data Standards

It is a difficult task to define data standards for cataloguing purposes. First of all, there are obviously many different layers of information to be filed. Second, once identified, each layer must be structured in an appropriate way, and once it is structured it must be filled with selected info.

Therefore, we can distinguish between three main categories of standards:
- Representation standards
- Descriptive standards
- Content standards.

Description, representation, content

Representation standards define with the logic and relational structure of the dataset. They provide the *Weltanschauung*[10]; the overall philosophy of the cataloguing system used. There are various representative standards in use. An interesting example is provided by the UNESCO ICOM standard called CIDOC CRM[11].

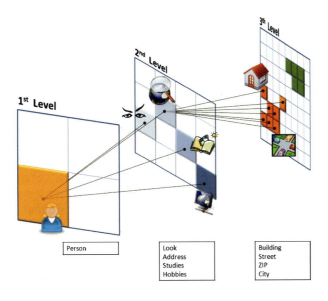

Fig. 24.1 Standard levels

---

10 The "vision of the world" that we would like to implement.
11 The *CIDOC Conceptual Reference Model* (CRM) is a formal ontology intended to facilitate the integration, mediation and interchange of heterogeneous cultural heritage information. The CRM is the culmination of more than a decade of standards development work by the International Committee for Documentation (CIDOC) of the International Council of Museums (ICOM). Work on the CRM itself began in 1996 under the auspices of the ICOM-CIDOC Documentation Standards Working Group. Since 2000, development of the CRM has been officially delegated by ICOM-CIDOC to the CIDOC CRM Special Interest Group, which collaborates with the ISO working group ISO/TC46/SC4/WG9 to bring the CRM to the form and status of an international standard.

The second level of standardisation involves populating the empty structure by adding specific description fields. These are the attributes, elements, categories and fields required to adequately represent any particular artefact.

This is the description level. One of reference standards at this level is, for instance, the *Categories for the Description of Works of Art* (CDWA), created by the J. Paul Getty Trust & College Art Association, Inc. in 1996, and recently revised (in 2005).

The third level of standardisation attempts to harmonise the terminology used by providing a set of vocabularies (thesauri). This supports both data entry and data retrieval phases.

24.2.1   Representation Standard: CIDOC CRM

The *CIDOC Conceptual Reference Model* (CRM) is a formal ontology that is intended to facilitate the integration, mediation and interchange of heterogeneous cultural heritage information.

The model was initially defined in order to provide a structured way to organise cultural information, and then a digital version was developed and implemented. The reference model enables information exchange and integration between heterogeneous sources of cultural heritage information. This model is crucial to the creation of museum information networks and intranets, since it provides the semantic definitions and clarifications needed to transform disparate, localised information sources into a coherent global resource. It explains the logic of what is actually documented, and thereby enables semantic interoperability.

The conceptual reference model was designed to be supra-institutional and abstracted from any specific local context; this goal deeply influenced the constructs and level of detail of the model. It outlines the semantics of database schemas and documents the structures used in cultural heritage and museum documentation in terms of a formal ontology. In addition it provides an optimal analysis of the intellectual structure of cultural documentation in logical terms[12].

Referring to the key document issued by the CIDOC CRM Special Interest Group:

The CRM aims to support the following specific functionalities:

- Inform developers of information systems as a guide to good practice in conceptual modelling, in order to effectively structure and relate information assets of cultural documentation.

---

[12]   The CRM is not optimised to implementation-specific storage and processing aspects. Rather, it provides the means to understand the effects of such optimisations on the semantic accessibility of the content.

III Exploitation, Applications and Services

- Serve as a common language for domain experts and IT developers to formulate requirements and to agree on system functionalities with respect to the correct handling of cultural contents.
- To serve as a formal language for the identification of common information contents in different data formats; in particular to support the implementation of automatic data transformation algorithms from local to global data structures without loss of meaning. The latter being useful for data exchange, data migration from legacy systems, data information integration and mediation of heterogeneous sources.
- To support associative queries against integrated resources by providing a global model of the basic classes and their associations to formulate such queries.
- It is further believed that advanced natural language algorithms and case-specific heuristics can take significant advantage of the CRM to resolve free text information into a formal logical form, if that is regarded beneficial. The CRM is however not thought to be a means to replace scholarly text, rich in meaning, by logical forms, but only a means to identify related data.

Users of the CRM should be aware that the definition of data entry systems requires support of community specific terminology, guidance to what should be documented and in which sequence, and application-specific consistency controls. The CRM does not provide such notions.

Due to its very structure and formalism, the CRM is extensible and users are encouraged to create extensions for the needs of more specialized communities and applications.

As stated in the report of the CIDOC CRM Special Interest Group:

The Intended Scope of the CRM may be defined as all information required for the exchange and integration of heterogeneous scientific documentation of museum collections. This definition requires further elaboration:

- The term "scientific documentation" is intended to convey the requirement that the depth and quality of descriptive information that can be handled by the CRM should be sufficient for serious academic research. This does not mean that information intended for presentation to members of the general public is excluded, but rather that the CRM is intended to provide the level of detail and precision expected and required by museum professionals and researchers in the field.
- The term "museum collections" is intended to cover all types of material collected and displayed by museums and related institutions, as defined by ICOM[13]. This includes collections, sites and monuments relating to fields such as social history, ethnography, archaeology, fine and applied arts, natural history, history of sciences and technology.

---

13 The ICOM Statutes provide a definition of the term "museum" at http://icom. museum/statutes.html#2.

24 *Cataloguing Standards and Archiving Tools*   257

- The documentation of collections includes the detailed description of individual items within collections, groups of items and collections as a whole. The CRM is specifically intended to cover contextual information: the historical, geographical and theoretical background that gives museum collections much of their cultural significance and value.
- The exchange of relevant information with libraries and archives, and the harmonisation of the CRM with their models, falls within the Intended Scope of the CRM.
- Information required solely for the administration and management of cultural institutions, such as information relating to personnel, accounting, and visitor statistics, falls outside the Intended Scope of the CRM.

The Practical Scope[14] of the CRM is expressed in terms of the current reference standards for museum documentation that have been used to guide and validate the CRM's development. The CRM covers the same domain of discourse as the union of these reference standards; this means that data correctly encoded according to any of these museum documentation standards can be expressed in a CRM-compatible form, without any loss of meaning.

24.2.2 Descriptive Standard: Categories for the Description of Works of Art (CDWA)

The *Categories* describe the contents of art databases by articulating a conceptual framework for describing and accessing information about works of art, architecture, other material culture, groups and collections of works, and related images. The CDWA includes 512 categories and subcategories. A small subset of categories are considered core in that they represent the minimum information necessary to identify and describe a work.

For a full discussion of CDWA, including basic guidelines for cataloguing and examples, see the CDWA website at http://www.getty.edu/research/conducting_research/standards/cdwa/.

24.2.3 Other Description Standards

Description standards aim to unify and homologate the information included in form fields and to provide some rules for inputting and retrieving information.

The Italian ICCD has developed a national standard of description based on the shapes and origins of artefacts. Ten categories were assigned to the entity

---

14 The Practical Scope of the CIDOC CRM, including a list of the relevant museum documentation standards, is discussed in more detail on the CIDOC CRM website at http://cidoc.ics.forth.gr/scope.html.

"immovable heritage": cataloguing code, object structure, structure of the assembly, structure of the aggregation, localisation, object, chronology, cultural definition, technical data, analytical data, administrative data, and documentation.

Canada has developed highly detailed description standards for managing artefacts and regulations that can be consulted online.

These standards are subdivided into twenty-one categories: management data, identification data, natural science data, artist/author, manufacture, market, additional contributions to production, date, dimensions, description, origin/destination, registration, property, references, actual location, estimated value, constraints/references, status, exhibits, etc.

ISO and the ISBN (International Standard Bibliographic Description) from the IFLA (International Federation of Library Associations and Institutions) are two of the main reference points for data standardisation and conversion.

24.2.4 Dublin Core

The *Dublin Core Metadata Element Set* is a vocabulary of fifteen properties for use in resource description. It is named "Dublin" because it originated at a 1995 invitational workshop in Dublin, Ohio; the term "Core" is used because its elements are broad and generic, and can therefore be used to describe a wide range of resources.

The Dublin Core Metadata Initiative (DCMI), as stated on their official website (Weibel et al. 1998), began in 1995 with an invitational workshop in Dublin, Ohio that brought together librarians, digital library researchers, content providers, and text markup experts in order to improve discovery standards for information resources.

The original Dublin Core emerged as a small set of descriptors that quickly drew global interest from a wide variety of information providers in the arts, sciences, education, business, and government sectors.

The Dublin Core is an example of an initiative that would be complementary to the definition of a general syntax standard such as RDF. The Dublin Core aims to identify domain-specific metadata elements that can be used to locate resources for any given community or application context.

This project was initiated by the OCLC (*Online Computer Library Center*) OCLC and is now also available as an IETF Internet Draft. This specification is being reviewed and adapted by a range of domain-specific communities, including those concerned with libraries, the visual arts, museums, galleries and slide libraries. Its focus on resource discovery means that it is ideally placed to form a link between the vast array of local standards currently in use, in a way which is particularly appropriate to the aims of the EU.

Although originally intended for bibliographic material, the mapping of key elements from metadata standards in a wide variety of domains to those (currently 15 elements) listed in the Dublin Core is now underway.

In the UK, the US and Australia, progress has been made in the identification of corresponding data elements used by museums and galleries.

24.2.4.1 Dublin Core Elements

In the element descriptions below, each element has a descriptive label that is intended to convey a common semantic understanding of the element, as well as a unique, machine-understandable, single-word name intended to make the syntactic specification of elements simpler for encoding schemes.

The list of key elements includes: *Title, Creator, Subject, Description, Publisher, Contributor, Date, Type, Format, Identifier, Source, Language, Relation, Coverage,* and *Rights.*

Although some environments, such as HTML, are not case-sensitive, it is recommended best practice to always adhere to the case conventions in the element names given below to avoid conflicts in the event that the metadata is subsequently extracted or converted to a case-sensitive environment, such as XML.

Each element is optional and repeatable. Metadata elements may appear in any order.

The ordering of multiple occurrences of the same element (e.g. *Creator*) may have a significance intended by the provider, but preservation of the ordering is not guaranteed in every system.

To promote global interoperability, a number of the element descriptions suggest a controlled vocabulary for the respective element values. It is assumed that other controlled vocabularies will be developed for interoperability within certain local domains.

Element Name: *Title*
   Label: Title
   Definition: A name given to the resource.
   Comment: Typically, *Title* will be a name by which the resource is formally known.

Element Name: *Creator*
   Label: Creator
   Definition: An entity primarily responsible for making the content of the resource.
   Comment: Examples of *Creator* include a person, an organisation, or a service. Typically, the name of a *Creator* should be used to indicate the entity.

Element Name: *Subject*
   Label: Subject and keywords
   Definition: A topic of the content of the resource.
   Comment: Typically, *Subject* will be expressed as keywords, key phrases, or classification codes that describe a topic of the resource. Recommended best practice is to select a value from a controlled vocabulary or formal classification scheme.

260   ***III** Exploitation, Applications and Services*

Element Name: *Description*
    Label: Description
    Definition: An account of the content of the resource.
    Comment: Examples of *Description* include, but are not limited to, an abstract, table of contents, reference to a graphical representation of content, or free-text account of the content.

Element Name: *Publisher*
    Label: Publisher
    Definition: An entity responsible for making the resource available.
    Comment: Examples of *Publisher* include a person, an organisation, or a service. Typically, the name of a *Publisher* should be used to indicate the entity.

Element Name: *Contributor*
    Label: Contributor
    Definition: An entity responsible for making contributions to the content of the resource.
    Comment: Examples of *Contributor* include a person, an organization, or a service. Typically, the name of a *Contributor* should be used to indicate the entity.

Element Name: *Date*
    Label: Date
    Definition: A date of an event in the lifecycle of the resource.
    Comment: Typically, *Date* will be associated with the creation or availability of the resource. Recommended best practice for encoding the date value is defined in a profile of ISO 8601 (W3CDTF) and includes (among others) dates of the form YYYY-MM-DD.

Element Name: *Type*
    Label: Resource Type
    Definition: The nature or genre of the content of the resource.
    Comment: *Type* includes terms describing general categories, functions, genres, or aggregation levels for content. Recommended best practice is to select a value from a controlled vocabulary [for example, the DCMI Type Vocabulary (DCT)]. To describe the physical or digital manifestation of the resource, use the *Format* element.

Element Name: *Format*
    Label: Format
    Definition: The physical or digital manifestation of the resource.
    Comment: Typically, *Format* will include the media type or the dimensions of the resource. *Format* may be used to identify the software, hardware, or other equipment needed to display or operate the resource. Examples of dimensions include size and duration. Recommended best practice is to

select a value from a controlled vocabulary [for example, the list of Internet media types (MIME) defining computer media formats].

Element Name: *Identifier*
Label: Resource identifier
Definition: An unambiguous reference to the resource within a given context.
Comment: Recommended best practice is to identify the resource by means of a string or number conforming to a formal identification system. Formal identification systems include but are not limited to the Uniform Resource Identifier (URI) [including the Uniform Resource Locator (URL)], the Digital Object Identifier (DOI), and the International Standard Book Number (ISBN).

Element Name: *Source*
Label: Source
Definition: A reference to a resource from which the present resource is derived.
Comment: The present resource may be derived from the *Source* resource in whole or in part. Recommended best practice is to identify the referenced resource by means of a string or number conforming to a formal identification system.

Element Name: *Language*
Label: Language
Definition: A language of the intellectual content of the resource.
Comment: Recommended best practice is to use RFC 3066, which, in conjunction with ISO 639, defines two- and three-letter primary language tags with optional subtags. Examples include "en" or "eng" for English, "akk" for Akkadian, and "en-GB" for English used in the United Kingdom.

Element Name: *Relation*
Label: Relation
Definition: A reference to a related resource.
Comment: Recommended best practice is to identify the referenced resource by means of a string or number conforming to a formal identification system.

Element Name: *Coverage*
Label: Coverage
Definition: The extent or scope of the content of the resource.
Comment: Typically, *Coverage* will include spatial location (a place name or geographic coordinates), temporal period (a period label, date, or date range), or jurisdiction (such as a named administrative entity). Recommended best practice is to select a value from a controlled vocabulary [for example, the *Getty Thesaurus of Geographic Names* (TGN) from the J.P. Getty Informa-

tion Institute] and to use, where appropriate, named places or time periods in preference to numeric identifiers such as sets of coordinates or date ranges.

Element Name: *Rights*
  Label: Rights management
  Definition: Information about rights held in and over the resource.
  Comment: Typically, *Rights* will contain a rights management statement for the resource, or reference a service providing such information. Rights information often encompasses intellectual property rights (IPR), copyright, and various property rights.
  If the *Rights* element is absent, no assumptions may be made about any rights held in or over the resource.

24.2.5 Content Standards

Content standards were first developed in the library sector in 1876. They later became widespread due to the advent of information systems.

Content standards are also known as *controller authorities*, *terminology standards*, *value standards* and *controlled vocabularies*. The latter is the term most commonly used to refer to content standards. A controlled vocabulary represents both a dictionary of synonyms and a classification system. However, it is worth noting that, while they are undoubtedly useful, controlled vocabularies inherently provide only restricted representations of the topics that they are associated with, in order to ensure standardisation.

There are a number of different kinds of dictionary or thesaurus. For example, the Anglo-American approach is based on the idea of controlling a huge number of terms in a structured and classified way, reflecting an encyclopaedic vision of the world.

The continental and Latin approaches, on the other hand, are based on themes, subjects, types of material and on gathering together sets of related words and then integrating them with definitions.

Controlled vocabularies are structured sets of preselected terms used by one or more authorities. If the terms in the controlled vocabulary are linked to each other by hierarchical or associative relationships, it can be termed a *thesaurus*.

These structural relations come in three different types:

- Equivalence
- Hierarchical
- Associational.

Equivalence relations refer to terms with similar meanings or synonyms (dialects, foreign words, etc.). Such relations make it possible to perform a linguistic check. One preferential term (the *descriptor*) will retrieve its synonyms (*nondescriptors*) and vice versa. A nondescriptor term should not be used as a preferential term.

24 Cataloguing Standards and Archiving Tools   263

Hierarchical relations lead to better comprehension of terms because they represent them in relation to super- or suborders instead of by themselves (which happens in a *glossary* for instance).

Associational relations are established between descriptors whose meanings are related in some way in order to help the user choose the appropriate term and during the data entry process (e.g. room, space, area, extent, etc.).

The use of different terms to refer to the same subject is forbidden, which makes it easier to compile forms.

The use of dictionaries guarantees lexical homogeneity regardless of the cultural background of the personal involved[15].

Visual Artefacts

For Western art, which mainly consists of visual artefacts, it is evident that one of the most significant and powerful search paths is based on the visual content of the artefact. Then, for example, if you wanted to gather information on paintings representing Leda and the Swan or Apollo and Daphne, you could simply type these names into a search box to receive a list of the images requested.

In order to implement this powerful type of search we must be able to automatically analyse and identify the visual content of artefacts. There are at least two main approaches that could be used to do this: the first is to automatically analyse the image and extract some features that enable subject identification; the second is to perform this task manually. However, whichever approach is used, the system will work better if there is a set of controlled vocabularies or thesauri acting as a general framework.

Some attempts to implement an automatic search are already being developed and tested. These mainly recognise the main components of the scene: trees, houses, etc. This should prove useful in other fields of investigation, but in the field of culture we need to identify each object in the artefact because some of them are clues that can be used to identify the meaning of the artefact (for example, an old man with white beard, a dove, or a triangle representing the Holy Trinity).

As already stated, most of the activities related to cultural heritage must be performed by skilled or expert people; there are very few tasks that can be performed by unskilled people. Even if the task is simply to merge pre-existing archives, some experience is needed in order to the harmonise data.

24.2.5.1 Iconclass

The reference work on this subject is undoubtedly *Iconclass*, an iconographic classification system originally developed by H. van de Waal, and published by the Royal Netherlands Academy of Arts and Sciences in Amsterdam from 1973 to 1983.

---

15 For example, the *Art & Architecture Thesaurus*, the *Union List of Artists Names* (ULAN) and the *Getty Thesaurus of Geographic Names* (TGN) from the J.P. Getty Information Institute.

The general reference framework of Iconclass is subdivided into nine main classes:
- Class 1: Religion and magic
- Class 2: Nature
- Class 3: Humankind, man in general
- Class 4: Society, civilisation, culture
- Class 5: Abstraction and concepts
- Class 6: History
- Class 7: Holy Bible
- Class 8: Sagas, legends and tales
- Class 9: Classic mythology and antiquity

These nine main classes are subdivided into first-level subclasses, second-level subclasses and third-level subclasses in order to be able to identify single objects.

Fig. 24.2 Detail of a mosaic in the Temple of Dafne, Athens (photo by the author)

It is also possible to combine more than one code in order to identify the compound presence of more than one theme or subject or in order to identify single subjects more accurately.

As an example *Class 9*, the classic mythology and antiquity class, contains terms related to classic mythology (subclasses 91–97) together with subjects related to Greek and Roman history (subclass 98).

Due to the complexity of the topic and the presence of multiple divinities in many artefacts, the authors of Iconclass proposed the use of a hierarchical system for classifying artefacts. This involves adding more and more numbers/letters to the code in order identify the content of the artefact more and more precisely. For example, he subject "Latona give birth to Apollo and Diana" is

24 Cataloguing Standards and Archiving Tools

classified under the code 92 B 31 1(note that 92 B 3 is the code for Apollo; see Table 24.1).

Table 24.1

Divineness of Heaven—Apollo	
Apollo	92 B 3
Apollo and Mercury	92 B 3 : 92 B 5
Apollo and Diana	92 B 3 : 92 C 3
Latona gives birth to Apollo and Diana	92 B 31 1

24.3   Searching for Items in the Catalogue

Catalogues that are created properly using dictionaries can easily be browsed by selecting appropriate search keywords (as derived from controlled lists).

The more general the keywords selected, the greater the number of search "hits". However, more general searches also give a greater proportion of "hits" that only vaguely correspond to what is being searched for; results of interest can be identified more rapidly by using more specific keywords.

Many search engines also offer a *full text search*; in this case, all of the text in the catalogue is searched. If a full text search is chosen, the user must be confident of their own knowledge of the specific domain; if the wrong set of words is chosen for the search the requested item will not be found. The user's data mining efficiency and accuracy will be related to their knowledge of keyword synonyms and their personal associational aptitude.

A hierarchy of terms is the only way to outline the relations between the main object and its subparts. If the information system does not use a hierarchical system, it will not be possible to launch thematic searches.

24.4   Some Basic Problems That Must be Solved When Cataloguing Historical Items

When cataloguing historical items we commonly encounter some specific problems.

First of all, identifying an object by name may prove difficult because it may have many names. This scenario can arise due to different dialects, foreign names (which are sometimes adapted to the local language), and alternate denominations. Sometimes the name of the object changes over the centuries.

Something similar can also happen for the author(s); they may use a pseudonym or nom de plume, or receive an alias as well as their real name. Sometimes the author is difficult to identify; an artefact may for example be attributed to a particular school (e.g. the school of Leonardo da Vinci) rather than a specific person (e.g. Leonardo di Vinci himself). Then of course there are the complete unknowns.

Even the time line can be difficult to manage. The artefact could be associated with a particular century (e.g. the twelfth century), a fraction of a century (e.g. the second half of the twelfth century), a decade (e.g. the 1920s), a particular year (e.g. 1478), and sometimes even an era (e.g. the Renaissance or the Middle Ages).

Furthermore, different cultures use different calendars, which sometimes overlap in terms of geographical regions (e.g. Europe and Muslims). This means that it is also important to consider historical atlases, multiple denominations and the politics of territories over the centuries. In other words, the context of the artefact is also significant: its historical background, milestones, the author's bio, related events, etc.

24.5 Catalogues and Database Management Systems

Once appropriate standards have been chosen, we must define an overall vision for this "world of data", a list of "fields" to be associated with each "data item" and a set of controlled vocabularies. How do we combine of these into an online catalogue?

Table 24.2

Name	Type	Length	Attribute	Vocabulary
Denomination	Alphanum	256	Multiple	Controlled
Author	Alphanum	256	Multiple	Controlled

Even if we start from Table 24.2, listing the set of fields describing the object plus their types (alphanumeric, numeric, etc.), their lengths (256 characters, integer, flag, etc.), their attributes (single, multiple field) and whether they have a controlled vocabulary or not, there is no direct and efficient transposition to a database management system.

Relational models versus object-oriented models, structured data versus raw data: knowledge should be represented as a network of nodes and connections. Information in cultural heritage is as well represented by a network connecting objects, people, events, times, places and more.

Although at first glance it seems to be an oxymoron, we must hide data in order to be able to find it efficiently. Storing information inside database management systems, whether relational or object-oriented in nature, has proved to be an extremely useful pursuit for information that is easily coded into data

Database management systems

structures[16] and for raw information[17]. The extensive use of RDF, XML and their derivatives usually offers an appropriate route to achieving this.

Museums often need to interchange or transfer data. When a museum moves from one computing system to another, it will need to migrate its data[18].

Museums currently often have one system for financial management, another system for membership, development and corporate communication[19], and yet another for collections management. These applications need to be able to interchange data.

If a museum lends out objects for exhibitions or borrows objects for research, it is useful for the museum to set up interchanges with other institutions[20]. An ability to interchange objects or data is also important when the interpretation of objects requires research into secondary sources, or when access to sources of standard vocabularies and authority files is needed in order properly index collection descriptions. We all know how the Internet has changed our approach to researching resources, libraries and archives.

Without a standard for such interchange, each interchange will require significant preparation and programming, or at least the time-consuming cut-and-pasting of single items of information. This may result in lost data, and ultimately in the cost of a one-off interchange outweighing its benefits.

With the adoption of interchange standards, the basic need to preserve museum information[21] and integrate museum functions will be met while the potential for scholarly information exchange will be enhanced.

---

16 By filing artefact forms.
17 Webpages.
18 Refer to Sect. 19 Long Term Preservation of Digital Archives
19 Museum websites for example (e.g. http://www.louvre.fr, http://www.louvre.edu and http://www.louvre.com).
20 For example, to obtain high-resolution images, multifrequency scanning, infrared, X-ray, colour filtering.
21 Migration is one of the potential solutions, together with standardisation (e.g. Internet standards).

25 Virtual Museum Networks

When designing virtual museums or, even better, a network of virtual museums, it is important to take into account the fact that a great deal of cataloguing work has usually already been done by museums or cultural institutions. Newcomers to the field of culture who are attempting to create ICT applications for it must make use of this work by including any pre-existing data.

However, this can lead to problems with the interoperability of data warehouses[22]. Other problems related to the management of different data structures associated with specific heritage families can arise. In the specific case of a network of museums, we may also have to deal with a number of heterogeneous (in terms of structure and technology) datasets distributed over an extended geographical network. Some issues related to the data structure that must be resolved include: "mapping" from one data structure to another; ensuring the use of a common bilingual *thesaurus* during data *retrieval*; and whether to use a meta-database[23] to add extra functionality (additional services) to the search engine[24].

Solutions adopted on a daily basis for these kinds of problems are based on a consolidated layout of information systems.

Museum portals act as a general index and switchboard between museums. Sometimes there is a need to preserve the look and feel of the original website and so the user is simply referred to the appropriate Internet address. At other times the results must be homogenised, and so a uniform portal interface is provided; the portal can then access (when allowed) single data components (e.g. text, pictures, etc.) and render them on the interface via shared style sheets.

---

22 Those problems may arise when accessing cultural heritage databanks implemented on hard/software that are different from those normally used to provide this service.

23 A "database of databases", which contains general descriptions of the contents of many different archives, and thus makes it easier and faster to search through multiple databanks for specific information.

24 Recent software technologies (e.g. XML) allow us to develop more flexible data structures that are more generally applicable compared to the rigid data structures hosted by DBMSs. Such flexible data structures tend to simplify the work involved in inserting data.

Fig. 25.1 Virtual Museums Network (MOSAIC Project)

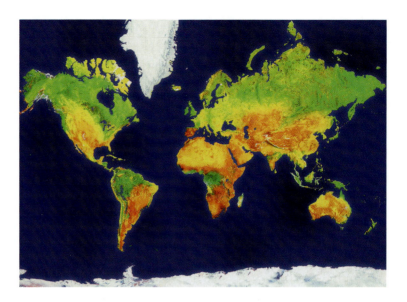

While we are on the subject of data access, it is worth mentioning Z39.2, which was an information exchange standard that was used in the field of cultural heritage for a long time. It was the data equivalent of Esperanto, since it allowed different data repositories to interchange their textual resources.

Z39.2[25] is the American equivalent of ISO 2709[26], and these standards are both representative of bibliographic and information (textual, descriptive data) interchange formats.

ISO 2709 is specifically intended for communications between data processing systems; it is not intended for application as a processing format within systems.

An ISO 2709 conformant record is a linear series of characters organised in a highly structured way that reflects its primary use: allowing information to be encoded sequentially onto magnetic tape.

A record contains both the data for transmission and information about the data, its structure and organisation for the data processing system to use.

Each record begins with a fixed-length record label that describes how long the record is, its status (i.e. new, amended, etc.), the location of the beginning of the data to be transmitted, and information about the record directory section that follows.

The variable-length record directory consists of fixed-length units which identify each field (element of information) by a three-character identifier or tag (practice dictates the use of a three-character identifier, but the original

---

25   ANSI Z39.2-1985.
26   ISO 2709-1981.

standard allowed implementations to specify the identifier length) and shows where each data field begins and how long it is.

The directory is variable in length since there can be any number of fields in a record. Following the directory are the data fields. There will be a data field corresponding to each field named in the directory for a given record. Each record is terminated by a record separator followed by another record if necessary.

Together with Z39.2, another standard is particularly interesting since it provided one of the first pillars of information retrieval from distributed databases: Z39.50[27] (*Information Retrieval Service Definitions and Protocol Specifications for Library Applications*). This standard allows an application on one computer to query a database on another. The protocol specifies the inter-system procedures and structures for submitting a search request in the native query syntax of the originating system, generating a response from the receiving system, and passing hits back to the originating system for display in its native format.

To date, service definitions have been written for catalogue and authority databases, and definitions for others are in development.

At the upper level, the level of content, one of the most commonly used solutions was developed by the OCLC working group, the *Dublin Core* introduced previously.

Another relevant solution was developed many years ago and recently tuned by the *Canadian Heritage Information Network*. The tuning was performed to update and upgrade online services. In the field of interoperability solutions, we should also mention the contributions made by some consortia such as CIMI, CHIO, MOSAIC and AMICO.

25.1 MCN and the CIMI Initiative

The Museum Computer Network (MCN) launched its *Computer Interchange of Museum Information* (CIMI) initiative in order to develop standards that can meet the requirements of museums.

The CIMI Standards Framework provides guidelines for museums, museum consortia, and vendors of museum services to define the purposes and contents of specific exchanges of data, and it positions them to take advantage of information industry-wide developments in interoperability. It allows individual museum institutions to be the beneficiaries of standards rather than having to bear the cost of developing software themselves.

Representatives from all of the major North American museum associations and network service providers attended meetings from 1990 to 1992 during which the framework for museum standards took shape.

The working group started their activities by identifying the types of interchanges that museums perform or require.

---

27 NISO Z39.50 or ISO 10162/63.

25 Virtual Museum Networks   271

The WG then examined national and international information standards to see whether pre-existing standards could be applied in this context, and used the Open Systems Environment (OSE) and the Open Systems Interconnection (OSI) models as benchmarks.

The WG concluded that certain classes of existing standards could serve museums and they discussed how applicable application standards should be selected.

The result of the activity, based on these findings, was a report on a standards framework for museum information interchange entitled *CIMI Standards Framework*.

This framework encompasses interchange protocols, interchange formats, and lower level network and telecommunications building blocks, as well as content data standards that provide the technical basis for museum information interchange[28].

There are two levels of implementation of the CIMI Standards Framework:
- The first is for museums to specify that their hardware and software acquisitions support the standards defined in the CIMI Standards Framework. This will ensure that the data can be interchanged even if all the institutional meanings cannot be.
- The second addresses the problem of agreeing on meanings by proceeding with the standardisation of data content (the fields of information) and data values (what goes in the fields).

25.2 Recent Applications

The introduction of the "X family" (XML, XSS, XSL, etc.) towards the end of the 1990s[29], together with enhancements in database interoperability[30], the tuning of the Resource Descriptor Framework (RDF) and the development of the Dublin Core Metadata Initiative, have resulted in great progress in the field of museum information sharing in recent years. DCMI is an organization dedicated to promoting the widespread adoption of interoperable metadata standards and developing specialized metadata vocabularies for describing resources that enable more intelligent information discovery systems.

---

28 Specifically, the CIMI Standards Framework adopts existing standards for the interchange of information at OSI levels 1–6, including FTAM for file transfer, X.400 and X.500 for messaging and directory services, and ISO 9040/41 for terminal access. It allows for the use of either OSI or TCP/IP. It recommends EDI for business transactions and ISO 10162/10163 for information retrieval. It provides rationales for using either ISO 2709, ISO 8879 SGML, ISO 8824 ASN.1 for building collections of databases or reference files.

29 XML was officially introduced at the 7th World Wide Web Conference held in Brisbane, Australia, on 14–18 April 1998.

30 For example Microsoft used ODBC then SOAP and other similar technologies.

The dream of interconnecting and sharing "museum information" is now much closer to becoming reality from a technological point of view. Other obstacles (such as investment in human resources, market models and rights and shares management) are still under discussion.

Case Study: MOSAIC
(Museums Over States and Virtual Culture)

MOSAIC[31], a European Commission Trans-European Network Telecom project developed in 1994 as an international follow-up to the Virtual Museums Network, introduces a new approach to the organisation, maintenance and promotion of arts and museums.

This approach is mainly based on two cool interactive technologies—hypermedia and telecommunications—and applies to museums, art galleries, archives, libraries, ancient buildings and other kinds of heritage and works of art.

Network access to museums and galleries offers both easier access to Europe's heritage and a method of generating new revenue for its preservation and display through access and reuse fees.

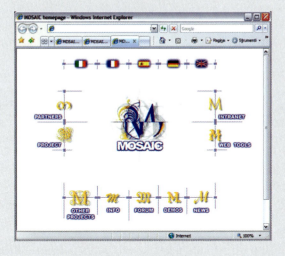

Fig. 25.2 MOSAIC project home page

---

[31] MOSAIC Consortium: Banca di Roma s.p.a (Italy), Joanneum Research—Forschungsgesellschaft mbH (Austria), Zentrum fur Graphische DatenVerarbeitung e.V (Germany), Cineca—Consorzio Interuniversitario per la Gestione Del Centro di Calcolo Elettronico dell'Italia Nord Occidentale (Italy), Politecnico di Milano, HMG Lab. (Italy), Infobyte s.p.a (Italy).

European museums and galleries hold the richest collection of objects, art and cultural wealth in the world, but much of it is not accessible to scholars and the general public because of lack of space and cost of travel. This is why MOSAIC, a "real virtuality" project, aims to develop a trans-European framework for electronic network access to museums and galleries by classifying and showing not only what is already presented to the public but also what is not visible due to a lack of exhibition space or because it is inaccessible (such as frescos in access-restricted buildings and private offices). The MOSAIC Consortium provides methods and tools that can be used to create and manage virtual museums.

MOSAIC can be considered to be an application layer between *content providers* and *end-users*, where *content providers* are museums, art galleries, collections, and regional and local institutions, while *end-users* are researchers, professors, teachers, experts, students, home users, etc. The project itself is structured into two different network layers: the physical network (ISDN, XDSL, ATM,...), which provides basic and advanced services, as well as an overlapping network of physical nodes called *Cultural Service Centres* that provide enhanced services such as video conferencing, virtual reality "visio rooms", pay per print services and more.

Both content holders and everyday users will benefit from using the *MOSAIC network*. Small- and medium-sized organisations will obtain enhanced visibility, a common solutions showcase, and training to start digital products. Large organisations will improve their investments by joining the *MOSAIC network* and hosting *MOSAIC Cultural Services Centres*. Experts and researchers will be able to use special tools and plug-ins to improve their productivity.

The main goal of this project is to improve the visibility of cultural heritage, to disseminate knowledge and to enhance cultural interchange amongst nations. One of the benefits of MOSAIC is that it can generate extra *revenue* for museums through network usage and information download charges.

Thanks to the high interoperability standard of the network, services that utilise pre-existing infrastructures will be offered by MOSAIC search engines. By following the international standard and utilising the specially developed research engines, the requested information will easily be obtained.

MOSAIC can offer multilanguage references to content holders inside the MOSAIC network in order to improve their visibility worldwide. In addition, the unrestricted sale of scientific-cultural images to network users in compliance with current regulations (intellectual property rights protection), as well as the advertising of specifically organised events on cultural issues to all of the network partners, promoting the visibility of all international and national cultural events, should be enabled by MOSAIC.

The most important MOSAIC tool will be the *online cultural browser*, *CUBE*, which will allow the information to be accessed through an adaptive graphic interface that provides the required information within an overall context (cultural, historical, geographical, etc.). For instance, the selection of various subjects (painting, sculpture, etc.) linked to a specific period and other parameters will cause the map to highlight the areas where information can be found. *CUBE* is based on *SUMS (System for Universal Media Searching)*, developed by Prof. Kim H. Veltman (Perspective Unit, National Library Toronto, Canada).

As future developments of the network, the ability to book and allocate tickets for exhibition visits and to sell merchandise online are forecast. A permanent thematic forum area is planned, as well as a news area. *Virtual Exhibitor* will permit the creation of exhibitions in a real or virtual context in order to create preview exhibition space or to announce forthcoming cultural initiatives during cultural events. MOSAIC partners are all signatories of the *Multimedia Access to Europe's Cultural Heritage MoU (Memorandum of Understanding)* and participate in various MoU working groups.

The project has been financed by the European Community (EC), represented by the Commission of the European Communities. Six companies constitute the industrial consortium involved in MOSAIC development.

The main issue that MOSAIC will face is: how can it spread knowledge of cultural heritage by creating a network framework that is capable of growing and financing itself?

Why is MOSAIC needed? To create a patchwork of titles (Cultural Service Centers) that are linked together and interoperable; to provide both generic services and application deployment; and to allow cultural heritage dissemination through a trans-European approach (MOSAIC 1994).

26 Unique Object ID

There is widespread agreement that documentation is crucial to the protection of cultural objects, for stolen objects that have not been photographed and adequately described are rarely recoverable by their rightful owners.

The idea of defining a set of information and features that enable an artefact to be identified should greatly aid the police in their fight against art thieves. Major police organisations all over the world, including *Interpol*[32], the *FBI* and *Scotland Yard*, have special teams devoted to art and cultural heritage crime. In Italy there is a very well known group of *Carabinieri* called the *Nucleo Speciale Tutela Patrimonio Storico*[33]. Their main role is to look after Italian historical patrimony and, in the case of theft, to carefully investigate the potential path followed by the artefact based on a good knowledge of the network of people potentially interested in it. One of the first recommendations of the Carabinieri is to take a clear photograph of the artefact that will aid them during investigation, identification and recovery. Obviously, the main information that can be gained from doing this is the visual content or visual aspects of the artefact. Of course, close cooperation between the Carabinieri[34] and the ICCD[35] is required because of the need to refer to a catalogue and a visual description of the artefact[36].

Interpol, FBI, Scotland Yard, Carabinieri

Unfortunately, very few objects have been documented to a level that can materially assist in their recovery in the event of theft. Indeed, even when objects have been documented in detail, the information collected is extremely variable. It is important, therefore, to make the public more aware of the need to make adequate, standardised descriptions of objects.

Different projects have been proposed and developed at European level, all of which are based on two main pillars: first, the use of advanced technologies[37] to extract special unique features of the artefact, and second, the use of technol-

---

32 http://www.interpol.int/Public/WorkOfArt/.

33 http://www.carabinieri.it/Internet/Cittadino/Informazioni/Tutela/ Patrimonio+Culturale/Articolazione/06_TPC.htm.

34 Nucleo Speciale Tutela Patrimonio Storico.

35 National Institute for Cataloguing and Documentation.

36 *Iconclass* is a content standard that provides a coding system for visual content— please refer to Sect. 24.2.5.1 Iconclass

37 Such as 3-D laser scanning, multi-spectral scanning, invisible water marking and tagging, embedded RFID, and other methods.

ogy to automatically identify the artefact based on such features, using printed images or invisible tags (e.g. RFID).

Fig. 26.1 Carabinieri: Nucleo tutela patrimonio storico (website)

Fig. 26.2 Interpol website: stolen artefacts

278 III Exploitation, Applications and Services

26.1 One of the Proposed Solutions

The illicit trade in cultural objects is now widely recognised as being one of the most prevalent categories of international crime. The proceeds from thefts, forgeries, ransoms and smuggling operations involving cultural objects are often used to fund other criminal activities, the objects themselves serving as both a medium of exchange between criminals and a means of laundering the profits of crime.

The police have long recognised the importance of good documentation in the fight against art thieves. Documentation is indeed crucial to the protection of art and antiques, for police officers can rarely recover and return objects that have not been photographed and adequately described. Police forces have large numbers of objects in their custody that have been recovered during the course of their investigations, but which cannot be returned to their rightful owners because there is no documentation that makes it possible to identify the victims.

In 1993 the Getty Information Institute initiated a collaborative project to develop an international documentation standard for the information needed to identify cultural objects. The new standard was developed in collaboration with police forces, customs agencies, museums, the art trade, valuers, and the insurance industry.

The contents of the standard were identified by a combination of background research, interviews, and, most importantly, by major international questionnaire surveys. In total, over 1,000 responses were received from organisations in 84 countries. The findings of these surveys, published in the document *Protecting Cultural Objects in the Global Information Society*, demonstrated that there was close agreement regarding the information needed to describe objects for purposes of identification. This resulted in the following Object ID[38] checklist.

26.1.1 Object ID Checklist

- *Take photographs*. Photographs are of vital importance in identifying and recovering stolen objects. In addition to overall views, take close-ups of inscriptions, markings, and any damage or repairs. If possible, include a scale or object of known size in the image.

Answer these questions:
- *Type of object*. What kind of object is it (e.g. painting, sculpture, clock, mask)?

---

38 *Object ID* is a trademark of the J. Paul Getty Trust. Use of this trademark is prohibited without permission from The Council for the Prevention of Art Theft, The Estate Office, Warminster, BA12 6QD, UK. © The J. Paul Getty Trust, 1999. All rights reserved.

- *Materials and techniques*. What materials is the object made of (e.g. brass, wood, oil on canvas)? How was it made (e.g. carved, cast, etched)?
- *Measurements*. What is the size and/or weight of the object? Specify which unit of measurement is being used (e.g. cm, in.) and to which dimension the measurement refers (e.g. height, width, depth).
- *Inscriptions and markings*. Are there any identifying markings, numbers, or inscriptions on the object (e.g. a signature, dedication, title, maker's marks, purity marks, property marks)?
- *Distinguishing features*. Does the object have any physical characteristics that could help to identify it (e.g. damage, repairs, or manufacturing defects)?
- *Title*. Does the object have a title by which it is known and might be identified (e.g. *The Scream*)?
- *Subject*. What is pictured or represented (e.g. landscape, battle, woman holding child)?
- *Date or period*. When was the object made (e.g. 1893, early seventeenth century, Late Bronze Age)?
- *Maker*. Do you know who made the object? This may be the name of a known individual (e.g. Thomas Tompion), a company (e.g. *Tiffany*), or a cultural group (e.g. Hopi).
- *Write a short description*. This can also include any additional information which helps to identify the object (e.g. colour and shape of the object, where it was made).
- *Keep it secure*. Having documented the object, keep this information in a secure place.

Object ID is an international standard for describing cultural objects. It has been developed through the collaboration of the museum community, police and customs agencies, the art trade, insurance industry, and experts in art and antiques.

The Object ID project was initiated by the J. Paul Getty Trust in 1993, and the standard was launched in 1997. It is being promoted by major law enforcement agencies, including the FBI, Scotland Yard and Interpol; museum, cultural heritage, art trade and art appraisal organisations; and insurance companies.

Having established the descriptive standard, the Object ID project now helps to combat art theft by encouraging the use of the standard and by bringing together organisations around the world that can encourage its implementation.

In 1999, the Object ID project found a new home at the *Council for the Prevention of Art Theft* (CoPAT). CoPAT was established in 1992 and is now a registered charity in the UK. Its mission is to promote crime prevention in the fields of art, antiques, antiquities and architecture. Its members are drawn from law enforcement, the crime prevention field, heritage organisations, historical house owners, the insurance industry and the art trade. CoPAT has participated in the project since its early stages and has played a significant role in the development of the standard.

Due to the relevance of the goal, other initiatives have been promoted at international level, including some European research projects that aim to develop a system that can extract unique features for each and every artefact. A number of different methods that work in both two and three dimensions have been proposed. Again, the basic idea is to automatically extract these features via scanners or similar technologies and to store them in a kind of object ID card[39]. Most of these features are not visible to humans and may be considered equivalent to fingerprints or DNA.

---

39 Some projects even foresee the use of RFID.

27 Different Channels and Platforms

A number of different technological channels and platforms are already available and a number of others are rapidly emerging. As often happens, there is no shortage of technology; the problem is that we don't know how to use it very efficiently for innovation.

A basic taxonomy of this field might be:

- Offline:
  - CD, DVD
  - MP3 players
  - MPEG Players
  - Podcasting (offline)
  - eBooks
  - Games platforms (offline)
  - Standalone applications
  - Offline info points
  - Interactive computer graphics installations
  - Others
- Online:
  - Wired
  - Desktops, workstations
  - Online info points
  - Games platforms (online)
  - Cable TV/interactive TV
  - Wireless
  - Smart phones
  - Palm computers
  - Games platforms (online)
  - Digital television (terrestrial DTT, satellite DST, phone DBV-H, etc.)
  - Other appliances (car sets, wearable devices, etc.)
- Cross-media:
  - Book + DVD
  - DVD + Internet
  - eBook + Internet
  - Other mixed media (e.g. RFID plus video wall etc.).

In conclusion, there are a wide variety of platforms that are potentially suited to cultural content. Some of these are multipurpose devices, while others specialise in one task, following the design trends already introduced in the chapter on *Interaction Design*.[40]

In the following case study an interesting unconventional platform is showcased: the father of "global interfaces", *TerraVision*.

Fig. 27.1
A multimedia player showing a picture (photo by Francesca Ronchi)

Fig. 27.2
A multimedia player showing a movie (photo by Francesca Ronchi)

---

40 Please refer to Chap. 12 Interaction Design.

Case Study: TerraVision

During the 1995 Telecom Conference a completely new interface concept was introduced to the expert audience. This interface was the forerunner of the *TerraServer*[41] and Google *Earth*[42] interfaces and systems in use today.

This project, called *TerraVision*[43], is a self-contained, virtual reality, one-to-one representation of our Earth. Using a stylised globe, users can zoom in on any location in the world and obtain incredibly detailed pictures (i.e. the application presents a virtual Earth). The original shape of the physical interface was a big track ball representing the planet and a wide screen that showed the requested view in real time.

The system offers not only satellite images and aerial photos but also geographically referenced data of all types, such as topographical or architectural schematic representations (e.g. temperature, weather forecasts, etc.). TerraVision was the first system to provide visualisation and unlimited freedom of navigation within an infinitely large spatial data environment. Providing visuals ranging from overviews of the Earth to extremely detailed movements in buildings, TerraVision provides smooth, real time pictures in a single comprehensive virtual reality system.

Fig. 27.3 *Terravision* project by ART+COM (Berlin, Germany, 1995)

---

41 Microsoft *TerraServer*: http://terraserver.microsoft.com.
42 Google *Earth* global geographical interface: http://www.googleearth.com.
43 ART+COM, Berlin, Germany: http://www.artcom.de.

Fig. 27.4 *Terravision* project by ART+COM (Berlin, Germany, 1995)

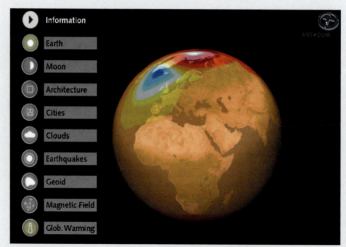

Fig. 27.5 a Berlin (D) **b** San Francisco (CA)

28 Intellectual Property Rights

This chapter provides an overview of one of the most important topics associated with the use of ICT in the field of culture. We all know that proper intellectual property rights management is one of the key requirements for a fruitful exploitation of cultural content. Copyright and copyleft are two sides of the same coin, but which is the most relevant... if any?

28.1 Introduction

Traditionally, *copyright* and *copyleft* have been regarded as absolute opposites: the former being concerned with the strict protection of authors' rights, the latter ensuring the free circulation of ideas. In addition, with specific reference to cultural topics, the Medicean[44] ideal—to allow all mankind, regardless of social status or worth, enjoy the beauty of art—seems to support free access to content.

Copyright and copyleft

While *copyright*—which seeks to protect the rights of inventors to own and therefore benefit financially from the new ideas and products they originate, thus encouraging further product development—is associated with a vast amount of legislation globally (leading to corresponding applicative complications), few studies have been made of *copyleft*. Indeed, a commonly held belief about copyleft is that it begins where the boundaries of copyright end, spreading over a no man's land of more or less illegal exploitation.

28.2 Copyleft

Let us start by examining copyleft and the beliefs of its sponsors. Copyleft, they say, is a zone of free creativity which anyone can access for their own personal benefit and/or the benefit of the community.

The copyleft phenomenon has recently exploded on the Internet after decades of "physical" exchanges of data and code within developer communities or special interest groups.

---

[44] The cultural patronage of the rich and powerful Medici family triggered the birth of the *Renaissance* in Florence.

Internet and broadcasting opportunities

The Internet has dramatically changed the information sector in a similar way to how commercial broadcasting televisions revolutionised the television sector. Now, not only media tycoons can access a broad audience, but "ordinary" webmasters and "Internauts" can too.

Before the Internet, newspapers, radio and television were the only media that enabled access to a broad audience. The Internet has made it possible to reach a wide audience simply by posting in a newsgroup or on a website.

However, the Internet not only offers infinite opportunities to exchange messages, find and publish information; it also provides free (at the moment at least) access to information that was once reserved for closed circles or specialised publications[45].

Freeware, shareware and trial versions

Free software ("freeware") has multiplied to such an extent that nowadays very few commercial software packages come without at least a free demo or trial version[46]. Easy access to new media and the changes in social behaviour caused by it are triggering changes in rights management. The two weeks dramatic rise in the consumption of digital music and movies is pushing major entertainment companies to change their policies and market models.

Free access to the network

Indeed, while market models (involving expensive subscriptions) once influenced access to the Internet, in recent years many telecom operators have made basic access free, conforming to the (free) "Internet market model"[47]. Free browser software and a huge number of free plug-ins have also become available.

So it can be said that the Net, with its ability to open up mass communication to all, has changed the balance in favour of *copyleft*, with its totally innovative dynamics.

How then can we reconcile a situation in which *copyright* is not cancelled but taken for granted, in which payment for access is abolished but the philosophy of profit-making according to market rules is retained?

The OCCAM–UNESCO Observatory[48] has been researching this phenomenon and here we provide a brief analysis of it (following Sect. 28.3 and 28.4), beginning with its principal tenets.

---

45 Sometimes important information is still locked within private sections of websites secured by passwords.

46 Shareware and free trial versions.

47 In Italy, a single operator, Tiscali, initially decided to provide access for free, and after two weeks all of the market had switched!

48 OCCAM–UNESCO Observatory: http://www.occam.org. Part of the UNO GAID project.

28.3 Free Access

Free access is now commonplace on the Internet, since the main providers must attract as many users as possible in order to demonstrate the "growth" of the company to the stock market, even if this is not related to actual income (i.e. the market values of such companies have not depended on their revenues or levels of production!). This need to attract users (no matter how long for) means that the providers must continually offer them more/better services and extras compared to other providers. Indeed, to keep one step ahead, many providers are now focussing on the next level of web communication: web "portals" and "social networking". These portals tend to offer an ever-increasing number of appealing services and frequently even software tools that can be embedded into or used as building blocks of personal websites or browsers (*YouTube*, *Google Earth* and *Skype* software tools for example), making it easy to build personal homepages that incorporate preferred websites and services (facebook, myspace, etc). The new market has thus created new rules and values.

The philosophy of *copyleft* has thus come to dominate the digital marketplace; value has shifted from products and the copyrights associated with them to the wishes of the users themselves. User habits are monitored in detail in order to pin down changing moods and whims, and then, based on this information, adequate and productive solutions are offered to them.

28.4 Freeware

Users have rushed to buy Microsoft products because they invented an interface that enabled humans to easily and intuitively use computers (and used this to generate hyperbolic profits—as though someone held the copyright to the English language and so all others that wished to use it had to pay, and then pay again when a more up-to-date English dictionary was released!). Because of Microsoft's market dominance, other software companies began to offer freeware components in order to get a hold on the market. This approach is obviously far cheaper than a big advertising campaign; it is often more effective too, since potential buyers can find it difficult to comprehend immaterial goods such as software when they are advertised conventionally.

Given the speed of evolution of these products, stable solutions can no longer be envisaged. However, browsers (Netscape and Explorer), where *copyleft* has become the guiding rule, provide an exception to this rule. The profit focus has thus moved from the product itself to its utilisation by the user.

This is even more evident and accelerated in the area of e-trading, which, through its online stock market service, transfers the added value from the software to the transactions performed.

28.5 Copyright

What is worth copying is probably also worth protecting. Protecting intellectual property involves two main tasks: protecting investments and creativity, and ensuring that the moral rights to original works are assigned to the authors of those works. This section provides a rough description of IPR management from both the European and American points of view.

28.5.1 Introduction

"New" intellectual property rights

When cultural materials are used in interactive multimedia it is necessary to acknowledge and/or negotiate *new* intellectual property rights. As cultural information has no geographical borders, legislation and agreements must be developed in international social and legal contexts. Differences in copyright laws between nations are currently a barrier to the development and distribution of multimedia products.

In most cases, museums want to distribute images and text related to their collections as part of their educational mission of making their collections physically and intellectually accessible. Nevertheless, in order to maintain the aesthetic integrity of the original work of art, they wish to exercise control over the dissemination and quality of this material. Licensing rights and reproduction fees are an important economic asset to most museums. Each museum will have to develop policies on and expertise in the implications of digital publishing (whether to get involved in joint ventures or to go it alone etc.), as museums have done previously with print, slides, film and video.

28.5.2 The Nature of Copyright

Integrity, piracy, reproduction, adaptation, distribution, ...

Copyright protects certain rights associated with all creative works. The copyright owner has the right to maintain the integrity of the work and protect it from piracy: to control the reproduction, adaptation, distribution, public performance and public display of a work, and to control the creation of derivative works. A widespread lack of understanding of the subject has led to an emphasis on copyright protection rather than the sensible and necessary exploitation of copyright. There is no required registration of copyright, no registration system and no central clearing house for information as to who owns or who can clear rights in relation to a particular work or performance.

Who are the authors/creators (copyright holders) of the digital form? This has become an even more complex question with the development of interactive multimedia, since it now involves authors of text and images: writers, museum databases, artists and the estates of deceased artists, photographers, museums as owners or controllers of photographic records of works, "subsidiary rights holders", including music, film and video, software authors, and the compilers of a new resource. Copyright may also be attached to the actual digital scanning of an image.

290   *III Exploitation, Applications and Services*

28.5.3 The Museum as Owner

To what extent does a museum own the works it shows? A museum has to consider the copyright and moral rights attached not only to the works held in the museum's collections, but also to other material that may be used in collection management systems and in other information systems or sources.

In general terms, the copyright and moral rights attached to a work of art *Copyright and moral rights* (including photographs) belong to the author or creator for the duration of his/her life or their lives and to his/her heirs for a period after their death[49].

Many works of art in museum collections will be out of authors'/artists' copyright and in the public domain. The museum (or other owner) may control physical access to the work but it does not usually own intellectual property rights.

The copyright attached to any photograph of the work of art likewise belongs *Copyright of pictures* to the photographer unless the photographer is an employee of the organisation for which the photograph was taken (e.g. the museum) or unless there is an agreement to transfer copyright to the organisation in question.

The control of access to the work of art may obviously represent a financial asset to the museum or other owner. It can also be seen as part of the museum's responsibility to preserve, authenticate and accurately represent material in their collections. This involves not only copyright but also moral rights: to protect the integrity of the images and the identity of the author/artist. It would be conducive to good working relationships for museums to take the initiative on the subject of rights agreements when new acquisitions enter the collection or new photographic records are commissioned, possibly utilising standard forms of rights agreement. This becomes even more critical when the museum may subsequently wish to disseminate images via a network, whether for collection management, research or public access.

28.5.4 The Museum as User of Copyright Material

Most museums are both providers and users of copyright material. Copyright protection arises when a work is "fixed" in any tangible medium of expression. Therefore, if the work is used without identifying the copyright owner (or his/her agent) and obtaining a license from them it may result in copyright infringement. As a general rule, it is safe to assume that any right not expressly granted is reserved by the copyright owner and that one does not have the right. All relevant rights should be expressly stated in a rights license. Multimedia and other applications of new media technology are not clearly covered in many traditional rights agreements.

---

49 Taking into account different continents, this time span is between 50 and 70 years.

28.5.5 Intellectual Property Laws

Two different approaches to IPR

Historically there have been two different European approaches to intellectual property rights.

Moral rights

On the one hand there are those countries for whom the concept of author's rights place emphasis on protecting the moral rights of the creator: the right to claim authorship, to insist on the integrity of the work and to prevent false attribution of the work (e.g. in France, where these rights are not assignable and continue in perpetuity).

Right to reproduce

On the other hand there are those countries who emphasise copyright law focussing on exploitation (e.g. Great Britain and the USA).

Copyright legislation in Great Britain and the USA now encompasses moral rights, but implementation is still not universal and the extent of moral rights protection varies from country to country. Other legal issues may be taken into consideration, such as privacy rights and publicity rights in the USA. One or both of the Berne Convention for the Protection of Literary and Artistic Works and the Universal Copyright Convention have been signed by most countries around the world (but have not been fully implemented in all aspects by all signatories), as has the Rome Convention for the Protection of Performers, Producers of Phonograms and Broadcasting. These conventions lay down only minimum terms of protection of the rights to which they refer, leaving the contracting States free to grant longer terms.

28.5.6 Regulation Initiatives

The Commission of the European Communities addressed the problems of harmonisation of copyright legislation within the European Union (EU) in a Green Paper in 1988, leading to legislation harmonising the terms of protection of copyright and certain related rights that has now been approved by the European Parliament for implementation in July 1995. While this represents a considerable step forward, these are minimal, only applying to the legislation of EU member countries (although many EFTA EEA countries will probably harmonise with the EU), and there are still many exceptions to the norm.

Table 28.1

Name	Authors	Photographers	Performers/ recordings
Berne Convention	50 years after death	25 years from making	
Rome convention			20 years from performance/fixation

Table 28.1 (continued)

Name	Authors	Photographers	Performers/recordings
EU harmonization	70 years after death	70 years after death	50 years from performance
USA	50 years after death/75 yrs from publ.	–	75 years from publication
Japan	50 years after death	–	30 years from performance/fixation

(Scans, like photos of photos, are not new works protected by IRC or neighbouring rights, if not precluded in contracts.)

The 70-year EU harmonisation will mean that some artists whose work is already out of copyright will come back into copyright. The EU Directive does not apply to works of non-EU origin, from countries that offer a shorter period of protection (e.g. the USA, life plus 50 years after death of the artist; see Table 28.1), where the protection will be for the shorter period. Copyright protection of computer programs was the first example of harmonisation in the field of copyright within the EC (1991), followed by rental and lending rights in 1992, and copyright related to satellite broadcasting and cable transmission in 1993. The EU has also published a draft Directive for harmonisation of the legal protection of databases, but has, so far, done very little on moral rights.

The administration of rights in the music industry (as compared with the visual arts) is much more developed, but highly complex. Attempts are currently being made to find workable solutions for music rights in the new situations arising from the development of interactive multimedia, including encouraging moves towards one-stop copyright clearance. Linear media in the film and TV sectors are also highly complex, and questions arise as to how interactive a use has to be before it becomes nonlinear.

28.5.7 Copyrighting Standards

A recent initiative (Samuelson 2006) launched in the USA is addressed towards protecting standards as intellectual products. Controversies over intellectual property (IP) in relation to standards have been common over the past decade. Most of those IT and standards disputes have mainly been about patents, although a new wave of disputes are now arising due to copyrights claimed by standard setting organisations (SSOs) regarding standards produced by committees formed by or under their aegis, especially when governments mandate use of these standards. These disputes are currently limited to the healthcare and eCommerce sectors, but should extend to other relevant sectors.

28 Intellectual Property Rights

28.6 Digital Uncertainties

Traditionally (analogue) media were segmented and had their own terminology and economics. While the content elements of digital multimedia do not cause new legal problems, the combination and uses of them do. The term "multimedia" can apply not only to text, images and music on hard disks, CD-ROMs, CD-Is, etc., but also to networked resources, video on demand and other interactive services. Questions to be answered are:

- Is multimedia a collaborative work (where the authors' rights belong to the different creators and have to be transferred by contract to the producer) or a collective work (where, from the outset, the rights belong to the publisher)?
- If multimedia were legally considered to be databanks, this would raise other sets of rights problems under existing national legislation and proposed EU harmonisation that is currently being discussed.
- Does the inclusion of a work in a multimedia resource constitute a new form of exploitation, or is it the adaptation of a pre-existing work? Many existing contracts have provisions for the assignment of unknown methods of exploitation, but most do not include rights of adaptation. Ancillary rights in existing contracts do not cover new media that are subsequently introduced.

Digital forms also introduce many new complications in relation to aspects such as image manipulation, downloading to disc or hardcopy printout, networking, etc. Reproducing a copyright protected work in electronic form is considered to be a restricted act, but in many EU and non-EU countries the status under copyright law of temporary (transient) electronic storage of protected works (i.e. in RAM memory) during acts of loading, transmission or screen display is currently being debated. With the rapid rate of technology development it is going to be necessary to regularly update agreements.

Multimedia is ravenous for content and, realistically, we have to start valuing the price of the various elements of content on a new basis.

28.7 Image Scanning and Image Security

Who should digitise: the museum or the developer/publisher? Ideally all scans, whoever makes them, should have integral header identification and information including the author/creator of the object or work of art, the title, date, owner and copyright owner. The security of digitised images from unauthorised use and piracy (which is a major economic problem in videotape and digital audio and video publishing) is made more problematic by the rapid development of networking, and is being explored through the development of a variety of technical devices. These include encryption systems and visible or invisible watermarking of images.

For instance, *CITED (Copyright in Transmitted Electronic Documents)* has been developed under the EU ESPRIT II program and represents a comprehensive system of controls over access and degrees of use of material within online and also CD-based multimedia resources, including audit trails—according to the password status of the particular user.

28.7.1 Recent Administrative Developments

The law follows technical development (although often much later). Most of the present copyright law does not adequately reflect current (and likely future) developments in digital publishing. Some people now feel that copyright will not be able to cope with digital developments in IT and will eventually be replaced by contract law or by copyright-on-demand arrangements. In 1993–94 the *CIAGP (Conseil International des Auteurs des Arts Graphiques et Plastiques et des Photographes)*, which comprises artists' rights societies from many countries, drew up draft proposals for agreements on digital imaging and interactive multimedia.

These proposals were considered by its parent body *CISAC (Confédération Internationale des Sociétés d'Auteurs et Compositeurs)* and were made available in 1995. Although they are unlikely to include recommended tariffs, they could and should provide a basis for an important step forward, providing the individual societies can, between themselves, agree on the terms and basis of implementation. In September 1993, the German Publishers Association has produced a *Guide to the Negotiation of License Agreements for the Utilization of Published Works in On-Line Databases*.

International conferences on interactive multimedia and on museums and information technology increasingly feature sessions on the topic of intellectual property rights and their implications, but there is still no sign of a basis for international proposals for model agreements. There have been a number of initiatives by consortia of museums in the USA that have set out to establish and protect the position of museums. Similarly there are initiatives by consortia of photographers in the USA.

The *Coalition for Networked Information*, Washington DC, produced an interesting research report on the *Rights for Electronic Access and Delivery of Information (READI)* project in September 1992. This has been followed by the deliberations and a preliminary report in July 1994 of the US *Working Group on Intellectual Property Rights of the National Information Infrastructure (NII) Task Force*, which highlight the problem that sources of valuable intellectual property are not being made available over the networks because of the absence of reasonable assurance that intellectual property rights will be respected.

READI

The *Multimedia Subcommittee of the Copyright Council* of Japan's *Agency for Cultural Affairs* considered the establishment of a centralised organisation for copyright information in a preliminary report in 1993. In 1994, the *Multimedia Committee* of Japan's *Institute of Intellectual Property* (MITI) proposed a *Digital Information Centre*, a collective administrative centre at which information on copyrighted works could be readily accessible and clearance approval efficiently obtained.

MITI

Copymart Also in Japan, *Copymart* is a contract-based model for the collective licensing of copyright, which would comprise two databases: the *copyright market (CRM)*, where rights holders can file their copyright information including a brief description of works and sale or license agreements, and the *copy market*, where copies of works are distributed to customers upon request and payment.

Multimedia clearinghouse In the US, there is a proposal for a *multimedia clearinghouse*, with copyright owners participating on a voluntary basis.

Photo library agencies *Photo library agencies* in the UK and the US are working with CD-ROM and on-line networking, providing clients with images that are copyright-cleared for the purposes declared online by the client followed by the payment of the appropriate fee by the client.

WIPO The *World Intellectual Property Organisation (WIPO)* is studying the establishment of an international system of assigning, on request, identifying numbers to certain categories of literary and artistic works and to phonograms. These identifying numbers may also be used for electronic (particularly digital) means to control the extent of use and, possibly, to identify the protected material used.

Within *WIPO*, the *Electronic Frontier Foundation (EFF)* stressed that the dream of making all published works available to everyone in the world was today available through technology. The digital world and the Internet provided the promise of universal access to knowledge stored in the world's libraries.

APP The French *Agency for Protection of Programs (APP)* has developed such an international identification system for software at the request of *WIPO*.

EC LAB Among recent specialist conferences, a significant one was *Legal Aspects of Multimedia and GIS,* held in Lisbon in October 1994 by the *Legal Advisory Board (LAB), DGXIII of the European Commission*. This included the presentation of drafts of several wide-ranging and, in some respects, controversial papers commissioned and now published by the Commission. Given that the clearing of intellectual property rights is currently complicated, time-consuming and therefore costly, there is an urgent need for simple, understandable licensing and model contracts on the part of the providers to encourage and facilitate integrity on the part of the users.

28.8 The Malaysian Experiment

The Multimedia Super Corridor (MSC) is Malaysia's most exciting initiative for the global information and communication technology (ICT) industry. It has been developed to act as a global reference centre for multimedia production. However, it has faced IPR and cyber law problems.

Conceptualised in 1996, the *MSC Malaysia* has since grown into a thriving dynamic ICT hub, hosting more than 900 multinationals, foreign-owned and home-grown Malaysian companies focused on multimedia and communications products, solutions, services, research and development.

Fig. 28.1
Malaysian *Vision 2020*

With this unique corridor, Malaysia continues to draw leading ICT companies of the world into locating their operations in the *MSC Malaysia* and to undertake research, develop new products and technologies and export from this base. The *MSC Malaysia* is also an ideal growth environment for Malaysian ICT SMEs to transform themselves into world-class companies. Furthermore, the *MSC Malaysia* welcomes other countries to use its highly advanced infrastructural facilities as a global testbed for ICT applications and a hub for their regional operations in Asia.

28.8.1 Infra- and Infostructure

The Malaysian government has equipped core areas in the *MSC Malaysia* with high-capacity global telecommunications and logistics networks. Emphasis has been placed on eco-friendly yet sophisticated urban structures for businesses, homes, education and recreation. The *MSC Malaysia* is also supported by secure cyberlaws, strategic policies and a range of financial and nonfinancial incentives for investors.

There are several compelling reasons for investors and ICT technopreneurs to conduct their business in the MSC Malaysia, including:

- Comprehensive package for investors
- Strong socio-economic fundamentals
- Firm commitment from the Malaysian Government
- Accelerated human resource training and development
- Competitive costs of doing business
- Ready access to the Asia-Pacific markets
- Widespread usage of English
- Superlative quality of life.

Compelling factors

The *Multimedia Super Corridor* is Malaysia's gift to the world—a growth area specifically designed to unlock multimedia's full potential by integrating innovative *cyberlaws* and outstanding infrastructure into an attractive and eco-friendly environment. The MSC Malaysia aims to revolutionise how Malaysians and others in the region conduct commerce in the digital age.

The *MSC Malaysia* has committed itself to fulfilling the following promises to ensure business success:
- Bill of Guarantees
- Infrastructure
- Cyberlaws
- Incentives.

28.8.1.1 Main Initiatives

Malaysia is a member of the *World Intellectual Property Organization (WIPO)*, *Paris Convention, Berne Convention* and a signatory to the *Agreement on Trade Related Aspects of Intellectual Property Rights (TRIPS)*.

With the implementation of the *Multimedia Super Corridor,* the Government has made a commitment to MSC Malaysia-Status companies in one of the *10-Point Bill of Guarantees* to provide a comprehensive regulatory framework of intellectual property protection and *cyber laws* to facilitate and assist the development of a truly ICT and multimedia environment.

A brief description of the Malaysian statutory framework for intellectual property protection and *cyberlaws* follows.

28.8.1.2 Intellectual Property Protection

The *Trade Marks Act 1976*, enforced on the 1st of September 1983, provides for a registration system for marks (e.g. logos, brands, signs) used in relation to goods and services. The registration of a mark in relation to specified goods or services is valid for ten years from the date of filing and is renewable for subsequent periods of ten years each, indefinitely. The registered proprietor is entitled to commence infringement action against others who use his mark without consent or lodge a complaint under the Trade Description Act 1972.

The *Patents Act 1983* came into force on the 1st of October 1986 to provide for a system of patent registration and utility innovations in Malaysia. The Act specifies, among others, what is meant by "patentable invention" and what are nonpatentable. Upon grant and if annual fees are paid, a patent is valid for twenty years from the date of application. The owner of a patent has the exclusive rights to exploit the patentable invention, assign or transmit the patent and to conclude licence contracts. Infringement proceedings can be instituted against those who have infringed or are infringing this patent.

The *Copyright Act 1987*, effective as of 1st of December 1987, confers the exclusive right to the owner of a copyright for a specific period. There is no system of registration for copyright in Malaysia. A work that is eligible (literary works, musical works, artistic works, films, sound recordings, broadcasts and derivative works) is protected automatically if sufficient effort has been expended to make the work original in character; the work has been written down, recorded or otherwise reduced to a material form; and the author is a qualified person, the work is made in Malaysia or the work is first published in Malaysia. The Act also specifies the circumstances amounting to and remedies for infringements and offences.

The *Industrial Designs Act 1996*, which is in force from the 1st of September 1999, implements a system for the registration of an "industrial design" in Malaysia, defined to mean the features of shape, configuration, pattern or ornament applied to an article by any industrial process which appeal to and are judged by the eye in the finished article. The registration is for five years from the date of application and renewable for two more periods of five years each. The Act further specifies the extent of rights granted to the owner and what amounts to infringement.

The *Layout Designs of Integrated Circuits Act 2000*, in force from the 15th of August 2000, set out, inter alia, the criteria for the protection of the layout design of integrated circuits and the extent of protection conferred upon the right holder. A layout design is valid for ten years from the date it is first commercially exploited. Notwithstanding that, the protection conferred by the statute will lapse fifteen years from the date of its creation.

The *Geographical Indications Act 2000,* which came into effect on the 15th of August 2001, specifies the process for registration of geographical indications, to prevent misuse of the names of places which identify both the geographical origins and the products.

The *Optical Discs Act 2000*, which is effective as of 15th of September 2000, provides for the licensing and regulation of the manufacture of optical discs, such as VCD, DVD, CDs, etc. in Malaysia. The Act represents one of the legislative initiatives taken to combat the piracy of copyright works in the form of optical discs and to strengthen the protection of intellectual property rights in Malaysia.

28.8.1.3 Cyberlaws

The *Digital Signature Act 1997*, enforced on the 1st of October 1998, is an enabling law that allows for the development of, amongst others, e-commerce by providing an avenue for secure online transactions through the use of digital signatures. The Act provides a framework for the licensing and regulation of *certification authorities*, and gives legal recognition to digital signatures. The *Controller of Certification Authority*, who has the authority to license and regulate Certification Authorities, was appointed on the 1st of October 1998.

The *Communications and Multimedia Act 1998,* which came into effect on the 1st of April 1999, provides a regulatory framework to cater for the convergence of the telecommunications, broadcasting and computing industries, with the objective of, among others, making Malaysia a major global centre and hub for communications and multimedia information and content services.

The *Malaysian Communications and Multimedia Commission* was appointed on the 1st November 1998 as the sole regulator of the new regulatory regime. Although regulation in the form of licensing is provided for, one of the cornerstones of the new regulatory framework is self-regulation by the various industries, including the ICT and multimedia content industries.

The *Copyright (Amendment) Act 1997* which amended the *Copyright Act 1987* came into force on the 1st of April 1999, to make unauthorised transmission of copyright works over the Internet an infringement of copyright. It is also an infringement of copyright to circumvent any effective technological measures aimed at restricting access to copyright works. These provisions are aimed at ensuring adequate protection of intellectual property rights for companies involved in content creation in the ICT and multimedia environment.

The *Computer Crimes Act 1997*, effective as of the 1st of June 2000, created several offences relating to the misuse of computers. Among others, it deals with unauthorised access to computer material, unauthorised access with intent to commit other offences and unauthorised modification of computer contents. It also makes provisions to facilitate investigations for the enforcement of the Act.

The *Telemedicine Act 1997* is intended to provide a framework to enable licensed medical practitioners to practice medicine using audio, visual and data communications. To date (November 2008), the Telemedicine Act has yet to be enforced.

28.9 Creative Commons

Fig. 28.2

As already stated, digital technology, and in particular the Internet, has completely overturned traditional ideas about distribution. Any work that can take a digital form can be infinitely reproduced and delivered directly onto desk or handheld appliances at minimal cost. In addition digital technology has enabled *new forms of expression* and *new classes of authors*. Digital music, video clips, animations, multimedia content are created and exchanged more easily, reaching a huge audience almost instantaneously. Peer-to-peer technology enables on-the-fly exchange of content, unleashing incredible opportunities to share personal content and activate added value chains of cooperation.

Intellectual property rights management and even the concept itself must be revised in order to better fit it to and minimise constraints to creativity and innovation. Cooperative and social products of creativity are boosted by the Internet and represent a completely new way to develop products.

In order to establish a similar scenario the *Creative Commons*[50] organisation was established some years ago.[51]

Creative Commons is a nonprofit organisation that offers flexible copyright licenses for creative works.

Creative Commons licenses provide a flexible range of protections and freedoms for authors, artists, and educators. The concept offers an extension to the "all rights reserved" concept of traditional copyright in order to offer a voluntary "some rights reserved" approach.

---

50 This section is derived from and directly related to the Creative Commons information set and website: http://creativecommons.org/.

51 Creative Commons' first project, in December 2002, was the release of a set of copyright licenses free for public use.

28.9.1 Baseline Rights and Restrictions in All Licenses

All *Creative Commons* licenses have many important features in common. Every license will help the author to:
- Retain their copyright
- Announce that other people's fair use, first sale, and free expression rights are not affected by the license.

Every license requires licensees:
- To get the author's permission to do any of the things that the author has chosen to restrict (e.g. commercial usage, creation of a derivative work, ...)
- To keep any copyright notice intact on all copies of the work
- To link to the author's license from copies of the work
- Not to alter the terms of the license
- Not to use technology to restrict other licensees' lawful uses of the work.

Every license allows licensees, provided they live up to the author's conditions:
- To copy the work
- To distribute it
- To display or perform it publicly
- To make digital public performances of it (e.g. webcasting)
- To shift the work into another format as a verbatim copy.

Every license:
- Applies worldwide
- Lasts for the duration of the work's copyright
- Is not revocable.

Note that this list of features does not apply to the *Public Domain Dedication*, *Sampling Licenses*, or *Founder's Copyright*.

28.9.2 Creative Commons Licenses

This paragraph describes each of the six main licenses offered when the author chooses to publish a work with a *Creative Commons* license. It is also helpful to know that there is a set of baseline rights that all six licenses offer to others. The licenses are listed below, starting with the most restrictive type that the author can choose and ending with the most accommodating type, and then the factors to consider before choosing a license are discussed.

28.9.2.1 Attribution Noncommercial No Derivatives (by-nc-nd)

This license is the *most restrictive* of the six main CC licenses, allowing redistribution. This license is often called the "free advertising" license because it allows others to download works and share them with others as long as they mention the author and link back to them, but they can't change them in any way or use them commercially.

28.9.2.2 Attribution Noncommercial Share Alike (by-nc-sa)

This license lets others remix, tweak, and build upon the work noncommercially, as long as they credit the author and license their new creations under identical terms. Others can simply download and redistribute the work just as under the by-nc-nd license, but they can also translate, make remixes, and produce new stories based on the work. All new works based on the author's will carry the same license, so any derivatives will also be noncommercial in nature.

28.9.2.3 Attribution Noncommercial (by-nc)

This license lets others remix, tweak, and build upon the author's work noncommercially, and although their new works must also acknowledge the author and be noncommercial, they don't have to license their derivative works on the same terms.

28.9.2.4 Attribution No Derivatives (by-nd)

This license allows for redistribution (commercial and noncommercial) as long as it is passed along wholly unchanged, crediting the author.

28.9.2.5 Attribution Share Alike (by-sa)

This license lets others remix, tweak, and build upon the author's work, even for commercial reasons, as long as they credit the author and license their new creations under identical terms. This license is often compared to open source software licenses. All new works based on the author's will carry the same license, so any derivatives will also allow commercial use.

28.9.2.6 Attribution (by)

This license lets others distribute, remix, tweak, and build upon the author's work, even commercially, as long as they credit the author for the original creation. This is the *most accommodating* of the licenses offered, in terms of what others can do with works licensed under Attribution.

28.9.2.7 Other Licenses

The Creative Commons organisation also offers a set of other licenses for more specialised applications.

Sampling licenses allow for snippets (not whole works) to be remixed into new works, even commercially. *CC Public Domain Dedication* allows works to be freed from copyright completely, and *CC Founders Copyright* does the same but after 14 or 28 years. Musicians looking to share their work with fans might want to look at the *Music Sharing License*.

The organisation has even considered one of the most relevant issues in fighting the digital divide and supporting developing countries. The *Developing Nations License* allows less restrictive terms to be offered to countries that aren't considered "high income" by the World Bank, and finally, for those licensing software, CC offers the GNU GPL and GNU LGPL licenses.[52]

28.9.3 Choosing a License

Offering your work under a *Creative Commons* license does not mean giving up author's copyright. It means offering some of the author's rights to any member of the public but only on certain conditions.

What conditions? All of the CC licenses require that attribution is performed in the manner specified by the author or licensor.

Attribution. The author allows others to copy, distribute, display, and perform their copyrighted work—and derivative works based upon it—but only if they give credit in the way requested by the author.

Example: Jane publishes her photograph with an Attribution license because she wants the world to use her pictures provided they give her credit. Bob finds her photograph online and wants to display it on the front page of his website. Bob puts Jane's picture on his site, and clearly indicates Jane's authorship.

Noncommercial. The author allows others to copy, distribute, display, and perform their work—and derivative works based upon it—but for noncommercial purposes only.

Examples: Gus publishes his photograph on his website with a Noncommercial license. Camille prints Gus' photograph. Camille is not allowed to sell the print photograph without Gus's permission.

No Derivative Works. The author allows others to copy, distribute, display, and perform only verbatim copies of their work, not derivative works based upon it.

Example: Sara licenses a recording of her song with a No Derivative Works license. Joe would like to cut Sara's track and mix it with his own to produce an entirely new song. Joe cannot do this without Sara's permission (unless his song amounts to fair use).

Share Alike. The author allows others to distribute derivative works only under a license identical to the license that governs their work.

---

52 GNU General Public License (GNU GPL or simply GPL) is a free software license, created by Richard Stallman for the GNU free operating system project. The GPL is the most popular and well-known example of a strong copyleft license that transfers the copyleft to all the derived works. The GNU Lesser General Public License (LGPL) is a more permissive version of the GPL. This licence was originally intended for software libraries.

Note: A license cannot feature both the Share Alike and No Derivative Works options. The Share Alike requirement applies only to derivative works.

Example: Gus's online photo is licensed under the Noncommercial and Share Alike terms. Camille is an amateur collage artist, and she takes Gus's photo and puts it into one of her collages. This Share Alike language requires Camille to make her collage available on a Noncommercial plus Share Alike license. It makes her offer her work back to the world on the same terms Gus gave her.

Also note that every license carries with it a full set of other rights in addition to the allowances specifically made here.

28.9.4   Taking a License

How does the licence work? When the author chosen a license, the appropriate license will then be expressed in three ways:
- *Commons Deed*. A simple, plain-language summary of the license, complete with the relevant icons.
- *Legal Code*. The fine print that is needed to make sure that the license will stand up in court.
- *Digital Code*. A machine-readable translation of the license that helps search engines and other applications identify the work by its terms of use.

Once the author has done this, they should include a *Creative Commons* "Some Rights Reserved" button on the site, near the work.

This button will link back to the Commons Deed, so that the world can be notified of the license terms. If the author finds that the license is being violated, they may have grounds to sue under copyright infringement.

28.10 The Products

Besides the traditional advertising information packs which have always been produced in the audiovisual field by governments and corporations, the web is being invaded by the free and subjective need of individuals to communicate and become active protagonists of communication, freed at last from media unidirectionality.

New forms of communication and expression are emerging, such as blogs, shared collections of photos and videos, shared surfing histories or personal video broadcasts[53].

---

53   See for example the photo archive at http://www.thesimplegallery.com.nyud.net:8080/pictures.php and the Slide Show Pro software available at http://slideshowpro.net, Flickr http://www.flickr.com/, YouTube www.youtube.com, etc.

Thoughts, emotions and beliefs become messages and works, sometimes of exceedingly high value, that are not linked to market values because they spring from primary exigencies of the creative self and community relationships.

28.11 Creativity, Production and Market

While in the previous century very few managed to get past the expensive threshold of production for a mass market, now we are entering a phase in which collective creativity can begin to produce for markets which are finely divided and sectorised.

We are thus passing from elite creativity for a mass market to mass creativity for elite markets. This new passage is irreversibly revolutionising our productive, distributive, communicational, educational and social worlds.

From being *generalist*, television is now becoming digital and thematic; broadcasting is changing to "narrow casting"; interactivity breaks down the unidirectional message into myriad fragments adaptable to each single user, who thus becomes the subject of the market rather than the object.

The selective capacity of the individual to latch on to tastes, trends, emotions and desires is such that anything may be custom-made, from clothes to gadgets, education or entertainment, and may be automatically renewed as required and promptly delivered to home.

The Web world, which has such a disconcertingly immense galaxy of options, may be comfortably controlled by selection on the part of each live user, whether an individual or a community, absolutely instantaneously, by paying rental services with minimum but constant fees, just like the mass fluxes which polarised the immense riches of the past.

New mass consumerism will therefore take the form of intelligent software, free and custom-made, which will remain with the customer in every phase of his or her life (and, very likely, post mortem too[54]) with all the solicitude of an old housekeeper, accustomed to anticipating future needs and whims, and able to regulate the purse-strings.

28.12 Final Considerations

This trend specifies how *copyright* and *copyleft* are twin faces of the same coin, complementary and equally necessary: it thus becomes evident that from the harmonic balance of these two exigencies a form of communication which is simultaneously open, free and democratic may arise.

The development of copyleft is thus functional to the new economy and should be incremented in order to increase access to the new media and raise

---

54   There are already post-mortem personal home pages, e.g. http://memorial.com/.

the educational level of the underprivileged classes, in the awareness that heavily unbalanced situations create social tension and war.

In this crucial era of globalisation in which we are living, it is necessary, without ignoring the dramatic game of rival markets, to be able to identify the weak points that the market can induce, if we do not wish to confine behind besieged bulwarks the few present users and abandon to dangerous *infopoverty* most of the world's population.

This is why the protection of *copyright*, if correctly applied, can valorise the creativity of all those with access to the new communication tools. This discriminating threshold can now be widened to very rapidly allow general entrance thanks to the use of *copyleft*.

28.13 Digital Rights Management and Clearance

It is reasonable that in the era of digital communication the management of IPR should be delegated to digital procedures. The amount of content and services produced and delivered in digital format is so huge that there is no chance to apply any traditional approach.

The use of *DRM* is sometimes the only way to enable content or service exchanges or the creation of compound services that *assemble* different contributions, sometimes even on the fly.

From a functional perspective, *DRM* means many things to many people. For some it is simply about the technical process of securing content in a digital form. To others, it is the entire technical process of supporting the exchange of rights and content on networks like the Internet. For convenience, *DRM* is often separated into two functional areas:

- The identification and description of intellectual property and rights pertaining to works and to parties involved in their creation of administration (digital rights management).
- The (technical) enforcement of usage restrictions (digital management of rights).

DRM may therefore refer to the technologies and/or processes that are applied to digital content to describe and identify it and/or to define, apply and enforce usage rules in a secure manner.

It is also important to distinguish between *access control*, *copy protection*, and *the management of intellectual property rights*, highlighting their respective boundaries.

Access control system   An *access control system* manages a user's access to content, usually through the implementation of some kind of password protection. However, once access to the content has been granted, no further protection is applied. Thus, once a user has access to the content, it is no longer possible to control what is done with that content. This type of protection is often employed on websites where a simple access control mechanism suffices.

Copy protection system   A *copy protection system* is designed to signal the extent of copying and serial copying permitted, if any, which is defined by the associated "usage information" with respect to any instance of delivered content, and to implement and enforce the signalled behaviour in consumer equipment. The notion of copy protection can be extended to control the movement of content within and outside the user domain, encompassing redistribution over the Internet.

A fully enabled *intellectual property rights management system* covers the processing of all rights information for the electronic administration of rights, sometimes including contractual and personal information, to enable end-to-end rights management throughout the value chain. By its nature, *DRM* may require access to commercially sensitive information (as opposed to copy information and usage signalling). The use of such a system will enable very granular control of content, enabling rights owners to apply sophisticated usage models.

IPR management system

This process of managing intellectual property rights inevitably involves the extensive use of *DRM* technologies. Such technologies can be embedded into many components, from those that reside on a single device, such as a *Personal Digital Assistant* (*PDA*), to those to be found in commercial Internet servers run by major companies and organisations.

28.14 Protecting Rights

How can we manage intellectual property rights in a global market, considering that *legal frameworks* differ from country to country, that some regions of the world *do not protect intellectual property by law*, and the rise of the *digital piracy phenomenon*?

It is obviously going to be difficult to develop a conventional market when there is an absence of a legal basis for protecting intellectual property. In such a scenario, specific content and entire products can be cloned and sold without infringing on any local laws; this has happened for software applications for example.

If we turn to consider differences between legal frameworks and digital piracy, a great deal of effort is currently being expended to harmonize the international regulatory framework (e.g. in the case of *Creative Commons* or WIPO*)*. There are even initiatives related to traditional IPR protection, such as *BSA* and *NetAssociate*.[55] Copyrighted products tend to have an explicit licence agreement that must be accepted before a new user can activate the application for the first time.

BSA and NetAssociate

In addition to the regulatory framework, IPR should be actively protected using methods such as:

Additional protection methods

- Watermarking and digital watermarking
- Trusted systems
- Encryption

---

55 BSA Business Software Alliance: *http://www.bsa.org*.
NetAssociate: *http://www.nai.com, http://www.mcafee.com/it/*.

- Hard keys
- Soft keys

Of course, nowadays we are interested in protecting not only *text*, *audio tracks*, *images* and *movies,* but also *three-dimensional models*, so major protection systems must be able to cope with all data types.

An additional key aspect that must be adequately taken into account is the availability of an unprotected preview of the content.

28.14.1 Watermarking and Digital Watermarking

Watermarking can be *classical* or *digital* (visible or invisible; see Table 28.2). The most effective watermarks must contain, in encoded form, the most important details of the copyright agreement, such as:
- Information about the owner of the rights
- Information about the customer
- Information about possible use
- Timeframe and validity.

Visible watermarking

Visible watermarking is mainly used by *image banks* or photographers to protect their own images. Note that the image may be highly compromised by the presence of the watermark.

Customers can only access the watermarked copy while they are deciding whether to order an image.

Table 28.2

Name:	Digital watermarking
Invention:	First related publications date back to 1979. However, it was only in 1990 that it gained a great deal of international interest.
Definition:	Imperceptible insertion of information into multimedia data.
Concept:	Insertion of information, such as a number or text, into the multimedia data through slight modification of the data.
Requirements:	Imperceptible. Robust or fragile, depending on application.
Applications:	Copyright protection, labelling, monitoring, tamper proofing, conditional access.
Commercial potential:	Unclear. Although many watermarking companies exist, few of them seem fully profitable for the moment.

Invisible watermarking is usually preferred because it enables visual material to be shown as is while still preventing unauthorised copying and redistribution.

Invisible watermarking

There are two distinct characteristics of such watermarks. On the one hand they must be *robust,* while on the other hand they must be *easily identified and managed automatically,* even in partial or modified copies of the original.

Robust means that even if we edit and modify the original image using digital filters or by lowering resolution, or even by cutting out parts of the image, the watermark will still be readable.

Robust watermarking

The ability to *manage* the information associated with the *digital watermark automatically* enables potential copyright infringements to be checked for automatically. This is one of the basic features required to make the protection process *economically valuable.* In addition, robust methods enable copyright to be identified even in reproductions made on different media (e.g. printed copies).

Of course, automation is the key; if it was not possible to automate the process of copyright identification, authors would have to collect books and magazines in addition to websites in order to identify potential infringements, and this would usually cost far more than simply paying for rights.

Automation is the key

This method is suited to most visual material. Some limitations with this approach are encountered in the field of motion pictures, where the most popular options are visible *watermarking* through the addition of logos or textual information to the movie, and data encryption that stops frames from unauthorised copies from being displayed.

28.14.2 Trusted Systems

This concept was developed many years ago. It is based upon the idea of establishing a "relationship of *trust*" between various interconnected devices. The devices involved in this relationship adhere to a *code of conduct*, which enables them to perform a set of basic actions such as *load in memory*, *save a copy*, p*rint*, d*isplay*, among others.

The processing of any kind of digital information within a trusted system must obey the code of conduct. A customised version of this approach was even included in some advance releases of the *MPEG* format.

28.14.3 Encryption

This method is suitable for any type of data—even for three-dimensional data models. It proved to be a very useful approach during the early years of Internet technology, when the bandwidth available to users was usually too low to enable the practical transfer of very large datasets across the Internet. To get around this issue, encrypted datasets were distributed on CD-ROMs and decryption keys for these datasets were sold on the Internet.

28.14.4 Hard Keys

The use of hard keys to protect digital content was one of the first protection methods to gain popularity. The hard keys were simply placed in a *special* floppy disk, embedded in the keyboard, linked to the CPU serial number, or installed in a chip that had to be permanently connected to an I/O port[56].

One of the major drawbacks of this method was that the keys frequently malfunctioned, causing registered customers a great deal of trouble.

28.14.5 Soft Keys

Soft keys are still one of the most popular methods used to access digital resources such as applications, data and services. This method is often enhanced by combining it with an internet connection; consider, for example, the online registration of software, the online activation of access credit (e.g. mobile phone prepaid cards).

28.14.6 Other Methods

There are a variety of slightly different technologies and methods aimed at IPR or data protection. Some of them mainly rely on software, some need to be associated with hardware components, while others use a combination of hardware and software components.

Some recent solutions have made use of *scratchable pre-paid cards;* for example, to access MP3 files over the Internet.

By following this approach we are now beginning to achieve the widespread application of secure identification and digital signatures.

28.15 Digital Object Identifiers

This topic is related to IPR to some degree. It addresses the following issue: how can we create a *robust* reference that points to a digital object? We all know all too well that any type of reference or link to a digital object is *fragile* information.

Digital objects are often created—without conforming to any "publishing protocol"—and then copied and moved from one website to another. This means that digital references are often unreliable or "fragile". So how can we create robust digital object references?

Physical objects are usually traced so that it is easy to find them. Paper-based documents are usually safely and systematically stored in archives or libraries,

---

56 One of the most popular protection devices used in the world of PCs was the Autodesk parallel port hard key.

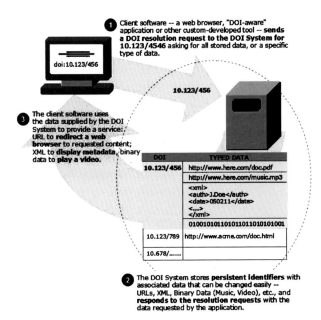

Fig. 28.3 DOI resolution schema (courtesy of the International DOI Foundation)

where they are easily retrieved by using the appropriate *inventory*. In addition, books, magazines, and so on are identified by information printed in the colophon and by a special code: the ISBN, ISSN, etc. ISBN is a global identification system that uses thirteen digits to identify any book printed on the planet.

Following this approach, the idea of associating *a unique alphanumeric code* with each digital object was borne. The European Commission eContent framework then converted this idea into reality, resulting in the *DOI System*. The *DOI (Digital Object Identifier) System* allows "content objects" to be identified in the digital environment. A *DOI name* is assigned to each entity used on the digital network.

The DOI system can also be used to provide information about the object, including where it (or information about it) can actually be found on the Internet. However, while information about the digital object (including where to find it) may change over time, its *DOI name* will not.

The DOI is a *unique name* (not a location) for an *entity* linked to the Internet. The application of *DOIs* to digital *objects* guarantees their persistent and actionable identification, and it also enables the interoperable exchange of managed information on digital networks.

As already expressed above, unique identifiers are essential for the management of information in any digital environment. While we can assign identifiers related to a specific context and time, consider the potential benefits of using *universal unique identifiers* (identifiers that can be re-used in a different context and at a different time without the need to consult the *official* content owner/publisher).

To achieve this goal we must design and manage identifiers that enable such interoperability and that can be used in services beyond the direct control of the issuing organisation.

Fig. 28.4 Crossref or DOI resolver

The need for interoperability requires that the identifier persists across time; once defined in relation to a digital object, the identifier is valid forever and will always refer to the same digital object.

Because of the independence of services from the issuing organisation, they are by definition arbitrary, and so interoperability implies the need for extensibility. Extensibility makes it possible to *extend* the description of the services provided.

Thanks to the design specification of the *DOI System* a *DOI name* can be a representation of any logical entity. *DOI* is a generic framework that is applicable to any digital object, providing a structured, extensible means of identification, description and resolution.

To ensure consistency the whole system is built on top of several existing standards that have been brought together and developed further. Indeed, the entire system has been accepted as an ISO standard (ISO TC46/SC9).

29 Technology and Privacy

In the near future, it will be necessary to find a satisfactory equilibrium between privacy and the "open" systems enabled by ICT.

On the one hand, these technologies should enable each of us to be more self-sufficient, and may indeed push us to become more "removed" or isolated from the rest of the world. On the other hand, they produce and store an incredible amount of "evidence" (files etc.) documenting our existence moment by moment.

The more technology we use, the more visible we become. High technology is now used to such an extent that it is often possible to *track* people using their devices. For example, in the United States, by law, the GSM mobile phone system must enable user localisation within a range of ten metres, while third-generation portable phones with AGPS make it possible to determine the position of the user with a high degree of accuracy, as do the GPS/navigation systems installed in many cars nowadays.

While accurate 2-D or 3-D positioning is now possible based on the use of from three to nine (or more) *visible* satellites, in the near future the European positioning system service, codenamed *Galileo*, will further improve the overall localisation performance, which will enable additional location-dependent services to be rolled out (these, such as natural disaster recovery, eHealth remote monitoring systems, etc., are actually already in the advanced beta-testing phase).

Internal and external video-surveillance systems connected to computer-vision-based systems are able to identify a person, a vehicle and their behaviour in both 2-D and 3-D.

ATM transactions and credit card usage indicate our movements, tastes and lifestyles. The contents of our PCs and our Internet activities are monitored by spyware, fished and hacked (in the most optimistic vision, such activities would simply lead to the creation of personal profiles for e-commerce applications, but that is a different topic altogether).

To illustrate this constant monitoring, a "total recall" digital memory system (similar in some ways to the—far more extreme—device used in Arnold Schwarzenegger's movie of the same name) was introduced by its inventor during the 2004 *World Wide Web Conference*. This wearable system is based on a CCD mounted onto thin glasses connected to a microcomputer with hundreds of gigabytes of memory. The system takes a picture every second (or some

Tracking and visibility

Fig. 29.1 Rolex wristwatch (photo by Francesca Ronchi)

Total Recall

other fraction of time). The inventor stated that *"if we lose something we simply have to press rewind"*.

Although this "total recall" system may appear to be just another new gadget, the privacy issues associated with it and other technologies are relevant to the field of culture, because of our ideas, attitudes, religions or general behaviour.

The issue of privacy in relation to technology extends far beyond user profiles and tracking. For instance, cultural databanks can contain sensitive information too—the exact location of an artefact[57]; the presence of a specific artefact in a temporary exhibition[58]; even the inclusion of a stolen artefact in the police's catalogue of thefts[59].

"Who's got the Rolex?"

There are also privacy concerns related to the general use of *RFID*. This technology effectively gives machines "X-ray vision". Cyber pickpockets can use it play "who's got the Rolex" or even simply "who's got the iPod" (Stajano 2005).

29.1 Privacy and Personal Data Management

Personal data

Due to the spread of online applications and the need to process and file personal information such as names, addresses, telephone numbers and email addresses, national authorities all over the world have started to look for potential infringements of privacy by hackers. Indeed, there have even been some international-level infringements; for example, the customer database belonging to a very well known underwear brand was cracked and personal information about various celebrities was made public.

Fig. 29.2 A security camera conected to a video surveillance system (photo by Francesca Ronchi)

---

57 Such as a Christian art artefact in a church or monastery.
58 Thieves may discover a lesser-known artefact in a minor art gallery or exhibit.
59 In the past this provided evidence of authenticity for both thieves and receivers. The same may happen for the Unique ID.

Rules and obligations may differ from country to country and from continent to continent, but the importance of keeping personal information private is always recognised and protected. It is mandatory to ask for explicit approval every time personal information is stored in any format. It is also mandatory to ask for explicit approval when the data is updated, communicated or transferred to a different organisation. In addition, an agent responsible for the personal information must be nominated and referenced by the organisation.

PDAs and mobile phones

In contrast, owners are responsible for managing the personal information stored in their PDAs and mobile phones.

30 Usability, Accessibility and Platforms

Usability[60] is strictly related to the concepts previously described in Chap. 12 Interaction Design. This chapter will briefly outline specific aspects of usability related to cultural applications.

Usability and cultural applications

In the general framework of interaction design principles, cultural applications and services must take into account the specific profiles of the personnel involved.

Starting from the basic requirement for "perceived utility" (PU), the design of any application must consider at least two classes of humans (the personnel working for the cultural institution and external users) as well as some machines (these machines were discussed in Chap. 16 Standards and Protocols for Interoperability[61]).

Perceived utility

The personnel at cultural institutions are usually more skilled in art history or artefact preservation than in information technology. Museum budgets are often prohibitive, and so personnel with specific ICT skills are rarely hired. Therefore, the custodians of museums must not be involved in rebooting systems or debugging applications.

Consequently, onsite applications must be designed such that they can be simply switched on and off daily. For this reason, as a temporary approach, DVD players suitable for the home market have been proposed as typical platforms for museum applications. The use of this platform has another advantage: most museum visitors are already familiar with such devices.

DVD players

---

60 There are some keywords related to the concept of usability, such as directness, multithreading, modelessness, responsiveness, observability, explicitness, simplicity, legibility, consistency, familiarity, informativeness, learnability, memorability, predictability, accessibility, adaptability, controllability, effectiveness, efficiency, error prevention, recoverability, flexibility, helpfulness, task conformance, perceivability, metaphoric design image, elegance, granularity, salience, dynamicity, acceptability, comfort, convenience, reliability, attractiveness, preference, satisfaction, marketing.

61 Museum networks, eCommerce (tele-ticketing, reactive museums, etc.).

In Chap. 12 Interaction Design[62], as well as *usability* we also discussed *accessibility to ICT*. However, the issue of cultural content access is somewhat more complex than basic ICT accessibility.

Cultural divide

Starting from the Medicean[63] concept—that culture is the patrimony of humanity and so everyone has the right to access and enjoy it, we must consider the potential "cultural divide" encountered by the disabled and other minorities that are unable, for whatever reason[64], to enjoy culture. Information and communications technology represents a great opportunity to try to bridge this gap.

Providing access to blind people

A number of different projects and pilot implementations have been developed in this area. Some of the most relevant are targeted at the *blind*, and attempt to render the beauty of a painting or the shape of a statue through different stimuli.

One recently tested pilot project[65] is based on the haptic perception of the relief associated with the features of the painting, along with a positioning system that links the position of the fingertip to a specific sound representing the *nuance* of the colour at that position on the original artefact.

Unfortunately, *nuances* are only comprehended by those who have experienced them, at least for a short time; people born blind usually do not appreciate nuances—brown is brown, green is green, and so on.

---

62 Sects. 12.5 Accessibility, 12.6 Usability

63 The cultural patronage of the rich and powerful Medici family in Florence (and later, with Catherine de'Medici, in France) resulted in the *Renaissance.*,

64 Remote location, lack of traditional sources, etc.

65 By Prof. Framcesco Antinucci, CNR Rome.

Case Study: Bridging the Island of the Colourblind

Another project addressing the same issue, *Bridging the Island of the Colourblind*[66], involves creating audio feedback from the output from a microcamera. This system even enables the user to become a *painter*. Bridging the Island of the Colourblind won a 2004 Top Talent Award (TTA) in the section *Content Tools & Interface Design*.

The inventor has also created a new device called the *Eye-Borg* that allows people with visual impairments, and even those that are totally blind, to experience the world in colour. The inventor has built a system that hijacks the user's other senses; it allows colour to be "heard".

In the system, a head-mounted camera reads the colours directly in front of the user. These colour data are then converted in real-time, via a computer, into sound waves. The inventor claims that the Eye-Borg creates a new sensation, a *cyborgian* extension of the human perception system that resides in both the brain and the hard-drive.

The translation of colour into sound was engineered with such high levels of functionality and usability that the product has already been integrated into the daily life of the colour-blind artist in its prototype version.

An increasing number of institutions and organisations are redesigning their own websites and services in order to comply with accessibility issues. As a positive side effect, accessibility improves multiplatform access to content and applications; scalable fonts, textual interfaces and easy navigation facilitate browsing from mobile phones or digital televisions.

Accessibility issues for institutional websites

Case Study: The Forbidden City in Beijing

Visitors do not like to have to wear much more technology than a traditional audio guide or MP3 player. In order to make it easier to use audio guides in the past, some museums have adopted multichannel infrared connections that each provide information on a specific object[67]. More recently, in Beijing automatic audio guides to the Forbidden City were designed to appear as small tablets that hang from the neck. Each tablet shows a plan of the site with red lights placed at the centre of each area

Forbidden City audio guide

---

66 Contact Adam Montandon: (13 Chard Road, Plymouth, PL5 2EG, UK; see http://www.plymouth.ac.uk/pages/view.asp?page=10944 for more information about this project.

67 For example the Mercedes Benz Museum in Stuttgart, Germany.

within the site. The appropriate language is automatically selected when the visitor rents the device. Each time the user enters a new area within the site, the audio guide starts the commentary on this area, including some in-depth information.

However, while there is an ongoing drive to increase usability, especially in the domain of culture, sometimes the results can seem to move in the opposite direction, yielding more services with decreased usability.

Fig. 30.1 Digital audio guide: Forbidden City Beijing (photo by the author)

Fig. 30.2 Digital audio guide: Forbidden City Beijing (photo by the author)

31 Content Repackaging

The idea of automatically reformatting, resizing and paginating text and graphics sounds attractive. Adaptive document layout has long proven to be an interesting field of investigation. However, even though it is recognised to be a key issue, no major breakthroughs have been achieved in this field in the recent past.

A special incentive to find a solution to this issue is provided by the massive use of web publishing to deliver content to different platforms (PCs, PDAs, smart phones, interactive televisions, games platforms, and more). In addition, we face the usual requirement to create a document from a webpage that is suitable for printing on the fly. Key software market players offer "off the shelf" solutions that aim to deliver the same content on different platforms (mainly different hardware platforms).

Multiplatform content delivering

The idea of creating and filing content in a common base format and adding one or more grid-based paging features to guarantee high-quality rendering on different devices in different formats is very alluring. The basic problem is very well known, which is the reason why many websites offer printable versions of their own pages.

Fig. 31.1 Newspaper and magazines

In addition, *cultural content users* tend to access information directly by interacting with precious ancient artefacts or by reading high-quality publications. High-quality layout and design are hallmarks of modern paper-based publications—they provide each book and magazine with its unique branding and visual style. This does not mean that *users* are more attracted to shape than substance; they simply appreciate quality standards.

Therefore, when the level of graphic design encountered is not comparable with paper-based publications (London Times, Newsweek, etc.), some major families of applications present on the Internet are easily recognisable, such as news, search engines, portals, etc.

Why online publications look less agreeable

There are at least two main reasons why online publications tend to look less appealing than paper-based publications from a pagination design point of view:

- *The traditional electronic publication process.* Even when supported by *ad hoc* software products and languages, the online publication process is mainly based on time-consuming manual activity. Consider the amount of time devoted to tuning and refining the pages of digital documents to optimise them for printing on paper, and extrapolate this to the effort required to do the same for online documents and future updates of them.

- *Current trends in viewing device production.* Due to advances in display technology and emerging markets, a number of different devices will be used to view online documents. Each of these devices has its own characteristics: screen size, ratio, resolution and palette of colours. While *PSP*, *iPod* or Archos media viewers/players are relatively popular and may become a relevant platform for the dissemination of quality content, their differing technical specifications provide a significant barrier to the multiplatform production of quality content.

Fig. 31.2 Basic layout styles used by news websites, search engines, portals, etc.

III Exploitation, Applications and Services

One of the most important page layout tools used by designers is an *underlying grid,* which helps them to organise the visual elements on a page into a coherent and pleasing display.

Organising visual elements

Some authors consider that *grid-based* graphical composition originated with visual research work carried out by Piet Mondrian, Le Corbusier and the Bauhaus school in Dessau (Germany) from the 1920s through to the 1940s. Their work was further developed and diffused after World War II.

Their approach, generally known as *rationalism,* spread across the world in the 1950s and 1960s and become the standard for paper-based publication design. A number of software applications devoted to document paging that follow the grid-based approach were developed for the custom paging machines that initially replaced the linotypes and mainframe computers (early paging systems).

Later on, the arrival of the *WYSWYG* approach and the drop in the prices of laser printers to generally affordable levels kickstarted the era of *desktop publishing* (DTP) on *personal computers*[68].

WYSWYG (what you see is what you get)

The first desktop publishing applications were completely different from world processors and editors. Two leading products in the early DTP market were *Aldus PageMaker* and *Xerox Xpress*. More recently, Microsoft brought out *Publisher,* and the previous two products merged into *Adobe's InDesign*.

Current market trends are leading to a rich selection of different viewers, such as Palms, Pocket PCs, handheld organisers, smart phones and media players, all of which are characterised by different input and output devices. The main output device, the display, can be obtained in different sizes and ratios, and with various resolutions and colour palettes. Input can be achieved through a microkeyboard, a virtual keyboard, a touch screen, a joggle, buttons, etc.

Palms, Pocket PCs, handheld organisers, smart phones, media players

The usual format in which the results obtained from a desktop publishing and paging system are "frozen" is *Adobe's Portable Document Format (PDF)*. The PDF format usually allows *glossy* document porting amongst different hardware and software platforms[69]. Unfortunately, due to differences between displays, the inflexibility of the PDF format can lead to a poor online reading experience, and few people currently want to read an entire book on a screen anyway[70].

Online HTML documents usually provide a limited degree of adaptability that is usually detrimental to the application of a *grid-based layout*, although it is possible to obtain a *grid-based layout* in HTML using tables. Unfortunately, HTML tables are not flexible enough to adapt to different viewer displays, and

---

68 PCs and Macs equipped with Aldus Page Maker or Xerox XPress (in the 1980s).

69 PDF readers are available for free on PCs, Macs, Pocket PCs, *Palm*s, smart phones, media players, etc., running different operating systems such as Linux, Symbian, PalmOS, etc.

70 This comment does not apply to multimedia technology and eBooks, which are specially designed to make them "easy to read".

31 Content Repackaging

their use creates functionality issues related to accessibility (e.g. for text-to-speech tools).

An "eXtensible" world
More recently, using the *eXtensible* approach, the use of the *Cascading Style Sheet (CSS)*, *Data Template Document (DTD)* and moreover *XHTML* technologies has enabled grid-based documents based on "content containers" and formatting rules to be published. This is the easiest way to change and adapt the document format; for example to turn webpages into printable documents.

There are additional important advantages to applying this *X approach* to document formatting, relating to accessibility. The use of *CSS* and *XHTML* enables the same content to be optimally *render*ed in slightly different ways in different web browsers, such as those with or without graphics, with special font sizes, colour contrasts, etc.

31.1   The Evolution of Hypertext Markup

The use of *tags*, as mentioned in previously, has a long tradition in information technology, and more specifically in textual document management. From the earliest technologies onwards, the basic methodology for the codification and storage of format features has been based on *visible tags*.

The invention of web languages
In this scenario, is quite evident that web "inventors" found a useful set of foundations on which to build more complex web languages in tags and early markup languages or metalanguages such as *SGML*. Following this philosophy, it took six/seven years to merge "web technology", which originated as an end-user-driven solution[71], with pre-existing computer science concepts, such as *data and code separation*, *inheritance*, the use of *include files*, *data structure declaration*, *separate format declaration*, *information management systems* and *data publishing systems*, and *dynamic libraries*.

First came the need to efficiently manage thousands of pages of content arose, and then later basic information technology concepts were applied to the solutions devised to fulfil this need. Most recently, it has become important to be able to clearly identify and retrieve each specific digital object *floating* in *cyberspace*. As we have seen, one of the proposed methods of achieving this is to assign a *DOI (digital object identifier) to each object*.

---

71 Starting with CERN employees, scientists and increasing numbers of end-users (philosophers, writers, engineers...) were attracted to the Web. During the first three Web Conferences (in 1991–1993) at least, the audience was a real mix of expertise.

III Exploitation, Applications and Services

32 Experiencing Cultural Content

Are museums, content providers and users ready and willing to use new technologies to explore cultural heritage? In the twenty-first century, the Information Society era, does the nineteenth century's *encyclopaedic* approach to museums still apply? Do ICT tools really help content holders and/or end-users?

In the last ten years, an increasing number of projects have taken advantage of computer graphics, hypermedia and telecommunications on a large scale to document, study and/or communicate cultural heritage.

Computer graphics, hypermedia and tele communications

In many countries around the world, projects that use technology to preserve and communicate cultural heritage are receiving increasing levels of financial support, as it is recognised that cultural heritage is a *vital national resource*[72].

Cultural heritage is a vital national resource

Fig. 32.1 *The Tribuna of the Uffizi* (1772–78) by Johannes Josephus Zauffely (1733–1810)

---

72 The key aspect in cultural heritage market evaluation is that revenues are not passed back to the major investors. Most of the revenue is shared between hotels, restaurants, travel agencies, merchandise, books, electronic media, etc. Please refer to recent studies included in the reference section.

Is cultural heritage merely an interesting field in which to apply computer graphics, multimedia and networking, or does it present unique research challenges? Are the basic tools and techniques used in cultural heritage adequately developed, or are they missing opportunities?

Technology is being used for a wide range of cultural heritage applications, including the digitisation and exploitation of museums, art galleries, architecture and other kind of works of art. Network access to museums and galleries seems to offer both easier access to cultural heritage and, potentially, additional revenues that can be directed towards its preservation and display. Many relevant players in both memory institutions and ICT have invested time and resources into creating pilot projects and applications in the field of cultural heritage, ranging from *3-D reconstruction* to *image-based rendering* to *virtual museums*.

Fig. 32.2 Palazzo Clerici, Milano (HMG Lab, 1995)

Fig. 32.3 Virtual restoration (HMG Lab, 1995)

Computer graphics research now includes methods and techniques for digitally reconstructing historical environments. Laser scanning technologies are used to "capture" the original artefacts.

These projects are appealing to people that work in computer graphics because of the sheer volume of results obtained. The results are used in museums and schools as a communication tool.

Restorations generated using computer graphics—so-called *virtual restoration*—have also become commonplace in television programmes about art and history. It is also possible to perform live events in virtual sets that are sometimes based on historical environments, such as Ancient Thebes in Egypt.

Virtual restoration

Are the techniques used to create feature films the same techniques that are needed to communicate cultural heritage?

Is this just another example of the use of computer graphics for *digital storytelling*, or are there other specific issues associated with communicating accurate reconstructions? Which types of representations and interactions are needed in these areas?

Digital storytelling

Should the application use a computer games approach to engage the audience, as in the case of *the Forbidden City*[73], or do we need another model to communicate heritage?

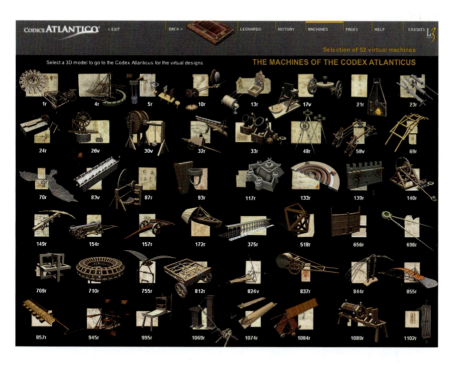

Fig. 32.4
Leonardo da Vinci:
Codex Atlanticus
(copyright Leonardo3, Italy;
http://www.leonardo3.net)

---

73 Early edutainment applications from Cryo: *Versailles*, *Forbidden City*, *Egypt* (published in the mid-1990s).

Less visible projects have investigated how graphics and multimedia technologies can be used by a variety of experts, such as historians, art historians, archaeologists, anthropologists, and architects, to study the past. Data visualisation techniques have been used to organise data collected from archaeological sites in order to yield new insights. Solid modelling software has been used for visual problem solving in order to attempt to understand how ancient structures and mechanisms were built, and how people may have used them.

The experts involved in these endeavours are very different to the engineers and technicians for which graphics tools have been designed in the past.

It is simply a matter of tailoring interfaces for specific applications? Or do we need fundamentally different ways of interacting with data and models? Are new devices or technologies needed?

We are now in a position to consider whether such approaches and ideas are effective; whether they really do increase and spread knowledge of the arts, sciences and history, and whether they satisfy users' requirements. Do ICT applications and virtual museums really provide added value to end-users? Are museums, content providers and users ready and willing to make use of new technologies for cultural heritage? What roles do wireless communication and mobile services have to play in cultural heritage?

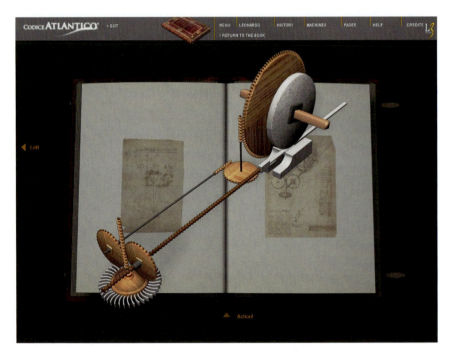

Fig. 32.5
Leonardo da Vinci:
Codex Atlanticus
(copyright Leonardo3, Italy;
http://www.leonardo3.net)

Other questions, which have already been outlined in DigiCULT reports, are:
- How do new technologies affect the core business and how can they be best integrated into the current workflow?
- Which new technologies can be expected and how can cultural heritage institutions avoid jumping on the wrong technological bandwagon?
- What kind of institutional changes are needed to adopt and adapt new technologies?
- How can small institutions manage to participate in the emerging Information Society?
- What is the potential to commercially exploit cultural heritage resources, and what are the future markets?
- What is needed to make cultural heritage services sustainable?

While we cannot answer this long list of questions with exhaustive replies, some *basic principles* could help us to frame the problem. In order to evaluate the potential benefits, we must refer to the added value applications and services that are enabled by new technologies. One of the main ways of evaluating the effectiveness of a (real or virtual) visit to a museum or general exhibit is to ask for feedback about it. Do users exiting the museum believe that they know or understand more about the exhibits than they did before the visit? How do they *score* the experience?

And what about feelings and emotions? Artefacts are mainly "communication objects", and so they must communicate with the visitors. ICT has to ease this process by breaking the barriers that sometimes disable the communication process.

Artefacts are "communication objects"

The communication process associated with cultural heritage involves a reasonable degree of complexity. We can present a work of art and propose an interpretation of it, or try to offer visitors all of the elements required to evaluate the work of art autonomously. Some of the main intrinsic difficulties with the cultural heritage communication process arise from the fact that the work of art usually pertains to a different historical and cultural context from its current situation; indeed, its original location may not be accessible anymore.

Predefined or self-interpreted?

Fig. 32.6 Bronze fragments from the third century B.C. (photo by the author)

How many times have we seen descriptions such as "Terracotta Fragment—Second Century", objects removed from their usual context or function, and artefacts on display without a "code" that can help us to understand their function or meaning? ICT should help to solve such problems, since it should provide context, customised information, references, virtual reconstructions and interactive applications.

Rebuilding the original context

One of the main roles of the communications manager must be to rebuild the original context of the work of art in such a way that it is possible to "communicate[74]" it together with all of the elements required to make an objective evaluation. Information science, specifically hypermedia and computer graphics, should offer a fertile field for developing such applications. When rebuilding the typical context of the work of art, another important aspect that is specifically linked to computer graphics and 3-D models is *space contextualisation*, which means the ability to place the digital 3-D object in the right location while preserving the full set of spatial relations between the model and all of the other objects in the scene.[75]

Space contextualisation

Of course, the implementation of these services will necessitate a different workflow, additional competencies and skills, and more exhibition space in order to host hi-tech installations.

Fig. 32.7 Terracotta fragments from the fourth Century B.C. (photo by the author)

---

74 Artefacts usually come from a different historical period to our own, and so we must re-enable communication between the artefact and the public.

75 As examples simply consider the following: Michelangelo's Mosè was originally created as a part of Julius II tomb in St. Peter cathedral butinstead was placed in the church of San Pietro in Vincoli as a single sculpture after the Pope's death.Michelangelo's Pietà Bandini was supposed to be placed on a tall basement, because this statue was sculptured in order to compensate the specific perspective effect.

In addition, one of the possible catalysts for the application of technology to cultural heritage is education. Technology-based cultural heritage services should be used at home, at school and on-site. Indeed, there are many digital cultural data repositories, usually websites, that could potentially be linked to form an educational service[76].

Educational service

One of the key approaches is to employ a set of methods and tools that can be used to select a limited amount of artefacts that comprise a "learning path".

Fig. 32.8 "3D Models" section of the CD-ROM *The Metopes of Selinunte* (V. Valzano, A. Bandiera, J.-A. Beraldin, (2006) Coordinamento SIBA University of Lecce, Italy, ISBN 8883050398)

Fig. 32.9 Leonardo da Vinci: *The Codex of Flight* (copyright Leonardo3, Italy; http://www.leonardo3.net)

---

76 See, for example, http://www.louvre.edu.

32 *Experiencing Cultural Content* 331

32.1 Impact of the Interface on the Enjoyment of Cultural Content

Cognitive "trails"

There is no doubt that ICT can aid the enjoyment of cultural content to some extent. Museums, for example, can offer explorative and cognitive *trails* that are created on the fly based on user profiles and the advice of communication experts and cognitive scientists.

The artistic and historical objects to be exhibited (ranging from architecture to sculptures, and from paintings to archaeological finds) could be exhibited using the most suitable technology in each case. In the case of architecture, in addition to the usual "movie maps [77]", 3D *modelling* techniques such as virtual reality, animation and digital movies are utilised, sometimes together with a 3-D plot (computer-generated *maquettes*), whilst volume rendering is much more appreciated in sculpture.

For paintings, aside from using high-quality digital images, methods of creating strong effects such as morphing, X-ray imaging, infrared imaging, chromatic variation and variations in perspective are used because they offer new and interesting ways of exploring the work of art. The *exploration* of a classic scene through 3-D or 2.5-D representations may help us to understand or *perceive* a painting. [78]

3-D or 2.5-D exploration

None of these features are gadgets but digital tools that aid our understanding, knowledge and studies of works of art, offering the visitor the opportunity to perform an immediate analysis.

Artefacts versus digital clones

There is no competition between artefacts and their *digital clones*, just as there is no competition between artefacts and art books, or books and CD-ROMs.

The application of ICT solutions to cultural heritage does not imply in any way diminish what can be gained from directly experiencing the work of art, and it does not involve reducing the artistic universe to a funfair with trivial content and approaches. Instead, the aim is to create an efficient hypermedia catalogue that does not just recreate an electronic version of traditional paper filing, based on the same methods, but instead provides an irreplaceable and unique working tool for the curator, the researcher and the common user [79].

---

77 *QuickTime VR*, Real *Vista*, *OmniView*, etc.

78 Some excellent examples are: The Tretyakov Gallery CD-ROM designed by the Russian National Multimedia Center of the Ministry of Education of Russia, or the Enciclopedia del Futurismo created by the International Multimedia Titles, Milan Italy.

79 Usually the tools and the methods used to access data are predefined by experts. It would be very interesting to offer a set of digital tools enabling personal analysis: the creation of links with attributes, comparison and analysis of parts of scenes in paintings, automatic validated translation from Ancient Greek and Latin or other languages, etc.

III Exploitation, Applications and Services

However the best way to start a revolution in this field is undoubtedly to use networks. These allow us to link *cultural heritage* to a wider range of topics and thus reach people that would not normally take much of an interest in cultural heritage, thanks to the relative ease with which websites can be created, together with the high degree of standardisation of formats and protocols.

The future of communications is undoubtedly *online*. Customised *cultural* search engines will make it possible to search through rich sources of knowledge such as museum databanks[80], not just through traditional searching on general-purpose engines and through lists of keywords, but also by data mining *weak* information[81], images, 3-D models, subtopics, etc. This approach will offer to researchers the ability to develop studies based on a wide range of online resources; for example, all of the paintings representing a specific subject, or all of the locations of Michelangelo's statues around the world. It will be possible to browse information on any work of art, wherever it is stored, and compare it with any similar artefacts.

"Cultural" search engines

Fig. 32.10 Ricci Oddi Art Gallery. This early online art gallery includes the Invisi(ta)ble Gallery showcasing the content of the art gallery warehouse. (HMG Lab, 1994)

---

80 At this point it may be necessary to underline the difference between online and offline information management and data publication systems. Information management systems include DBMSs (database management systems), while data publication systems include the Web, CD-ROMs, electronic hosts and other interactive and nonadvertising formats. In the early phase of the Web the difference between these types of system was not clear; webmasters tended to place a lot of content online without providing any tools to manage it.

81 In other words poorly structured "raw" information.

Lost in cyberspace

However, we are yet to reach this goal. Currently, and probably in the near future too, the richness of online data and references is also causing a number of problems. One of these is the syndrome commonly termed "lost in cyberspace", which has resulted from the uncontrolled proliferation of links, references, and unstructured websites. This problem highlights the benefits and the importance of using *information frameworks*, clear references, and customised search engines connecting objects, people, events, times, and places.

Validity and reliability of information

Other important aspects to consider are the *validity* and the *reliability* of the information uploaded as well as the compliance of the published data to patrimonial and moral rights[82].

32.2   A Quick Overview

From one point of view, choosing the right *navigation tool* can be highly beneficial to a data processing solution, since a highly appealing or user-friendly navigation tool can greatly increase the popularity of a particular solution. However, the rapid obsolescence of interface solutions and the evolution in the abilities and tastes of users themselves also dictates that they should be interchangeable. Many different types of user *interface* have been used to represent cultural content over the years, starting from the standard textual structure with references and logic connections, and including much more recent highly graphical interfaces that are realised using *QTVR-like* or *VRML-like* environments. The classification of navigation interfaces and metaphors used for cultural heritage is rich and full of interesting entries, beginning with the first tests carried out in the field of virtual reality with the *Padiglione d'Arte Contemporanea (Contemporary Art Gallery, HMG Lab. 1993)* and the *Basilica Superiore di Assisi (Infobyte 1993), and then moving* onto the Internet and online applications such as *the unofficial Le Louvre*[83] and the *Galleria d'Arte Moderna Ricci-Oddi (Ricci-Oddi Modern Art Gallery, HMG Lab. 1994)*, the *Palazzo Grassi (Grassi Palace Venice)*, and finally mentioning relatively innovative navigation interfaces, such as *Smithsonian Without Walls—Revealing Things (Smithsonian 1997)*, *History Wired (Smithsonian 1999)* as well as the *Uffizi 3D Tour (Uffizzi Lab. & Centrica)*, *Hermitage*[84], *Eternal Egypt*[85] and *Musei Vaticani (Musei Vaticani, All Media, 2003–2007)*.

In such a context, it is evident that while search engines and associated keyword masks are very useful and absolutely necessary, they are a less desirable method of locating data than simply navigating through the data structure by

---

82   Please refer to Chap. 28 on IPR for more information on this topic.

83   Developed by a French student.

84   See http://www.hermitage.ru; from IBM.

85   See http://www.eternalegypt.org; from the Egyptian Ministry of Culture in cooperation with IBM.

III Exploitation, Applications and Services

browsing through its contents. Such an approach may represent the key to the success of a museum site too.

However, the free and direct access to information enabled by the World Wide Web has certainly (and almost *unintentionally*) greatly contributed to its success, since it has removed the barrier represented by the database query mask. Based on these considerations, a large number of online museum sites have adopted a "double access" approach to data searches: they allow users to search either by query or by browsing.

Fig. 32.11
Tate Gallery website

Fig. 32.12
Tate Gallery website registration form

32 *Experiencing Cultural Content* 335

Years ago, in 1994, during the *Virtual Museums Network* project, the concept of *user profiling* was developed in the field of culture. This involved defining several user profiles, ranging between *researcher* and just *curious*. Later on, during the *EC MOSAIC project* (in 1995) and some online training courses, some features devoted to *user tracking* and *adaptive multimedia were added*.

Tailor-made content and interface

At that time, the main developmental path envisaged was to take advantage of structured content in order to enhance the application of user profiles that tailor both the content and the interface to the needs of the user. Most of this task would be carried out in the background, using *intelligent agents* and *user tracking* methods.

The final aim was to tailor the cultural information system output to the user's requirements, by providing the right content within the right format and interface. Based on the specific user profile, the *weights* of some of the interface components are changed in order to enhance the visibility of frequently browsed sections, and some shortcuts (hyperlinks) facilitating navigation through the Web can be established.

Case Study: Aram Khachaturian: The Life and Works

The CD-ROM devoted to the world-famous Armenian musician Aram Khachaturian is a significant example of the balanced use of multimedia content. As stated in the official presentation of the product:

"It is always hard to add virtual dimension to music, but this project succeeds in creating that, by interactively presenting not only his music, but also sources of inspiration of this great composer, the facts of his life and surrounding musical environment, that inspired and made possible such a synthesis."

Aram Khachaturian: The Life and Works [86] succeeds in immersing the user in a captivating journey into the world of the composer. The product is dedicated to the 100th anniversary of Aram Khachaturian (1903–1978), who was the first composer to significantly combine symphony music with the musical tradition of the East.

The composer's life and works are presented through his letters, photos, a biography, an archive, his contemporaries' memories, video material, in-depth commentary, personal recollections and, most importantly, his music.

This project reveals how Khachaturian absorbed the Eastern and Western cultures that were present in his native city of Tiflis. It was this

---

[86] Producer: ITE CJSC, Garegin Chugaszyan, Republic of Armenia; see http://econtent.am/?p=77&ln=en&module=001.

extraordinary cultural heritage that inspired him to create his unique blend of symphony music.

A time line is one of the entry points to the digital content; all the major events and milestones of Khachaturian's life are aligned along the time axis of a sheet of music. This tool helps us to clearly understand the various musical influences that provided the sources of inspiration of Aram Khachaturian. The choice of music accompanying each section gives us a clear understanding of the exceptional mix of Oriental melodic traditions with Occidental symphony techniques that make the work of Khachaturian so unique.

Case Study: Vatican Museums Website

Here we encounter one of the most unique and rich collections of cultural heritage in the world. The Vatican Museums[87] host an incredible number of collections and unique artefacts, range from Etruscan relicts to geographic maps to the Sistine Chapel. These artefacts have come from all over the world and are on display for visitors from around the globe. Some of the key points about this project are: the huge amount of information to be managed and linked; the relevance of the content; the multicultural approach needed; the need to carefully consider the management and evolution of the application, at least from a mid-term perspective.

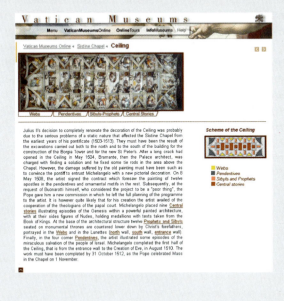

Fig. 32.13 Vatican museums official web site—Sistine Chapel, Doom day

---

87 Vatican Museums website: http://www.vatican.va/.

Fig. 32.14 Vatican museums—Sistine Chapel

In recent years, the Vatican's visitors have been demanding an increasingly exhaustive knowledge of the collections and better assistance when viewing the collections. This requirement has become an incentive to integrate traditional communication channels with the use of the Internet. The exceptional characteristics of the Internet have helped erase barriers related to time and space, making it an extraordinarily effective way of spreading knowledge and culture. Furthermore, thanks to the Internet, the invaluable artistic heritage that has been preserved and protected in these museums for five centuries, defined by UNESCO as "humanity's artistic legacy", will be made available to all of the Web users around the world.

The development of the Vatican Musuems website was assigned to a company called All Media[88] by the Direzione dei Musei Vaticani, and it took over three years to complete. The website can be explored in five languages: Italian, English, German, Spanish and French.

Due to the incredible richness of the content available, the initial phase of the project mainly involved highlighting some of the most popular collections, such as the Sistine Chapel, Raphael's Rooms and the Pinacoteca, as well as recent renewed and enriched sections, such as those of the Gregorian Egyptian and Etruscan Museums and the Ethnological Missionary Museum.

During the five-hundred-year anniversary of the establishment of the Vatican Museums (in 2006), the official website was enriched with another 4000 HTML pages (corresponding to more than 3400 conventional pages of text) written in Italian, English, German, Spanish and French, containing 215 explanatory items, 165 high-definition images and 95 medium-resolution ones. The development of the Vatican Museums website required the coordination of a group of Vatican Museum experts, who were responsible for the scientific and artistic aspects of the website, with the employees of All Media, who provided the technological and communications expertise.

The complexity of the iconographic contents of the pictorial cycles of both the Sistine Chapel and Raphael's Rooms required that a great deal of effort was expended to provide exhaustive as well as didactically accurate artistic and historical descriptions together with high-quality images and details. Some high-quality two- and three-dimensional representations of the rooms allow the viewer to rapidly scan through the pages via a considerable number of links. An additional aspect that we should emphasise here is the ability to cross-reference the biblical texts that provide the inspiration for the episodes depicted in the frescoes.

---

88 All Media website: http://www.allmedia.it.

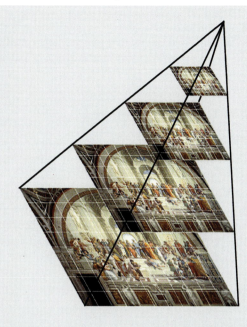

Fig. 32.15 Vatican museums—Sistine Chapel

The Pinacoteca is approached through an introductory overview with a list of the most important paintings present in each of the 18 rooms, accompanied by a detailed analysis of the most significant works of art and related images, which can be enlarged in order to visualise the tiny details. Other museum sectors can be explored in a similar way to the Pinacoteca, with the main works exhibited in each room listed so that they can be looked at and analysed in greater depth.

Due to the technical specifications employed[89], the Vatican Museums website can easily be explored on mobile platforms, both palm-sized computers and smart phones. Several applications have been developed in order to enable users to take multimedia guided tours on palm-sized computers with the Pocket PC operating system connected to WiFi access points, or GSM/GPRS/UMTS smart phones. This approach will enable access to the most important works and useful information about the Vatican Museums; soon this information will also be accessible in many areas served by public "hot spots" controlled by different operators.

The Vatican Museums website is scientifically and didactically accurate, so in terms of content quality it is comparable to those designed for other great museums. The online service is also intended to provide

---

89 In other words the size of each webpage and the possibility of viewing the pages with any mobile device.

certified, validated and upgraded content to curators, who represent the foremost experts in their field, given that many other websites refer to the Vatican Museums' works or collections in inaccurate or incomprehensible ways.

Case Study: Virtual Viking Village

One of the first forays into virtual reality in the field of archaeology was developed by Ola Odegard with the support of Telnor, the Norwegian telecom operator, in 1993.

Virtual Viking Village 1.0 can be experienced using HMDs on the SGI ONYX platform running *Performer*. Thanks to interactive virtual reality, the user can explore a Viking village just as it (probably) appeared in ancient times. The complexity of the geometrical model and the quality of texturing was limited by the technological approach of that time.

Case Study: Cluny Abbey

As computer graphics and solid modelling became more popular, a number of digital reconstructions of historical buildings and monuments were created. One of the first high-quality digital reconstructions was the movie in which *Cluny Abbey* (most of which no longer exists) was recreated. IBM France provided the authors of the digital model with the equipment used to model the architectural details[90].

Cluny Abbey was one of the greatest and most important churches in Christendom during the eleventh and twelfth centuries. In 1793 Cluny Abbey was demolished by French revolutionaries rebelling against the clergy; all that remains of it today is the south portion of the main transept and the octagonal bell tower.

The project was originated by a thesis written by two engineering school graduates from the province of Cluny, who had built a database of all of the architectural information on the original abbey compiled between 1928 and 1984 by Conant.

Starting from the available resources, a team of technicians rebuilt Cluny Abbey by offering a live digital experience to the public. The

---

90 This televirtuality application was created by a real mix of expertise, including IBM France's database muscle, Medialab's televirtuosity, France Telecom's ISDN bandwidth, and the collected notes of the late Harvard architecture professor John Kenneth Conant. The chief coordinator was the leading French VR guru Philippe Queau, a researcher at the Institut National de l'Audiovisuel.

digital movie was created in order to promote the historical monument and generate revenue for an association. The movie included a dynamic walkthrough and a detailed exploration of the original shape of the church, including animated actors like pigeons and even a nun walking over to her own burial stone at the end of the movie. The same approach was later adopted to finance the reconstruction of another relevant monument: the *Dresden Frauenkirche*.

In addition, during IMAGINA 1993 (held in Monaco), Father Di Falco exchanged his vestments for a head-mounted display, while six hundred miles away in Paris, at the other end of a pair of ISDN lines, Dominique Vingtain, a curator from the Musee d'Ochier in Cluny (in eastern France), tested the torque on her joystick. Minutes later, both Dominique and the priest were time-travelling together online; they gradually floated 860 years back down the timeline and then toured through a virtual model of the famous Cluny Abbey.

Case Study: From Ruins to Reality—The Dresden Frauenkirche

A similar project was realised in 1993 by the Frauenkirche Foundation with the support of IBM Germany (Collins 1993). The basic idea was to support fundraising for the reconstruction of a church destroyed in World War II by providing a digital reconstruction of the original shape of the church and a digital movie describing the history of the Frauenkirche in different sections: its status after World War II, its reconstruction and its future shape.

The movie was an important promotion tool for the fundraising campaign.

32.3 Advanced Interaction Models for Cultural Content

This section will sketch the state of the art in the field of advanced user interfaces that ensure the interoperability of heterogeneous distributed datasets and their querying interfaces, describing recent solutions and implementations and outlining future trends and approaches.

The arrival of the *networking era* after more than thirty years of standalone data management has highlighted the need for information interchange and interoperability between systems. This issue is most relevant in the data management sector; interoperability amongst huge databanks may unleash unpredicted benefits.

Consider, for instance, cultural heritage databanks. Such datasets hold various information types, ranging from alphanumeric data to images or computer-generated movies. Experts in cultural heritage started to define data structure and formats many years ago in order to promote standards enabling information storage and exchange.

The chance to use a *common access interface* to the whole set of cultural heritage data will enable us to easily retrieve very useful results, and it should become important components of virtual exhibitions and online cultural services that specifically reference to the European culture.

Let us consider some of the most relevant shifts in the domain of advanced interaction models:
- From alphanumeric to visual/graphic (multimedia)
- From unrelated data to related and complex data (hypertext/media)
- From standalone DBMSs to distributed heterogeneous DBMSs
- From querying to dynamic "browsing".

The tip of the iceberg Navigation tools, interfaces and metaphors should be considered to be just the tip of the iceberg of the information system. However, users judge the application or service that they are using starting from the interface. The weight attributed to the interface is increasing every day. The shift from textual interfaces to visual interfaces and from alphanumeric content to multimedia content has enhanced the relevance of the interface.

The use of hypertext and, later on, hypermedia has unleashed the possibility of relating and linking information while allowing all of the information to be transferred in a structured and related format, skipping the usual linear deconstruction phase.

Fig. 32.16 Indigo Media, Mexico (http://www.reporteindigo.com/)

The structured information transfer offered by information technology is a powerful opportunity; the usual transfer protocol applied is *serial*, like writing and speaking.

Structured information transfer

The resulting web of links might *represent knowledge that connects concepts* and relevant items together into predefined "trails".

In addition, while standalone data processing characterised the past, the explosion in Internet-based working has forced the issue of data exchange amongst heterogeneous databases to be addressed. To some extent, at least conceptually, this has unleashed incredible potential in the *info domain*.

Info domain: from standalone to networked data

Skipping over the complexity involved with managing these functionalities at the DBMS level, let now focus on interface issues.

Bill Hewlett used to say that one graph is much more meaningful than a thousand numbers, immediately illustrating the power of graphics.

	2004/2003	2005/2004	2006/2005	2007/2006
Austria	2.3	4.6	6.0	5.9
Belgium/Luxembourg	3.1	3.8	4.0	6.1
Denmark	3.6	4.6	4.2	3.6
Finland	3.4	4.2	4.0	4.1
France	2.9	5.3	3.4	3.9
Germany	1.8	2.8	2.6	3.0
Greece	2.9	4.7	5.3	6.2
Iceland	5.4	5.7	8.1	5.4
Italy	1.2	2.3	1.7	2.5
Netherlands	1.6	4.7	5.5	6.5
Portugal	2.3	5.0	2.7	4.5
Spain	3.6	7.0	5.6	5.9
Sweden	1.3	4.7	2.8	3.3
United Kingdom	4.0	5.5	4.1	4.2
Czech Republic	14.3	9.9	10.1	9.6
Estonia	24.2	11.3	6.0	8.2
Hungary	16.9	7.0	6.9	7.5

Table 32.1 IT market growth by country in Europe (source: EITO)

Table 32.1 (continued) IT market growth by country in Europe (source: EITO)

	2004/2003	2005/2004	2006/2005	2007/2006
Latvia	18.2	15.1	9.8	9.5
Lithuania	23.3	17.0	11.8	9.4
Poland	21.0	21.6	12.1	9.1
Slovakia	20.7	9.4	11.7	10.4
Slovenia	14.7	6.6	6.1	4.0
EU	3.1	4.7	3.8	4.2
Norway	4.8	5.2	4.2	3.3
Switzerland	1.1	3.5	3.7	4.7
All	2.6	4.4	3.6	4.0

Hypertext plus multimedia multiplies the results

In addition, the use of hypermedia extensions gives us the opportunity to use the most appropriate medium for each specific information transfer, according to the rule that the use of "hypertext plus multimedia multiplies the results", enhancing the communication.

VR: ultimate interface

Even the use of *virtual reality*, which could be considered to be the *ultimate medium* for multimedia, provides many benefits in the field of education and training because it simplifies the information transferring process, especially when it is necessary to deal with structured complex data. In such cases the information can be transferred "as is": with all concepts and relations included.

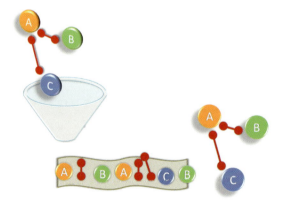

Fig. 32.17 Serial communication process: knowledge transfer

III Exploitation, Applications and Services

The classic way to access information within databases is to create a query using single or multiple keywords and type this into a form. This approach requires a good knowledge of both suitable keywords and the properties of the query language. Querying can be a frustrating task, because we may know that interesting data are inside the database, but we may not know the correct query to use to retrieve that data. Of course, in this case we could bypass this problem by using an appropriate interface to the database.

Querying databases or browsing data?

Fig. 32.18 Tate Gallery website: search by colour

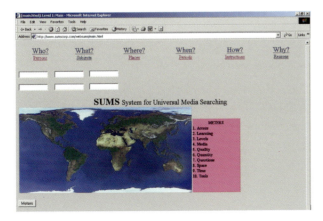

Fig. 32.19 The original SUMS interface based on: Who, What, Where, When, How, Why (developed by Kim H. Veltman)

32 Experiencing Cultural Content

The "direct query" approach is suitable for experienced *infosys* users but is too complicated for general users interested in accessing cultural content.

Following relevant discussions on data structures, interoperability and data management (OODBMS, XML, CIMI, Dublin Core, CIDOC and others), websites devoted to cultural content now tend to offer a query form based on a list of selected entries, such as *Artist Name*, *Work Title*, etc.

The invisible universe of data

However, interactions achieved through the use of a set of interrelated *keywords* do not offer a comprehensive view of the network in terms of relations and references. It often happens that we jump from no results to hundreds of links—an *invisible* universe of data is again beyond our reach.

A common solution to this problem is to give the user hints and *cues* about this *invisible world of data*. This means dynamically updating the list of available keywords with the most relevant choices, or in a graphic environment the links and data distribution around the focus of the query can be displayed.

When dealing with cultural content it is important to outline some relations or at least make them visible. One of the most important early experiences in this field is named *SUMS*.

The *System for Universal Media Searching (SUMS*[91]*)* was chosen as one of the reference solutions for G7 Pilot Project 5: *Multimedia Access to World Cultural Heritage*.

Fig. 32.20
MOSAIC query form (1995)

---

[91] In 1991 Prof. Kim H. Veltman developed the concept of SUMS at the Perspective Unit of the McLuhan Institute, Toronto, Canada, refer to www.sumscorp.com.

SUMS offers interesting opportunities for advanced conceptual navigation in cyberspace. The Internet has magnificent resources, but it is chaotic because its basic tools are too primitive. There are home pages: but the notion of a page with a few *hotwords* becomes impractical in the case of a museum with thousands of paintings or a library with millions of books.

Present browsers search keywords alphabetically and usually give us an enormous amount of references we don't want. There are bookmarks that help us to remember a site that we have found, but if we do a lot of searching, the resulting pages and pages of bookmarks soon become overwhelming.

SUMS provides a methodology for tackling these problems. It is a systematic tool for finding, retrieving and organising material on the Internet, linking your own local collection of facts with the external electronic universe. The system is based on a primary set of references: *who, what, where, when, how, why*, etc.

A customised browser that used this approach was released during the *MOSAIC*[92] project. The evolution of SUMS and SUMMA projects was the "Digital Reference Room" elaborated by Prof. Kim Veltman in the 1990s.

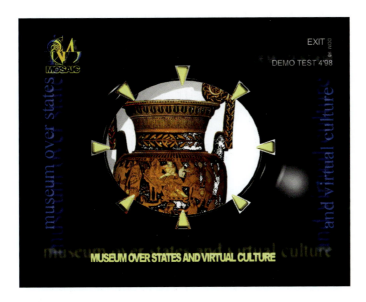

Fig. 32.21
MOSAIC concept, early demo (1995)

---

92 *Museums Over States and Virtual Culture* (an EC Ten Telecom project), 1995.

32 Experiencing Cultural Content ▪ 347

Case Study: Smithsonian Without Walls—Revealing Things

An interesting project that considered how to preserve the richness of relations and offer the opportunity to browse content by following a series of possible connections, and even change the point of view, was carried out by the *Smithsonian Institution* and presented during the *WWW7 Culture Track* in 1997.

Smithsonian Without Walls—Revealing Things

The resulting application was named *Smithsonian Without Walls— Revealing Things*[93]. Users could browse the site using both a graphical representation of the structure of the data and a set of filters and keywords that could be tuned in order to encompass or filter out information.

The application screen was ideally subdivided into three main sections: navigation tools, content preview, content publication. The first section, navigation tools, was structured into three main functional areas. The first area provided an outline of the items, concepts and relations within the data via a 3-D "look and feel" graph; the second area included some *sliders* that filtered themes, eras, objects and data shading. By moving each slider the user was able to increase or decrease the *weight* of the related filter. A search field was also provided. The final navigation tool was a strip of thumbnails representing the top of the list of selected items. Users were able to click on any of the thumbnails to select the corresponding item.

Fig. 32.22 Smithsonian Without Walls: *Revealing Things* (1997)

---

93   The project was presented by Judith Gradwohl of The Smithsonian Institution (http://www.si.edu).

348   *III Exploitation, Applications and Services*

While some "basic" users encountered some difficulties with it, this application allowed enhanced interaction with a dataset. Users could move from one reference entity to another one by following a relation (e.g. from blue jeans to the 1970s before finally reaching a guitar).

Fig. 32.23 Smithsonian Without Walls: *Revealing Things* (1997)

Fig. 32.24 Smart Money website: *The Map of the Market*, a tree map (1998)

Fig. 32.25
Smithsonian Institution:
Historywired (1999)

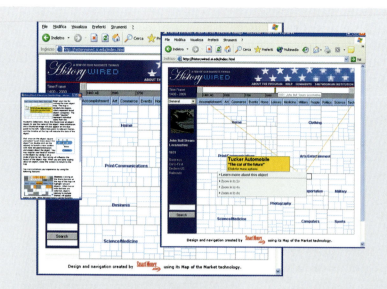

This approach combined the power of DBMS querying with the friendliness of browsing; visitors were able to follow their own lines of thought. Nevertheless, this approach, while a flexible one for a specific collection such as *Revealing Things*, is not easy to extend to multiple collections due to the complexity of the web of links that connect the artefacts.

A second project was also developed by The Smithsonian in order to overcome these limits. While looking for a suitable interface paradigm, they found the SmartMoney.com website and its *Map of the Market*. In this map, a patchwork of coloured rectangles represents the stock exchange market. The map is subdivided into macro areas (energy, food, ICT, etc). Each single tile represents a company and the size of the tile the value of the company. The colours range between green and red and represent stock health. Users can zoom into a specific section of the market, and when a tile is selected some more options are made available.

This interface concept is based on Benjamin Shneiderman's concept of *tree maps*. The application of this approach to multiple museum collections led to the creation by The Smithsonian of *HistoryWired*, which comprises a set of elastic links to a set of keywords pertaining to the selected collection or object.

Case Study: Ename 974

The *Ename 974* project represents a typical example of the added value use of technology in the field of archaeological sites and monument communication, providing contextualised visual and textual information to visitors and students.

In 1997, during the MEDICI meeting on Virtual Museums, Dirk Callebaut, the project leader and senior staff member of the Institute for Archaeological Heritage of the Flemish Community of Belgium (IAP), introduced the concept of the ENAME 974 project:

At Ename, a number of extremely important and varied monuments have been preserved from both the early-medieval occupational phase and the period of the medieval and post-medieval abbey. This rich evidence of continuous occupation has enabled the Ename 974 Project to reconstruct the history of this living community and its environment over a span of more than a millennium. This story involves not only wars and kings and emperors, but also the lives of countless common people who adapted to their environment and altered the surrounding landscape to fit their changing needs.

The mission of the ENAME project is to define the basic objectives and principles of site interpretation in relation to authenticity, intellectual integrity, social responsibility, and respect for cultural significance and context. It recognises that the interpretation of cultural heritage sites can be contentious and should acknowledge conflicting perspectives.

The interpretative program of the Ename 974 Project focuses on four points of archaeological and historical importance, all situated within walking distance from each other: the archaeological site, the Saint Laurentius Church, the Ename Provincial Museum and the "Bos t'Ename". In the present section we will mainly focus on the archaeological site and the Saint Laurentium Church.

The archaeological site of Ename (covering an area of eight hectares) has been developed as an open-air museum. It is often the case that open-air museums and archaeological sites are not, to use an ICT term, very "user friendly".

One of the usual challenges related to archaeological sites is to make complex and poorly preserved archaeological remains comprehensible to the general public.

Archaeological remains are rarely recognisable (as churches, houses, workshops, etc.) to those working outside of the field. Fragments of walls, columns and floors do not provide enough information to allow the casual observer to figure out the original shape and sometimes even the type of building that the fragments refer to.

In the case of Ename, visitors see a labyrinth of partially preserved walls and courtyards. These are the foundations of the Benedictine abbey that dominated life in Ename from 1063 to 1795. The remains of the early-medieval trade settlement (975–1050) are not visible, since they consisted largely of soil layers and traces of decomposed wood that were removed in the process of excavation.[94]

---

94 From the official description of the project.

The Ename 974 project has developed a computer-based presentation technique that allows archaeological sites to be interpreted in a variety of ways, by different audiences, without damaging or performing dubious physical reconstructions of the archaeological remains. As the official description of the project explains:

The first prototype of this non-intrusive interpretation system, called *TimeScope*, was installed at the Ename site in September 1997, using the foundations of the abbey church as the basis for virtual reconstruction. The initial concept, called *TimeFrame*, by John Sunderland and André De Clercq (Barco), was technically developed by IBM and further refined by Daniel Pletinckx of the Ename 974 team. The project was commissioned by the government of the Province of East-Flanders. The Institute for Archaeological Heritage of the Flemish Community of Belgium (IAP) was responsible for providing the archaeological data used in the computer reconstructions.

The current TimeFrame on the site was the first of its kind worldwide. In the beginning the visitors were asked to evaluate the system and assess the concept. The reactions were enthusiastic and are best summarized with the words of a visitor: "*I have been to the site many times before, but this is the first time I really understand what is actually shown here.*" [95]

TimeScope shows a semi-solid 3-D plan of the Saint Salvator church precisely superimposed on a real-time video image of the archaeological foundations visible at the site. This composite image is observed by visitors standing in a kiosk at the same vantage point implied by the video image. Together with narration, images and other architectural reconstructions, the TimeScope presentation offers a clear and vivid interpretation of the evolution of the archaeological site over the last thousand years.

As the site is developed further, new additional TimeFrames will be installed all around the excavations to give the visitors a comprehensive idea of the history of the site.

TimeScope 1: The Concept

The *TimeScope 1* system consists of a video camera, a computer system, two monitors, and a touch screen. A specially designed on-site kiosk houses the system and protects visitors from the elements. The video camera is directed toward a particular section of the archaeological remains (for instance the visible foundations of the Saint Salvator church) and it

---

95 From the official description of the project.

transmits real-time video images of those remains to the monitor screens in the kiosk.

Through the use of a series of touch screen icons on the main monitor screen, visitors can view computer reconstructions of the structures that have successively stood on that spot, superimposed precisely on their excavated foundations.

In this way, the TimeScope 1 system helps visitors to understand the labyrinth of the archaeological remains at a site and to visualise how the original structures might have appeared when standing.

By using real-time images of the archaeological remains as a background for the reconstructions and multimedia presentations, the Time-Scope 1 system offers visitors a sense of immediacy and realism in which the actual weather, sky conditions, and angle of sunlight at the time of their visit serve as a background for the virtual reconstructions.

The touch screen also allows visitors to select programmes that deal with various historical subjects and offer other perspectives on the virtual reconstruction. For example, when a structure from a certain period has been "built" over its visible foundations, viewers can explore its interior rooms and furnishings. In this way, a multimedia presentation with photos, plans, drawings and animated virtual images describing the evolution of the site and its buildings is shown on the same screen.

In the *TimeLine*, interactive virtual reality is used to place various excavated objects in their historical context and thereby help the visitor to gain an understanding of the living world of Ename over the last thousand years. A traditional, chronologically arranged display of excavated archaeological artefacts is juxtaposed with a virtual reality application. On one side of the exhibit room, the artefacts are presented in small exhibit cases. On the other, a computer application places each of these objects in its original spatial and chronological context (where was it discovered? What culture or activity did it belong to?). Through these virtual images the object can be placed in the historical milieu in which it was used.

This system offers an effective means of archaeological presentation: it can be continuously updated and expanded as additional discoveries are made. An additional program is currently available at the museum in which the excavations and restoration work at the nearby Saint Laurentius church are shown and regularly updated.

TimeFrame III

A new TimeFrame was set up in the west choir of the Saint Laurentius church that allows individual visitors as well as guided groups to explore the history of the church in an interactive way. Guided by their own interests, the visitor actually puts the story together and is shown an optimal presentation not only of the monument, its history and its significance, but also of the restoration and the excavations.

The TimeFrame technology also takes into consideration the fact that the monument is used as a church. The visitors use audio guides so that the noise of the presentation does not disturb the character of the church as a place for prayer. The TimeFrame also gives a good idea of the church before the restoration. Thus the technology ensures that the architectural evolution of the building up to its present state is not wiped out.

In this way, experience and expertise has been gained in applying virtual reconstruction methods, creating user interfaces for exploring virtual reconstructed worlds in time and space, in the use of the Internet for heritage presentation and in on-site outdoor interpretation systems. Applied technologies include:

- Websites
- Timescopes
- Character-based interpretation
- Audio interpretation
- CDs and DVDs
- 3-D
- Graphical panels.

During the MEDICI meeting, some future developments of the TimeFrame concept were outlined. An interesting "movable window" showing the past and created by combining the technology developed by ART+COM in Berlin (for *Virtual Vehicle*[96]) with the TimeFrame concept was outlined. The user explores the scene via a movable window (plasma screen) that presents selectable *layers* of the past superimposed onto the actual view. Such an application can be used to offer a complete recontextualisation of scattered objects or to integrate different relicts within their original environment.

Case Study: CREATE (Constructivist Mixed Reality for Design, Education, and Cultural Heritage)

This project represents an excellent case study in the field of interactive virtual reality. It enables full interactive navigation in complex scenarios enriched with both autonomous actors and multisource audio feedback.

---

[96] The *Virtual Vehicle* (1997) developed for Daimler Chrysler is an interactive presentation system for viewing and configuring the entire model range of a given vehicle. It was designed for use in showrooms and at trade fairs. See http://www.artcom. de.

The virtual environment enables re-lighting, photorealistic rendering, population and sound so that it can provide a highly realistic experience while supporting interactive use.

In addition, an ad hoc haptic interface enables physical interaction with the model. Thanks to force feedback the user can actually "grab" objects in the scene and replace them. A typical use for this is in anastylosis[97], where archaeological ruins are reconstructed from the original material. Of course, this feature can also be used for didactical purposes, enabling a kind of assembly box for classical temples to be created.

CREATE[98] (Constructivist Mixed Reality for Design, Education, and Cultural Heritage) aims to develop a mixed-reality framework enabling highly interactive real-time construction and manipulation of realistic virtual worlds based on real sources. This framework has been tested and applied to two prototypes: a cultural heritage/education application with a haptic interface, for students and the general public, and an architectural/urban planning design review application incorporating an autonomous crowd of people and multiple sources of sound, for use by decision makers and the general public.

To develop these applications, the project follows a "constructivist" approach, combining innovative work in VR, simulation, data capture, visualisation graphics, and interface design to provide highly realistic yet interactive experiences where users actively participate in the construction of environments. Development will be driven by actual user requirements, through careful analysis of each case, and evaluated for its effectiveness.

Case Study: The Foundation for the Hellenic World

The Foundation for the Hellenic World (FHW) is an interesting initiative that illustrates the active role of private foundations in the field of culture. The Foundation of the Hellenic World was envisioned, founded and funded by the family of Lazaros Efraimoglou, and is a privately funded not-for-profit cultural institution based in Athens. Its foundation was ratified in 1993 by a unanimous vote of the Hellenic Parliament.

---

97 Anastylosis from the Ancient Greek: αναστηλωσις, -εως; αυα, ana = "again", and στηλόω = "to erect (a stela or building)". Archaeological term referring to a reconstruction technique where a ruined monument is restored.

98 Consortium partners: Centre Scientifique et Technique du Batiment (CSTB; France), Realviz (France), University of Cyprus (Cyprus), Scuola Superiore di Studi Universitari e di Perfezionamento Sant'Anna (Italy), Institut National de Recherche en Informatique et en Automatique (INRIA; France), Foundation of The Hellenic World (Greece).

The official mission of the FHW is the preservation of Hellenic history and tradition, the creation of an awareness of the universal dimension of Hellenism and the promotion of its contribution to cultural evolution. Its aim is to provide an understanding of the past as a point of reference for the formation of the present and future, such that contemporary thought may once again be inspired by the Hellenic spirit. The dissemination of Hellenic history in any way possible is the principal objective through which the aim of the Foundation will be achieved.

The Foundation is located in Athens on the way to Piraeus; the building hosts several different installations and services, ranging from multimedia desks to virtual theatres and a CAVE.

Case Study: Eternal Egypt

Eternal Egypt[99] is a multilingual website (provided in English, French and Arabic) that uses a number of interactive technologies to offer users from around the world the experience of learning about ancient Egypt. High-resolution imagery, animations, virtual environments, remote web cameras and three-dimensional models all combine to provide a rewarding interactive learning experience.

The user can explore the site by taking a guided tour and selecting the highlights of Egyptian civilization in addition to a number of valuable search possibilities.

Eternal Egypt brings to light over five thousand years of Egyptian civilization. It is a living record of a land rich in art and history, people and places, myths and religions. It is not an easy task to provide intuitive and consistent access to this rich content spread over a time span of five thousand years and thousands of square kilometres of territory along the River Nile.

There are many ways to begin your journey through Eternal Egypt. The guided tour is a quick way to experience the best that the site has to offer. You can also begin with one of the cultural highlights, like specific objects or places, or make your own discoveries using one of the many other ways to explore. Choosing the last option, the basic ways to explore Egyptian History are across time or space.

An interactive timeline provides one of the key routes to accessing the web content. The *Timeline of Egyptian History* allows users to place the stories, artefacts, characters, and places of Egyptian culture in their

---

99   Company: CULTNAT Fathi Saleh in partnership with Editions du patrimoine Commission du Vieux Paris, Arab Republic of Egypt; see http://www.eternalegypt.org.

356 ⋮ *III Exploitation, Applications and Services*

chronological contexts. Additional controls, such as zoom or contextualised combo boxes, allow the user to adjust what is displayed on the timeline. Clicking on any entry included in the timeline provides access to additional information.

An interactive map enables spatial contextualisation; interactive labels show the names of different places. A single click on a label opens a combo showing different entries. A large number of interactive panoramic views are included in the tour.

Of course, due to the richness of the multimedia content, a specific entry point that allows the user to directly access the multimedia objects is available. In order to enable direct access to specific topics, an index by type (artefacts, characters and places) is also available.

On the occasion of the Tunis phase of the World Summit on the Information Society, an innovative application devoted to the exploration of ancient papyri was shown for the first time. The application is based on an in-depth interactive multimedia presentation of papyri content presented on a panoramic 180-degree screen.

Fig. 32.26 Eternal_Egypt web page

33 Cultural Tourism

Cultural tourism is a market-share development strategy that focuses on promoting the unique cultural aspects of a city or region in order to draw tourists interested in those particular cultural subjects to the area. This strategy is gaining widespread acceptance by tourism bureaus that are anxious to promote their cities, regions and states as being desirable tourist destinations in an increasingly competitive marketplace.

Action in the field of ICT for tourism is targeted at developing new components and distributed architectures for tourism information and communications systems that support users and businesses, by offering value added services and multimedia information on accommodation, events, culture and leisure, together with booking and payment facilities. Applications mainly focus on the customisation of data-mining techniques, intelligent, multilingual, agent-based technologies and positioning systems.

Fig. 33.1 Smart phone equipped with keyboard and camera (photo by author)

Integration of emerging technologies and processes

The emphasis is on the integration of emerging technologies and processes. Integration will improve interaction processes and customisation of services, as well as ensure the quality of information. In this convergent scenario, all types of tourism services will be accessible through different channels, including of course mobile/handheld platforms.

Tourists visiting museums should be informed about current local tourism initiatives, such as entertainment and educational experiences which combine the arts with natural and social heritage, history and the discovery of monuments and sites. It would be even better if, in addition to timely information provided through regular online updates, they could enjoy location-dependent information and services (e.g. via GPS).

Cultural tourism encompasses an incredible variety of topics and unique artefacts and events:
- Local history, including visible reminders
- Language or dialects spoken by the residents
- Traditions and folklore
- Methods of work and products or technology
- Art or music
- Styles of dress
- Distinctive architecture
- Environmental and natural resources
- Educational systems
- Religion, including visible manifestations
- Leisure activities
- Handicrafts
- Gastronomy or food preparation
- Festivals or celebrations.

Educational tourism, nature-based tourism and ecotourism

Cultural tourism can be considered to be a dynamic tourist activity that is closely linked to physical experiences. Cultural tourism itself can be subclassified into *educational tourism*, *nature-based tourism* and *ecotourism*.

We can also distinguish between "soft tourism", which aims to minimise the negative effects of tourism on the visited culture and area (i.e. by maximising sustainability and ecocompatibility and by encouraging tourists to comply with local customs), and mainstream tourism, which is generally far less concerned about the effects of tourism on the culture involved.

If we consider cultural tourism services from the end-user side, we can distinguish:
- *Information services* (business-related information, transport, hospitality, itineraries, cultural and business tourism, virtual visits, etc.)
- *Booking services* (entrance tickets, guided visits, etc.); purchases (e-commerce, catalogues, tourist packets, merchandising, etc.).

Furthermore, there is the possibility of exploiting information tools in order to direct and enlarge the demand, for example within the framework of large-scale cultural initiatives such as Jubilees, Expos and the Olympics.

Case Study: Lascaux Cave: Conservation or Consumption?

Lascaux Cave[1] represents one of the first examples of the use of the digital virtual reconstruction of artefacts or environments in order to preserve the original ones by reducing or avoiding the "anthropic risk" resulting from mass tourism.

The same approach was later applied to the Tomb of *Nefertari* (Egypt), the *Last Supper* by Leonardo da Vinci in Milano, the *Scrovegni Chapel Frescos* by Giotto in Padua, as well as the lesser known *Byzantine Crypt* in Carpiniano and the *Cave of the Deers* in Porto Badisco, Salento.

Displaying a replica in order to safeguard the original is a traditional conservation approach that has been used extensively in Western countries, although Eastern countries such as China are also familiar with it.

The horses on the *San Marco Cathedral* in Venice, the *Statue of Marcus Aurelius* in Campidoglio in Rome, and even some of the statues from the *Terracotta Army*[2] in Xian are replicas. Displaying high-quality replicas rather than originals resolves one of the basic conflicts encountered in the field of cultural heritage: should we conserve the artefact or allow it to be experienced? Should we grant everybody access to all of our cultural resources, as mankind's patrimony, or restrict access to a carefully selected group of experts?

The increasing number of cultural tourists and visitors has turned this problem into one of the most significant ones found in the field of culture in the twenty-first century.

Sometimes this problem can be partially solved by diverting some of the visitors towards a "minor" cultural attraction. In Xian for instance, another more recently discovered terracotta army from the Han Dynasty draws some of the tourists away from the better-known Qin Terracotta Army.

Lascaux[3] Cave was discovered in 1940. It comprises an incredible set (hundreds) of graffiti from the Palaeolithic period (17,000 years ago) representing animals and hunt scenes—one of the few such examples of Palaeolithic art remaining. The archaeological site was open to the public until 1963, at which point the Ministry of Culture decided to close it to the public because of the results from research into the impact of tourists on the cave. While this decision was made to ensure the preservation of the

---

[1] See http://www.culture.gouv.fr/culture/arcnat/lascaux/en/.

[2] The Terracotta Army was buried with the Emperor of Qin (Qin Shi Huangdi) in 210–209 BC.

[3] Dordogne Department, west-central France.

relics, it did have a negative impact on visitors and citizens' livelihoods, and so in 1980 the regional government decided to launch a project to recreate the original cave artificially and then open this to visitors.

The double of the Lascaux cave was named *Lascaux II* and was created two hundreds metres away from the real one, partially below ground level.

The "fake" Lascaux cave was opened to the public in 1983. It provides an accurate replica of the two main volumes of the cave: the *Great Hall of the Bulls* and the *Painted Gallery* (*Diverticule Axial*). The original cave was surveyed by the French National Geographic Institute (IGN), who acquired contour data every 50 centimetres so that they could build a theoretical 3-D model of the cave. The existence of the double reactivated tourism to the area, providing useful evidence of the power of the replica approach. Some ten years later, thanks to the emergence of virtual reality technology and the efforts of Benjamin Britton[4], a second clone was developed, this time using virtual reality. The virtual Lascaux cave developed by Ben Britton was, at that time, one of the most successful applications of VR to cultural heritage. It showcased the potential use of this technology to overcome similar problems. In addition to simulating a visit to the real cave using the virtual environment, a set of multimedia effects were used to present the relic.

Approximately ten years later, the *Byzantine Crypt*[5] in Carpignano was digitally reconstructed in a similar way, taking advantage of laser scanners and ad hoc software applications. More recently, another virtual cave has been developed by the same research team. It is modelled on the *Cave of the Deers* in Porto Badisco, Salento. The process was again achieved using laser scanners and cloud-of-points post-processors.

---

4   Benjamin Britton, computer artist and Associate Professor of Fine Art at the University of Cincinnati.

5   Coordinamento SIBA, University of Salento, Italy. Contact: Dr. Virginia Valzano.

33.1 Application Trends

Travel and tourism are highlighting how *e-commerce* can radically change the structure of a traditional industry and, in the process, create new business opportunities.

Some time ago, because of the rise in travel facility sharing and the number of travellers in general, an intermediary between travel companies and travellers was established: *the travel agency*.

The travel agency provided a worldwide distribution channel that aided both companies and travellers; it removed the need to go to Cunard or (later on) *TWA* ticket counters, for example. The work done by travel agencies become an *information-based business*, encompassing more and more services, such as hotel booking, excursion and special event reservation. Their products became "confidence goods"—it was impossible to achieve a comprehensive quality assessment a priori.

The travel agency

While choosing the product, only an abstract model of it is available. Most of the work done by both sides (the agency and the traveller) of the transaction is qualified information gathering, involving, in addition to quality and best offer estimation, some special evaluations of risks, strikes, security and even weather conditions.

This business has, however, changed significantly in the last decade due to the creation of some specific online services[6]. On the one hand, *low-cost carriers*[7] have begun to provide on-line offers with electronic ticketing[8] to business travellers, while on the other *on-line travel agencies* are now offering leisure travellers with low-cost special offers and "last minute" bundle services.

The low-cost formula

Smart *e-travellers* are able to create their own tour package simply by surfing the web. Online services mainly provide e-travellers with "best choices" based on a real-time analysis of commercial offers.

e Travellers

The emerging scenario is based on flexible network structures (both wired and wireless) on the one side and an increasing number of potential consumers that are deeply involved in the use of these network structures and services on the other.

If we refer to the actual trend for experience extension through digital services, the tourist market can be represented as shown in Table 33.1.

Experience extension

---

6 For example the lastminute.com (http://www.lastminute.com), Expedia (http://www.expedia.com) and volaregratis.com (http://www.volaregratis.com) websites, and various online travel agencies from Virgin (http://www.virgin.com).

7 Mainly, but not only, air carriers and railroads.

8 Sometimes provided as a mobile phone SMS message.

Table 33.1

Pre-tour	On-site	After tour
Online service platform		
Tour planning Marketing eCommerce	On-site planning On-site infoservices Marketing Monitoring	Tour experience extension After-tour services

The "pre-tour" phase involves information gathering (locations, accommodation[9], travel, highlights, historical background, cultural background, electronic visas, weather conditions and sometimes customised application downloads for portable devices[10]). The marketing of different offers and online reservations and payments conclude the pre-tour phase.

During the tour, tourists may need further assistance in order to plan local excursions and visits or to participate in typical events. In addition, once they choose a visit, additional information services could enhance the experience and improve their understanding of it. A recent development in this field is induced by "proximity" services. Thanks to GPS position tracking the user may be constantly informed about relevant (accordingly with the specific user profile) interest points and events close to his/her actual location. Such e-services may be accessed via Internet cafes, mobile phone networks or other wireless connections if available[11].

---

9 Websites full of tourist feedback on locations, accommodation, restaurants and extra tour excursions are now accessible online.

10 Such as Pocket PCs, Navigators, smart phones.

11 WiFi, WiMax, WiBro, etc.

Case Study: Stelvio Swiss National Park

An interesting example of onsite information services is provided by *Stelvio Swiss National Park*, which offers a wireless information system to its visitors.

Stelvio Swiss National Park

Tourists can hire "off the shelf" wireless GPS palmtops equipped with ad hoc software for few euros per day. This solution offers an easy-to-use navigation system that enables the user to retrieve a great deal of information about different tours and trails through the Park, including three-dimensional maps, actual positions, real paths, Z-contour, and more.

A special section is devoted to visitor-specific information on typical flora and fauna found in the Park. The flora section starts with a set of flower colours, and once the visitor selects a colour the system shows him different shapes of flowers with this colour in the park. The user then chooses the shape and the system provides the full set of information on that specific flower.

Case Study: Archeoguide Project

Another project that takes advantage of positioning systems in order to provide information targeted at tourists has been developed through the European Commission IST Framework. This project is called *Archeoguide*[12]. One of the proposed applications offers a tablet computer equipped with GPS and an e-compass that provides visitors to archaeological sites with location- and orientation-dependent information. Thanks to enhanced reality technology, some specific appliances even offer an "ancient view" of the area that is superimposed onto the real-time view of the site.

Archeoguide

This feature—originally based on the use of head-mounted displays, wearable computers, GPS, an e-compass, and a wireless network—was later extended to other appliances. One of the key aspects of such enhanced reality applications is the real-time alignment of the real and virtual world. In order to avoid the unwanted effect where the virtual world "floats" over the real one, the two images are often merged into one unique digital image containing both the real and the virtual worlds.[13]

---

[12] Contact: Nikos Ioannidis, Intracom Development Programmes Department, PO Box 68, 19.5 Km Markopoulou Avenue, 19002 Peania, Greece. Email: nioa@intranet.gr.

[13] Please refer to Sect. 11.4 Enhanced Reality.

Fig. 33.2a–c ARCHEO-GUIDE: an augmented reality-based system for personalized tours in cultural heritage sites

In order to enhance the accuracy with which the exact position and orientation of the user are pinpointed, Archeoguide also refers to a second positioning system built on top of a structured database of pictures representing the panorama from an extended number of perspectives. Thus starting from the position and the orientation acquired by the electronic devices, the system searches for similar images in the database, and once some common features have been identified it calculates the exact location and orientation of the user.

Case Study: Phone Guide: Museums Guide Through Mobile Phone

Phone Guide

The *Phone Guide: Museums Guide Through Mobile Phone* application developed by the Bauhaus University of Weimar (Germany, 2007) is an interesting example of the use of image recognition on mobile appliances. This approach is based on the idea of assigning a "visual tag" to every object exhibited in the museum, even the smallest one. The visual tag is essentially a photographic image of the object taken with the visitor's mobile phone. The application compares that picture, with those in a stored image bank using a neural network. Once the object has been identified, the systems links to the corresponding information. The kernel of the application, the neural network, runs on a smart phone, and requires around 100 kB of memory. A small Bluetooth ID device is also available if an additional way to identify single objects is required.

Fig. 33.3 Bauhaus-University Weimar (Germany): *PhoneGuide* (a museum guide by mobile phone; photo by the author)

Moving on to the topic of easy-to-use applications that are designed to fit on handheld terminals such as smart phones, PDAs, navigators or even MP3 players, we note at least two interesting fields of application: audio-visual guides based on very popular multimedia development tools such as Macromedia *Flash/Flex* and similar technologies[14], and easily accessible digital audio guides that can be played on MP3 players.

eTourism using smart phones, PDAs or MP3 players

Fig. 33.4 *GiraMilano Palm Guide* (by G. Bettinelli, M. Forni, C. Galimberti)

---

14   W3C SMIL standard.

33 Cultural Tourism

Fig. 33.5 Ultraportable PCs: a SONY VAIO running Microsoft Windows Vista (photo by author)

The concept here is that the information sets are available both online and on-site. If the tourists are interested in preparing for their journey in advance, they simply browse the relevant website and declare their specific interests (monuments, museums, art galleries, exhibits, shows, etc., or simply curiosity). Once downloaded onto the portable system (installation is usually not required[15]), the application will perform as an interactive audio or audio/video guide.

Some early experiments on audio video guides were carried out in the era of Pocket PCs in order to provide an updated, online interactive guide and catalogues for relevant exhibitions through IRDA interfaces[16].

The potential benefit of such an approach is that users can use their own terminal and therefore pay only a small fee in order to access audio/video guides (e.g. via prepaid cards with access codes). Access points (e.g. newspaper kiosks) or telephone service providers may offer a similar service on-site. Audio guides played on MP3 players have been around for some time already and perform adequately.

The challenge of choosing the right platform

The challenge associated with such approaches is always the same: to use the right device at the right time. Ensuring that the solution available to the market at the right time is a key factor. As already demonstrated a number of times, solutions that are developed too far in advance are sentenced to death. Smart phones or navigators could replicate the success story of MP3 players provided that the critical mass of owners is reached.

---

15 Although a media player must be installed, e.g. Flash player, mp3 player, etc.
16 IRDA at that time, and Bluetooth later.

Fig. 33.6a,b ARIANNA by econoetica Firenze (I)

Case Study: Arianna

Consider an example: the application called *Arianna* developed by a company called Econoetica. The project started from the idea of building a tourist guide providing multimedia location-dependent information that is frequently updated via wireless connectivity on top of a smart device that originally consisted of a navigation system and a Pocket PC, and now includes a third-generation smart phone equipped with wireless connectivity.

The system provides a mix of information related to culture, shopping, curiosities, accommodation and restaurants, live events, temporary exhibitions, and more.

The intended architecture of the system includes a main server that manages all of the digital content pertaining to different cities and areas. Portable clients can download updated content almost anywhere and at any time via WiFi connectivity.

The digital content can be subdivided into two main categories: long-term content and news. As a potential start-up solution, hotels may provide the device to their guests along with WiFi connections in their rooms (in order to update, browse, make Skype phone calls, etc.).

The main market model involves local agreements with content providers. Content providers can create their own tourist-targeted services using a set of digital templates and an ad hoc authoring tool.

Turning our attention back to the general scenario, the common pervasive network infrastructure is becoming more and more transparent or invisible to the user. An "infosphere" around the user enables the user to access information services at home, outdoors, in the car, while travelling, etc. Ubiquitous computing is becoming a reality.

The infosphere

In such a scenario, tourist applications may use processes that cross company borders, including the travel agency, carrier, hotel, local tour operator, and thus leading to *business-to-business-to-customer* (B2B2C) applications. Technology must provide some basic contributions in this case; most added value services are built on top of various distributed

B2B2C

Scalability and interoperability

heterogeneous databanks (e.g. transportation, accommodation, weather forecasts, museums, etc.), and they combine, assemble and process the information provided. This leads us to two of the most important features that support distributed data sources, heterogeneous data formats and business functions and ensure structured access to such resources: scalability and interoperability.

As a natural consequence, the integration of different channels and platforms is foreseen. This will allow the creation of added value solutions that are mosaics of well-defined contributions/tiles.

Multilayered systems

On the content/service side, one current trend is to take advantage of online information systems and soft intelligence in order to offer updated and tailored services covering a range of interests. This approach dispenses with monothematic tours for a person or a family in favour of a mix of different cultural opportunities designed to satisfy multiple interests and enrich the experience of each person. In addition, the services offered will be influenced by the calendar and even the weather.

Lack of leading authorities in service provision

Due to the fact that there are usually no clear leading authorities among the set of entities involved in service provision, technology must ensure full autonomy to all of the participants and also promote cooperational behaviour[17].

Fig. 33.7 Smart Phone displaying the dome of the historical Gellert Hotel in Budapest (photo by Francesca Ronchi)

17 In terms of data structure, access, security and last but not least management.

It is also important to remember that technology must allow the proper evaluation, in terms of costs and rights, of the various tasks performed in such services. A proper business model must accompany the proposed service. A lack of a proper business model or difficulties in identifying individual contributions to the product (among other issues) have heavily contributed to the downfalls of many such initiatives.

Don't forget the business model

Case Study: Paris, a Roman City

Paris Ville Romaine[18] (*Paris, a Roman City*) is an incredibly rich and well-designed online resource developed by the French Ministry of Culture and Communication[19] in partnership with Editions du Patrimoine Commission du Vieux Paris.

This resource represents a significant example of the efficient information management and communication of urban and landscape historical content.

Visitors to *Paris, a Roman City* website can explore the main monuments of *Lutetia Parisiorum* from the early Roman Empire, which have now completely disappeared. Users can navigate through numerous relics and locations such as the forum, the theatre, the amphitheatre (*Les Arenes de Lutece*) and the baths (*Les Thermes de Cluny*). The forgotten past is brought back to life and rediscovered. A secret map hidden by centuries of history and a great number of events that changed the shape and appearance of the city are made visible and visitable.

Users can satisfy their curiosity by interacting with objects discovered during archaeological excavations, such as a fibula, a statuette, a vase, and a pocketknife.

As an additional tool, users can make use of overlay maps to move backwards and forwards in time in order to discovering what was and what now is present at a specific location. A similar effect was realised in the middle of the 1990s by CINECA by utilising different 3-D models of buildings present in the city centre of Bologna over the centuries, generated in a VRML reconstruction.

For those who want to make a "real" visit to Roman Paris, an information guide is provided which leads travellers through the streets of modern Paris, pointing out traces of the past along the way.

---

18 See http://www.paris.culture.fr/en.
19 Christophe Dessaux and Martine Tayeb at the French Ministry of Culture and Communication.

Fig. 33.8a,b Paris Ville Romaine Ministry of Culture and Communication—Christophe Dessaux, Martine Tayeb

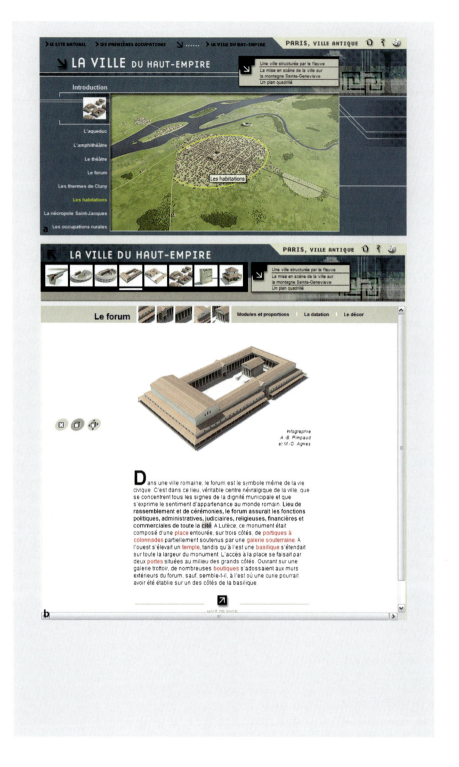

Case Study: Invisible Shape of Things Past and CyberCity Berlin

How can we turn film or video clips into interactive virtual objects characterised by a specific shape, location and orientation in the virtual space of a digital model? This concept was defined and developed by Joachim Sauter and Dirk Lüsebrink – ART+COM[20] research centre in Berlin for the *Invisible Shape of Things Past* project, which was used for the first time in 1995. This technique enables the creation of a virtual visual documentation layer on top of a geographical information system. The visual documentation layer comprises three-dimensional objects that represent camera movements, close-ups, etc. This spatial/temporal concept makes it easy to organise and navigate through film objects (ART+COM used historical documentation for Berlin).

The transformation into virtual objects is performed based on the camera parameters relevant to a particular film sequence on screen: movement, perspective, focal length. The individual frames of the film are lined up along the path of the camera. The angle of the individual frames relative to the virtual camera path depends on the view from the actual camera, whilst the sizes of the individual frames depend on the focal length used. The rows of pixels at the edges of the frame define the outer membrane of the film object.

The project devoted to Berlin covers all of the urban development phases from 1900 onwards in the vicinity of the Museum Island and Potsdamer Platz. Starting from an accurate three-dimensional model of the area representing all of the urban development phases, the movie film documentation available was turned into virtual 3-D film objects and positioned according to their virtual location (determined by when and where they were shot). In this way, users are able to move through the documentation within time and space, interacting with the film objects and different time-layers of the model.

This project is closely related to *CyberCity Berlin*, probably the first immersive multimedia application to enable an interactive walkthrough, in this case of a three-dimensional model of the museum area of Berlin. The application, which runs on a SGI Onyx, offers the opportunity to click on each building or monument and access in-depth multimedia information on it, such as pictures, text and 3-D models.

The final stage involved building an interactive installation and a solid architectural model based on individual film objects.

---

20 ART+COM AG, Kleiststrasse 23–26, 10787 Berlin. See http://www.artcom.de.

Fig. 33.9a–c *Invisible Shape of Things Past* by Joachim Sauter and Dirk Lüsebrink (ART+COM, Berlin, Germany, 1995)

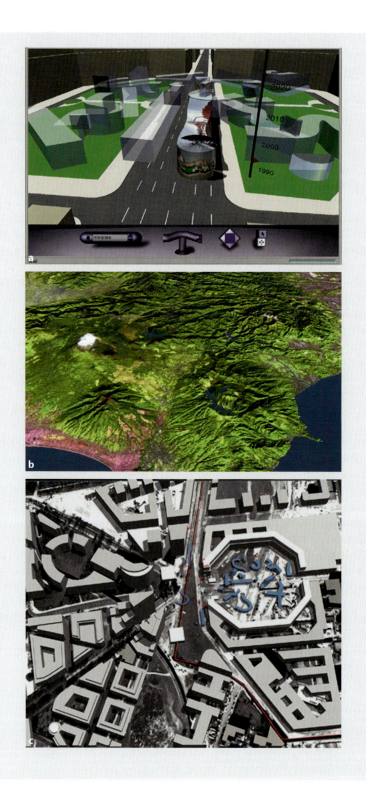

34 Games and Edutainment Applications

Edutainment is potentially a new field of development for software applications. This type of "value added" game will provide an "intelligent competitor" to common "shoot and kill" games, adding some useful content like historical background to the entertainment. This approach should also prove useful in the field of cultural heritage since edutainment applications linked with artworks or archaeological sites can be developed. One of the first examples of such software were presented at Imagina INA '97 in Monaco.

For example, the application, entitled *Versailles 1685: A Game of Intrigue at the Court of Louis XIV*, is mainly based on a digital 3-D reconstruction of the Palace of Versailles as it was in the seventeenth century, fitted with original paintings and furniture. The development of this game presented one major challenge: how to reconcile gameplay requirements with the constraints of historical fact—in other words, how to create an attractive game while still communicating historical data, which is, by its very nature, rigid and unwieldy. These two imperatives must be combined without allowing either one to cancel out the other. This game is an incredibly effective means of reconstructing a Versailles that no longer exists. It enables us to explore the chateau exactly as it was in 1685, to infuse the often staid documentation with new life and to inject the hum and throb of life back into the chateau.

Versailles 1685: A Game of Intrigue at the Court of Louis XIV

New technology enables us to make Versailles better known to the public by leading them away from the beaten track. Even the chateau that hosted the *Roi Soleil* is not very well known, with the exception of the State Apartments and the Hall of Mirrors. Given that the game takes place in 1685, its authors recreated different locations exactly as they were at that time, whereas the chateau and the gardens were actually continually being modified. In such a historical reconstruction the documentation (in the form of engravings, paintings, architectural elevations, memoirs, etc.) is sometimes contradictory or incomplete and requires rigorous collation.

The player must solve a plot to kill the King while taking part in the main ceremonies and events linked to the King's everyday life. A QuickTime VR-like environment allows the user to walk through the palace, looking at frescos and asking for further information about artefacts and architecture. The King's day dictated life at Court, so it naturally directs the way that the game unfolds. As a result, the historical reality of life in the chateau at that time is intimately recreated by the game. Similarly, anecdotes recounted by chroniclers of the time have also been integrated into the story.

Fig. 34.1
Rome: Caesar's Will by Cryo Interactive

Egypte: L'Énigme de la Tombe Royale

Rome: Caesar's Will

This application enables us to rediscover Versailles and provides an astounding comparison between the reality of existing places and the regeneration of those that have disappeared. The regeneration provides detail, allowing us to contemplate the variety of the décor, its beauty and its quality. The user can also discover astonishing things that would otherwise be difficult to imagine at Versailles, such as the spiral staircase.

Such experiments bring the monuments back to life by redecorating rooms and reinstalling paintings that are presently scattered around different museums. Paintings are placed in their original locations and textiles are fully restored in order to recreate the monument as it was at the time.

Later on, the same group of investors, Cryo, Réunion des Musées Nationaux and Canal+ Multimedia, developed two additional products named *Egypte 1156 A.C.: L'Énigme de la Tombe Royale* and *China: Crimes in the Forbidden City*. Due to the interest generated by edutainment applications, additional players then joined the group, such as Montparnasse Multimedia, and an application named *Rome: Caesar's Will* was introduced to the public at MILIA 2000.

Another interesting cultural heritage application addressed at the SOHO (small office/home office) market is *Roma: Duemila Anni Fa* by Fratelli Carraro, Editalia Multimedia and Sacis. This is a full three-dimensional interactive application that recreates ancient Imperial Rome with palaces, houses and monuments in their original colours.

The next step in the evolution of such games are role-playing games and interactive stories that merge visual simulation with the virtual actor's behaviour and everyday life at the time.[21]

Fig. 34.2 *Rome: Caesar's Will* by Cryo Interactive

---

21 In the general contest of edutainment we cannot forget to mention a special artefact, the movie "Russian Ark" by Alexander Sokurov. A full immersion in the Russian history shot in one day at the Hermitage museum St. Petersburg.

376 ■ *III Exploitation, Applications and Services*

Fig. 34.3a–c Gulliver's World—a Multimedia Theatre, by Ars Electronica Futurelab, Linz Austria

Case Study:
Gulliver's World—a Multimedia Theatre

Gulliver's World[22] is a unique and innovative exhibition model for interactive digital environments. It features a total of seven "experience stations" whose intuitive, user-friendly interfaces make it easy for visitors to get into the swing of hands-on experimentation. This simplifies the process of learning to create a complex and individualised mixed-reality environment. Users can give free reign to their imaginations in designing and exploring virtual worlds and their inhabitants. Any journey through Gulliver's World therefore features a challenging but enjoyable series of highly technical procedures that even kids can master.

Gulliver's World thematicises the relationship between virtual and material reality, and the reality that is a blend of these two components.

In conjunction with the 2002 Ars Electronica Festival, *Hidden Worlds1* was installed as the first permanent exhibition based on mixed reality technology. The following year, the Ars Electronica Futurelab collaborated with Prof. Hirokazu Kato (Osaka University, Japan) to expand on this research effort and developed *Gulliver's Box2* for the 2003 Ars Electronica Center Exhibition. This set-up is also a multi-user mixed reality system, and one that has been astounding visitors from wide variety of backgrounds on a daily basis ever since.

From its very inception, Gulliver's Box was conceived as an experimental platform on which new interfaces and approaches to interaction could be tested in a laboratory setting as well as in actual use by the general public. However, in spite of the installation being a prototype,

---

[22] Producers: Ars Electronica Futurelab, Stefan Feldler, Peter Freudling, Thomas Grabner, Roland Haring, Horst Hörtner, Andreas Jalsovec, Hirokazu Kato, Daniel Leithinger, Christopher Lindinger, Christian Naglhofer, Christine Pilsl, Robert Priewasser. See http://futurelab.aec.at.

Gulliver's Box developed into one of the top attractions at the Museum of the Future. Furthermore, the experience derived from this exhibition led to insights that have made a key contribution to the work that the Ars Electronica Futurelab is currently doing. Motivated by this success, staffers took another long look at the concept and expanded it in several directions.

Probably the most important new feature added to Gulliver's World is that users are no longer limited to preset environments and characters; instead, they are called upon to design the artificial world and its components themselves. This was accomplished by the development of intuitive editors with which the environment can be totally revised and customised anew each time. When dealing with the individual interfaces, users are introduced into mixed reality environments at different levels of interaction.

35 Hands-On and Interactive Museums

This chapter explores a different approach to the traditional function of museums, starting from some early experiences that were to some degree directly derived from the historical "scientific cabinets" and other traditional ways of enjoying experiences directly.

Fig. 35.1 *Exploratorium*: The Museum of Science Art and Human Perception in San Francisco (photo by the author)

Fig. 35.2 Joseph Wright of Derby (1768): *Experiment With the Vacuum Pump*

35 Hands-On and Interactive Museums   379

35.1 Science and Technology Museums

An evolution of the historical approach invented by the Deutsches Museum in Munich in the nineteenth century led to the "hands-on" approach that was greatly advocated[23] by Frank Oppenheimer (1969) for the Exploratorium in San Francisco and the many technology and science centres all over the world that were derived from it.

This sector, museums of science and technology, has always been one of the most innovative and active. Even when, as happens in the rest of the cultural sector, no communications experts are involved in the design and development phases of the exhibit, the effort and interest directed into spreading knowledge of and educating visitors in the fields of science and technology are evident.

Science and technology museum "protocol"

Science and technology museums have fine-tuned a well-tested mechanism where visitors' experiences are enriched by actively involving them in phenomena and providing tutors, text and images in order to transfer knowledge actively and thus attract more visitors. Nothing similar, or in any case that satisfies the same goals, has actually been implemented in the other fields of "culture".

Fig. 35.3 Hands-on experience with magnetic fields at the Città della Scienza Naples (photo by the author)

---

23 Relevant experiences in this field include those associated with the Chicago Museum of Science and Industry (1933), Palais de la Découverte (1937), the National Museum of Science and Technology: Leonardo da Vinci (Milan 1939), the Exploratorium (San Francisco 1969), La Villette (Paris 1986), Città della Scienza (Naples 1992).

At a basic level, a structured set of information is provided to the visitor:
- How the direct experience works
- What to do
- What to observe
- Why it happens.

This information is often printed on forms that are sometimes shown as a series of video clips.

By following this protocol, there is a reasonable chance that visitors will derive the maximum benefit from the experience because they will assimilate information more easily by playing an active role than by watching a movie or reading a book.

Fig. 35.4 SONY Wonder Technology Laboratory in New York City (photo by the author)

Fig. 35.5 Liberty Science Centre in Jersey City (photo by the author)

Tutors and infotrainers

If the experience is basically a mass experience then continuous video training is preferable.

Sometimes this approach alone is not enough and we need a *tutor* in order to improve comprehension of the topic. These tutors, who are usually called infotrainers, can approach their task in two different ways: *solicited* or *unsolicited*.

Sometimes a kind of reticence or nervousness about getting directly involved with exhibits keeps visitors away from them. Therefore, the unsolicited approach involves actively approaching visitors, getting them involved in the experience, and trying to keep their interest during it.

The solicited approach involves waiting near the item of interest and providing timely support to visitors already interested in the experience. This is a softer approach; solicited tutors will simply suggest *how to, what to observe* and *why this happens*.

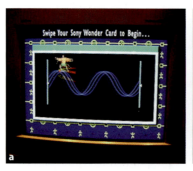 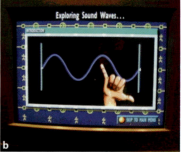

Fig. 35.6a,b Basics of acoustics at the SONY Wonder Technology Laboratory, New York City (photo by the author)

Fig. 35.7 Hands-on experience with magnetic fields at the Exploratorium, San Francisco (photo by the author)

III Exploitation, Applications and Services

35.2 Theme Parks

The introduction of a wide range of methods and technologies used in theme parks, hands-on experiences, 3-D theatres, interactive experiences, digital storytelling, etc. represented a significant innovation in content communication.

The idea of devoting an entire park to a specific topic, exploring all its possible aspects, is itself highly innovative. From its origins in the 1950s[24] up to the present day, theme parks have attracted increasing numbers of visitors and generated many advanced methods and technologies.

It is therefore hardly surprising that some players within the field of culture have started to wonder: "Why not re-use some of the experience gained from creating theme parks in order to better communicate cultural content?"

Of course this is not a simple task; we do not want to turn a high-quality cultural experience into a "Back to the Future"-style ride.

We probably need to divide the theme park methodologies between two main tasks:
- "Communicating" the cultural objects to the visitors
- Immersing visitors in cultural contexts and enabling virtual time travel.

A recent example of the second approach, even though it is limited to a pilot implementation, is the *Time Elevator* experience available in Rome. Time Elevator Roma is a tourist attraction based on an active theatre (Imax-like) with a panoramic screen and surround sound that projects a movie about the evolution of the city of Rome from its earliest origins to recent times.

Time Elevator

Fig. 35.8 PassPort: *Time Elevator Roma* (photo by the author)

---

24 Tivoli Park in Copenhagen, and later Disneyland in Anaheim, Los Angeles, CA.

Fig. 35.9 PassPort: *Time Elevator Roma* (photo by the author)

Special effects (such as dynamic seats, water spray and smoke) are used to underline key narration points. Direct interaction is not required in order to capture and involve the audience; it is enough to use motion picture techniques properly.

It can be trickier to use theme park methods to "communicate" artefacts and cultural content rather than traditional methods because much more room is required. In this context there is no relation between a virtual theatre and a glass exhibition case filled with dozens of artefacts.

Case Study: Scrovegni Chapel, Padua

There are already some experiments in this area, such as the *Scrovegni Chapel* in Padova or, in a different cultural context, the *Museum of the Future* in Linz.

In March 2002, the Scrovegni Chapel in Padova was reopened to the public after a long restoration period. In order to better preserve the chapel and particularly Giotto's frescos in it, a maximum of 25 people were allowed inside at a time for no more than 25 minutes. A group of researchers from CNR ITABC (Roma, Italy)—Maurizio Forte, Claudio Rufa and Eva Pietroni—developed a project entitled *Musealising the Virtual: the Virtual Reality Project of the Scrovegni Chapel of Padua*[25] that enriches the experience of visiting the chapel. The idea is to boost the learning experiences of visitors by establishing to a "virtuous loop" between computer-assisted briefing and the frescos. Each time one of the two forms of the chapel (i.e. the real and the virtual chapels) is approached, detailed, in-depth information about it is made available.

Fig. 35.10a,b Cappella Scrovegni multimedia room (Assessorato ai Musei, Politiche Culturali e Spettacolo Comune di Padova)

Fig. 35.11a,b Cappella Scrovegni after restoration (Assessorato ai Musei, Politiche Culturali e Spettacolo Comune di Padova)

---

25 See http://www.itabc.cnr.it/VHLab.

Case Study: Museum of the Future in Linz

The Museum of the Future in Linz is another significant example of this type of experience. The Museum is actually another name for the Ars Electronica Center. Ars Electronica, the organisation that maintains it, originated more than 20 years ago in Linz (Austria) through a collaboration between governmental bodies, a national television company, a telecommunications company and other partners. The Ars Electronica Festival occurs every September, and offers a unique opportunity to experience the best of eArt. The whole city of Linz is the perfect stage for the festival: narrow old-fashioned streets, historical squares, the Gustav Mahler Auditorium, the former industrial area.

The Festival is the key event all over the world for eArtists and creative people. To be included in the restricted number of selected products is equivalent to winning an Oscar. Artefacts and installations hosted by the Museum of the Future represent the best of digital art around the world. A visit to the Museum is a must for creative people.

Conservation activity

In terms of the "conservation" role of this museum, we all know that the long-term preservation of interactive installations is one of the biggest challenges of the digital era.

For this reason they launched a project entitled *Archiving Media Art*:

The Linz-based Ludwig Boltzmann Institute Media.Art.Research was founded in October 2005. It is managed by a partner consortium comprised of the Ludwig Boltzmann Society, the Linz University of Art, the Ars Electronica Center and the Lentos Museum of Art.

Fig. 35.12 ARS Electronica Linz: Museum of the Future

The institute's mission is the scholarly processing, mediation, archiving and publication of works of media art and media theory, in particular, the extensive holdings of the Ars Electronica Archive and works submitted for prize consideration to the Prix Ars Electronica. The aim is to develop not only long-term archiving methods for media art but also tools to enable scholars to work with these pieces in accordance with the criteria of art history and media theory. The Ars Electronica Center's existing online archive will be enhanced by the inclusion of this material.

Fig. 35.13 ARS Electronica Linz: Museum of the Future (photo by the author)

Fig. 35.14 ARS Electronica Linz: *Life Spacies* interactive installation (photo by the author)

A key task is the conservation of entries to the annual Prix Ars Electronica. Artists from more than 80 countries have submitted approximately 30,000 works to the Prix Ars Electronica since its founding in 1987, which makes it the world's oldest media art competition. It is also the highest endowed.

The submissions are presently being stored in files and cartons. Each respective entry includes an entry form on which the work is described by the person submitting it and, in numerous instances, supplementary material such as photos, slides and folders as well as data storage media containing documentation about the work.

Over the past 20 years, submissions have utilized an extremely wide variety of data storage media, operating systems, programs and file formats, a consequence of, among other factors, the competition's wide-ranging categories: Computer Animation, Digital Music, Interactive Art and Net Vision. Thus, virtually every single entry calls for custom handling in order to make it accessible, to describe it and to conserve it.

Another problem is the life expectancy of the particular data storage medium: 20 years in the case of magnetic tapes; only 5–10 in the case of diskettes, CDs and DVDs. These magnetic tapes have by now been archived for nearly 20 years; some of the CDs have been on hand for over 10 years. The upshot is a paradoxical situation in which the later submissions on CD and DVD, due to their shorter life expectancy, have to be transferred immediately to another medium to avoid loss of the data, whereas it is reasonable to proceed under the assumption that the magnetic tapes can still remain in service for some time.

Fig. 35.15 Museum of the Future: a visitor is suspended from the ceiling in order to navigate in a virtual reality

One of the difficulties of archiving and conservation efforts in the field of media art is preserving the data in such a way that the work can be run or displayed as its creator intended. Indeed, some pieces in the Prix Ars Electronica Archive, above all, installations in the Interactive Art category, can be documented solely on the basis of their description and archived only as such, since it would be much too costly to conserve such an installation in its original configuration.[26]

Case Study: The Science of Aliens

Our conceptions of aliens and what they might actually look like provide the theme of the exhibition *The Science of Aliens* that ran at the London Science Museum from October 15, 2005 to February 26, 2006. The exhibition combined the latest scientific insights with the vivid fantasies of filmmakers.

Fig. 35.16 *Alien World* by ART+COM: interactive installation for the exhibition "The Science of Aliens"

---

26 Description provided by Guenther Kolar, responsible for content management systems, databases and formats at the Ludwig Boltzmann Institut Media.Art.Research (see http://media.lbg.ac.at), at the Asolo Meeting held in September 2006.

For this show, ART+COM created an interactive room where visitors could directly contact aliens. The creatures living on the planets Aurelia and Blue Moon, move dynamically through virtual landscapes. They are generated in real time. Visitors interact with the two worlds via a touch-sensitive surface two metres wide and 7.5 metres long, developed by ART+COM. They can watch the aliens as well as influence the creatures' behaviour and actions.

The Science of Aliens is said to have been the biggest exhibition of its kind. Created as a touring show, the strange creatures are currently visiting different cities around the world.

Case Study: Visite+ at the Cité de Science in Paris

Visite+ is a typical example of post-museum visit support service. Some of these types of service even aim to create an active community.

Not too far from one of the beating hearts of Paris, the Marais, a few stops from Place de la Bastille, the Cité de Science (City of Science) is an important example of a science centre that offers both hands-on experiences and digital content both on-site and online. The Cité consists of different "nodes" and "paths": the main buildings, which host permanent and temporary exhibits, the Geode (a dome theatre), a real submarine, and others.

Fig. 35.17 Visite+ – Cité de Science, Paris

III Exploitation, Applications and Services

In order to offer new services and enhance the post-visit experience, some years ago the Cité implemented an additional service, Visite+. Using the "Visite+ code" associated with their entrance ticket, each visitor can log on to a private section of the museum website and access a set of information related to their own visit (*carnet de visite*).

This personal dataset includes a description of the visit, the scores achieved by the visitor in tests and games, digital documents created during the visit and some in-depth information on the main topics tackled during the visit.

When the visitor becomes a member of Visite+, he or she can create their own portal. Access to the personal portal is actually granted by their email address and a password, not their entrance code. The personal portal hosts all of the logs of the different visits made to the Cité (*cyber carnets*) by the visitor, and all of the pictures taken during the visits are accessible through the portal. Subscribers receive emails containing detailed information about upcoming exhibitions, descriptions of relevant sections of temporary exhibits and a significant bibliography. Examples of topics covered by this service include *Biométrie, le corps identité; Ombre à la portée des enfants. L'homme et les gènes.*

When a temporary exhibit ends its run, the information associated with it pass into the archives of the service. Indeed, the historical archive already contains information on the following previous exhibits: *L'homme transformé; Le cerveau intime; Opération Carbone; Soleil, mythes et réalités; Téléphonie mobile: Tout capter; La population mondiale… et moi?*

Once a direct link to the visitor has been established, a rich set of newsletters (city, college and education newsletters) is also made available.

Fig. 35.18 Han Dynasty tomb: virtual theatre (Xian, China – photo by the author)

Case Study: Jurascopes at the Berlin Museum of Natural History

Jurascopes are "telescopes" augmented by e-media that enable visitors to the Berlin Museum of Natural History to peer back in time to the Jurassic period, when the dinosaurs ruled the Earth. They provide a link between the familiar pictures of dinosaurs seen in the movies and the original dinosaur exhibits in the museum. When the visitor looks through the telescope, a photo of the skeletons in the dinosaur hall initially appears. One of the animals can then be selected, and the animation begins: its skeleton grows muscles and skin, and then the dinosaur is transplanted into its natural habitat and starts moving, feeding, and hunting. The dinosaur display also provides a realistic soundtrack corresponding to its natural habitat for the benefit of visitors.

New media can make long-dead animals come alive again and take visitors on a trip to the origins of our solar system. The dinosaurs in the central hall are made to look much fitter and more dynamic than before, and all of the exhibits deal with one general theme: evolution in action.

Fig. 35.19a–c Berlin Museum of Natural History: *Jurascopes* by ART+COM (Berlin, Germany, 2007)

These new exhibits combine original objects and new media in a presentation full of creative ideas, making the displays highly attractive to visitors of all ages. Nevertheless, the museum remains true to its history by making the actual remains or physical objects the highlights of the exhibitions. The dinosaur skeletons, the animals on display and the meteorites have always been the stars of the show, and will always remain so.

The Jurascopes make it possible to view Tendaguru (in Tanzania) as it is thought to have looked 150 million years ago.

The highlight of this hall is the Berlin-based specimen of *Archaeopteryx*. This early bird did not live at Tendaguru, but existed at around at the same time as the dinosaurs from that location. For the first time ever, the original *Archaeopteryx* slab has been placed on display.

35.3 From Conventional to Hi-Tech Exhibits

While it is apparent that the proper use of technology, to transfer information and knowledge, should bring many potential benefits for museums, exhibits and even the thematic park approach, are there any drawbacks to the rising use of technology in this arena?

One downside, as highlighted by exhibits that are already using cutting-edge technologies, is that each exhibit requires more space, since briefing areas, immersive rooms, multimedia theatres and more are often required. Another obvious disadvantage is that such exhibits require technical support and on-site assistants. Indeed, at times it may be necessary to change the entire exhibit, including most of the equipment.

In the middle of the 1990s, Disney started to experiment with some hi-tech entertainment—flight simulators, virtual reality worlds—in their conventional theme parks, like Epcot and Walt Disney World.

The results of the trial led to a radical reshaping of the traditional theme park. There was a move away from the "village-like" arrangements of traditional theme parks, with visible reference points such as Snow White's castle (at Walt Disney World) or the "big ball" (at Epcot), and opening hours and entrance policies were changed, along with the target audience.

The result of this revolution was DisneyQuest, a blue cube close to the waterfront of the Village Lake in Downtown Disney (Orlando, Florida, USA).

Visitors entering this theme park at ground floor level are seamlessly lifted up to the fourth floor by simply entering a big room/elevator with two big aquariums full of swimming fishes on the side walls in order to boost the idea to "stand still". DisneyQuest is designed to make the visitors lose themselves in the three-dimensional space. The space inside the cube is arranged in order to ease the transition from one immersive adventure to the next completely different one. This theme park has reduced opening hours (10 am to 10 pm) compared to traditional Disney parks (8 am to 1 am), the entrance ticket is cheaper, and a year ticket costs less than three days' worth of tickets.

Lastly, and probably most importantly, the technological equipment was completely redesigned in order to meet the needs of a huge number of users, such as ease of use, robustness, safety and hygiene.

Fig. 35.20 DisneyQuest in Orlando, FL, USA

36 Educational Market

During the opening ceremony of the *World Forum of UNESCO Chairs*, which took place on the 13th November 2002, Mr Koichiro Matsuura, Director-General of UNESCO, emphasised the need to make educational materials freely available on the Web and the real possibilities of being able to do so. As a result, the *Open Educational Resources initiative* was launched as a cooperation mechanism for the open, noncommercial use of educational resources.

The new technologies have helped create a culture for learning in which the learner enjoys enhanced interactivity and connections with others. Rather than listen to a professor regurgitate facts and theories, students discuss ideas and learn from one another, with the teacher acting as a participant in the learning. Students construct narratives that make sense out of their own experiences. Initial research strongly supports the benefits of this kind of learning (Tapscott 1999).

The increasing demand for high-quality digital content

We are already in the Information Society era, and we are now evolving towards a *Knowledge Society* (KS) and beyond (to, say, a "Consciousness Society"). One of the keys to establishing a KS is the creation of high-quality digital content. This means that there will be an increasing demand for high-quality, enriched digital content. Furthermore, lifelong learning is no longer just a buzzword; the high technological turnover rate has already made continuous learning a necessity.

The solution: the silver bullet or the magic recipe

eLearning is an umbrella term that covers a wide range of applications and services. There is no "silver bullet" or "magic recipe" that is applicable to all circumstances or that is able to solve all problems perfectly. The method of eLearning required changes from subject to subject, from audience to audience and from goal to goal. Workshops and laboratory-based subjects must be managed in different ways than theoretical subjects. Conventional classrooms (e.g. university degree courses) require different approaches and solutions than lifelong learning groups or corporate/institutional training courses (e.g. training courses for sales managers or public administration officers). A fully online approach without any interpersonal relationship between the learner and the teacher works quite differently from blended resources that are a mixture of the two approaches.

Under the "umbrella" we find classical courses as well as educational applications for science and technology centres, training courses for paramedics and eHealth podcasting for citizens, virtual reality simulators and serious games. A complete, updated and comprehensive taxonomy appears to be one of the most urgent and important requirements of this sector.

The evaluation phase

Evaluating the results is always a challenge; users may prefer self-assessment and evaluation methods, while sometimes person-to-person evaluation is required.

eLearning resources must be appealing and effective

Representatives of both developers and users highlight the need to provide high-quality content and services. eLearning resources must be *appealing* and *effective*. Users, especially those that are working, do not want to waste time getting to grips with an eLearning application.

They stress the need to use multidisciplinary teams when developing eLearning services. This means bringing on-board experts in the specific topic, experts in the pedagogical aspects of eLearning, experts in eLearning course structures, experts in learning object creation, experts in forms of communication, such as digital storytelling, digital movies, digital imaging and others.

Resources and related costs

This immediately leads to another aspect of eLearning: *required resources and related costs*. It is clear that eLearning requires more resources and is more expensive than traditional education. From the start, one of the ideas was to share products and costs amongst different potential users. Unfortunately this has not been possible as frequently as we would like.

Different viewpoints, different requirements and constraints

This again is due to the sheer diversity—an archipelago—of eLearning applications. In the field of corporate applications, for example, cost is not a major constraint for sales personnel working for large distribution chains. They can employ a well-known movie director to create educational video clips or shorts to be included in the eLearning application.

Long-term content versus short-term content

Again, in an attempt to provide a reference framework, we can consider medium- and long-term educational content or short-term information content. A typical example might be the issue of providing privacy regulations on the fly for all employees. The most important aspect here is to be prompt in order to satisfy the immediate need.

The relevance of tutors

There is a need to create specific professional profiles for *tutors*, who provide the link between teachers and learners. They must be able to integrate the service and motivate students to use online resources.

The are another two aspects that should not be neglected:
- *Students/users* are continuously evolving in terms of skills, approaches and requirements. We have already entered the "digital native" era, where young people are using digital resources and technology in a very natural and proactive way.
- *Experts* do not necessarily make excellent professors, and neither experts nor professors are necessarily great (multimedia) communicators.

In addition, the author should be invited to attend his own eLearning course in order to experience the student's side of the service.

Microlearning as a new platform

Microlearning applications appear to be another useful format for accessing eLearning resources. They provide a sequence of simple concepts to be learned via SMS or other short messaging services.

396 ⋮ *III Exploitation, Applications and Services*

Moving back to the main topic, it appears that only specific sectors are currently obtaining clear added value from using eLearning. Sometimes people involved on both sides seem to use it as a backup solution rather than an added value opportunity.

Through the centuries we have experimented with mentors, ateliers and masters, private trainers and schools. Will eLearning be the next step towards the integration of traditional educational resources?

Case Study: The Mobile Learning Engine

The *Mobile Learning Engine*[27] (MLE) was awarded a Top Talent Award in the category of Mobile Content in 2004. It provides the user with the freedom to learn in any place and at any time using just a mobile phone. This makes it possible to learn during times that would otherwise be "wasted" waiting for an event, no matter where you are.

The Engine transfers computer-aided and multimedia-based learning to the mobile environment, using a server on the Internet. The technical solution exploits the Pocket PC power of smart phones, the newest generation of mobile phones. The MLE communicates with the learning platform through HTTP and XML, making it possible to use existing learning management systems as a mobile learning platform.

Although originally developed to teach a medical topic, the MLE can be applied to any specific theme. Learning objects can easily be created for almost every type of content. The application provides a wide range of functions, such as a multimedia forum, hypermedia systems and learning communities.

The Mobile Learning Engine illustrates the progression of mobile-learning technology and its potential.

---

27 Author: Matthias Meisenberger, Alte Poststrasse 147–149, 8020 Graz, Austria (see http://www.mlearn.net/).

36.1 The Role of Memory Institutions

Education and memory institutions are in a prime position to deliver the kind of unique learning resources that are needed at all educational levels. Information communication and knowledge technologies will play a major role in creating structure for and delivering this new content, which goes far beyond the current stage of providing access to raw information.

Such services will be supported by intelligent tools and agents that help end-users to locate the required information and knowledge fragments in a structured format via multichannel/media interactive/immersive communication.

Deeply immersive environments will make end-users check out virtual worlds they could not experience anywhere outside of the digital realm.

Visibility of the overall scene
Thanks to the work carried out by the Council of Europe and the European Commission in the field of ICT for cultural heritage (e.g. the EC's *DigiCULT* framework, the CoE's *Vital Links* report) and educational multimedia (e.g. the Multimedia Educational Task Force), this scene is currently highly visible to the public. In addition, the European Information Technology Observatory (EITO) is considered to be a defining reference work on the European ICT market.

Even if we do not consider its main museums and collections, such as the Louvre, Uffizi, Prado, Hermitage, and the National Gallery, to mention but a few, the regional and local cultural heritage of Europe, as already stated, is one of its greatest economic assets. Cultural institutions can utilise information and communication technologies as effective instruments to fulfil some of their primary aims, to disseminate and educate, by providing contextual information enlightened by narratives and visualisations with computer-aided renderings and displays.

Digital storytelling, for instance, is an extremely powerful tool. Film-makers have recently adopted the digital storytelling approach used in video games as a powerful medium to promote new productions.

Appropriate use of ICT increases interest in the original collection
As experience has shown, the appropriate use of ICT increases interest in the original collection, and cultural heritage institutions should not ignore this opportunity to add value to their holdings. Nevertheless, the potential of ICT in this arena is very far from being fully exploited.

Education and training are undergoing a dramatic process of transformation due to the emergence of new media and communication processes. Students are looking for different approaches to gaining information and knowledge; there is a considerable efficiency gap between some new and effective communication channels and the traditional educational ones.

Different media, direct access to "certified" information resources, interactivity and virtuality are power tools in information and knowledge transfer. Virtuality and digital simulation should re-enable the transfer of knowledge and skills based on direct experimentation and trial and error, which is a very powerful type of learning, and one that harks back to traditional atelier methods.

All of these technologies must be as unintrusive as possible, and invisible to the user, in line with the ideas of The Disappearing Computer interest group. Invisible technology is usually the best technology available. This is usually the natural extension of basic technology; in the beginning technology offers an increasing number of options and functions, and later on technology is instead used to perform tasks and services transparently.

A basic example is the evolution of software suites: they started by offering an increasing number of options and services, and then the number of options immediately available to the user was rationalised and some background services were implemented, such as real-time spell checking, type checking, etc.

Case Study: Da Vinci's Workshop

Leonardo da Vinci's Workshop[28] is a compound product that includes a book with 3-D images, an interactive CD-ROM and paper models. It represents a new approach to the educational market; students (although not only students—adults are often interested in these products too) are immersed in an interactive and stimulating learning environment. The book presents a reconstruction of the workshop in Milan Castle where Leonardo planned and produced his inventions and works of art. It is virtual workshop and its rooms represent all of the places where he worked at different times in his life before moving to France. A "learning by doing" approach predominates; the user can read the book, which introduces Leonardo's marvels via 3-D computer graphics, or perform the "entry test" on the CD-ROM. The captivating 3-D graphical reconstructions allow pupils to see how Leonardo invented his amazing machines, beginning with the simplest and continuing through to those that are the strangest and most fascinating.

Fig. 36.1a,b
Da Vinci's Workshop
(copyright by Leonardo3, Italy; http://www.leonardo3.net)

The CD-ROM really brings the book to life, so that the user becomes involved in an interactive game that lets pupils explore every corner of the entire workshop. If they pass the test, which checks for a basic know-

---

[28] Available from Leonardo3, Milano, Italy: http://www.leonardo3.net.

ledge of mechanics by making the user choose the right mechanism, they can move on to more exciting experiences, such as creating their own mechanical inventions from scratch! Once the invention has been constructed using 3-D graphics they can try it out in a real-time simulation.

Pupils can also construct paper models of three of the machines: the Cart, the Aerial Screw and the Swing Bridge.

At the end of the interactive experience, a certificate including the plans for the invention is made available for printing. This approach, which mixes interactive 3-D graphics with physical models and paper-based visual publications, seems to be highly appreciated by learners.

Case Study: Participatory 3-D GIS Modelling Exercise for Resource Use, Development Planning and Safeguarding Intangible Cultural Heritage in Fiji[29]

Experimentation with this methodology started in the late 1980s; since then it has become much refined and more accessible, and this deployment has been enormously successful in demonstrating valuable cultural assets clearly and informatively using state-of-the-art technology.

Different groups of inhabitants (elderly people, young people, etc.) are involved in an innovative exercise to "draw" their own personal map of their territory, pinpointing relevant locations or events.

This participatory GIS (PGIS) scheme is the result of a spontaneous merger of participatory learning and action (PLA) methods with geographic information technologies and systems (GIT&S) in order to compose peoples' spatial knowledge in the forms of virtual or physical two- or three-dimensional maps. These are then used as interactive vehicles for discussion, information exchange and analysis, and to aid advocacy, decision-making and action-taking. The result supports local communities in developing resource management and simultaneously developing plans for preserving local cultural heritage, both tangible and intangible.

Preserving and presenting cultural heritage in line with the challenges of the future is very much the foundation of the PGIS Project in Ovalau Island, Lomaviti Province, Fiji. The project's objective was to support community-based biodiversity conservation in order to ensure food security and sustainable livelihoods. The interactive tools used for spatial learning in this project are geared towards community empowerment through measured, demand-driven, user-friendly and integrated applications of GIT&S; maps provide a major conduit in this process.

---

29 See: http://www.iapad.org/applications/plup/ovalau.htm.

400 *III Exploitation, Applications and Services*

37 Culture Counts[30]: the Economic Dimension

The present paragraph refers to one of the most misjudged but nevertheless important aspects of culture and cultural services: *the economic dimension*.

We all know that "La culture, ce n'est pas une marchandise comme les autres", and that those that work in the field of culture usually try to shield it as much as possible from the world of money and business. Of course, such actions are admirable, but we cannot ignore the fact that money has a huge influence on the everyday work of cultural institutions; it impacts on the restoration, conservation, care, protection, research and enjoyment of cultural content.

Return on investment

Very often cultural heritage, tangible heritage especially, is perceived as a pure cost—something we are committed to investing in without any actual or future *return on investment* (ROI). This sometimes happens because those that earn money from cultural heritage are often not the same people that are willing to invest in and preserve cultural heritage. Depending on the country, most of the revenue from cultural heritage is usually shared among travel agencies, hotels, restaurants, merchandise suppliers, etc. Direct revenue, such as entrance fees, usually represents a minor or even insignificant part of the revenue.

Early experiences

This was one of the key problems in the early days of eCulture—although cultural heritage enthusiasts created websites, they were often only interested in the cultural value of these websites and so largely ignored the issue of how to make such websites sustainable over the long term (i.e. revenue generation). Such applications and services were very hard to maintain; banners and online advertisements were not enough. Even market models, which were widespread at that time and were based on subscriptions or e-commerce of images and reproductions, did not succeed.

Revenue from images, the first idea

The idea of obtaining revenue from the high-quality digital reproduction of artefacts was the reference market model for quite a long time. Museum curators and superintendents were concerned about the digitisation of artefacts, although not because of any potential damage to the physical object during the digitisation process. Concerns mainly focussed on potential losses of control

---

30 Culture Counts is actually the title of an international conference on culture that was held in Florence in 1999.

37 Culture Counts: the Economic Dimension   401

over or "ownership" of the artefact. Nevertheless, high-quality digital reproductions represented the core business of the digital division of museums for a decade.

Fig. 37.1
Musei Online, Italy

Fig. 37.2 *Art Museum Network*, USA

This business wasn't easy to manage: some of the issues that had to be dealt with included advertisements, IT experts and data management, small payments, and media and/or reproduction delivery. In the middle of the 1990s, one potential solution to these issues was to look for a trusted institution with IT skills and an ability to manage complex IT systems, that is also adept at handling small payments and at customer care, and that also possesses a network point-of-presence in the same territory. The best fit to these criteria would appear to be *banks*.

Even IT companies tried to enter this business, although some of them quickly reshaped the business into a "museum Yellow Pages", supported mercly by banners, while others that tried to maintain enhanced services decided to open up the service in order to provide a wide range of e-commerce offers, including ticketing, books, cultural travel, merchandise and other related goods, high-quality documentation and services.

The most active players in this field tried to improve their budgets by attempting to manage the "memory institution" by applying a more up-to-date organisational model and adding a marketing branch and a sales branch to the usual cultural expertise branch. They started to expand their offers in both the *B2B* and the *B2C* directions. In this case, the business-to-business market includes temporary "turnkey" exhibits that can be offered to other museums, agreements with tour operators, television programmes, "the making of" shows, high-profile stages for advertisement, ticketing and info services, among other sources of revenue.

Memory institutions and B2B, B2C

Temporary "turnkey" exhibits

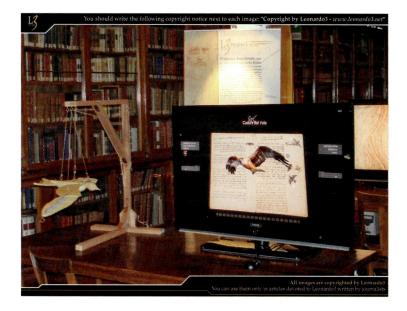

Fig. 37.3
Leonardo da Vinci:
The Codex of Flight
(copyright Leonardo3, Italy;
http://www.leonardo3.net)

Of course, ICT plays an important role when implementing these strategies; a key aspect of designing temporary turnkey exhibits is the availability of digital originals and their derived products for lease or sale with the exhibits.

The business-to-customer market includes merchandise, restaurants, bars, post-visit services, annual subscriptions, special events and other services.

37.1 Some of the Basic Conditions Required to Develop the Cultural Heritage Market

Close and effective cooperation

The first condition for the development of this market is close and effective cooperation between those actors who are custodians of the cultural heritage (mainly of course museums, galleries and archives), and those actors who provide the means for disseminating ICT (mainly commercial companies operating in the fields of information technology, telecommunications, broadcasting, etc).

Different "business cultures"

This is a major challenge, due to the completely different "business cultures" of these two sectors and their different knowledge backgrounds and expertise. Historically, museums have been suspicious of industry, since they have been fearful of vulgarising heritage and of being commercially exploited; in turn, industry has accused museums of being impractical and out of touch with harsh commercial reality.

Some conditions to be fulfilled

In order to make the successful development of this market possible a number of conditions must be fulfilled. Potential investors need to understand the potential return on their investments. Companies should look at their investments in the field of art as not only philanthropic programmes but also as multipliers for potential market actions.

A fair return on investment

While indeed many museums and galleries in Europe operate on a nonprofit basis, this is obviously not true for the companies that develop and market the technology necessary for the multimedia exploitation of European cultural heritage. These companies must be assured that a fair return can be made on investment.

The effective deployment of products and services in this sector requires the effort of many actors on the industrial, cultural, legal and even governmental sides. When there is a mutually understood scenario, this effort will take place with the necessary degree of cooperation and subsequent effectiveness.

Open market

Technology should permit the interoperability of different systems in order to keep the market open to all potential actors, including SMEs, and thus allow worldwide access to European cultural heritage. A closed system over which one actor or group of actors has exclusive rights would evidently seriously restrain the growth of the market.

The legal framework

The legal framework must be clarified, particularly in the field of IPR. Museums are especially in need of orientation in an environment where the technical capacity exists to duplicate and transport images and intellectual content freely and without restraint.

37.2 Cultural Heritage as Value Generator in a Post-Industrial Economy[31]

We, the government of the state, wish to put an end to the unhealthy practice which has created much disgust, because it permits buildings to be destroyed and thereby robs the town of its majestic appearance. Therefore we command that buildings constructed by the old shall not be desecrated. Those police officers who do not intervene when monuments are threatened by violence shall, after they have been whipped, have their hands cut off.

Julius Valerius Maiorianus (Roman Emperor 457–461)[32]

37.2.1 Economics, Value and Socioeconomic Theory

Each time cultural heritage contributes to artistic, educational or social development, it is a source of value: aesthetic value, experience value, existence value; its production implies economic movement, and not to take this into consideration would lead to a lack of fundamental understanding (MCC 2003).

In order to set the value of cultural heritage objects we must make use of *socioeconomic theory*. Cultural heritage must be treated as (*consumable*) goods. Further, according to socioeconomic theory, cultural heritage objects are "common goods".

Cultural heritage as consumable goods

Common goods are characterised as being (Narverud and Ready 2002):

Common goods: nonexclusive, nonrivalling

- *Nonexclusive*: goods are nonexclusive when a user cannot technically be stopped from enjoying/consuming those goods
- *Nonrivalling*: the level of enjoyment/consumption of the goods by a user is not reduced when other people consume it at the same time.

The private (and profit-driven) market cannot produce or supply sufficient nonexclusive common goods. The reason for this is simple: if you cannot force someone to pay to consume specific goods you cannot generate any profit!

---

[31] This section (37.2) is based on a paper written by Dr. Terje M. Nypan from the Directorate for Cultural Heritage, Norway; see Nypan (2005) and http:// www.nba. fi/tiedostot/b425fd75.doc.

[32] Survival of several of his legislative enactments, known as "Novels", which were preserved in the Breviarium, a compilation of Roman law published by Gallo-Roman jurists in 506 under the authority of the Visigothic king Alaric II (484–507). These laws may have made their way into Gallic archives during the course of Majorian's stays in Gaul during the years 458–461. They demonstrate the increasingly pervasive problems that the emperors had with maintaining the functioning of the imperial bureaucracy as self-interest and corruption became more and more rampant among government officials.

37 Culture Counts: the Economic Dimension

If profit cannot be achieved for specific goods, then the mechanisms of the private market ensure that such goods are not offered on this market. Therefore, if the mechanisms of the private market alone decided which (immovable) cultural heritage objects should be protected, only those with a high market value would be. This logic applies to all common goods.

Now, if this is the position of cultural heritage in the marketplace, how can we find out the *values* of these goods? From the perspective of *value creation/ definition*, there is no defined and unified methodology for specifying the socioeconomic values of cultural heritage objects. However, standard economic calculation methods can be used to define the value of a cultural heritage object, or—better—an aggregated group of cultural heritage objects.

The value a consumer gets by consuming a market good is equal to the highest sum of money the consumer is willing to pay to secure that good for his own consumption (Narverud and Ready 2002).

Nonmarketable goods and nonrenewable goods

Consequentially, the value of a cultural heritage good is the highest sum of money that a consumer is willing to pay to consume the good. This is the use value of the good. However, just as for other common goods, cultural heritage objects are *nonmarketable goods* and also *nonrenewable goods*.

Note that the values of such goods must be defined by analysing two types of values: the *use value* and the *non-use value*. In this section we will concentrate on trying to analyse the use value of cultural heritage from a socioeconomic perspective. The non-use value is a value that must be added to the use value to be able to accurately gauge the total value of cultural heritage to society. This is not done in this publication.

Usual indicators

Usually studies of cultural heritage and its economic effects make use of the following indicators: *turnover*, *employment* (direct and indirect) and *frequentation* (number of visitors). Such studies also make use of a number of different approaches, such as basic cost studies, economic impact studies, contingent valuation and choice modelling and regression analysis. There are also hedonic, travel cost and property value studies. In this work we have chosen to analyse the sector using its *turnover* and *employment capacity* as primary indicators.

37.2.2 Turnover of the Cultural Heritage Sector

Cultural heritage is of great value to other industries. Cultural landscapes, townscapes and individual buildings are used as inputs or backdrops for many PC games, by the film and television industry, and by businesses in their marketing and customer-relation-building activities when they organise spectacles and PR/reception activities for clients in old monuments. While this use value is not calculated here, it should be mentioned.

Cultural tourism

The tourism sector is the industry that makes the most extensive use of cultural heritage as support for its backbone activities, like hotel accommodation, transport and catering.

Cultural heritage is a major contributor to the income from tourism, which stands at 5.5% of the EU's GDP, generates more than 30% of its revenues from trade in external services, and employs 6% of the EU workforce. The expected growth rate of tourism is 57% over the period 1995–2010[33].

There are clear indications that the dedicated cultural heritage tourist spends more money when travelling than other tourists. Data from New Jersey (USA) shows that their daily spending is 60% higher than other tourists or travellers. The high employment levels associated with tourism are caused by the cultural tourism production line; cultural heritage increases the number of employees needed for hotels, restaurants and in the transport sector.

The value of cultural heritage *flows to other businesses rather than cultural heritage itself*. Even in those cases where entrance fees are demanded in order to access a cultural heritage site, the problem of defining the total value based on earnings from tickets, souvenirs or other activities that generate revenue at the site remains.

The Value flows to other businesses

The reason for this is the difference between spending at the site (*direct earnings*) and spending away from the site. The total sum of money that a visitor will spend on getting to the site, eating and (possibly) staying overnight constitutes the *sum of money that the consumer is willing to pay to secure that good for their own consumption*. This sum total is part of the economic value of that cultural heritage site.

However, we know[34] that only 6–10% of the total spending is performed at the site. It is also interesting to note that only 16.3% of the total number of jobs generated by cultural heritage are situated at the heritage sites themselves (Greffe 2002).

To arrive at a figure for the turnover of the cultural heritage sector, we used the following approach. We took the number of tourists to arrive in Europe in 2002, and we assumed that they stayed for 16 days on average and that they visit at least one museum or historic building during their stay. We also estimated their daily spending (overnight, food and drink) to be 150 Euros per day per person. We did not include the cost of travel to the destination or any travels between different destinations during the stay. Local transport use as well as one entry to a museum[35], etc., was calculated per stay[36].

So this gave us an idea of the total amount of money spent, but how much of this sum can be assigned to cultural heritage?

---

33 From the EU High Level Group working on the 1999 Eurobarometer (see http://ec.europa.eu/public_opinion/index_en.htm).

34 Studies done by English Heritage and the Norwegian Directorate for Cultural Heritage.

35 Local transport and sundries at 20 Euros per day, museum/gallery visits at 20 Euros per stay.

36 We also know from other studies that cultural heritage can potentially for be greatly rationalised and its maintenance can be made much less costly, saving 1.9 billion Euros. This sum was added to the total value. (Data from the Norwegian Directorate for Cultural Heritage in 2001).

37 Culture Counts: the Economic Dimension 407

Fig. 37.4 Elements in the turnover of the cultural heritage sector

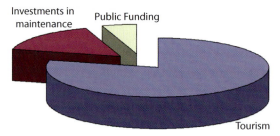

Consumption of cultural heritage

Here we were forced to define the *consumption of cultural heritage* and subsequently how much of their time tourists spend consuming this good. We defined consumption of cultural heritage as visiting museums and sites, obviously, as well as visiting cafés close to historical, architecturally interesting or beautiful landscapes. Sitting down to eat or drink, or simply walking and "taking in" the surroundings is therefore cultural heritage consumption.

Based on this, we stipulated that, on an average, 30% of a tourist's time is spent consuming cultural heritage. In total we found that the turnover from cultural heritage-related tourism is around 338 billion Euros in Europe[37].

Seventy-nine percent of this turnover comes from tourism, while 16% derives from contributions from private owners, charities, foundations, etc., and the remaining 5% is invested by public and governmental bodies.

37.2.3 Employment in the Cultural Heritage Sector in Europe

Based on a survey carried out in the spring of 2003, we received information on the cultural heritage sector from Norway, Sweden, Finland, Denmark, The Netherlands, the United Kingdom and France. We used this information to estimate the numbers directly employed in this sector in those countries that did not participate in the survey. According to our calculations, the number of people *directly employed* in this sector in Europe is 306,000 (although the actual figure is probably even larger). Furthermore, *indirect employment* by this sector amounts to 7.8 million man-years. In *total*, more than eight million jobs in the EU are provided by the cultural heritage sector.

For example, in France, a study shows that more than 40,000 craftsmen work on repairing and maintaining cultural heritage (French Ministry of Culture and Communication 2001).

---

[37] Here "Europe" is taken to include EU countries, EEA countries and the countries that joined the EU in June 2004.

Another important element to consider in our post-industrial economy is the labour-intensiveness of the sector. In all major industrial sectors, the trend is towards increasing production while reducing the workforce. This is a general trend, and is partly responsible for the unemployment problem Europe is facing today.

However, the cultural heritage sector, including tourism, is highly labour-intensive. Furthermore, there is a huge backlog of maintenance work that needs to be done in this sector, so it also has the potential to employ many more people.

Looking at Fig. 37.5, we can see that the cultural heritage sector creates approximately 26.7 jobs for every direct one, which can be compared to the auto industry, for example, where this factor is only 6.3. Of course, these figures would be more accurate if more data were available, but they are still excellent indicators of the employment potential of cultural heritage maintenance.

The ability of those working directly in a sector to create additional employment is called the *multiplier effect*. The size of this multiplier is heavily debated. Different studies come up with different numbers, depending on their analytical approach and/or the site being studied. The multiplier in the French study by Greffe is 17.1%. It is interesting to note that only 9–16.3% of the jobs associated with cultural heritage are situated on the cultural heritage site itself (direct employment).

Multiplier effect

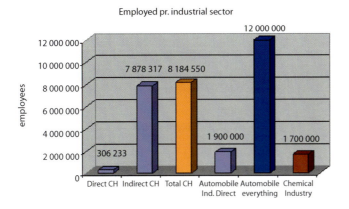

Fig. 37.5

37.2.4 Methodological Research Considerations

It is clear that the number of economic studies of culture and cultural heritage are on the increase. Cultural heritage is increasingly seen as a tool for employment creation and regional development.

However, the methodology is still being developed, and in most cases the empirical data is lacking or impossible to obtain. As stated by Randall Mason in a paper on the subject (Mason 2005):

The economics of preservation is an embryonic field compared with research in other economic disciplines, and the research is currently weighted heavily towards advocacy. The paper concludes with a call for more development in the field to be able to more objectively answer the question: Does preservation pay? Toward that end, the paper calls for a hybrid of the most promising methods and more collaboration across research fields.

By combining methods, the particular shortcomings or blind spots of different methods can perhaps offset one another. Without further refinement, the ability to make conclusive, generalized statements about the economics of preservation will remain elusive.

We should also emphasise the following important facts, which are also weaknesses of this study. These studies and the figures given are of an explorative nature. From a social science methodology point of view, the empirical data is insufficient to be able to satisfactorily verify the figures and conclusions.

Follow the money In this section we have chosen to use the approach sometimes called "follow the money". We have calculated tourist spending conservatively, but we have made an assumption about time spent consuming cultural heritage. We require more data in order to substantiate the consumer patterns of tourists.

On the other hand, we have sufficient data to develop hypotheses for which can then be tested. This is exactly what needs to be done.

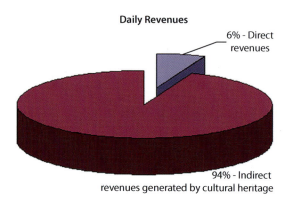

Fig. 37.6 Daily Revenues

More research needs to be done to verify what the present explorative study expounds. The first step would be to collect all of the empirical data that is presently sitting in national administrations, tourist institutions and NGOs working with cultural heritage.

We have tried to make conservative estimates and to avoid exaggerating, considering the methodologically inadequate empirical data and the subsequent need for calculations and stipulations. Similarly, our conclusions are also based on not wanting to exaggerate. In all we believe that the figures are conservative rather than radical. However, these findings need to be substantiated using more valid and reliable empirical data.

Only 6–10% of the daily spending of visitors to cultural heritage sites is actually spent at the site; the remaining money flows into the society around the site. Only 10–15% of all jobs in the cultural heritage sector are performed directly on the site or are directly related to the site. Sometimes these two aspects cause some trouble with local communities (e.g. in emerging countries).

37.3 Economic Promotion of Cultural Heritage: Problems and Issues

Its regional and local cultural heritage (defined in a broad sense, from museums to regional gastronomy and folklore) is one of Europe's greatest economic assets. Information and communications technology (ICT), along with other advanced technologies, can potentially dramatically increase our ability to exploit this cultural heritage, although we are still far from achieving this aim. Up to now, the application of ICT to cultural heritage has all too often failed to provide valuable economic results, due to a number of problems, and it has generated disappointment among the potential players and beneficiaries.

The main problems are listed below:

Main problems

- In general at the regional and local levels there is shortage of experience and expertise regarding the use of ICT in relation to cultural heritage. Therefore, local and regional administrators have to rely on ICT vendors and consultants, who are often only able to suggest general-purpose solutions that are not optimised for this particular sector. Even the large and well-known consultant companies only rarely have consolidated expertise in the field of cultural heritage.
- If we consider "conventional" cultural heritage (museums and galleries), this sector lacks expertise and experience in marketing and business promotion, which also makes it difficult to develop credible business models and plans, and to attract investment;
- There are analogous problems in the cultural tourism sector. There are hundreds of projects and initiatives related to cultural tourism in Europe, but they have often been designed based on "supply-oriented" thinking; the needs of the customer, the *cultural tourist*, are rarely investigated.
- More generally, the problem of a lack of mutual understanding between the cultural sector, the service industry and ICT experts, due to their different

ways of thinking, makes it difficult to achieve fruitful cooperation in areas ranging from education to multimedia production, where the availability of cultural heritage content could open up very promising development perspectives. In order to be able to develop innovative and marketable products and services with real cultural added value, the personal and direct involvement of experts from the relevant cultural area is absolutely required. Despite the abovementioned issues, there are nevertheless a number of interesting examples and initiatives, on various scales, of the successful economic promotion of cultural heritage in Europe and around the world. Unfortunately, they often have only local or regional visibility, and their positive (and negative) experiences cannot be fully exploited and shared by other projects. As a consequence, the same mistakes continue to be made; in short, the wheel keeps on being reinvented.

37.4 Cultural Services and Markets

The new century has not started well for the ICT industry. After a decade of strong growth, for the first time the sector has experienced a severe slowdown and stagnation, resulting from an exceptional combination of adverse factors, including a global economic slowdown after the 9/11 terrorist attacks and the uncertainty in the financial markets that followed the drop in *blue chip stocks* and over-investment. Nevertheless, the usage of ICT by both enterprises and SOHOs has still increased. European enterprises have reached a maturity level in terms of their basic ICT infrastructure and their connectivity to the Internet. According to the statistical data from Eurostat, over 95% of companies in the EU Member States use computers, and more than 85% have access to the Web. These are average figures, and local rates are even higher; in some countries, as well as for larger enterprises[38], the saturation level (almost 100%) has practically been reached.

Looking at the scenario from a different point of view, we are only just starting out on a revolution resulting from a set of converging technologies. Previously, innovations took many years to impact on the general public: seventy years for printing; fifty for commercial flights and the telephone; thirty years for the Internet; fifteen years for PCs.

It is worth noting that we are probably in a kind of "Middle Ages" of technological communication—we are still looking for a proper multimedia format to use (Ronchi 2003). Although we are not completely sure about where the current technological revolution will take us, we do know we are experiencing a deep transformation due to the convergence of goals and technologies in the fields of communication, information technology and entertainment.

---

[38] In some countries, small-to-medium-sized enterprises were the first to adopt ICT.

First we experienced the merging of IT and TLC; then ICT merged with entertainment, and then wireless communication, handheld location-based services, among others.

Technological convergence and "pointing towards the stars but looking at our fingers"

As is usually the case for such technological trends, even for "fake" revolutions[39], initially we overestimate technology and underestimate its potential influences and transformation on culture and society—*although we are pointing towards the stars with our fingers, we are still looking at the fingers*. As a consequence, the general view is limited to a short-term perspective, leading to premature or limited applications and effects.

Consider the revolution resulting from the invention of the transistor, one of the most important and pervasive technologies of the last century. It was originally developed and patented as a device to fight deafness. Wireless communication was developed in order to allow ships crossing the oceans to communicate, but a "bug" in the technology did not allow private communication (for military purposes anyway). This bug is now called *broadcasting*, and it provides the bedrock of radio and television services.

Revolutions and "bugs"

37.5 Emerging Professional Profiles

The end-goal of economic promotion is to create conditions for the development of new economic activities that are able to enhance our enjoyment of our cultural heritage and to create new employment opportunities in its corresponding sectors. Cultural heritage plays a key role in our lives since it links us with our *roots*. In the millennium of globalisation and the aggregation of countries into "continental states", local and regional culture represents an essential building block of future society.

In order to reach this goal, our cultural heritage evidently needs to be made available in a sustainable way and to the greatest extent possible in both real and virtual formats. Of course, any form of economic exploitation must take fully into account the overriding need to preserve cultural heritage for future generations.

Education and training are the basic steps required to understand and protect our cultural identities and heritage. A true commitment to preserving cultural assets comes from knowledge and understanding. Furthermore, in order to fully enjoy the opportunities unleashed by technology, a fruitful cooperation must be established between technologists and experts in cultural heritage.

Today, the preservation and revitalisation of our cultural heritage has acquired major significance, and these aims, at least in a pan-European context, will be characterised by the utilisation of our cultural heritage.

---

39 Associated with "overhyped" technologies.

37 Culture Counts: the Economic Dimension 413

Cultural market indicators

There are number of powerful indicators of our utilisation of cultural heritage:

- Culture is becoming an increasing important element of our leisure time
- Cultural tourism is a relatively stable sector of the tourism industry that is characterised by high quality and is largely independent of unpredictable climatic conditions, expensive wage costs in Europe, or low transport costs to international destinations
- In a worldwide context, culture is one of the most powerful resources within Europe
- Our cultural heritage is the basis for regional identity in the European Union, enabling not only sustained socioeconomic use, but also, particularly within the framework of the economic unification of Europe, countering the destabilising effect of this process on regional identity
- Within the fairly sizeable niche market for the sustained use of our cultural heritage, almost the entire spectrum of information technologies can be used in a productive manner.

Specific professional profiles

One strategic issue associated with the utilisation of applications and services from the ICT and emerging technologies market in the cultural heritage sector is the availability of persons with specific professional profiles; particular attention will be need to given to identifying these profiles and defining suitable study curricula at various levels. In particular, the courses for humanistic and classical studies must be re-evaluated in order to promote the use of ICT for innovative research in these areas.

Multidisciplinary approach

The specific field of "cultural content communication through new information technologies" is strongly based on a multidisciplinary approach, including the basics of computer science, multimedia, computer graphics, data acquisition, legal aspects and IPR, social sciences, psychology and cognitive sciences, visual communication, pedagogy and more. Up to now there have been almost no opportunities to match these competencies with existing courses at both graduate and postgraduate levels.

Such profiles are usually built on top of traditional curricula by achieving cross-sector competencies through self-managed ad hoc training processes. The starting points are mainly traditional courses, such as architecture, art history, cultural heritage, archaeology and, less frequently, computer science.

Professionals can acquire some of the required interdisciplinary competencies by taking postgraduate courses, which are sometimes financed by the European Social Fund. Of course, the cocktail of competencies required must be tuned to the specific field of interest: conservation, communication, education, etc.

More recently, some new and specific courses in digital communication have been created, with sub-branches in education, culture, entertainment, etc. These courses can be studied as first- and second-level degrees and sometimes to PhD level. This revised educational approach represents the first step towards a completely new set of careers.

37.6 Cultural Services and Markets: the Challenge

In order to explore this sector, let us now recall some of the events and documents introduced in the "Background" chapter of this book.

The general theme that links *Universal Access to Information*, launched during the 32nd UNESCO General Conference, as well as the World Summit on the Information Society, and the implementation of the documents adopted by the Summit, is the need to focus on both technological and cultural aspects simultaneously.

During the Special European Council held in Lisbon on 23–24 March 2000, a guideline document titled *eEurope* was launched. This document provides some guidelines for developing e-society, including making Internet access cheaper, accelerating e-commerce, providing fast Internet for researchers and students, producing smart cards for secure electronic access, making risk capital available for high-tech SMEs, promoting e-participation for the disabled, bringing healthcare and government online, and creating intelligent transport.

37.6.1 Lisbon Council and European Strategy

The outcome of the Lisbon Council was an agreement on a new strategic goal for the Union in order to strengthen employment, economic reform and social cohesion as part of a knowledge-based economy.

Thus, the strategic goal for the EU "to become the most competitive and dynamic knowledge based economy in the world capable of sustainable economic growth with more and better jobs and greater social cohesion" was set for this decade (2000–2010).

One important aspect of this new strategic goal of the EU was to *create a climate conducive to investments, innovation and entrepreneurship*. An additional component of the new strategic goal was to implement *sustainable development based on culture and education*. *Cultural patrimony* is a vital resource for achieving this strategic goal. Another goal was to activate local (rural and urban areas) initiatives founded on sound democratic processes.

In March 2004 a program was initiated in order to review the Lisbon Strategy in 2005. So far, innovation and entrepreneurship initiatives that target sustainable development based on culture and education seem to be a main focus of the European Strategy. Cultural assets are fundamental building blocks for creating a cohesive Europe and for the further development of Europe. The challenge of creating a proper market based on cultural heritage starts here.

The Lisbon conference was held during a period in which Europe was witnessing many changes. The European Union was in the process of admitting ten new Member States, a new European Parliament had been elected, and a new European Commission had been appointed at almost at the same time.

The entry of the new Member States[40] into the EU has had a profound impact on European society, and this will last for decades. The EU has not only grown in size, but has also become more varied in terms of the cultures, languages and opinions included within its borders. Promoting social cohesion between the different cultures that represent contemporary Europe and ensuring social and economic progress requires tremendous energy and commitment from the Member States and European institutions.

Changing patterns of media usage

Citizens are increasingly accessing information through a range of different platforms. In many ways these new platforms are changing the patterns of media usage, especially in the younger generations.

- In the political field, the European Union has set new objectives to improve the quality of European society. Besides the Lisbon objectives and the development of a high-quality Knowledge Society, the European Union also wants to improve European citizenship within a community of values where all of the different cultures can flourish.
- As a result of globalisation and the expansion of Europe, cultural identity has become increasingly important as a reference point for the wide variety of cultural communities within European society. Local production and Europe-wide exploitation of content represents a vital source of internal pluralism and guarantees that European citizens have access to a diverse range of quality services that reflect their cultural heritage and cultural identity.

In 2000, the Council of Ministers in Lisbon concluded that by 2010 Europe must become "the most competitive and dynamic knowledge-based economy in the world". It should be capable of creating sustainable economic growth along with improved employment opportunities and social cohesion.

As we creep closer to the deadline (2010) set by the Lisbon programme for the European Union to be transformed into the most dynamic Knowledge Society, it is clear that some positive steps toward this goal have been taken, but also that there are some unsatisfactory delays, partly due to the economic slowdown.

A range of goals remain unfulfilled that will need to be driven forward if Europe is to enjoy the maximum benefits from economic growth and technology.

Towards the Knowledge-Based Economy and Society

During the IST conference Towards the Knowledge-Based Economy and Society, held in December 2001, Erkki Liikanen[41] outlined some strategic aspects and goals related to the Lisbon strategy by stating that "we're talking about a long-term perspective as we are re-designing the processes of work, production, trade, education, and governance. These are largely social and societal changes which take time before they deliver their full benefits", and

---

40 Cyprus, Czech Republic, Estonia, Hungary, Latvia, Lithuania, Malta, Poland, Slovakia, Slovenia.

41 Member of the European Commission responsible for Enterprise and the Information Society.

416 *III Exploitation, Applications and Services*

that "Lisbon is about the structural change towards the Knowledge Society, about the very architecture of our economy and society for the emerging knowledge society".

Liikanen's analysis shows that in order to fulfil these objectives some (at least six) pressing challenges must be overcome:
- Telecom liberalisation must be completed
- The digital divide must be bridged by providing everyone with skills
- eCommerce must be accelerated
- Security and confidence must be built up
- Content must be promoted
- Governments must migrate online.

At least two of these challenges are directly related to our topic: bridging the digital divide by providing everyone with skills, and promoting content[42].

Digital divide and quality content

Sociodemographic characteristics continue to have a considerable impact on whether individuals access the Internet. It all starts at school. Schools must provide all young Europeans with the digital skills that they need to live and work in the digital age. This very much depends on the equipment available in the schools. The target of having all schools online by the end of 2004 was almost achieved (note that 90% of schools were online in May 2001).

But connecting schools is not enough. The integration of the Internet and IST into teaching methods and tools is still limited and requires that courses are adapted and, of course, that teachers and tutors are trained. Simple availability of new technologies and tools is not enough if they are not used positively and valuably.

Training trainers: teachers and tutors

Governments and institutions must also ensure that people already on the job market are employable. Better living conditions, the increase in our average life spans and the consequent extension of our working lives, together with the acceleration in the fields of technology and science and the growth and harmonisation of markets all mean that we must constantly update and improve our knowledge. This calls for the promotion of *life-long learning* programmes for all Europeans.

Lifelong learning programmes

The challenge of promoting content will also have to be faced:

Now assume we have genuine and fair competition, and a high level of security and privacy. This is still not enough to ensure the long-term development of the infrastructure. You don't sell a service simply because it's cheap and safe.

The thrill is in the content. If we want an Information Society for all, content must be in mother tongue, rich, diversified, and it must meet specific cultural demands[43].

In conclusion, the Information and Knowledge Society is and will remain a top priority for the EU. The ICT industry is asking for a clear relaunch of

---

42   All of these are the goals of the World Summit Award initiative.
43   From Erkki Liikanen during the IST conference Towards the Knowledge-Based Economy and Society, held in December 2001.

37 *Culture Counts: the Economic Dimension*   417

the Lisbon mission, focusing on more specific targets and defining specific processes for reaching them. There is also a need to monitor progress through benchmarking results in Member Countries and in local government, and for more specific definitions and verifications of accountability and responsibilities. To reach the objectives of the programme, the EU Council should fix clear parameters that must be followed by Member States. In the meantime, the i2010 strategy has already been extended to i2020.

37.7 The European ICT Market

The previous part of this chapter was devoted to introducing and historically framing the legal and institutional background of ICT and cultural products and services. Let us consider now the effects of having such a framework and the actual playground.

One of the main infrastructures emerging at European level is broadband, both wired and wireless. Over the past few years, broadband access has grown at a very high rate in Europe[44].

Broadband residential penetration in Europe, according to the special study into *Convergence and the Digital World* at EITO 2004–05, has already grown from 12% in 2003 to 23% in 2006, and it will be 40% in 2010 and 100% in 2020.

However, the study indicates that there is a gap of two years between the US and Europe in terms of broadband penetration of online households. DSL technology represents the major driver for accelerating convergence with digital TV.

Broadband access (over two megabits) is causing a revolution in multimedia convergence. It is opening up a wide market for interactive digital content. Together with VoIP, high-speed DSL, WiFi, WiMax, WiBro and fibre optics, widespread broadband access will transform information/transaction flows within all organisations. A number of traditional telecom operators are entering the market due to this multimedia convergence, offering not only Internet access but event entertainment and eCommerce services, thus essentially becoming *media companies*.

---

44 Please refer to the EITO reports and specific documents included in the references at the end of the chapter.

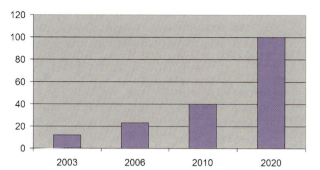

Fig. 37.7
Broadband penetration

At the same time, the diffusion of third- and fourth-generation wireless technologies will permit the expansion of mobile commerce, mobile banking, mobile government, mobile entertainment, mobile work and mobile education. Sometimes wireless connections are competing directly with wired, offering similar performances at reasonable prices.

Broadband requires proactive government policy action and incentives to promote wide coverage across all European regions, thus avoiding the creation of areas of broadband divide. Triple and quadruple players are a natural consequence of the availability of wireless broadband; mobile phone operators are widening their own markets.

In this convergent scenario, *virtual operators*—commercial entities without any technological infrastructure—are the new players that are enhancing the competition. Some of them are also key players in other sectors, such as mass distributors of goods or banks.

Virtual operators

Once the different "piping" systems are ready, we need something desirable to transfer. In this case we need *added value content and services*, so digital content and services are two of the main drivers of market innovation. *High-quality eContent* is one of the keys to the implementation of the Knowledge Society and the fruitful exploitation of broadband services[45].

Piping, quality content and services

The EITO thematic study on *Convergence and the Digital World* highlights the development of a *digital value chain* that is changing the traditional business models of various players.

The most successful convergence driven by digital technology is not that of physical devices or network infrastructures, but mainly that of content and services, as well as business processes.

---

[45] During the first WSIS a global contest called the World Summit Award was launched in order to select the best eContent from the sectors of eBusiness, eCulture, eEntertainment, eGovernment, eHealth, eInclusion, eLearning and eScience from around the world.

Convergence can be defined as: "The phenomenon by which the evolution and/or the integration of technologies with different origins allows infrastructure, delivery devices and applications to provide existing or new functionalities". This introduces the concept of multiplatform access to the same digital content/service and the idea that effective convergence is achieved by the end user.

Of course there are some undesirable side effects of this convergence. For example, even though most people consider movies to be artistic works, the movie industry was moved under the "ICT" umbrella in the EU because movies can be transferred via broadband.

Due to the spread of broadband lines and wireless networks, there is a huge opportunity to build a large European industry and market for digital content/ services. This requires policies for promoting a new wave of start-ups, as well as new entrepreneurship and risk capital initiatives for developing new digital content/services and opening new markets, especially in the digital consumer field.

To gain a better understanding of digital convergence we must analyse the *consumer electronics* (CE; palmtops, camcorders, DVD readers, set-top boxes, digital cameras, MP3 players, multimedia players, navigators, etc.) markets in Europe, focusing on the main convergence trends between ICT and CE, with the aim of evaluating future areas of growth in digital content/services based on various platforms.

There are already interesting trends coming from the shared media (i.e. memory cards) and wireless communication device (WiFi, Bluetooth, etc.) markets.

37.8 A European Knowledge Society

Europe must not lose momentum at the beginning of the new development cycle, just as growth and change in North America and East Asia are speeding up. Europe has the potential to reach ambitious targets in becoming a prosperous Knowledge Society of 500 million people.

However, we need pride and vision to overcome the challenge presented by the Lisbon programme. We must make the right structural reforms to remove obstacles to change, reducing rigidity and increasing adaptability to change in work organisations, making European administrations less bureaucratic, reducing overregulation and not overburden Internet IPR and privacy regulations, implementing proactive and ex-post communications regulations that favour digital convergence and market development, and investing in skills and preparing all citizens and workers for the new scenario.

2004 was the year in which the European Union was enlarged, bringing new expectations and new challenges for both the new Member Countries and also the old ones. That event must mark the start of a new cycle for the construction of a European Knowledge Society.

37.9 The Challenge: Fostering Creativity

Let us recapitulate some of the concepts already mentioned. In the new scenario of an enlarged Europe there is a need to catalyse a common understanding where the enriching kind of cultural diversity is encouraged and the divisive kind of cultural diversity is censured, thus providing a common vision of European society.

Young people and their potential creativity could play an important role in such a scenario, particularly if supported by digital technologies. One of the goals is to promote creativity by maximising the cultural and educational potential of new technologies.

Promoting creativity

Digital technology now affects our whole lives, not only in terms of our health, security, safety, work and similar fields, but even more importantly in our cultural interests, creativity, entertainment, communications and relationships.

Digital media have dramatically increased the possibilities open to the artist, either by creating new forms of expression or by bringing the costs of production within reach of individuals[46].

New forms of expression

As well as specifically digital media, music, still images and video are three significant areas where the costs of producing a finished work have dropped so radically that new young talents are emerging.

Digital technology, and in particular the Internet, has completely overturned traditional ideas about distribution. Any work that can take a digital form can be infinitely reproduced at minimal cost.

Digital distribution channels

Young people especially will be galvanised if they feel that others will see their efforts. The instant global network of the Internet has made the building of *special interest groups* (SIGs)[47] unprecedentedly easy. These spaces are where artists talk, and are excellent places to gauge the state of a scene.

Peer-to-peer technology enables on-the-fly exchange of content, unleashing incredible opportunities to share personal content and to activate added value chains of cooperation. Creativity and high-quality content are key aspects for the future of technology and the Knowledge Society.

Peer-to-peer

Initiatives and projects must take into account some concerns within the context of the youth sector:

- The development of sustainable ways for cultural diversity to flourish
- Public access to information and freedom of expression

---

46 Such as computer graphics, mixed media, online publishing, video and audio tools and editors, etc.

47 This is even true for hackers (see http://www.blackhat.com, http://www.ccc.de, http://www.defcon.org, http://www.hack.lu, http://www.whatthehack.org for example)!

- The capacity to innovate in terms of the creation and distribution of cultural goods and services
- The encouragement of partnerships between different segments of the value chain
- The impact of new technologies on opportunities for teaching and learning, including self-directed education.

Creativity must be encouraged and new interactive cultural expressions must be stimulated. Knowledge is not about the *circulation of information*. It is *about adding value to ideas*. The younger generations are digital natives—they are not immigrants into the brave new world. They need a different approach; different applications and services. They use technology seamlessly. A new model for communication processes is required—it's hard to live between two different realities: the digital and the traditional worlds.

A Knowledge Society must provide people with opportunities to think in new ways. Some technologies are still being used to create "libraries without books" (i.e. applications with no real added value), while ICT companies are still looking for "killer applications". However, there are some applications and technologies on the horizon that could potentially provide useful services to users, although these are not yet well focussed or developed.

The availability of software is very patchy. The least widely available software are video/audio authorware, programmes for music composition, computer graphics and 3-D modelling.

The lack of a main actor   One of the weaknesses of the cultural market is the lack of a *main actor* in the exploitation and fruitful promotion of cultural products. We miss the presence of a *marketing manager*; the markets includes scientists, technicians and salesmen, but there is no one devoted to marketing the product, defining product specifications, tuning the product to user expectations and requirements.

Production,   Mature markets always involve at least three main actors: *production, mar-*
marketing and sales   *keting* and *sales*. Harmonious cooperation between them is a key factor in the success of the company. If one of these actors is missing, the circle is broken and some relevant input is lost. Without sales we do not have direct access to customers and feedback about products, customer expectations and satisfaction is lost.

Technologists and danger   To let technologists decide about user needs and requirements is a very risky approach: the statements "I know what they really need" or "they do not understand what they really need" are very common and dangerous.

Technicians and experts are always so involved, even emotionally, in their own work that is almost impossible for them to consider something to be a final product that is suitable for the market. They are always thinking that the next generation will be better and is therefore probably the right product, and so they never meet the market.

On the other hand, a proper organisation where sales people inform marketing managers about user requirements and expectations, and marketing managers define strategies and guidelines for actual and future products, will tend to produce the right product at the right time for the market.

Fig. 37.8

Culture and cultural heritage has incredible economic potential, surely enough to sustain the sector. Consider the incredible sales opportunities generated by the *Da Vinci Code* or *Alexander* phenomena and their follow-ups; these are able to attract customers and provide significant revenue to a broad market ranging from "cultural tourism" to merchandise.

One emerging service offered by mostly medium-sized companies involves providing *integral assistance* to cultural asset managers who wish to outsource activities. The integral service provider offers assistance and expertise in buying or selling artefacts, restoration, maintenance, safe storage, exploitation and rental of exhibits, among other services[48]. The question is: are these companies going to play the role of the main actor in this field?

An emerging business

37.10 The Art Market and Digital Media

There are at least two main factors affecting the use of interactive digital media in the art market. First, this technology is not yet fully accessible to authors and end-users. Second, and just as importantly, *digital art* or *computer art* is not yet a mature market standard.

However, it is worth noting that it took some time to find the proper formats and markets for some earlier technologies such as movies or photographs too. The acceptance of the movie format was initially aided by its similarity to the structures of books—the same linear structure in terms of time, (This of course ignores the use of flashbacks and other nonlinear tricks in movies) Photography replaced some types of paintings, such as portraits and visual documentation, and retained the important role of the author, just like in painting.

---

[48] For example Open Care in Italy, see: http://www.opencare.it.

Fig. 37.9 *neoart3*, a virtual museum for digital and virtual artefacts by Mario Taddei & Edoardo Zanon

Which market aspects influence the value of artefacts? Do we consider the economic value of a work of art the one reached during a Sotheby's auction?

Aspects influencing the value of an artefact

There are a number of different aspects that influence the value of the artefact:
- Number of "originals" created by the author[49]
- Intellectual property rights management
- Expected lifespan of the artefact
- How it is experienced (one-to-one, one-to-many, etc.)
- And last but not least, the "immaterial essence" of this type of art.

It was a long time after the initial work of Daguerre before photographers such as Ansel Adams[50] were considered to produce works of art that were suitable for inclusion in Sotheby's auctions. Should Henry Cartier Bresson's[51] shots become much more valuable if they only a limited number are made available or not? Negatives and original prints still somehow retain a closer link (perhaps due to their physicality) to the original scene than digital images.

The concept of "original"

When we use digital media we lose the unique physical nature of the artwork; we create a completely different class of objects from an ontological point of view. The copy is exactly the same as the original, so part of the problem is transferred to IPR management.

What about expected lifespan? Traditional artefacts, even those considered fragile or delicate, tend to last for a very long period of time, ideally indefinitely.

Digital objects seem to have timestamps and expiration dates. People do not expect a PC-based application to last forever, or consider DVDs to provide

---

49 Six to eight copies are still considered to be "originals" in the fields of sculpture or painting.
50 Ansel Adams: www.anseladams.com.
51 Fondation Henry Cartier-Bresson: http:\\www.henrycartierbresson.org.

eternal media. Technological obsolescence, physical obsolescence, media aging and other factors lead us to expect a limited digital life. Art is a long-lasting concept; a *pietà* is forever, as is Mozart's *Zauberflöte*.

Another property that influences value is the number of people that can potentially experience the artefact simultaneously: one person or many people. Interactive virtual reality is often limited to one main user and at least some passive partners that can share the experience. These are some reasons and factors that are probably stopping virtual reality from becoming a "front-line tendency" in the art world.

Fig. 37.10 *Tondo 2006* by Piero Fantastichini (Atelier in Nice; http://www.pierofantastichini.com)

38 Quality

Quality of electronic content is not easy to evaluate and measure. First of all we must adequately take into account different platforms and their related capabilities and aims; then we need to separately evaluate the quality of the pure content and that of the container.

Content and container

One of the potential starting points is to refer to ISO[52] norms on software quality, even though e-content products and services represent more than simply software.

In order to estimate multimedia products, we must extend our software evaluation criteria by taking into account the following:

Evaluation criteria

- Evaluation must not be biased by personal taste or specific attitudes (e.g. cutting edge technologies). We must refer to a method that is not influenced by the evaluator/s; that is as objective as possible.
- A clear metric must be defined; each criterion must be measured within a proper range with well-defined thresholds. The metric must define "what" and "how" to measure quality in the most accurate way. These criteria must be applied to both technical[53] aspects and different interaction and communication aspects[54].
- The "quality" of content or services must be considered, if requested, by specific panel experts. Evaluation criteria can vary from case to case; they can take into account the proper use of multimedia objects[55] and hyperlinks and/or the completeness of information and/or the ability to provide comprehensive background or context and/or the cultural added value.
- In order to rate the products a uniform score criterion is needed. At the end of the evaluation, single scores must be merged into one single index. This means we need a scoring system that permits an absolute rating. If the metric and threshold differs from criterion to criterion a weighted score may be used.

---

52 ISO (International Organization for Standardization): http://www.iso.ch.
53 Platform, technical quality of different media, compliance to standards, e.g. WAI SigACCESS, interoperability, etc.
54 Interaction design, accessibility, usability, etc.
55 Checking the technical quality of the medium used was covered in the previous point.

One potential side effect of the evaluation methods should be close cooperation between evaluators and developers during both the design and the development phases in order to improve the final result through assessment/feedback cycles.

Quality assessment

This means that both the rationale beyond the method, the criteria and the metrics must be exploited and included in the technical specifications. This kind of quality assessment must contribute to the final overall quality of the product by providing clear guidelines for analysis and testing tasks.

Absence of biases

From a practical point of view, the first requirement—an absence of biases—will be ensured by basing the method on different criteria and metrics. Some of the criteria used to evaluate applications should be:

Some criteria

- Quality and comprehensiveness of content
- Ease of use: functionality, navigation and orientation (usability—interaction design)
- Value added through interactivity and multimedia
- Attractiveness of design (aesthetic value of graphics/audio)
- Accessibility (e.g. according to the W3C, http://www.w3.org)
- Quality of craftsmanship (technical realisation)
- More specific criteria of evaluation (if any)
- ...

In addition, we can add some more criteria that focus on additional attributes, such as:
- Strategic importance of the product from a cultural and social point of view
- Multilinguism/different cultural models.

Not forgetting one of the most important checkpoints:
- Sustainability/quality of the market model.

If we consider the evaluation procedures to be part of the design phase, an objective evaluation of the economic value of the product is undoubtedly one of the best contributions to this phase.

Depending on the nature of the content and/or service, an additional parameter may be:
- Portability and technological updatability.

This last parameter measures the ability to migrate the product to new technological standards and formats.[56]

The economic dimension

It is often the case during multimedia development, and even more so when developing multimedia-based cultural products, that authors are so fixated on their enthusiasm for the cultural value of the product that the economic dimension is completely ignored.

---

56 Please refer to Chap. 19 Long Term Preservation of Digital Archives.

III Exploitation, Applications and Services

This has been one of the key problems encountered during the creation of some museum networks. While these are very attractive from a cultural point of view, they proved very hard to maintain—banners and online advertising did not generate enough revenue. Even market models based on subscriptions or e-commerce of images and reproductions did not succeed.

In some cases these businesses were reshaped into "museum Yellow Pages" supported solely by banners, while others attempted to maintain enhanced services by opening up the service to e-commerce, by offering books, cultural travels, merchandise, high-quality documentation and services[57].

Sound market models and business plans together with "swot"[58] analysis and other tools are good friends of eContent developers.

"Swot" analysis and other tools

Going back to the criteria, we should note that the different platforms and channels used will also influence the relevance or even the inclusion of some criteria.

Online products could take advantage of connectivity; interactions with *digital terrestrial television* (DTT) services must be metered differently to broadband applications. Computer games require an additional criterion: *playability*.

Lastly, when considering performance features of the product (enhancements or constraints), we need to distinguish between those that are market- or technology-related, which can rapidly disappear due to changes in the rules of the game[59], and those that are "absolute".

Market or technological constraints

Abbreviation	Name	Website
ANEE	Associazione Nazionale Editoria Elettronica	http://www.anee.it
SIAE	Società Italiana Autori ed Editori	http://www.siae.it
BVDW (formerly DMMV)	Bundersverband Digitale Wirtschaft	http://www.bvdw.org
AFEM	Association Française de l'Edition Multimédia (ex-AFEE)	http://www.afem.org
ASEDEM	Asociación Española de Empreseas de Multimedia	http://www.asedem.com
SIMA	Swiss Interactive Multimedia Association	http://www.sima.ch

Table 38.1 Some organisations associated with the field of (quality) multimedia

---

57 For example the Artbank Old Master website (http://www.artbank-oldmaster.com/), which provides the history of the auction prices related to a specific artefact upon payment.

58 Strengths, weaknesses, opportunities and threats.

59 Due to technological enhancements or revolutions or to dramatic changes in commercial policies.

Table 38.1 (*continued*) Some organisations associated with the field of (quality) multimedia

Abbreviation	Name	Website
BIMA	British Interactive Multimedia Association	http://www.bima.co.uk
AIMIA	Australian Interactive Multimedia Industry Association	http://www.aimia.com.au
AMC	Association for Multimedia Communications	http://www.amcomm.org
NBMA	North Bay Multimedia Association (California)	http://www.nbma.com
EADiM	European Academy of Digital Media	http://www.eadim.org
ICNM	International Centre for New Media	http://www.icnm.net

38.1 Affective Quality

"Affective" quality, mood, emotions, and feelings

While at first glance *affective* quality might not seem very applicable to interaction design and human computer interactions, it is an emerging attribute of digital products. Users do not always view technology completely rationally; in fact, emotions play an important but largely overlooked role in users' acceptance of technology (Zhang and Li 2005).

The term "affective" encompasses moods, emotions and feelings (Norman 2002)—the remit of the left side of the brain—which also influence our reflexes, perceptions, cognition and behaviour.

Affective quality can influences job satisfaction, decision-making behaviour and consumer shopping behaviour. The affective quality of a product may depend on its shape, colour, feel, or even just the feelings inspired by the product.

Consumer satisfaction and experience

New trends in consumer satisfaction have led to the idea of the consumer "experience" being a key factor. Consumers are looking for new experiences that can be shared with and recommended to relatives and friends, some of which are merely extensions of experiences that they have already had. In this way, the affective quality is ability of a product to affect human emotions.

There is no direct evidence that human–computer interactions are influenced by the affective/hedonic quality of the interface, and there is no direct relation of this quality to the perceived usability of the product. However, there is a long tradition, which probably started from the Ancient Greek motto "Καλός καί Αγαθός"[60], relating human "beauty and goodness" to quality or perfection

---

60 This means "beauty and goodness".

III Exploitation, Applications and Services

of design, such that beautiful things work better (Norman 2002), are easier to learn[61], influence our choices, and produce better results.

It is well known that affect and emotion play a significant role in design as well as usability, and that they, together with aesthetics, are instrumental to the creation of pleasurable products. The role of affect in design has already been mentioned in Chap. 12 Interaction Design. Design assumes a key role when the product has entered the mature phase of its lifecycle, which is when the mass market becomes less interested in pure performance.

Let's have a look at some of the key terms and criteria associated with this specific domain of quality evaluation. There are few data on whether or not *perceived affective quality* influences user perceptions of product usefulness and ease of use. The first key term is *perceived usefulness* (PU), which represents the improvement in job performance perceived by the user due to the utilisation of the product. A second key term is *perceived ease of use* (PEOU), which represents how easy the user believes that a particular system is to use. To some degree the PU and PEOU predict the user's acceptance and actual usage of the product.

Perceived usefulness

A third key term is the *core affect*[62], which is a neurophysiological state that is consciously accessible as a simple nonreflective feeling. The affective quality is then the ability to cause a change in the core affect of a potential user/buyer.

Core affect

Affective quality

As a result, a number of existing studies on user IT evaluation and acceptance underline that PU has a strong impact on *behaviour intention* (BI) to use IT; PEOU has an impact on PU; PEOU can have some impact on BI and BI is a strong indicator of actual use behaviour. *Perceived affective quality* (PAQ) directly influences both PU and PEOU in a positive way, so PAQ influences BI.

Behaviour intention

Some studies have already investigated the affective constructs and affective qualities associated with IT products (see Table 38.2).

Table 38.2

Study	IT and context	Affective construct	Affective quality/feature
Kim et al. (2003)	Home page	Secondary emotions	Shape, texture and colour of title, menu and main images
Mundorf et al. (1993)	Screen-based information services	Hedonic quality	Colour, graphs, music

---

61 Pleasing and attractive things, or things that are managed or presented in a pleasing and attractive manner, are easier to learn. This is the potential key to the success of edutainment and eContent in general.

62 Also known as mood, affect, feeling.

Table 38.2 (continued)

Study	IT and context	Affective construct	Affective quality/feature
Shenkman and Jonsson (2000)	Telecommunications, electronics or other companies' websites	First impression	Beauty, mostly illustrations versus mostly text, overview and structure
Tractinsky et al. (2000)	ATM machine	Perceived aesthetics	Layout
Van der Heijden (2003)	A generic portal website in Netherlands	Perceived visual attractiveness	Layout and colour

Case Study: Women in the Mediterranean Area

This project[63] is a clear example of the application of ICT to both cultural content and the field of inclusion actions. Today's great challenge is to encourage tolerance and peaceful coexistence of different cultural identities. Mutual knowledge and information is the foundation for a good relationship, since we are less likely to feel uncomfortable with or even threatened by things we don't know. Schools are key to whether this challenge is overcome, since they are the main crossing points between different cultures and people. Therefore, our future is strongly reliant on education at school.

The aim of this project is to set up a teaching path, based on multimedia content that can be accessed over the Internet or distributed to schools across the country.

Among several aspects of the different cultures, the project focuses on the female condition from both diachronic and synchronic perspectives within the different realities in which women in the Mediterranean area live and work. The main themes, which were chosen with the cooperation with experienced professors in anthropology, sociology, history, language and literature, law and ICT, are the use of the veil, the institution of marriage and the marriage ceremony, the dissolution of marriage, and the social and ethical values that characterise different ways of living in each country.

This kind of approach is very useful for promoting mutual knowledge in order to increase the value of similarities and positive differences.

---

63 By Rossana Valenti, Università Federico II, Naples, Italy (see http://www.donnamed.unina.it/).

This new teaching proposal, from a wide European and Mediterranean perspective, highlights the multiculturalism that has long been a historical tradition of this region. Studying the history of multiculturalism might help to correct the current pervading view of a "clash of cultures", which is reinforced by the images of violence (and related deaths) between cultures that we see in the media. Therefore, the different political and economic interests are hidden. In schools that attempt to teach principles and values that apply to all, multicultural teaching emphasises the fact that cultures are not absolutes; they change over time, losing and gaining new elements. The classic authors, who mediate between conflicting ideologies and provide wise advice, are centuries-old witnesses to multiple traditions, exchanges and merges of languages, cultures and identities in a process of continuous change.

The website associated with the project contains many entries. The main metaphor used for the organisation of the website is a magazine containing a series of subjects, where it is possible to delve deeply into each subject. Therefore, the structure comprises several themes, and historical ages are ignored, thus avoiding a restrictive chronological approach. The themes cover five main subjects related to female life:

- *The veiled body*. Two bodies face-to-face: a male one, glorified by classical art, looked at with admiration, and a female body, covered by a long dress and a veil typical of Muslin women. These contrasting images of the two bodies mark the starting point for the exploration of Mediterranean women.
- *The marriage ceremony*. What is a ceremony? What is the link between this word and terms like "liturgy", "holiday" and "rite"? Studying the etymologies of such words may help us to define their meaning.
- *Marriage as an institution*. In the last 40 years, in all European countries, social changes have greatly modified how marriage is perceived. Indeed, all of the countries have enacted radical reforms to family laws, thus modifying the principles by which relationships between husbands and wives, and between parents and their children are conducted.
- *The dissolution of marriage*. The choice of the term "dissolution" comes from the wish to analyse the multiple historical and social aspects associated with the severance of marriage, including both the similarities and the deep differences between various Mediterranean cultures in this respect.
- *The prospective of social and ethical values*. This section, which is still under development, stresses the social and cultural changes that are currently affecting the female condition. The stereotypes applied by the Western world to the Islamic world are examined, and new scenarios that call for new values and new roles for the women are predicted and outlined.

Using this kind of approach, the similarities between cultures are underlined rather than the differences and the distances between Mediterranean countries. On the website, each theme is structured such that a series of entries are shown on the left frame:

- An editorial introducing the theme
- History
- The words (the specific terms)
- The stories (interviews and literary passages)
- The news (including a selection of newspapers)
- The Italian laws (relating to each theme)
- Expert opinions
- Teaching tools.

The latter includes "learning paths" for the students, and a game played after learning material that is downloaded and assembled in class.

The different sections offer various kinds of learning tools that can be downloaded by the students and the teachers. Thematic learning paths include thoughts and documentation for the teachers; operating proposals include several kinds of drills, often with their solutions, for the students.

The game, *Itineraries in the Mediterranean*, involves moving along four different paths around the Mediterranean basin. The players must fulfil their itineraries and collect pictures of the countries that they pass through. Questions about geography, history, languages, culture and rites must be answered; these questions are related to the items covered on the website. All of the material, including the game board, the questions and the pictures, can be downloaded from the website.

Fig 38.1 Women in the Mediterranean Area

39 Conclusions and Future Trends

We have now reached the end of this book. We have travelled a long path, starting from early experiences in cultural data filing and the first attempts to use digital technology to both communicate cultural content and perform cultural education, and finally exploring current and predicted applications of ICT to cultural heritage.

The exploitation of multimedia communication, computer graphics, virtual reality and the Internet has significantly improved the use of information technology in the cultural field, potentially providing added value and useful services. It has been at least twenty years since ICT was first applied to the field of cultural heritage, and during this period of time many important players in both the "memory institutions" and the ICT community have invested a great deal of time and resources into creating pilot projects and applications. Some of the most significant experiences are outlined in the present publication. Some of them are described in case studies; others are just remarked upon or mentioned as suggested solutions.

Within the book we have addressed some fundamental questions. Do virtual museums really provide added value to end-users? Are museums, content providers and users ready and willing to use new technologies to explore cultural heritage? Do ICT tools really help content holders and/or end-users?

Fig. 39.1 ICT for Masses: The Manthan Award eContent for Development in India – created by the Digital Empowerment Foundation (www.manthanaward.net, www.difindia.net)

Shall we now try to provide some answers? Have we mastered the general framework? Is the necessary technological framework already in place?

Information and communications technologies should only be considered to be powerful tools for achieving important results; ICT tools will never compete with content and skills.

Technology is not a constraint: digital services, networking, wireless connections, instant communication, cooperative and knowledge management tools are more than enough to fulfil our needs. The challenge now is how to take advantage of these tools by channelling their use into creating true innovation. We must work out how to positively influence society by making use of new opportunities, and how to reverse the *digital divide* in order to create *digital opportunities*.

References

21 Content, Communication and Tools

M. Lunghi (ed.)(2007) Cultural heritage on line: The challenge of accessibility and preservation. Fondazione Rinascimento Digitale, Firenze

J.-P. Mohen, M. Menu, B. Mottin (2006) Mona Lisa: Inside the painting. Abrams, New York

A.M. Ronchi (2001b) Evoluzione delle tecniche di comunicazione alla luce delle nuove tecnologie informatiche. In: M.A. Crippa, C. Alessandri (eds.) I nuovi metodi di indagine e comunicazione della storia dell'architettura. Sinai Edizioni, Milano, pp. 45–53

A.M. Ronchi (2003a) Digital communication: the long way toward the proper format. In: Proc. Global Forum 2003, Rome, Italy, 6–7 November 2003 (see http://www.items.fr/IMG/doc/GF2003/Presentations%20GF03/Day%202/Session%206/RONCHI_GF2003.pdf)

A.M. Ronchi (2003b) On culture in a worldwide Information Society: Cultural diversity, technology and formats. Proc. CIDOC 2003, St. Petersburg, Russia, 1–7 Sept. 2003, pp 165–179 (see http://confifap.cpic.ru/upload/spb2004/reports/doklad_173.doc and http://cidoc2003.adit.ru/eng/default.asp)

22 Exploitation, Applications and Services;

23 Prioritisation in Digitalisation

Digicult Special Issues: http://www.digicult.info/pages/special.php

Digicult Technology Watch: http://www.digicult.info/pages/techwatch.php?PHPSESSID=bcdde8db2d6fd5b0324708ec13360305

Digicult Thematic Issues: http://www.digicult.info/pages/themiss.php

Eurobarometer: http://ec.europa.eu/public_opinion/index_en.htm

A. Granelli, F. Traclò (eds.)(2006) Innovazione e cultura. Il Sole 24 Ore, Milano

Lund principles: http://www.cordis.lu/ist/digicult/lund-principles.htm

MINERVA eC (the MINERVA Project was enlarged to MINERVA eC—MInisterial NEtwoRk for Valorising Activities in digitisation, eContentplus—supporting the European Digital Library in Oct. 2006): http://www.minervaeurope.org

24 Cataloguing Standards and Archiving Tools

Art & Architecture Thesaurus (AAT; from the J.P. Getty Information Institute): http://www.getty.edu/research/conducting_research/vocabularies/aat

M. Baca (ed.)(1995) Categories for the description of works of art (report of the Art Information Task Force). J.P. Getty Trust, Art History Information Program, Los Angeles, CA

D. Bearman (1987) Towards national information systems for archives and manuscript repositories: The NISTF papers, 1980–1984. Society of American Archivists, Chicago, IL

D. Bearman (1989) Archives and manuscript control with bibliographic utilities. Am. Archivist 52:26–39

D. Bearman (1990) Archives and museum data models and dictionaries (Tech. Rep. 10). Archives & Museum Informatics, Pittsburgh, PA

D. Bearman (1991a) Museum information standards: Progress and prospects. In: S.M. Spivak, K.A. Winsell (eds.) A sourcebook of standards information. G.K. Hall, Boston, MA, pp. 253–264

D. Bearman (1991b) Computer interchange of museum information. Bull. Am. Soc. Inform. Sci. 18(2):14–16

D. Bearman (1992a) Information exchange requirements of archives and museums. In: D.A. Roberts (ed.) Proc. Int. Conf. "Sharing the Information Resources of Museums", York, UK, 14–18 Sept. 1989

D. Bearman (1992b) CALS '91 and CIMI efforts. Paper distributed to CIMI Committee, Halifax, NS, Canada, 8 Jan. 1992

Bildarchiv Foto Marburg's image index of art and architecture: http://www.bildindex.de

Canadian Heritage Information Network (CHIN): http://www.chin.gc.ca

C.F. Cargill (1989) Information technology standardization: Theory, process and organizations. Digital Press, Bedford, MA

Categories for the Description of Works of Art (CDWA): http://www.getty.edu/research/conducting_research/standards/cdwa/definitions.pdf

E. Chouraqui (1973) The index and filing system used by the "Inventaire General des Monuments et des Richesses Artistiques de la France". Comput. Humanit. 7(5):273–285

W. Crawford (1984) MARC for library use: Understanding the USMARC formats. Knowledge Industry Publ., White Plains, NY

W. Crawford (1986) Technical standards: An introduction for librarians. Knowledge Industry Publ., White Plains, NY

Definition of the term "museum" by ICOM: http://icom.museum/statutes.html#2

R. Denenberg (ed.)(1990) Library Hi Tech Consec. Issue 32(8)

Extranet de l'Inventaire general du patrimoine culturel (France): http://www.culture.gouv.fr/culture/inventai/extranetIGPC/index.html

J.A. Fincher (1990) The ISO edi conceptual model activity and its relationship to OSI. Library Hi Tech 32(4):83–91

G. Geser et al. (2003) Towards a semantic web for heritage resources. DigiCULT Thematic Issue 3 (see http://www.digicult.info)

Getty Thesaurus of Geographic Names (TGN; from the J.P. Getty Information Institute): http://www.getty.edu/research/conducting_research/vocabularies/tgn

J. Henshall, S. Shaw (1988) OSI explained. Ellis Horwood, London

P. Homulos, C. Sutyla (1988) Information management in Canadian museums. Communications Canada, Ottawa, ON, Canada

Iconclass: http://www.iconclass.nl

Iconclass Libertas browser: http://www.iconclass.nl/libertas/ic?style=index.xsl

International Committee for Museum Documentation (CIDOC): http://cidoc.mediahost.org

Inventare General des Monumentes et Richesses Artistique: http://www.culture.gouv.fr/culture/bdd/index.html

ISBN (International Standard Book Number): http://www.isbn.org or http://www.isbn-international.org

Istituto Centrale per il Catalogo e la Documentazione (ICCD; Central Institute for Cataloguing and Documentation): http://www.iccd.beniculturali.it

Joconde: Catalogue des collections des musees de France: http://www.culture.gouv.fr/documentation/joconde/fr/apropos/presentation-joconde.htm

Learn about the Getty vocabularies (from the J.P. Getty Information Institute): http://www.getty.edu/research/conducting_research/vocabularies

D.P. Ledrick, M.B. Spring (1990) International standardized profiles. Comp. Stand. Interf. 11:95–103

Le portail de la Culture (France): http://www.culture.fr

C.A. Lynch (1990) Information retrieval as a network application. Library Hi Tech 32(4): 64–72

J. Moline (1991) Using standards to facilitate access and reuse of museum information. In: D. Bearman (ed.) Hypermedia and interactivity in museums. Archives & Museum Informatics, Pittsburgh, PA, pp 307–315

Museum Documentation Association (MDA): http://www.mda.org.uk

T. Oren (1990) Towards open hypertext: Requirements for distributed hypermedia standards. In: J. Moline, D. Benigni, J. Baronas (eds.) Proc. Hypertext Standardization Workshop, Gaithersburg, MD, 16–18 Jan. 1990 (NIST Publication 500-178)

J. Perkins (1990; 1991) Report of the First CIMI Meeting; Report of the Second CIMI Meeting. (Both unpublished)

J. Perkins (1991; 1992) CIMI News 1 (January 1991); 2 (August 1991); 3 (January 1992). Committee on Computer Interchange of Museum Information, Halifax, NS, Canada

J. Perkins (1992) The CIMI Standards Framework: A briefing paper on options for computer interchange of museum information. (Unpublished)

D.A. Roberts (ed.) Proc. Int. Conf. Collections Management for Museums, Cambridge, UK, 26–29 Sept. 1987

A.M. Ronchi (2001) Sistemi informativi multimediali per il patrimonio architettonico: i progetti BAA, SIRCoP e MIMS. In: Proc. "Un archivio per la città", Udine, Italy, 1–2 December 2000

C.M. Sperberg-McQueen, L. Burnard (eds.)(1990) Guidelines for the encoding and interchange of machine-readable texts (draft version 1.1). University of Virginia, Charlottsville, VA

L. Swain, P. Tallim (1990) X.400: The standard for message handling systems. Library Hi Tech 32(4):43–55

The CIDOC—Conceptual Reference Model (CIDOC CRM): http://cidoc.ics.forth.gr

Union List of Artists Names (ULAN; from the J.P. Getty Information Institute): http://www.getty.edu/research/conducting_research/vocabularies/ulan

Various authors (1989; 1990) Am. Archivist 52(4); 53(1) (these two issues are devoted to archival standards and have useful articles, a glossary, a checklist of standards, and a bibliography)

S. Weibel, J. Kunze, C. Lagoze, M. Wolfe (1998) Dublin Core metadata for resource discovery. RFC 2413 (see ftp://ftp.isi.edu/in-notes/rfc2413.txt)

25 Virtual Museum Networks

Art Museum Image Consortium (AMICO, 1997–2005): http://www.amico.org

G. Bernbom, D. Cromwell (1993) Data architecture in an open systems environment: http://www.educause.edu/ir/library/text/CEM9346.txt

Coalition for Networked Information (1994) Project CHIO: Cultural heritage information online: http://www.cni.org/pub/CIMI/project.CHIO.html

Consortium for the Computer Interchange of Museum Information (CIMI): http://www.cni.org/pub/CIMI

B. Davis, J. Trant (eds.)(1996) Introduction to multimedia in museums. ICOM Multimedia Working Group, Paris (see http://www.willpowerinfo.myby.co.uk/cidoc/introtomultimediamuseums.pdf)

G7 multimedia access to world cultural heritage (MOSAIC Consortium): http://mosaic.infobyte.it/project/wp1100/anx1.html

A. Granelli, F. Traclò (eds.)(2006) Innovazione e cultura. Come le tecnologie digitali potenzieranno la rendita del nostro patrimonio culturale. Il Sole 24 Ore Pirola, Milano

Information and documentation—Format for information exchange ISO 2709-1996: http://www.iso.org/iso/iso_catalogue/catalogue_tc/catalogue_detail.htm?csnumber=7675

Information Interchange Format ANSI Z39.2 (the basis for the MARC—machine-readable catalog—record, this standard specifies the requirements for a generalized interchange format that can be used for the communication of records in any media): http://www.niso.org/kst/reports/standards

International Standard Maintenance Agency Z39.50 (NISO Z39.50 or ISO 10162/63): http://www.loc.gov/z3950/agency

MOSAIC: http://www.arenotech.org/mosaic98_ingles/MOSAIC_ingles_998.htm

Museums and interpretation centers (on the Vilau website): http://www.vilaumedia.com/data/docs/pdf_museosen_68427.pdf

Museums around the world (ICOM): http://www.museum.ru/mirror/vlmp/world.html

Open Systems Interconnection (OSI; Webopedia definition): http://www.webopedia.com/TERM/O/OSI.html

A.M. Ronchi et al. (1998) Considerazioni riguardo il presente ed il futuro dei musei virtuali. Sistemi Intell. 2

A.M. Ronchi (1999a) Tecnologie e progetti per il patrimonio culturale. IF Riv. Fondazione IBM Italia 2:14–27

A.M. Ronchi (1999b) Distributed heterogeneous data base access and query: Centralised versus distributed contents. In: Proc. Int. Conv. DEXA QPMIDS "Distributed heterogeneous DB: interoperability of systems", Università di Firenze, Firenze, 3–4 Sept. 1999 (see http://www.ifs.tuwien.ac.at/dexa99/Conference-Workshop.html)

A.M. Ronchi (1999c) A framework for cultural co-operation in the field of new technologies in South-East Europe (final report of the MEDICI joint working session during the Council of Europe Meeting 1999): http://www.search.coe.int/texis/search

A.M. Ronchi (2000) Networked arts: basic issues and achievements. In: Proc. WWW9, Amsterdam, The Netherlands, 15–19 May 2000 (see http://www.medicif.org/Events/MEDICI_events/WWW9/Sessions/networked.htm)

A.M. Ronchi (2001a) Culture and digital media. In: Creative Digital Media: Keio University Center of Excellence International Symposium (CD-ROM). Keio University Press Inc., Tokyo, pp. 92–101

A.M. Ronchi (2001b) [ars.edu] European network of cultural heritage education centres. In: Proc. ICHIM 01 "Cultural Heritage and Technologies in the Third Millennium", Milano, Italy, 3–7 Sept. 2001 (see http://www.archimuse.com/publishing/ichim01_vol2/ronchi.pdf)

K.H. Veltman (1999) Digital reference rooms: Access to historical and cultural dimensions of knowledge: http://www.isoc.org/inet99/proceedings/2b/2b_1.htm

K.H. Veltman (2001) La crescita nel settore dei musei virtuali (Developments in virtual museums). In: Museo contro Museo. Le strategie, gli strumenti, I resultati. Giunti, Firenze, pp. 263–286 (see http://www.mmi.unimaas.nl/people/Veltman/veltmanarticles/2001%20Developments%20in%20Virtual%20Museums.pdf)

26 Unique Object ID

Comando Carabinieri Tutela Patrimonio Culturale: http://www.carabinieri.it/Internet/Cittadino/Informazioni/Tutela/Patrimonio+Culturale/Articolazione/06_TPC.htm

CoPAT (Council for the Prevention of Art Theft): http://www.museum-security.org/object-ID-and-Copat.htm#copat or http://www.buildingconservation.com/directory/ad230.htm

Object ID: http://www.object-id.com/about.html

Object ID by ICOM (a project developed through the collaboration of the museum community, police and customs agencies, the art trade, the insurance industry, and valuers of art and antiques; it helps to combat art theft by encouraging the use of the standard and by bringing together organisations around the world that can encourage its implementation): http://icom.museum/objectid

Stolen Works of Art (on the Interpol website): http://www.interpol.int/Public/WorkOfArt

R. Thornes (1997) Protecting cultural objects in the global Information Society: The making of object ID. J.P. Getty Trust, Los Angeles, CA (see http://icom.museum/objectid/final/index.html)

27 Different Channels and Platforms

ART+COM (company based in Berlin that researches and develops interactive media solutions for industry, culture and the research sector): http://www.artcom.de

M.C. Bueti, M. Obiso (2005) Ubiquitous network societies: the case of the Italian Republic. ITU, Geneva (see http://www.itu.int/osg/spu/ni/ubiquitous/Papers/UNSitalycasestudy.pdf)

Google Earth global geographical interface (offers maps and satellite images for complex or pinpoint regional searches): http://earth.google.com

TerraServer USA (formerly Microsoft TerraServer): http://terraserver-usa.com

28 Intellectual Property Rights

Agency for the Protection of Programs (Geneva): http://app.legalis.net/geneve/gb/indexgb1.htm

Agreement between the World Intellectual Property Organization and the World Trade Organization (1995): http://www.wipo.int/treaties/en/agreement/trtdocs_wo030.html

Berne Convention for the Protection of Literary and Artistic Works (Berne Convention 1886): http://www.wipo.int/treaties/en/ip/berne

D.M. Berry, M. McCallion (2005) Agenda: Time to examine the debates about the ownership of intellectual property. Eye Mag. 55 (see http://www.eyemagazine.com/opinion.php?id=117&oid=290)

CIAGP (Conseil International des Auteurs des Arts Graphiques et Plastiques et des Photographes): http://www.arsny.com/cisac.html

CISAC (Confédération Internationale des Sociétés d'Auteurs et Compositeurs): http://www.cisac.org

Convention establishing the World Intellectual Property Organization (1967, 1979): http://www.wipo.int/treaties/en/convention/trtdocs_wo029.html

Creative Commons information set and website: http://creativecommons.org

Digital Object Identifier System: http://www.doi.org

EC (2001) Directive 2001/29/EC of the European Parliament and of The Council 22 May 2001 on the harmonisation of certain aspects of copyright and related rights in the information society. Off. J. Eur. Commun. 167:10–19

Electronic Frontier Foundation (EFF): http://www.eff.org

International Convention for the Protection of Performers, Producers of Phonograms and Broadcasting Organizations (Rome Convention 1961): http://www.wipo.int/treaties/en/ip/rome/trtdocs_wo024.html

Legal Advisory Board (LAB, on the Information Society website): http://ec.europa.eu/archives/ISPO/legal/en/lab/labdef.html

Main Italian regulations: Law no. 633/1941; Law 18 August 2000, no. 248, art. 2575/2594 codice civile; Decreto Legislativo 2 Febbraio 2001, no. 95

Multimedia Committee of Japan's Institute of Intellectual Property (MITI): http://www.japaninc.com/cpj/magazine/issues/1995/jun95/06piracy.html

Multimedia Super Corridor (MSC): http://www.msc.com.my

A. Nimus (2006) Copyright, copyleft and the creative anti-commons: http://subsol.c3.hu/subsol_2/contributors0/nimustext.html

OCCAM–UNESCO observatory: http://www.occam.org

Rights for Electronic Access to and Dissemination of Information (READI): http://www.cni.org/projects/READI

P. Samuelson (2006) Copyrighting standards: Should standards be eligible for copyright protection? Commun. ACM 49(6)

What is copyleft? (author: R. Stallman): http://www.gnu.org/copyleft

World Intellectual Property Organisation (WIPO): http://www.wipo.int/portal/index.html.en

29 Technology and Privacy

P.E. Agre, M. Rotenberg (1999) Technology and privacy: The new landscape. MIT Press, Cambridge, MA (see http://polaris.gseis.ucla.edu/pagre/landscape.html)

Intel POLS (Privacy-Observant Location System): http://pols.sourceforge.net

Italy's new data protection code (Il Garante della protezione dei dati personali): http://www.garanteprivacy.it/garante/navig/jsp/index.jsp or http://www.garanteprivacy.it/garante/document?ID=1219452&DOWNLOAD=true

Joint Supervisory Authority: http://www.schengen-jsa.dataprotection.org

G.T. Marx (1990) Privacy and technology. The World and I Sept. 1990 (see http://web.mit.edu/gtmarx/www/privantt.html)

V. Otsason, A. Varshavsky et al. (2005) Accurate GSM indoor localization. In: M. Beigl et al. (eds.): Proc. UbiComp 2005: Ubiquitous computing (Tokyo, Japan, 11–14 Sept. 2005). Springer, Berlin, 3660:141–158

RemoteSensing.org (website that hosts and supports various open source software projects related to remote sensing, GIS, mapping and advanced image processing; see the project links for a list of projects, their associated webpages and download areas): http://www.remotesensing.org/

Schengen Information System (SIS): http://www.garanteprivacy.it/garante/doc.jsp?ID=1042728#uk

F. Stajano (2005) RFID is X-ray vision. Commun. ACM 48(9)A. Varshavsky, M.Y. Chen et al. (2006) Are GSM phones THE solution for localization?: http://www.stanford.edu/~haehnel/papers/100620061635_346.pdf

30 Usability, Accessibility and Platforms

Ars Electronica Center (Linz): http://www.aec.at/de/index.asp

Bridging the island of the colourblind (author: Adam Montandon): http://www.adam-montandon.com/index.php/2008/03 and http://www.toptalent.europrix.org/tta05/2004/8030_16.html

Human Computer Interaction Laboratory (University of Maryland): http://www.cs.umd.edu/hcil

MIT MediaLab: http://www.media.mit.edu

Nielsen Norman Group: http://www.nngroup.com

S. Pemberton (2005) Usability, accessibility and markup: http://www.w3.org/2005/Talks/11-steven-usability-accessibility

The Human Interface Technology Lab (HITLab, University of Washington): http://www.hitl.washington.edu/home

Usability.gov (official U.S. Government website managed by the U.S. Department of Health and Human Services): http://www.usability.gov

Webusability: accessibility and usability services: http://www.usability.com.au/index.cfm

31 Content Repackaging

S. Adler (2001) Extensible Stylesheet Language (XSL) version 1.0 (W3C recommendation): http://www.w3.org/TR/xsl

A. Borning, R. Lin, K. Mariott (2000) Constraint-based document layout for the Web. Multimedia Syst. 8(3)

C. Jacobs, W. Li et al. (2003) Adaptive grid-based document lay out. ACM Trans. Graph. 22(3)

C. Jacobs, W. Li et al. (2004) Adaptive document layout. Commun. ACM 47(8)

XHTML 1.0—The Extensible HyperText Markup Language (Second Edition): http://www.w3.org/TR/xhtml1

XHTML.org (website that provides information related to XHTML): http://www.xhtml.org

XHTML tutorial: http://www.w3schools.com/xhtml

32 Fruition of Cultural Content

B. Collins (1993) From ruins to reality: The Dresden Frauenkirche. IEEE Comp. Graph. Appl. 13(6):13–15

33 Cultural Tourism

All Media website: http://www.allmedia.it

F. Antinucci (2005) Comunicare nel museo. Editori Laterza, Roma

F. Antinucci (2007) Musei virtuali. Come non fare innovazione tecnologica. Editori Laterza, Roma

ARCHEOGUIDE (will build a system providing new ways of accessing information at cultural heritage sites in a compelling, user-friendly way through the use of advanced IT, including augmented reality, 3D-visualization, mobile computing, and multi-modal interaction): http://archeoguide.intranet.gr/index.htm

Arianna (video guide): http://www.ariannaguide.com

Ars Electronica Center (Linz): http://www.aec.at/de/index.asp

M. Bergamasco, A. Dettori et al. (2003) The CREATE (Constructivist Mixed Reality for Design, Education, and Cultural Heritage) project: Mixed reality for design, education, and cultural heritage with a constructivist approach: http://ieeexplore.ieee.org/iel5/8784/27815/01240721.pdf or http://cordis.europa.eu/data/PROJ_FP5/ACTIONeqDndSESSIONeq112422005919ndDOCeq499ndTBLeqEN_PROJ.htm

B. Britton (1995) The Lascaux Cave in virtual reality: http://www.mediamente.rai.it/mmold/english/bibliote/biografi/b/britton.htm

Cappella Scrovegni Wiegand Multimedia Room: http://www.padovanet.it/salamultimediale/index.htm

Cave of Lascaux: http://www.culture.gouv.fr/culture/arcnat/lascaux/en

C. Christodoulopoulou, J. Garofalakis, T. Giannakoudi, A. Koskeris (2006) Innovative ICT applications to support the tourism sector of Ionian

Islands: cc.europa.eu/regional_policy/conferences/od2006/doc/articles/koskeris_article.pdf

Cité des Sciences et de l'Industrie: http://www.cite-sciences.fr/english/indexFLASH.htm

B. Collins (1993) From ruins to reality—The Dresden Frauenkirche. IEEE Comput. Graph. Appl. 13:13–15

Council of Europe (1999) Digital culture in Europe: A selective inventory of centres of innovation in the arts and new technologies. Council of Europe Publishing, Paris

Council of Europe (2001) New information technologies and the young. Council of Europe Publishing, Paris

CyberCity Berlin (1995, ART+COM project): http://netzspannung.org/cat/servlet/CatServlet?cmd=netzkollektor&subCommand=showEntry&entryId=113713&lang=en

Ename 974 website (Ename is a unique archaeological site where a fragment of the medieval world has been uncovered and preserved): http://www.ename974.org/Eng/pagina/index.html

Eternal Egypt (from Egyptian Ministry of Culture in cooperation with IBM): http://www.eternalegypt.org

Exploratorium—the museum of science, art and human perception: http://www.exploratorium.edu

F. Fischnaller (ed.)(2006) eART società e democrazia nell'era della rete. Editori Riuniti, Roma

Foundation of the Hellenic World (a foundation aiming to promote historic, educational and social activities so that modern thought can be inspired by the Hellenic spirit): http://www.fhw.gr/index_en.html

L. Genevriez (1991) Cluny Abbey digital reconstruction: http://www.mediaport.net/CP/CyberScience/BDD/fich_054.en.html

J.G.M. Gonçalves, V. Sequeira (2001) 3D reconstruction applied to virtual heritage and cultural conservation. In: Proc. Int. Cultural Heritage Informatics Meeting (ICHIM) '01, Milano, Italy, 3–7 Sept. 2001 (see http://www.archimuse.com/publishing/ichim01_vol2/goncalves.pdf)

Hermitage: http://www.hermitage.ru

HistoryWired—A Few of Our Favorite Things (an experimental program that allows you to take a virtual tour of selected objects from the vast collections of the National Museum of American History): http://historywired.si.edu

Human Computer Interaction Laboratory (University Maryland): http://www.cs.umd.edu/hcil

INFOBYTE S.p.A.: http://www.infobyte.it

Invisible Shape of Things Past (1995, ART+COM project): http://www.artcom.de/index.php?option=com_acprojects&page=6&id=26&Itemid=144&details=0&lang=en

Leonardo da Vinci (on Leonardo 3 website): http://www.leonardo3.net

Louvre: http://www.louvre.fr

Louvre educational resources: http://www.louvre.edu

R. Makkuni (1998) The Crossings Project. Xerox PARC, Palo Alto, CA (see http://www.sacredworld.com)

Metropolitan Museum of Art: http://www.metmuseum.org

MIT MediaLab: http://www.media.mit.edu

A. Mulrenin, G. Geser (2002) DigiCULT report: Technological landscapes for tomorrow's cultural economy: Unlocking the value of cultural heritage. European Commission (Directorate General for the Information Society), Brussels

Museo Nacional del Prado: http://www.museodelprado.es/index.php?id=49&L=5

O. Odegard (1994) Virtual Viking village: http://heim.ifi.uio.no/~sigar/vroslo/vr.oslo.program.html

Paris Ville Romaine: http://www.paris.culture.fr/en

Phone Guide (mobile phone enabled museum guidance): http://www.uni-weimar.de/medien/ar/PhoneGuide/index.htm

Revealing things (a Smithsonian Without Walls project, director: J. Gradwhol): http://www.si.edu/ripley/eap/sww.htm

A.M. Ronchi (1997) Introduction to digital reconstructions of cultural heritage. In: D. Bearman, J. Trant (eds.) Museum interactive multimedia 1997: cultural heritage systems design and interfaces. Selected papers from ichim97. Archives & Museum Informatics, Paris (see http://conference.archimuse.com/biblio/introduction_to_digital_reconstructions_of_cultural_0)

A.M. Ronchi (2000a) Il sistema informativo a supporto della conservazione programmata. In: Polo Regionale della Carta del Rischio del patrimonio culturale. Regione Lombardia Istituto Centrale per il Restauro, Milano

A.M. Ronchi (2000b) Managing monuments: ICT Tools. In: First Int. Conf. Monumentenwacht, Amsterdam, 15–16 Sept. 2000 (see http://www.monumentenwacht.be/nl/uploads/b180.pdf)

A.M. Ronchi (2001a) Evoluzione delle tecniche di comunicazione alla luce delle nuove tecnologie informatiche. In: M.A. Crippa, C. Alessandri (eds.) I nuovi metodi di indagine e comunicazione della storia dell'architettura. Edizioni Sinai, Milano, p. 45, 53

A.M. Ronchi (2001b) Culture and digital media. In: Creative Digital Media: Keio University Center of Excellence International Symposium (CD-ROM). Keio University Press Inc., Tokyo, pp. 92–101

A.M. Ronchi (2001c) [ars.edu] European network of cultural heritage education centres. In: Proc. ICHIM 01 "Cultural Heritage and Technologies in the Third Millennium", Milano, Italy, 3–7 Sept. 2001 (see http://www.archimuse.com/publishing/ichim01_vol2/ronchi.pdf)

A.M. Ronchi (2006) New technologies and art dissemination (workshop at the Beijing Museum of Natural History, 15–19 June 2006): http://www.leonardonline.info/rivista/7_7_2006/doc/N7_A2ApprVirtual_Museums_China_sistemato.pdf

B. Shneiderman (updated by C. Plaisant, 2008) Treemaps for space-constrained visualization of hierarchies: http://www.cs.umd.edu/hcil/treemap-history

SIBA Coordination (2002) Carpiniana: A virtualized Byzantine crypt (DVD). SIBA Coordination, Lecce (ISBN 8883050053)

SmartMoney Map of the Market: http://www.smartmoney.com/marketmap

H. Tardif (1993) Liaison de télévirtualité par Numeris entre Paris et Monaco. In: Actes Imagina 93, Monte Carlo, Feb. 1993, p. 91

The First Emperor China's Terracotta Army: http://www.britishmuseum.org/whats_on/all_current_exhibitions/the_first_emperor.aspx

The Human Interface Technology Lab (HITLab, University of Washington): http://www.hitl.washington.edu/home

The National Gallery: http://www.nationalgallery.org.uk

The Smithsonian Institution: http://www.si.edu

Uffizi Gallery: http://www.uffizi.com

V. Valzano, A. Bandiera, J.-A. Beraldin et al. (2003) Carpiniana: A virtualized Byzantine crypt. In: Proc. EVA 2003 Conf., Florence, Italy, 24–28 March 2003, pp. 169–173

Vatican Museums: http://www.vatican.va

K.H. Veltman (1996) SUMS (System for Universal Media Searching). SUMS Corporation, Toronto (see http://www.sumscorp.com)

K.H. Veltman (1997) Frontiers in electronic media. ACM Int. 4(4):32–64 (see http://delivery. acm.org/10.1145/260000/259353/p32-veltman.pdf?key1=259353&key2=3670700021&c oll=portal&dl=ACM&CFID=4847400&CFTOKEN=67787081)

K.H. Veltman (2000) Frontiers in conceptual navigation for cultural heritage. Ontario Library Association, Toronto (see http://www.mmi.unimaas.nl/people/Veltman/books/2000%20 Frontiers%20book%20March%202004.pdf)

34 Games and Edutainment Applications

F. Bellotti, R. Berta, A. De Gloria, M. Margarone (2003) MADE: developing edutainment applications on mobile computers. Comput. Graph. 27(4):617–634 (see: http://www.science-direct.com/science?_ob=ArticleURL&_udi=B6TYG-49036X1-3&_user=2620285&_rdoc=1&_fmt=&_orig=search&_sort=d&view=c&_acct=C000058180&_version=1&_urlVersion=0&_userid=2620285&md5=0824314e074a36ef2fe9450b9bcb8796)

China: The Forbidden City (1998, Canal+Multimédia, Cryo Interactive Entertainment, Réunion des Musées Nationaux): http://www.mobygames.com/game/china-the-forbidden-city

A. Damala, H. Kockelkorn (2006) A taxonomy for the evaluation of mobile museum guides: http://delivery.acm.org/10.1145/1160000/1152283/p273-damala.pdf?key1=1152283&key 2=2405940021&coll=GUIDE&dl=GUIDE&CFID=12483301&CFTOKEN=79267296

Egypt 1156 B.C.: Tomb of the Pharaoh (1997, Canal+Multimédia, Cryo Interactive Entertainment, Réunion des Musées Nationaux): http://www.mobygames.com/game/egypt-1156-bc-tomb-of-the-pharaoh

Egypt II: The Heliopolis Prophecy (2000, Cryo Interactive Entertainment, DreamCatcher Interactive Inc.): http://www.mobygames.com/game/egypt-ii-the-heliopolis-prophecy

J.L. Encarnação (2007) Edutainment and serious games—Games move into professional applications: http://www2.acae.cuhk.edu.hk/~edutainment2007/plenary%20talk1.pdf

Gulliver's World—A multimedia theatre (Ars Electronica Futurelab): http://www.aec.at/en/futurelab/project.asp?iProjectID=12800

LibroVision—Gesture controlled virtual book (Ars Electronica): http://www.aec.at/en/futurelab/project.asp?iProjectID=12339

Rome: Caesar's Will (2000, Montparnasse Multimedia): http://www.mobygames.com/game/rome-caesars-will

S. Sauer, S. Göbel (2003) Focus your young visitors: Kids innovation fundamental changes in digital edutainment: http://www.archimuse.com/mw2003/papers/sauer/sauer.html

F. Tinelli (2001) The RENAISSANCE project: A virtual journey in a Renaissance court: http://www.cultivate-int.org/issue3/renaissance

Versailles 1685: A Game of Intrigue (1997, Cryo Interactive Entertainment, Réunion des Musées Nationaux): http://www.mobygames.com/game/versailles-1685/release-info

Versailles II: Testament of the King (2002, Cryo Interactive Entertainment, Réunion des Musées Nationaux): http://www.mobygames.com/game/versailles-ii-testament-of-the-king

35 Hands-On and Interactive Museums;

36 Educational Market

Ars Electronica Center (Linz, Austria): http://www.aec.at

ART+COM (Berlin, Germany): http://www.artcom.de

Cité des Sciences et de l'Industrie (La Villette, Paris, France): http://www.cite-sciences.fr

Città della Scienza (Naples, Italy): http://www.cittadellascienza.it

Ciutat de les Arts i les Ciències (Valencia, Spain): http://www.cac.es

Codex on Flight (on the Leonardo 3 website): http://www.leonardo3.net/leonardo/home_eng.htm

DisneyQuest (Orlando, FL, USA): http://disneyworld.disney.go.com/wdwi/en_GB/entertainment/entertainmentDetail?id=DisneyQuestIndoorInteractiveThemeParkEntertainmentPage

Epcot Center (Orlando, FL, USA): http://disneyworld.disney.go.com/wdwi/en_GB/parks/parkLanding?id=EPLandingPage

Exploratorium (San Francisco, CA, USA): http://www.exploratorium.edu

Futuroscope (Poitiers, France): http://www.futuroscope.fr

Heureka (Finnish Science Center in Vantaa, Finland): http://www.heureka.fi

Inventure Place—National Inventors Hall of Fame (Akron, OH, USA): http://www.invent.org

Jurascopes exhibit at the Berlin Museum of Natural History (2007, ART+COM project): http://www.artcom.de/index.php?option=com_acprojects&page=6&id=59&Itemid=144&details=0&lang=en

Liberty Science Center (Jersey City, NJ, USA): http://www.lsc.org

Mobile Learning Engine: http://mle.sourceforge.net/demo.php

Museu de la Ciència de la Fundaciò "La Caixa" ("Cosmocaixa"; Barcelona, Spain): http://www.cosmocaixa.com

Museo Nazionale del Cinema (Turin, Italy): http://www.museonazionaledelcinema.org/en/cover_en.php

Museum Arbeitswelt Steyr—working_world.net (Ars Electronica): http://www.aec.at/en/futurelab/project.asp?iProjectID=13474

National Museum of Emerging Science and Innovation (Tokyo, Japan): http://www.miraikan.jst.go.jp

newMetropolis (now NEMO) Science & Technology Centre (Amsterdam, The Netherlands): http://www.e-nemo.nl

New York Hall of Science (New York, USA): http://www.nyhallsci.org or http://www.try-science.org

Pacific Science Center (Seattle, WA, USA): http://www.pacsci.org

Sacred World Foundation: http://www.sacredworld.com/

Smithsonian (Washington, DC, USA): http://www.si.edu

Sony Wonder Technology Lab (New York, USA): http://sonywondertechlab.com

Tech Museum of Innovation (San Jose, CA, USA): http://www.thetech.org

The Exploratory (science centre in Bristol, UK): http://www.exploratory.org.uk

The Science of Aliens (2005, ART+COM project): http://www.artcom.de/index.php?lang=en&option=com_acprojects&id=43&Itemid=144&page=6

Wellcome Wing Project at the Science Museum (London, UK): http://www.sciencemuseum. org.uk/about_us/doing_business_with_us/corporate_and_private_events/venues/well-come_wing.aspx

Virtual Codex Atlanticus (on the Leonardo 3 website): http://www.leonardo3.net/Atlantico/ index_eng.htm

Virtual Heritage Laboratory (CNR, Rome, Italy): http://www.itabc.cnr.it/VHLab

37 Culture Counts

BDRC Ltd. (2001) The development of broadband access platforms in Europe: Technologies, services, markets. European Commission (Directorate General Information Society), Brussels

Council of Europe (2000) Maximising the educational and cultural potential of new information technologies. Council of Europe Publishing, Paris

Council of Europe (2001a) Digital culture in Europe. Council of Europe Publishing, Paris

Council of Europe (2001b) New information technologies and the young. Council of Europe Publishing, Paris

EC (2000) eEurope—An Information Society for all (Communication on a Commission Initiative for the Special European Council of Lisbon, 23 and 24 March 2000). European Communities, Brussels

EITO-EEIG (2004) European information technology observatory 2004. EITO-EEIG, Frankfurt

P. Fantastichini (2006) Tondo: http://www.pierofantastichini.com

French Ministry of Culture and Communication (2001) Les vieilles pierres valent de l'or. J. Dimanche, 11 February 2001

X. Greffe (2002) La valorisation économique du patrimoine. Ministère de la Culture et de la Communication, Dep et à la Dapa, Paris

Hackers websites: http://www.blackhat.com, http://www.ccc.de, http://www.defcon.org, http://www.hack.lu, http://www.whatthehack.org

IST Advisory Group (2003) Ambient intelligence: from vision to reality (for participation—in society and business; draft report). European Commission, Brussels (see ftp://ftp.cordis. europa.eu/pub/ist/docs/istag-ist2003_draft_consolidated_report.pdf)

Italian Broadband Task Force (2003) About broadband in Italy. Ministry of Communications and Ministry for Innovation and Technologies, Rome (see http://www.fub.it/it/pubblica-zioni/dossier or http://www.fub.it/it/pubblicazioni/quadernitelema or http://www.fub.it/it/ osservatori/rapporti)

L. Jeffrey (2001) Vital links for a knowledge culture. Council of Europe Publishing, Paris

E. Liikanen (2001) Towards the knowledge-based economy and society: http://europa.eu/ rapid/pressReleasesAction.do?reference=SPEECH/01/603&format=HTML&aged=0&la nguage=EN&guiLanguage=en

R. Mason (2005) Economics and historic preservation: A guide and review of the literature. The Brookings Institution, Washington, DC

MCC (2003) Culture et development, No 141. Ministere de la Culture et du Communication (MCC), Direction de l'administration générale, Département des études et de la prospective, Paris

References 449

S. Narverud, R.C. Ready (2002) Valuing cultural heritage. Edward Elgar, Cheltenham, UK (ISBN 1-84064-079-0) X. Greffe (2002) La valorisation économique du patrimoine (MCC/DAPA report). Ministère de la culture et de la communication (MCC), Paris

T.M. Nypan (2005) Cultural heritage monuments and historic buildings as value generators in a post-industrial economy. Directorate for Cultural Heritage, Oslo, Norway (see http://www.nba.fi/tiedostot/b425fd75.doc)

Office of Strategic Planning and Policy Analysis and International Bureau (2003) Broadband internet access in OECD countries: A comparative analysis (staff report). OECD, Paris (see http://www.caltelassn.com/reports/BroadbandOECD7Oct03.pdf)

OpenCare (global services for art and museums): http://www.opencare.it/2006/index.html

A.M. Ronchi (2001) Business opportunities from cultural heritage. In: Proc. MEDICI Panel at CeBIT 2001, Hannover, Germany, 21–28 March 2001 (see http://www.medicif.org/Events/MEDICI_events/Cebit2001/Ronchi.htm)

A.M. Ronchi (2003a) On culture in a worldwide Information Society: Cultural diversity, technology and formats. In: Proc. CIDOC 2003, St. Petersburg, Russia, 1–7 Sept. 2003, pp. 165–179 (see confifap.cpic.ru/upload/spb2004/reports/doklad_173.doc)

A.M. Ronchi (2003b) MEDICI Framework and infopoverty. In: A Regional Workshop on Human Security and Local Initiatives in Development, International Center, Chiang Mai University, Chiang Mai, Thailand, 5–7 Dec. 2003 (see http://coe21-policy.sfc.keio.ac.jp/ja/event/20031205.html)

A.M. Ronchi (2003c) Heritage, identity and education. In: UNESCO World Summit on the Information Society, Geneva, Switzerland, 9–13 Dec. 2003 (see http://www.wsis.org)

D. Tapscott (1999) Growing up digital: The rise of the Net Generation. McGraw-Hill, New York

38 Quality

ArtBank Old Master (provides the auction price history of a

specific artefact for a fee): http://www.artbank-oldmaster.com

CHI 97 electronic publications (tutorials): http://www.acm.org/sigchi/chi97/proceedings/tutorial

Copyright Progetto Manuzio: http://www.liberliber.it/progetti/manuzio/index.htm

Glossary of CD and DVD technologies: http://www.cd-info.com/tech/index.html

Glossary of CD and DVD technologies (at Webopedia): http://www.webopedia.com/DidYou-Know/Hardware_Software/2003/DVDFormatsExplained.asp

D.S. Hands (2004) A basic multimedia quality model. IEEE Trans. Multimed. 6(6):806–816 (see http://ieeexplore.ieee.org/iel5/6046/29822/01359861.pdf)

ISO (International Organization for Standardization): http://www.iso.ch

Multimedia authoring web: http://www.mcli.dist.maricopa.edu/authoring/index.html

Multimedia glossary: http://www.multimediaglossary.net

Multimedia glossary (at UCSC): http://media.ucsc.edu/glossary.html

MultiMediator (Canadian multimedia guide): http://www.multimediator.com

New Media Links (Toronto): http://www.newmedialinks.com/index.html

D.A. Norman (2002) Emotions in design: attractive things work better. Interactions Mag. IX(4):36–42 (see http://delivery.acm.org/10.1145/550000/543435/p36-norman.pdf?key1=543435&key2=7901240021&coll=GUIDE&dl=GUIDE&CFID=12367524&CFTOKEN=56179308)

useit.com (Jakob Neilsen's column on Web usability): http://www.useit.com

W3C quality assurance tools: http://www.w3.org/QA/Tools

W3Schools: Web quality—Standards: http://www.w3schools.com/quality/quality_standards.asp

Women in the Mediterranean area (project leader: R. Valenti): http://www.donnamed.unina.it

P. Zhang, N. Li (2005) The importance of affective quality. Commun. ACM 48(9):105–108 (see http://melody.syr.edu/pzhang/publications/CACM_04_Zhang_Li_ImportanceOfAffectiveQuality.pdf or http://delivery.acm.org/10.1145/1090000/1081997/p105-zhang.html?key1=1081997&key2=5590240021&coll=GUIDE&dl=GUIDE&CFID=12367160&CFTOKEN=88950760

Subject Index

3D
- Glyph, Anaglyph   45, 116
- Threedimensional   115, 124, 365

A

access
- accessibility   186, 199, 256, 319
- electronic access   XV, 295, 415
- free access   287, 289
- information access   31
- Internet access   XV, 415, 418
- multimedia access   XII, 275
- public access   XVIII, 24, 25, 421
- universal access   XI, XVI, 4, 296, 415

added value   6, 21, 25, 164, 238, 250, 350
- added value application   66, 329
- added value chain   13, 34, 300, 421
- added value service   9, 35, 190, 369

AMICO   271, 440

archaeology   17, 257, 340, 414
- archaeological   18, 45, 242, 254, 350, 361, 365, 371

B

briefing
- briefing area   393
- briefing session   167

C

Canadian Heritage Information Network (CHIN)   73, 252, 271

catalogue   61, 252, 266, 271, 277, 314, 332, 368

CIDOC Conceptual Reference Model (CRM)   255, 256, 346, 439

classification   17, 129, 183, 197, 237, 240, 263, 334

Coalition for Networked Information (CHIO)   271, 440

Computer Interchange of Museum Information (CIMI)   271, 440

conservation/preservation
- conservation/preservation of artefacts   203, 243, 245, 361, 386, 400

context, contextual   3, 21
- contextualisation   351
- spatial context   22, 330, 357

D

dark ride   166, 167

Deutsches Museum   380

digital
- digital actors   65
- digital audio   85, 156, 320, 367
- digital communication   21, 33, 414
- digital content   3, 30, 156, 203, 337, 369, 390, 418
- digital convergence   40, 64, 420
- digital divide   XIV, 5, 35, 64, 302, 417, 436
- digital duplicate   XIV
- digital heritage   19
- digital image   84, 92, 332, 365
- digital landscape   IX
- digital library   243, 259
- digital literacy   14
- digital media   13, 21, 69, 203, 249, 421

Subject Index   453

- digital movie   332, 341, 396
- digital music   288, 300, 388
- digital objects   22, 81, 178, 211, 311, 424
- digital opportunities   5, 436
- digital originals   81, 207, 249, 404
- digital preservation   82, 215, 240
- digital signature   211, 299, 310
- digital storytelling   160, 327, 396, 398
- digitisation   XIV, 81, 94, 237, 249, 326, 402
Disney Quest   126, 166

E
economics   405, 410
edutainment   155, 157, 375
eInclusion   XVIII, 7, 419
eLearning   395
enhanced reality   22, 131, 210, 365
exploitation   238, 245, 287, 294, 404, 413, 422
Exploratorium   179, 380, 445

F
force feedback   51, 102, 122, 129, 163, 355

G
games   70, 102, 126, 155, 210, 327, 375, 429
- serious games   157, 395
- simulation games   173, 177
Getty, J. P.
- Getty Information Institute   279
- Getty Thesaurus of Geographic Names (TGN)   438
- J. Paul Getty Trust & College Art Association   256

H
haptic
- haptic device   163
- haptic feedback   102
- haptic interface   102, 355
- haptic perception   318

Hermitage   77, 334, 398
hypermedia   40, 68, 189, 210, 325, 330
hypertext   55, 62, 188, 324, 342, 344

L
Lascaux Cave   361
laser   118
- laser camera   98
- laser printer   105, 323
- laser scanning   94, 98, 327, 362
- laser show   179
Louvre Museum, Musée du Louvre, Louvre   334, 398, 445

M
market
- marketing   143, 181, 364, 403, 411, 422
- market models   6, 63, 239, 246, 273, 288, 401, 429
- marketplace   42, 175, 289, 359, 406
mobile
- mobile commerce   419
- mobile content   11, 178, 397
- mobile learning   397
- mobile phone   35, 81, 107, 143, 178, 319, 397
- mobile platform   339
- mobile services   328
MOSAIC
- MOSAIC (Browser)   62
- MOSAIC (Museum Over Stated and Virtual Culture)   271, 273, 336
motion capture   103
Museum Computer Network (MCN)   271

N
National Gallery   99, 398, 446
native   81, 82, 110, 271
- digital native / native digital   83, 396

network, networked
- digital network   5, 311
- human network   14, 289
- museums network   269, 273, 336, 429
- network technologies   61
- neural network   163, 175, 366
- sub network   61

O
ontology   255
- ontology web language (OWL)   192

P
Pacific Science Center   448
Pompei   XV
Prado Museum   398, 446

Q
quality content   9, 27, 69, 239, 322, 421

R
rendering
- fur rendering   118
- image-based rendering   21, 103, 118, 326
- photorealistic rendering   146, 355
- volume rendering   332
RFID radiofrequency identification   35, 183, 314
- passive RFID   183

S
satellite   6, 30, 52, 61, 285, 293, 313
scanner
- colour scanning   92
- flatbed scanner   93
- image scanning   290, 294
- ranging scanning   96, 97
- raster scanner   93
- scanning   94
- scanning device   98
- telemetric scanning   94
- VASARI scanning   99
Scrovegni Chapel   361, 385

semantic
- semantic interoperability   186, 256
- semantic revolution   148
- semantic web   23, 30, 148, 187, 191, 241
senses   41, 50, 81, 103, 124, 319
simulation
- natural phenomena simulation   163
- realistic simulation   119
- simulation device   168
- simulation game   161, 173, 177
- simulation theatre   166
- simulator   119, 131, 160, 164, 393, 395
- visual simulation   104, 376
Smithsonian Institution   348, 446
social   238, 257, 288, 306, 360, 405, 410, 414
solid modelling   102, 144, 328, 340
Stelvio Swiss National Park   365

T
tags
- active tag   183
- data tag   187
- markup tag   190
- passive tag   183
- semantic tag   196
- smart tag   183
theme park   34, 70, 126, 155, 167, 179, 383, 393
time of flight   94, 96
Trans-European Telecom Network, TEN Telecom (EC framework)   273
treemap   31, 446
triangulation   94, 97

U
ubiquitous
- ubiquitous computing   4, 201, 230, 369
- ubiquitous network   4, 441
Uffizi Gallery   99, 334, 398, 446

V

Vatican Museums, Vatican 334, 337, 447
virtual reality 127
– HMD (head-mounted display) 120, 131, 165, 224, 340, 365
– VRML 126, 334, 371
visualisation, visualization
– data visualization 113, 328
– stereo visualisation 115

W

Web 2.0 148, 193
wireless
– WiBro 418
– WiFi 339, 369, 418
– WiMax 418
– wired connection 107
– wireless broadband 419
– wireless communication/connection 33, 35, 53, 61, 184, 328, 364, 369, 413, 419, 420, 436
– wireless devices 34
– wireless information system 365
– wireless networking 238
– wireless sensor network 184
– wireless technology 419

Printing and Binding: Stürtz GmbH, Würzburg